Film History Theory and Practice

Robert C. Allen
University of North Carolina, Chapel Hill

Douglas Gomery
University of Maryland, College Park

McGraw-Hill, Inc.
New York St. Louis San Francisco Auckland Bogotá
Caracas Lisbon London Madrid Mexico City Milan
Montreal New Delhi San Juan Singapore
Sydney Tokyo Toronto

First Edition

FILM HISTORY
Copyright © 1985 by McGraw-Hill, Inc.

Library of Congress Cataloging-in-Publication Data

13 14 15 16 17 18 19 20 21 BKMBKM 9 9 8 7

Allen, Robert Clyde, (date).
  Film history: theory and practice / Robert C. Allen, Douglas
Gomery
      p.   cm.
  Originally published: 1st ed. New York: Knopf, c1985.
  Includes bibliographical references and index.
  ISBN 0-07-554871-2
  1. Motion pictures—History. 2. Motion picture plays—History and
criticism. I. Gomery, Douglas. II. Title.
PN1993.5.A1A47   1993
791.43'09--dc20   93-6198

Cover design: Lorraine Hohman.
Cover photo: Marc Wanamaker, Bison Archives, Beverly Hills, California.

Preface

As recently as 1960, few universities offered courses of study in cinema. Film scholarship was the province of film buffs and a handful of brave academics whose love for the movies prompted them to write and teach film "on the side." Today, there are few major universities that do *not* list at least one course in film, and nearly 100 colleges grant degrees in film studies and/or production. Library shelves groan under the proliferation of books on film published over the past twenty years, and a wide variety of academic journals showcase more specialized studies of the cinema as art form, industrial institution, medium of mass communication, and social force. In short, the movies have come of age as a field of academic inquiry.

One of the signs of maturity of any new discipline is a consciousness of its own methods and approaches, successes and shortcomings. We believe that film history has reached the point that it deserves an examination of the historical questions that have been asked about the cinema's past and of the approaches that have been and might be taken in answering them. It is this function that *Film History: Theory and Practice* attempts to serve.

Because this is the first book of its kind, a few words about its goals are necessary. First, it is not a chronological history of the cinema; rather, it establishes a context within which film history might be more profitably read and conducted. Our subject in this book is the historical study of film, not film itself. While we cover specific examples drawn from film history to illustrate issues, problems, and approaches, in no way do we pretend to have surveyed the whole of cinema history.

The primary impetus for this book came from our frustrations as teachers of film history. Our students were all too eager to regard what they read in film history books as the single, indisputable truth, and most of them thought it heretical to question the film historian's methods, philosophical orientation, evidence, or conclusions. Survey texts contributed to the problem by remaining silent as to the process by which historical questions are posed, research conducted, evidence analyzed, and generalizations drawn. We felt a work was needed that would (1) place film history within the context of historical research in general; (2) acquaint the reader with the specific and, in some cases, unique problems confronting film historians; (3) survey the approaches that have been taken to the historical study of film; and (4) provide examples of various types of film historical research. Our goal, then, is to enable the student of film history to become a more sensitive and discriminating reader of film historical works and to enable him or her to conduct and write film history. Since fascination with film history greatly exceeds its study in the college classroom, we also believe such a book will prove useful to any reader interested in the movies and the serious study of their past.

One exciting thing about film historical research that sets it apart from some other branches of history is that it can be conducted nearly anywhere. Although some film historical research projects do require the use of rare films or data from film archives, others depend only on sources of data available in almost any community—and, of course, on the imagination and perseverance of the researcher. For this reason we hope to break down the distinction between producers of film history (writers of film history books and teachers of film courses) and consumers of film history (readers of film books and students of film history). Students should be encouraged to leap across this barrier by investigating aspects of film history at the local level. Therefore, Chapter 8 contains several examples of local film historical research and a guide to local resources. Actually doing film history is the best way we know to discover that film historians are not infallible deities, but merely inquisitive mortals.

This book does not attempt to establish *the* way of conducting film historical research. There is no one correct approach to film history, no one "superhistory" that could be written if only this or that "correct" perspective were taken and all the "facts" of film history uncovered. All models and approaches—even the ones we adopt in the following chapters—have their advantages and disadvantages. All make certain assumptions and are based on certain notions as to what makes history "work." As for obtaining all the "facts" of film history, this is a futile task, since the domain of "all the facts" is infinite. We hope to show that film historians do not work in a vacuum, nor do they approach the study of film history uninfluenced by their culture, tastes, and philosophical orientation. Doing history requires judgment, not merely the transmission of the facts. Similarly we attempt to demonstrate that reading film history is an act of judgment, requiring the active involvement of the reader.

We recognize that film is and has been a multifaceted phenomenon: art form, economic institution, cultural product, and technology. Traditionally, each of these facets has been treated as a separate subdiscipline in film history. In recognition of this fact, we have divided our discussion of film historical research into aesthetic, technological, economic, and social chapters. Although this is certainly not the only division that could have been made, it does represent the major lines of film historical research to date and provides a useful way of grouping the methods, problems, and opportunities associated with a wide range of film historical studies. However, the explanatory convenience of these categories should not hide the fact that, at any given time, film is *simultaneously* all these things: It is a system. Understanding how that system operates and how it has changed over time means understanding not only the workings of those individual parts but their interaction as well. Chapter 9 is an attempt (however preliminary) to address the systemic nature of film history directly and to end the book on an integrative note.

The obvious American focus of the book as a whole is by design. Most general readers and students of film history are far more familiar with Hollywood than with other national cinemas. Thus we can take a certain amount of basic film historical knowledge on the part of the reader for granted. Most survey histories of film available in English, whether American or international in scope, foreground the American cinema. Since this book is in part a guide to reading film history, it seemed to us best to emphasize those historical phenomena the reader would encounter most frequently in the survey work. The American focus also facilitates a certain amount of continuity among chapters and case studies, enabling the reader to see relationships among various historical periods and approaches to film history. Perhaps the most historically cogent reason for this focus is the fact of Hollywood's economic, aesthetic, and cultural impact on the history of world cinema. The economic power of American media, which began with the emergence of Hollywood as a major film-producing center in the 1910s, has been such that some scholars have called it "cultural imperialism." "Hollywood style" is a term apropos not only of films made in the United States, but of many produced in Moscow, Tokyo, and Bombay, as well.

A few notes are called for on the organization of this book. Although each chapter is autonomous, later chapters do rely somewhat on the concepts and vocabulary explained earlier. Hence the reader will probably find it helpful to read the chapters in order. The book is divided into three parts. Part One (Chapters 1, 2, and 3) considers the nature of film history as a scholarly discipline: its relation to the more general field of history, the special research problems involved in conducting film historical research, the influence of culture on the writing of film history, and the issues readers should be aware of as they read any film historical work. Part Two (Chapters 4, 5, 6, and 7) discusses the methods, problems, and opportunities involved in aesthetic, technological, economic, and social film history, respectively. Part Three (Chapters 8, 9, and 10) examines how one might study the historical impact of the cinema on a given community, attempts a reintegration of film history presented from a Realist philosophical perspective, and concludes with a bibliographic essay.

The authors served as partners in the planning and production of this volume. Each of us takes responsibility for individual chapters: Robert Allen for Chapters 1, 3, 4, 7, and 9; and Douglas Gomery for Chapters 2, 5, 6, 8, and 10. The material for the Durham case study in Chapter 8 is based on unpublished research by Robert Allen.

ACKNOWLEDGMENTS: Robert C. Allen

Although we shared the planning for this book and reviewed each other's work, the research for and writing of our respective chapters necessarily proceeded independently. Thus we have two lists of colleagues and friends to thank for their help. Much of the material that forms the case studies I wrote (those for Chapters 3, 4, 7, and 9, and the research for the Durham, N.C., study in Chapter 8) represents original research, and I have a number of individuals and organizations to thank for their assistance. Among the latter are the North Carolina Collections of the University of North Carolina Library and the Durham Public Library, the Manuscripts Division of the Library of Congress, and, for their help in locating and duplicating photographic materials, the Museum of the City of New York and the Museum of Modern Art.

Dan and Kathy Leab graciously provided me with a New York "home" during my frequent research trips there. My parents-in-law, Dick and Kitty Adams, allowed me to combine always pleasant visits to my Washington "home" with the business of research. Patricia Zimmerman shared her research on cinema verité and amateur filmmaking practice and offered constructive comments. Robert Drew granted me an extensive interview and provided the photographs that accompany Chapter 9. I drew upon Joanne Yeck's encyclopedic knowledge of 1930s Hollywood in my research on Joan Crawford. I was extremely fortunate to be able to call on three resourceful and dependable graduate students during the course of my research: Laurie Schulze, Robbie Burton, and Mark West. Edward Branigan and Roberta Kimmel surely deserve canonization for taking me in and nursing me for three days when my Hollywood research trip was aborted by an automobile accident.

Other individuals provided support and assistance over the course of this book's preparation. At UNC I was (and am) blessed with a supportive and sensitive department chairman, John R. Bittner, and with helpful colleagues, especially Gorham Kindem. Roy Armes enabled me to revise my chapters in London, a city I will always associate with Jane Douglas's remarkable kindness and hospitality. Charles Reed gave Chapter 1 a much-needed historian's reading. I am sure Doug joins me in thanking our manuscript reviewers: Phil Rosen,

Clark University; Marshall Deutelbaum, Purdue University; Kristin Thompson, University of Wisconsin; and Janet Staiger, New York University. Their many insightful comments and apt, gentle criticisms were enormously beneficial.

Finally, at the risk of lapsing into cliché, I reserve special thanks for two people: my mother, whose loving support and encouragment long predate this particular effort; and my wife Allison, who read, reread, critiqued, proofed, and consoled for four years with a grace and good humor that are surely unique.

ACKNOWLEDGMENTS: Douglas Gomery

I have many people whom I would like to thank for their help with the preparation of *Film History: Theory and Practice.* Much of the material that forms the case studies for Chapters 2, 5, 6, and 8 is based on research I have conducted during the past ten years. I wish to thank all those persons, too many to list individually, who helped with my numerous research trips, archival visits, and interview sessions. Special thanks go to the folks at the Museum of Modern Art, Georgetown University, the Theatre Historical Society, and the Library of Congress.

I wish to thank Thomas Aylward, my former chair, for providing me with release time to work on this project. Thanks also go to my current chair, Patti Gillespie, for providing the appropriate incentives, and to Larry Lichty for explaining to me how the world really works.

Like Bobby, I wish to thank those who read and reviewed the manuscript: Phil Rosen, Clark University; Marshall Deutelbaum, Purdue University; Kristin Thompson, University of Wisconsin; and Janet Staiger, New York University.

Finally, I wish to dedicate this book to Marilyn Moon. She provided useful scholarly advice and supplied needed sympathy. However, her greatest contribution came from the inspiration of her own work, which is a model of clarity and insight. It is the work of Marilyn Moon that gave rise to whatever first-rate contributions I was able to make in this book. Thank you, Marilyn.

Chapel Hill, North Carolina   R. C. A.
College Park, Maryland   D. G.
September 1984

Contents

PART ONE

Reading, Researching, and Writing Film History

1

Film History
as History

What is film history? This might well seem an unnecessary question, given the fact that books announcing themselves as "film histories" have been published since the early 1910s. Every college library in the United States and Europe today contains hundreds of such works, most of whose authors are confident that their readers know what a film history is. Do we really need yet another film history book, especially one that asks such an elementary question? The question, What is film history? does need to be addressed, in large measure because the superficial consensus suggested by hundreds of film history titles belies considerable disagreement among scholars as to what film history is all about. Furthermore, any scholarly discipline that is to be taken seriously must define and continuously redefine its object of study, goals, scope, and methods.

An examination of the assumptions and approaches that lie behind all works that call themselves *film history* should enable the person interested in the history of the movies to make better use of any of them. Thus the object of study in this book will be historical writing on the cinema: *film historiography*. Although several specific case studies will be presented in subsequent chapters, the primary concern of this book is with the "big picture"—the larger questions that transcend any particular example of film historical writing. What, precisely, does film history claim to study? What is the nature of the knowledge gained through the study of film history? What materials do film historians work with? What approaches have film historians taken in their work? How might these approaches be critiqued?

We might begin by asking the most basic of film historical questions: What is film history? The term itself suggests a two-part definition. Film history involves the study of the phenomenon we commonly refer to as "film" (or cinema, the movies, motion pictures—these terms will be used interchangeably). Further, it involves studying film from a particular perspective and with particular goals in mind—perspective and goals that are historical. In Chapter 2 the *film* component of film history will be considered: those problems and opportunities film presents as an object of historical investigation. This chapter examines what it means to study anything *historically*. By calling themselves "film historians," and their works "film histories," film historians, whether they choose to acknowledge the fact or not, involve themselves in issues, controversies, and problems that reach far beyond the study of film itself and have been debated by historians and philosophers of history for centuries.

Every piece of film historical writing, no matter how modest, implicitly is based on a set of assumptions about history. Thus before discussing any particular approach to film history, even before discussing film at all, it is necessary to examine the sorts of assumptions historians (including film historians) make. Having been warned that the first chapter of this book on film history has little to do with film, the reader should further be warned that this chapter is perhaps the most abstract and "theoretical" of the entire book. However, if the historical issues outlined here were not important, they would not have been the subject of debate since Aristotle. If film history is to be more than a topic of cocktail-party chatter, then it too must be brought into the vital discussion of the nature and purpose of History with a capital *H*. Rest assured that the path of our discussion will lead eventually (if circuitously) back to the movies.

FILM HISTORY AS A BRANCH OF FILM STUDIES

Before discussing the relationship of film history to history in general, it might be helpful to locate film history within film studies. Film history traditionally has been thought of as one of the three major branches of film study, along with film theory and film criticism. The boundaries among the three are by no means fixed, but the three terms do delineate primary areas of research emphasis and form the basis for curricular divisions in many colleges.

In *The Major Film Theories*, Dudley Andrew argues that film theorists "make and verify propositions about film or some aspect of film."[1] Film theory takes as its domain the nature, qualities and functions of film in general. What *is* film? How are we able to derive meaning from a film? How can it be used? Which are its unique properties, and which does it share with other communications media, art forms, and modes of representation? Until fairly recently film theory has been almost exclusively aesthetic in orientation, attempting to determine the unique properties of film as art, define the types of art film might produce, and prescribe (in some cases) how the filmmaker might realize film's artistic potential. Within the past fifteen years some film theorists have asked, "How does film produce meaning?"or "How is a film grasped by a particular audience?" rather than "How is film art?" This shift in theoretical orientation will be taken up in Chapter 4. Regardless of orientation, however, theorists deal with film in the abstract. Seldom do they analyze individual films except as examples of a particular category of filmic potential or as an illustration of a more general proposition.

Where film theory deals with commonalities among films, film criticism concerns itself with the particular qualities of individual films or groups of films. The critic asks, "How do the various elements of filmmaking come together in a given film?" "How does a particular film *work* as a visual experience, as a story, as an artwork?" To some (but by no means all) critics, the purpose of their analysis of individual films is aesthetic evaluation: the determination by some aesthetic criteria of the relative merits of a film as a work of art.

Although film theorists and critics have influenced film history and sometimes involved themselves in historical controversies, neither branch of film studies has as its primary domain the temporal dimension of the cinema: how film as art, technology, social force, or economic institution developed over time or functioned at a given moment in the past. This is the domain of film history. Rather than analyze one film or reflect on the nature and potential of all films, *the film historian attempts to explain the changes that have occurred to the cinema since its origins, as well as account for aspects of the cinema that have resisted change.*

For example, in the late 1920s, many film theorists and critics wrote essays in response to one of the most important changes in the history of the cinema: the advent of commercially viable synchronous sound. Theorist Rudolph Arnheim lamented the passing of the silent film and the possible loss of what he saw as an entire set of aesthetic possibilities from the cinema. Filmmaker and theorist Sergei Eisenstein, along with two colleagues, issued a manifesto on the aesthetic opportunities and limitations of sound. American and European critics alternately excoriated the "talkies" for their static theatricality and hailed the coming of sound as ushering in a new artistic era for the movies.[2] Whereas Arnheim, Eisenstein, and the others treated the coming of sound as a given, as a development to be integrated into their respective theoretical or critical systems, the film historian is interested not only in the fact that sound was developed, but how and why synchronous sound came about when and where it did. In order to answer questions about the cinema's past, the film historian must not only be a *film* scholar, but a *historical* scholar as well.

THE NATURE OF HISTORICAL INQUIRY

What distinguishes film historical questions from theoretical and critical ones, then, is the goal of explaining change and stasis over time. But how does this historical enterprise proceed? Put another way, how does any historian, regardless of his or her object of study (film, art, politics, technology), explain the past? This question has occupied historians and philosophers for centuries, and it is certainly beyond the scope of this book to address it in the detail it deserves. However, it might prove useful to begin a book on film history with a brief discussion of some of the philosophical issues that underlie any type of history.

We might first ask, What is a historian? At the most elementary level, a historian is someone who studies the past. Obviously this definition is too broad, since not everyone who studies the past is a historian. For example, collectors often possess extraordinarily detailed knowledge about objects from the past. A film collector might own hundreds of rare films or have committed to memory all the dialogue from *Casablanca*, but the collector's possession of and knowledge about historical objects do not in themselves make him or her a historian, any more than the collector of first editions is necessarily a literary historian. The collector finds an intrinsic fascination in old things—in their beauty, rarity, or merely the fact that they are old. The historian's study of the past seeks to explain why a particular set of historical circumstances came about and with what consequences. The historian's interest in the past stems directly or indirectly from the belief that an understanding of the past is useful in understanding the present.

What links the collector with the historian are those artifacts that survive from the past. To the collector they are valuable in themselves, sometimes monetarily so (Dorothy's slippers from *The Wizard of Oz* are worth thousands of dollars); to the historian they are a vital source of information about the past. Unlike sociologists or geographers, historians cannot observe directly the phenomena they seek to explain. They cannot transport themselves back in time to take notes on the Battle of Waterloo or sit in on an MGM story conference. They must rely on those artifacts that have lasted until the time of investigation: in the case of film history, films, production records, newspapers, government documents, and even old buildings that once served as movie theaters, among many other types of artifacts.

Without thinking about it too much, most of us place great emphasis on the role of artifacts in explaining the past. We have learned from high school history classes that the proper study of history consists in uncovering all the relevant facts about a particular historical question and presenting them in as dispassionate and "objective" manner possible. The job of the historian, we are taught, is to act as collector and organizer of historical evidence. Interpretation is relegated to a much lower level of importance, and, in fact, might even be unnecessary, since once the facts are properly arranged they can "speak for themselves." In this admittedly caricatured version of what I am calling "high school history," the truth of history is knowable on the basis of the incontrovertible facts of history, and this truth exists entirely separate from the interpretations of any historian. Historical truth is presented as something indisputable and reducible to true-or-false questions on a final exam.

The general assumptions most of us make about the nature of historical inquiry derive from a philosophical position known as *empiricism*. Empiricist history, says historian E. H. Carr, is "common sense history," in that it conforms to what our unreflective common sense tells us historical explanation must be like. Indeed, the basic tenets of empiricist history would seem, at first glance at least, to be borne out by our everyday experience of interpreting the past. Without being too metaphysical about it, we can agree that certain events did actually occur in the past. The D-Day invasion, the construction of Chartres, the release date of *Gone with the Wind* all have objective status as "facts" of history. Further, in trying to make sense of a phenomenon we cannot directly observe, the more facts about it we can collect, the more certain we are apt to be about its true nature—what "really happened."

What, then, could be the objection to a philosophy of history that (1) sees the facts of history as existing entirely apart from the historian who uses them, (2) argues that the truth of history emerges from these facts, (3) limits the historian's role to that of disinterested collector and arranger of the facts, and (4) regards "theory" as being, at best, secondary and, at worst, unnecessary to the objective enterprise of historical explanation? Many contemporary historians (both empiricist and otherwise) would argue that the "common sense" legacy of nineteenth-century empiricist history is not so much "wrong" as it is simplistic. Carr, for example, questions the extent to which the material of history, the "facts," are independent of the researcher using them.

How should we define a "fact" in history? In his book, *What is History?* Carr makes a useful distinction between *a fact of the past* and *a historical fact*. Everything that has ever happened is a fact of the past, and thus is potentially, at least, a source of historical data. However, history could not possibly consist of all the facts of the past, even those facts of which traces have survived. They would be so numerous as to be meaningless. A fact of the past becomes an historical fact when a historian decides to use that fact in constructing a historical analysis.[3] Medieval history provides an excellent example of how our knowledge of the past is determined by which pieces of evidence came to be saved. Much of our picture of medieval life concerns religious life: theological debates, ecclesiastical politics, the relationship of church to worshippers. It is unlikely that people in the Middle Ages were markedly less secular than people from other eras in European history; it's just that most of our information about medieval life comes from material saved in later years by the church. Those "facts" became historical facts while others documenting more mundane aspects of medieval history were simply not deemed worthy of preservation.

Hence, Carr and others make the point that the historian's role is not quite so simple or innocent as the description, "collector and passive transmitter of the 'facts,' " would suggest. Historians also select from among all the available historical data only those historical facts they see as important. The facts of the past do not "speak for themselves"; the historian makes them speak as part of a historical argument.

Many contemporary historians also question the extent to which the historical enterprise can be said to be "objective" or value neutral. Long before the current challenge to empiricist history, Hegel said of historians, "Even the average and mediocre historian who perhaps believes and pretends that he is merely receptive, merely surrendering to the data, is not passive in his thinking."[4] The very recognition that historians select facts and use them in historical arguments in addition to collecting them reveals history to be a more subjective and theoretical undertaking than the empiricist view allows. Historians are not identical automotons all programmed to view the world in the same way.

Differences in philosophical orientations among historians produce different sets of beliefs about what is important in history, different views as to what makes history happen. As we shall see in later chapters, the same film historical change might be attributed to the actions of a powerful individual, economic forces, aesthetic "fate," or social pressures, depending on what factors each historian sees as being most determinant in film history. One of the difficulties in film history is that frequently the writers of books on film history do not explicitly state what theory(s) of historical change they adhere to. Carr suggests that any time we read a historical work we should be listening for the "buzz" of the historian's interpretive stance—his or her argument as to how pieces of data are related. "When you read a work of history, always listen out for the buzzing. If you can detect none, either you are tone deaf or your historian is a dull dog."[5]

In recent times historians have also become aware of the influence on historical interpretations by the pressures, concerns, tendencies, and frames of reference of the historian's age and culture. Culture conditions the way historians look at the world, what they think is worth writing about, what they take for granted, and how they analyze data. These cultural or ideological factors express themselves not only in the historian's conscious method and philosophical positions, but more importantly in areas the historian might not even be aware of: those vague, unarticulated notions of "how things are supposed to be," "the way people act in most cases," and "how the world works." In *Catherine, Empress of all the Russias,* Vincent Cronin explains Catherine's twenty-two-year correspondence with Frederick Grimm, a German journalist, as follows: "A woman autocrat tends to feel lonely, because the woman longs to lean and the autocrat cannot."[6] Cronin reveals much more about his (and his culture's) attitude toward women than he explains about this autocrat's decision to correspond with someone.

At the very least, then, empiricist history presents a somewhat simplistic view of the nature of historical evidence and the role of the historian. *Facts of the past* do exist independently of the mind of the historian, but *historical facts* are only those data selected from the past that a historian finds relevant to his or her argument. The historian can never know the past "as it really was," but only how it might have been, since our information about the past is partial and inevitably mediated. Because the historian's job requires selection, interpretation, appraisal, and judgment, he or she is never totally "objective." As early as the 1930s, noted American historian Charles Beard challenged his colleagues in the American Historical Association to rethink their empiricist assumptions about history:

> History, as it actually was, as distinguished, of course from particular facts of history, is not known or knowable, no matter how zealously is pursued "the ideal of the effort for objective truth.". . . The historian seeking to know the past, or about it, does not bring to the partial documentation with which he works a perfect and polished neutral mind in which the past streaming through the medium of documentation is mirrored as it actually was. Whatever acts of purification the historian may perform he yet remains human, a creature of time, place, circumstance, interests, predelictions, culture.[7]

HISTORICAL KNOWLEDGE AND SCIENTIFIC KNOWLEDGE

It is easy enough to see the inadequacies of the bowdlerized version of historical empiricism taught us in high school history classes. It would also be unfair to end this discussion of empiricism having effortlessly dispensed with this intellectual straw man. As you might expect, challenges to the empiricist position have prompted a response, one that cannot be so easily dismissed. Empiricist historians and philosophers of history, chief among them Carl Hempel, have maintained that despite the historian's innate "subjectivity," history still has as its goal the production of verifiable information about the past. The historian, they argue, faces many of the same problems as the physical scientist and should strive for explanations about history as "scientific" as those fashioned by the biologist about the structure of the cell. It behooves us to consider (albeit briefly and incompletely) the relationship Hempel and others would posit between historical knowledge and scientific knowledge, since it forms the philosophical core of modern historical empiricism and, indeed, for much of American social science in general. Equally important for the purposes of our discussion, the nature of scientific knowledge is the philosophical issue seized upon by those philosophers we will call *conventionalists*, who base their radical critique of all empiricist endeavors (including historical empiricism) on the rejection of the empiricist view of science.[8]

For the scientist, explanation takes the form of universals or covering laws under which a given phenomenon can be placed. These laws are expressions of regularities that the scientist has observed or has produced in experimental situations. There cannot exist any cases in which a particular law does not work, and so the law can be used to predict the same phenomenon in the future. For example, under the general laws of thermodynamics we know that a volume of water heated beyond 212 degrees Fahrenheit will change into a gas, assuming that other "normal" conditions hold (atmospheric pressure, for example). Every instance of heated water can be subsumed under this principle—no exceptions are known; and should we wish to test the law experimentally (by making a cup of tea), we can confidently predict that the law will come into play once more.[9]

In the empiricist model of science, the role of the scientist is twofold. First, he or she usually creates experimentally a situation in which the regularity can be observed. This means establishing a *closed system* in which all conditions save one (the independent variable) have been controlled. Second, the scientist is the careful observer and recorder of the results of the experiment. To the scientist, the facts "speak for themselves," in the form of covering law regularities. What the facts "say" is limited to the recognition of a regular (predictable) relationship between isolated events in controlled situations. When a phenomenon (boiling water, the movement of fluids across cell membranes) has been subsumed under a covering law, it has been "explained." The scientist's job is then finished. According to the empiricist view it is not the purpose of science to go "behind" or "beyond" observable phenomena in trying to explain them.[10]

Although Hempel and other empiricist historians pose the scientific method and scientific explanation as ultimate models for history, they recognize several difficulties in trying to hold historical research to the same standards of rigor. For example, scientists assume that except for the variable being tested all other conditions can be controlled. A *closed system* can be created. Thus experiments can be replicated and the same results produced, time after time. History, on the other hand, is an *open system*, not a closed one. Two experimental situations can be made operationally identical, but no two historical events are ever the same, no matter how similar they might appear to be to the historian.

Scientists can "create" an experimental situation to test hunches and hypotheses in a way historians never can. The scientist can ask, "What would happen if I poured hydrochloric acid on a piece of zinc?" and find out by doing so. The historian is stuck with the existing traces of what was. Speculation as to what might have been "if it had only been different" is not historical. As David Fischer points out, "All historical 'evidence' for what might have happened if John Wilkes Booth had missed his mark is necessarily taken from the world in which he hit it."[11] In short, scientists enjoy the luxury of being able to replicate the situations they wish to study; historians do not.

Furthermore, the historian's observation of the phenomenon under study is much less direct than the physicist's, since the historian cannot "see" a historical event directly, but only the traces of it that remain. In this respect, historians are more like detectives than physicists: They always arrive at the scene after the murder (event) has been committed and must try to reconstruct the crime from whatever bits of evidence have been left behind. Empiricist historians would thus admit that there are few if any instances of historians deriving "laws" with the predictive power of a scientific covering law. Usually any attempt to produce a historical universal ("whenever x occurs, y is invariably a consequence") will result in a formulation either so inclusive and vague as to be useless, or so specific as to be inapplicable beyond a single case.

How, then, can historical knowledge even begin to approach the level of scientific knowledge? Modern empiricist historians generally agree that the historian seldom if ever explains the past with scientific certainty. However, they contend, the historian can offer explanations based on an event's probability. Unlike the covering law explanation, the *probabilistic* or *statistical* explanation does not say, "Given X, Y will invariably occur," but "If certain specified conditions are realized, then an occurrence of such and such a kind will come about with such and such statistical probability."[12] We encounter probabilistic explanations frequently in history. Any time historians say, "X was likely to have occurred," or "We can be relatively sure that Y did not occur," they are relying on a probabilistic explanation. Given the incomplete evidence historians must work with and the uncontrollable factors present in any single historical situation, stating an explanation in terms of its likelihood of happening is probably as close to "knowledge" in an empiricist scientific sense as the historian can come.

To Hempel and other modern empiricist historians, the covering law in science represents a level of explanatory power to which history should aspire. Historical knowledge for them consists in explaining an event, in Hempel's words, "by showing that, in view of certain particular circumstances and general laws, its occurrence was to be expected (in a purely logical sense), either with deductive certainty or with inductive probability."[13] Empiricist historians minimize the effects on historical explanation of the historian's culture or philosophical orientation, just as empiricist scientists argue that regardless of cultural, political, or moral differences among researchers, science is still an "objective" enterprise. They would acknowledge the fact that the historian cannot use the same tools as the experimental scientist, but would contend that this should not prevent the historian from making explanation of the past as much like scientific knowledge as possible.

THE CONVENTIONALIST CRITIQUE OF EMPIRICISM

Empiricism in history and science (both physical and social) is predicated on the belief that reality exists independently of the human mind, and that reality can be known and explained by scientific observation of events. Since the early part of the twentieth century, these twin tenets of empiricism have been radically questioned by a number of philosophers, scientists, and historians who hold that what we take as "scientific" descriptions of reality derived from observation and experimentation are, in fact, artificial constructs (conventions) that cannot be validated. *Conventionalists* argue that science or history is not a value-neutral enterprise, a transparent window through which the investigator observes and describes reality or the past, but rather a set of lenses and filters interposed between the investigator and reality. The distorting effects of the "scientific" method, the investigator's cultural and philosophical orientation, even language itself, are so bound up with any attempt to explain reality (past or present), conventionalists would claim, that scientists or historians with differing outlooks "see" the world in different terms. Taken to its logical extreme, the conventionalist position holds that scientists and historians construct the worlds they seek to explain. Any attempt to validate a theory by reference to "the facts" is doomed, since "the facts" do not exist apart from the conventions the investigator uses.[14]

In film study and in social science in general, much of conventionalism's original impetus was provided by the work of Swiss linguist Ferdinand de Saussure. When Saussure began his career around the turn of the century, linguistics was principally concerned with the historical development of individual words. ("Where did the word *pajamas* come from?") Language itself was conceived of as a fairly straightforward process: a word stood for a thing in the real world.

To continue our metaphor, language was regarded as the mind's transparent window on reality. What struck Saussure about language was not its transparency but its opacity, not its connection with the world of things but its separation from it. Verbal language, said Saussure, is *arbitrary* in its relationships with the things it represents. There is no natural or necessary relationship between the letters c-o-w and a cow. We might just as well substitute b-a-r-f for c-o-w—the latter is no more "cow-like" than the former. The word *cow* takes on its meaning by convention and not by any connection of it with any qualities of a real cow. Further, what *cow* stands for is not a flesh-and-blood cow but the concept of a cow; it stands for whatever we endow with the qualities of "cowness." Note that the very concept of "cowness" is itself somewhat arbitrary, being quite different in parts of India than in Europe and America. *Cow* means whatever it means because it is part of a system of relationships among words, a system of similarities and differences that allows us, for example, to distinguish *cow* from *cot*. All meaning, claimed Saussure, occurs within and by virtue of this system. In the words of Terence Hawkes, Saussure's revolutionary discovery was that verbal language "allows no single, unitary appeal to a 'reality' beyond itself. In the end, it constitutes its own reality."[15]

Saussure also distinguished between any particular use of the word *cow* and the system of language of which it is a part and which necessarily precedes it. We can control what use we wish to make of language in any particular utterance (as I am doing by writing this sentence), but we cannot control the system that *is* language. It is impervious to whatever alterations or mutilations we might want to make of it.

Structural linguistics, the school of thought that grew from Saussure's work, has had an enormous impact on many fields of study, including film. Saussure's legacy to film study will be considered in both Chapters 4 and 7. For present purposes, Saussure can be seen as laying the groundwork for conventionalism through his insistence on the active role of language in conferring meaning on the world and on the cultural basis of language. If the world is constructed by and through language, then we do not speak it so much as it speaks us. Both the world and our place in it are determined by language.

Probably the most influential of the conventionalist accounts of science is Thomas Kuhn's *The Structure of Scientific Revolutions*. At any given time, Kuhn argues, science is governed by a set of conventions that form a paradigm (or model) of what science is all about. This paradigm determines what questions are viewed as important, what explanations can be seriously considered for a phenomenon, and what criteria should be used in evaluating scientific research. Scientific "advancement" occurs not through a process of knowledge accumulation, but when the governing paradigm begins to lose its hold on the scientific community and is replaced by a new paradigm. The new paradigm is not necessarily more valid than the old one; it is merely a different way of constituting the questions science asks. Alternative paradigms are not only incompatible, says Kuhn, they are "incommensurable" with one another. Different sets of conventions cause scientists to "see" the world differently.[16] To Kuhn, the world is constructed by scientific theories, not explained by them. When conventions change, reality changes.

To the conventionalist, there is no factual test or standard of ultimate truthfulness by which to judge one theory as preferable over another, since "reality" cannot be known apart from theory. Instead, one theory or explanation is chosen over another because of its internal logic (coherence, consistency, inclusiveness), aesthetic qualities (elegance, style), or usefulness. Taken far enough this relativism leads to philosopher P. K. Feyerabend's "anarchistic theory of knowledge," whereby

> without universally enforced standards of truth and rationality, we can no longer speak of universal error. We can only speak of what does, or does not, seem appropriate when viewed from a particular and restricted point of view, different views, temperaments, attitudes giving rise to different judgments and different methods of approach.[17]

THE REALIST RESPONSE

It might well seem that the preceding discussion has little to do with film history. Certainly few film histories address these philosophical issues directly. However, it is because most film history books treat questions of historical evidence and explanation as if they were unproblematic that it is necessary to devote this admittedly tortuous discussion to them: Film histories are works of historical explanation, and as such cannot escape basic questions of historiography. Further, it might seem that after this long historiographic journey the reader is left either to accept the limitations of empiricist history or embrace the extreme view that, as one philosopher of history put it, history is a "child's box of letters with which we can spell any word we please."[18]

Both empiricism and conventionalism recognize important aspects of the scientific and, by extension, historical enterprise. Facts *do* matter, and, as will be discussed in Chapter 2, evidentiary problems afflict film history with particular severity. The empiricist concern with collecting and arranging data is a necessary component of film historical research. Conventionalism quite justifiably warns us that the facts do not explain themselves, and that theory, far from being an unwarranted and unnecessary intrusion of the historian's subjectivity into the pure world of "objective" history, is the indispensable application by the historian of discernment, judgment, and reasoning to the raw data of historical evidence. By the same token, to assume that there exists no "world out there" that is at least in part knowable and against which theories can be tested reduces history to little more than navel-gazing.

Over the past two decades a new philosophy of science has emerged: *Realism*. This theory offers the prospect of fashioning an approach to history which preserves the notion of an independently existing past, while taking into account the necessity and complexity of theory in historical explanation. Realism is offered here not as a final solution to the empiricism/conventionalism conflict or as *the* way to conduct film history, but rather as an emerging (and hence preliminary) alternative philosophical formulation that seems particularly applicable to film history.

First, it must be pointed out that the term is an unfortunate one when applied to film because of other, quite different meanings "realism" already has in film studies. In traditional film theory, for example, realism is the name given to the aesthetic theory of André Bazin, who suggested ways in which the cinema could be made closer to our experience of the phenomenal world. The approach to history outlined here is derived from a realist philosophy of science as developed by Roy Bhaskar and Rom Harré. It has only the most tenuous of connections with cinematic realism. To keep things straight, "Realism" as a philosophy of science and history will be designated in this book as a proper noun; other uses of the term will not.[19]

Realism takes as its starting point a fundamental agreement with empiricism. Realism asserts that there is a world that exists independently of the scientist. Furthermore, like empiricism, Realism sees the goal of science as the explanation of that world. Thus theories must be assessed by reference to the "real" world. Realism departs from empiricism over the nature of that reality and what constitutes explanation of it. To the empiricist, explaining a phenomenon ends with the observation of regularity: when it is subsumed under a covering law.

The Realist believes this view of reality explanation to be limited in two ways. First, it conceives of reality as the one-dimensional realm of observable phenomena. Second, a description of regularity is not explanation of what causes that regularity. To the Realist, reality is complex and only partially observable, even with the most sophisticated scientific tools. The level of observable phenomena is but one of a multilayered structure. The event the empiricist describes is the *effect* of processes and mechanisms at work in other layers of reality. Explanation for the Realist consists of describing not only the observable layer of reality but also the workings of the *generative mechanisms* that produced the observable event.

The Realist position asserts that answers to *why* questions (Why did an event take place?) require answers to *how* and *what* questions.[20] One of the chief proponents of Realism is British philosopher Roy Bhaskar. His summary of the Realist position, taken from *A Realist Theory of Science*, deserves quoting in full.

> The world consists of mechanisms not events. Such mechanisms combine to generate the flux of phenomena that constitute the actual states and happenings of the world. They may be said to be real, though it is rarely that they are actually manifest and rarer still that they are empirically identified by men. They are the intransitive objects of scientific theory. They are quite independent of men—as thinkers, causal agents and perceivers. They are not unknowable, although knowledge of them depends upon a rare blending of intellectual, practico-technical, and perceptual skills. They are not artificial constructs. But neither are they Platonic forms. For they can become manifest to men in experience. Thus we are not imprisoned in caves, either of our own or of nature's making. We are not doomed to ignorance. But neither are we spontaneously free. This is the arduous task of science: the production of the knowledge of those enduring and continually active mechanisms of nature that produce the phenomena of our world.[21]

Realism therefore takes as its object of study the structures or mechanisms that cause observable phenomena—mechanisms that are rarely observable directly. It is the role of theory to offer descriptive models of these mechanisms.

To the Realist, models are not mere abstract ruminations, but hypothetical descriptions of actually existing mechanisms. It is in the crucial role of the scientist (or historian) as active theorizer and interpreter that Realism joins with conventionalism. Like the conventionalist, the Realist insists that every theory carries with it a set of implications and assumptions derived from culture, language, and the governing scientific paradigm of a given time. The Realist also sees the act of scientific investigation itself as carrying its own implications and assumptions. To the Realist, theory is not an unnecessary intrusion of subjectivity into an otherwise "objective" enterprise, but a necessary component of scientific explanation. Since explanation involves the description of directly unobservable mechanisms that cause events, the scientist must theorize about what he or she cannot "know" by observation alone.

Realism breaks with conventionalism in asserting that while science is inevitably laden with values and assumptions, it does not follow that we must embrace Feyerabend's anarchistic theory of knowledge and presume that one theory cannot be more valid than another, only more logical, elegant, or useful. Certainly, the Realist contends, a theory should be internally logical, consistent, and coherent, but in the end a theory must be tested by external criteria:

"Scientific theories must be objectively assessed by reference to empirical evidence. This evidence is such that all scientists who are competent, honest, and lacking in perceptual deficiencies can agree upon it, though not necessarily with total certainty."[22] One such way of testing a theory is by the principle of *noncontradiction*. Frequently the same phenomenon will be investigated by scientists with differing philosophical orientations, theories, and methods. On most points we would expect the resulting explanations to differ as well. Where they do not, where there is noncontradiction among them, there is evidence of a finding that is valid: one not merely a product of the theoretical model imposed by the scientist.[23]

REALISM AS A THEORY OF FILM HISTORY

A Realist approach to history, specifically film history, would view the past as having an existence independent of the historian and would regard historical evidence as the partial, mediated, yet indispensable record of the past. Evidence provides the historian access to the facts of history; it enables the historian to describe historical events so that the existence of those events can be agreed upon by other historians. However, in the Realist view, the events or facts of history in no way speak for themselves, nor is the historian's job finished when a chronology of events has been compiled. The object of historical study for the Realist is not the historical event in itself, but the generative (causal) mechanisms that brought that event about. To adopt a phrase from Bhaskar, the world of history consists of mechanisms not events. Usually a historical event is the result of more than one causal factor. The generative mechanisms of history operate at a number of levels and with uneven force, so that it is the historian's job to understand these mechanisms in their complexity rather than to isolate a single "cause" for a given event.

In contrast to the experimental scientist, the historian never deals with a closed system. History is always an open system beyond the historian's control. The same causal mechanisms might be at work in a number of historical events, but those events (the results of the operation of those mechanisms) might be very different. This is because generative mechanisms in history do not operate in isolation from each other; they *interact* to produce "the flux of phenomena that constitute the actual states and happenings of the world." Seldom, then, do historical events provide illustrations of universals or covering laws. The historian simply cannot hold other factors constant so that the operation of a covering law can be seen in splendid isolation.

The Realist approach to history is particularly applicable to the history of the cinema, since film is a complex historical phenomenon (an art form, economic institution, technology, cultural product) which, since its inception, has participated in many networks of relationships. In other words, film is an *open system*. It is not just a set of components forming a whole, but an *interrelated* set of components that condition and are conditioned by each other. The artistic effects that can be achieved in the cinema at any given time are in part dependent on the state of film technology. Technological developments are conditioned in many instances by economic factors. Economic decision making occurs within a social context, and so forth. Furthermore, historically film can never be separated from other systems: the popular entertainment industry, other forms of mass communication, national economies, or other art forms. In the 1950s, for example, the American cinema underwent a transformation because, in part, of its role in the system of American popular entertainment. The acceptance of television as a leisure-time activity altered every component of that system: film, radio, the recording industry, advertising, theater, even sporting events. Thus from the Realist perspective it is the frustrating but exciting task of the film historian to describe the working of the generative mechanisms in film history in general and the particular conjunction of those mechanisms in any given film historical phenomenon.

A Realist approach to film history insists that historical explanations can and should be tested by reference both to historical evidence and to other, competing explanations. Where explanations from differing theoretical positions agree, we have, in the words of Terry Lovell, "a residue of theoretically grounded 'observations' which may be taken as the testing ground for any given theory at any given point in time."[24] This Realist principle of noncontradiction is particularly important in film history, where, as we shall see in later chapters, scholars hold a wide variety of philosophical positions, and even a variety of notions of what constitutes film history itself.

Finally, is there a specific method for conducting film history suggested by Realism? It is not at all the aim of this book to impose a single working method or approach on film history. History in general and film history in particular admit to a number of methods of historical explanation, the major categories of which will be outlined in the following chapters. Although Realism as a theory of science is just beginning to be applied to the study of history, it is possible to extrapolate a general historical method from the overall precepts of Realism. Briefly outlined here, it will be put into practice in the case study on cinema verité documentary, which constitutes Chapter 9. This Realist approach to film history, adapted from the work of Roy Bhaskar, should not be thought of as the only film historical method or even the only possible Realist method, but rather as one way of approaching the complexities of film history.[25]

Faced with the task of explaining a particular phenomenon or event (the invention of the motion picture apparatus, the coming of sound, the use of deep-focus photography, the 1948 Supreme Court decision in *U.S.* v. *Paramount, et al.*, the production of a given film), the historian first recognizes that the event under study is not a one-dimensional "thing" but the point of convergence for various lines of historical force. The event thus requires what Bhaskar calls "causal analysis": a redescription of the event so as to uncover the possible causal mechanisms responsible for it.

To give a very truncated example, let us take as a film historical "event" the first successful commercial exhibition of projected motion pictures in the United States: the public debut of the Edison/Armat Vitascope projector at Koster and Bial's Music Hall on April 23, 1896, in New York City.[26] Since 1894 the Edison Company had been commercially exploiting motion pictures, but only as a peep-show device. During the summer of 1895, two Frenchmen, Auguste and Louis Lumiere, had developed and demonstrated a motion picture projector. Other inventors in England, Germany, and the United States were also on the verge of solving the problems of screen projection. Edison had contracted with two businessmen, Norman Raff and Frank Gammon, to market his peep-show. By the summer of 1895, however, the market for the Kinetoscope, as the device was called, had nearly dried up—patrons had grown tired of seeing the same brief film "loops" shown over and over again.

Raff and Gammon realized that the only hope for their failing movie business lay in persuading Edison to develop a projection system. Edison, deeply

Koster and Bial's Music Hall in New York City, site of the debut of the "Edison" Vitascope on April 23, 1896.

Photograph by Byron, the Byron Collection, Museum of the City of New York

involved in a host of other invention projects and disappointed by the financial return on the Kinetoscope, refused their entreaties to act quickly before others entered the projection market. In December 1895, just as Raff and Gammon were contemplating selling what remained of their Kinetoscope venture, they came upon news of a projector invented by two Washington, D.C., men, Thomas Armat and Francis Jenkins. Raff and Gammon secured the rights to the device, the Vitascope, and persuaded Edison to manufacture it and supply them with new films. The Vitascope was demonstrated for the New York press in early April of 1896 and was touted as "the latest invention of Wizard Edison." The exhibition at Koster and Bial's, a prominent New York vaudeville theater, was the public debut of the Vitascope.

Even this brief and greatly simplified account of the Koster and Bial exhibition reveals something of its historical complexity. To the Edison Company, which had not invented the Vitascope but manufactured it, the exhibition provided exposure for yet another piece of Edison-manufactured technology and an opportunity to rejuvenate the flagging market for motion pictures, in which Edison had a considerable stake. To Raff and Gammon, the Koster and Bial showing represented the inauguration of their campaign to sell franchises for the Vitascope before other projectors were launched on the American market. To Koster and Bial, the Vitascope premiere meant the display of a novelty act on their vaudeville program, the hoped-for publicity of which might give them an edge in the highly competitive New York vaudeville market. To the patrons of Koster and Bial's on that April evening, their first glimpse of projected movies meant several things: the latest miracle from the "Wizard of Menlo Park," one of a series of technological novelties they had seen on the vaudeville stage, and an extension of popular photography, among others.

The redescription of the event under examination exposes the range of possible causal mechanisms responsible for it. The second stage of historical explanation involves analysis of these individual mechanisms. In the case just mentioned, this would include (but is not necessarily limited to) the organizational structure of vaudeville, the dynamics of technological change, the conventions of still photography, the constitution of the vaudeville audience, and the economics of popular entertainment. This stage might well require turning to other fields of inquiry for theories on the operation of the various generative mechanisms involved. In Chapter 5, for example, a theory from the field of industrial economics is used to help explain the coming of sound motion pictures. In the preceding case, theories of technological innovation, the history of visual representation, and marketing might help explain the circumstances under which American audiences first viewed projected motion pictures.

Third, the historian must take into account the fact that these generative mechanisms or causal factors do not operate in isolation from one another, but are interrelated. For example, the initial impetus for the development of the motion picture apparatus was scientific: an attempt to use photography to study motion. This scientific research formed the basis for the first movie camera, the

Edison Kinetograph, even though Edison's aim was primarily economic (to develop a visual accompaniment for the phonograph, another Edison invention that was hugely successful as a popular entertainment novelty). As Chapter 3 demonstrates, Edison's inventions (or, in the case of the Vitascope, inventions marketed under Edison's name) were eagerly accepted by the American public in part, at least, because of a climate of opinion that glorified the machine and inventors.

Finally, Realism recognizes that the force or causal power of generative mechanisms is uneven in any particular historical event. It is the historian's task not only to identify the range of causal factors responsible for any given event, but also to assess their relative force or importance. A generative mechanism primarily responsible for one event might not be nearly so important in another, apparently similar event because of a different relationship between that mechanism and the others involved. For example, the formal or aesthetic qualities of the films shown on the first Koster and Bial program seem not to have been a major determinant of their success—that first audience was fascinated by the very fact of moving images regardless of the relative simplicity of those images. It was not long, however, before aesthetic differences between films became considerably more important.

By the same token, where the historian observes the same generative mechanism at work in the same manner in a variety of historical events, it is possible to develop models of that mechanism and test those models in still other historical cases. For example, it is difficult to deny the central role played by economic forces in the historical development of the American cinema. No film is made without an economic commitment of some kind, and, given the fact that by 1910 commercial films already were costing more to make than the average worker made in a year, it is not surprising that a great deal of film production has been the province of profit-seeking companies. Time and again in film history we can see film companies acting in ways that they believe will result in the greatest long-term profitability. This is definitely not to say that all film history can be explained by economic forces alone. Economics is but one among a number of generative mechanisms involved in the history of the American cinema, and its relative force varies considerably from event to event. However, the consistency with which economic factors arise in film history enables us to develop models of the operation of economics in film history that can be applied to various specific cases.

Chapters 4 through 7 discuss the four major areas of film historical investigation to date: the study of the cinema as technology, economic entity, social institution, and art form. This division might also be seen as establishing four major categories of generative mechanisms in film history: technological, economic, social, and aesthetic. Some film historians regard these areas as separate objects of historical study, claiming, for example, that the history of film as art has little to do with the history of film as a business enterprise. However, a historical understanding of the cinema ultimately involves all of these factors; they are all threads of the same cloth. The question is not *if* they are all part of film history, but *how* they operate as individual generative mechanisms in specific historical cases, and, beyond that, how they are interrelated. The interrelation of these areas from a Realist perspective is the subject of Chapter 9. It is not necessary that the reader share this Realist approach to film history in order to make use of this book. It is used in this book to suggest one possible approach to film history—an approach that is empirically grounded, theoretically informed, and capable of accommodating a number of historical interests and orientations. For those readers who do not find Realism valuable as an approach to film history, it is hoped that the following chapters will still provide a useful introduction to the field of film historical investigation.

By taking up philosophical issues first, this book has begun at a rather abstract level—a level above that of the specific concerns of film history, even, at times, above those of history in general. Some readers might feel the issues dealt with in the preceding discussion were *unnecessarily* abstract for the person just beginning a study of film history. However, film history is not a list of film titles or an academically respectable trivia contest. It has the much more important and complex task of explaining the historical development of a phenomenon on which billions of dollars and countless hours have been spent. Film is thought by some to be the representative art form of the twentieth century, yet it has also prompted riots and demands for censorship. Film is an entertainment form we have taken for granted for more than eight decades, yet it has undoubtedly changed the way we perceive the world around us. Thus readers of film history, even first-time readers, cannot afford to assume that the nature of this serious undertaking is unproblematic, even if film historians sometimes do.

NOTES

1. Dudley Andrew, *The Major Film Theories* (New York: Oxford University Press, 1976), p. 3.
2. See Rudolph Arnheim, *Film As Art* (Berkeley: University of California Press, 1966 [originally published in 1930]); Jay Leyda, ed. and trans., "A Statement on the Sound-Film by Eisenstein, Pudovkin, and Alexandrov," in *Film Form* (New York: Harcourt, Brace and World, 1949), pp. 257–260; for the response of American reviewers to sound, see Stanley Kauffman, ed., *American Film Criticism: From the Beginnings to* Citizen Kane (New York: Liveright, 1972).
3. Edward Hallett Carr, *What Is History?* (New York: Vintage Books, 1961), pp. 7–9.
4. Quoted by John A. Passmore, "The Objectivity of History," in *Philosophical Analysis and History*, William H. Dray, ed. (New York: Harper and Row, 1966), p. 76.
5. Carr, *What Is History?*, p. 26.
6. Vincent Cronin, *Catherine, Empress of All the Russias* (New York: Morrow, 1978), p. 233.

7. Charles Beard, "Historical Relativism," in *The Varieties of History*, Fritz Stern, ed. (New York: Meridian Books, 1956), p. 324.

8. See Carl Hempel, "The Function of General Laws in History," *Journal of Philosophy* 39 (1942): 35. Empiricism in the social sciences is discussed by David and Judith Willer in *Systematic Empiricism: Critique of a Pseudo-Science* (Englewood Cliffs, N.J.: Prentice-Hall, 1973); and Richard Bernstein in *The Restructuring of Social and Political Theory* (New York: Harcourt Brace Jovanovich, 1976), pp. 3–54. The Willers call empiricism "an approach so all-pervasive [in American social science] that, although the commitment to it is only partially conscious, it enters unknowingly into the most diverse activities. . . . It determines what is today sociologically legitimate and is even the basis of the evaluation of historical works" (p. 1).

9. Louis O. Mink, "The Anatomy of Historical Understanding," in Dray, *Philosophical Analysis and History*, p. 166.

10. Russell Keat and John Urry, *Social Theory as Science* (London: Routledge and Kegan Paul, 1975), p. 4.

11. David Hackett Fischer, *Historians' Fallacies: Toward a Logic of Historical Thought* (New York: Harper and Row, 1970), p. 16.

12. Hempel, "Explanation in Science and in History," in Dray, *Philosophical Analysis and History*, p. 100.

13. Hempel, "Reasons and Covering Laws in Historical Explanation," in Dray, *Philosophical Analysis and History*, p. 92.

14. Keat and Urry, *Social Theory as Science*, p. 5.

15. Terence Hawkes, *Structuralism and Semiotics* (London: Methuen, 1977), p. 22. Hawkes's book provides a good overview of the schools of linguistic and cultural analysis that grew out of Saussure's work.

16. Thomas S. Kuhn, *The Structure of Scientific Revolutions*, 2nd ed. (Chicago: University of Chicago Press, 1970).

17. Paul K. Feyerabend, "Against Method: Outline of an Anarchistic Theory of Knowledge," *Minnesota Studies in the Philosophy of Science* 4 (1970): 21.

18. James Anthony Froude, quoted in Carr, *What Is History?*, p. 30.

19. Roy Bhaskar, *A Realist Theory of Science* (Atlantic Highlands, N.J.: Humanities Press, 1978); and Rom Harre, *Philosophies of Science* (Oxford: Oxford University Press, 1972). My discussion of Realism is also based on: Terry Lovell, *Pictures of Reality: Aesthetics, Politics and Pleasure* (London: British Film Institute, 1980); Ted Benton, *Philosophical Foundations of the Three Sociologies* (London: Routledge and Kegan Paul, 1977); and Keat and Urry, *Social Theory as Science*. Gregor McLennan's *Marxism and the Methodologies of History* (London: Verso Books, 1981) interprets Marxist historiography from a Realist perspective. As he notes, "a systematic realism is only now coming onto the agenda in historiographic thinking" (p. 66).

20. Keat and Urry, *Social Theory as Science*, pp. 5–32.

21. Bhaskar, *A Realist Theory of Science*, p. 47.

22. Keat and Urry, *Social Theory as Science*, p. 44.

23. Benton, *Philosophical Foundations*, p. 196.

24. Lovell, *Pictures of Reality*, p. 22.

25. This method is adapted from Bhaskar's "four stages in the explanation of an open-systemic event" in *A Realist Theory of Science*, p. 125.

26. This discussion of the Koster and Bial exhibition is based on: Robert C. Allen, *Vaudeville and Film 1895–1915: A Study in Media Interaction* (New York: Arno Press, 1980).

2

Researching
Film History

In an attempt to define film history, this book has dealt thus far with the "history" part of that term, that is, those historiographic issues film history shares with all other types of historical analysis. This chapter examines those issues, problems, and opportunities that make the study of the cinema's past a distinctive branch of historical research: the "film" part of film history. As you read film historical works, you will find that some periods, issues, films, and personalities have received considerable attention, while other large areas of possible investigation have remained virtually untouched. The entire project of film historical research—what topics receive scrutiny, which questions get asked, which approaches are taken—is conditioned by (1) the history of film history and film studies as an academic discipline, (2) the perceived cultural status of film as an art form and industry, and (3) the particular research problems presented by the nature of film technology and economics.

THE HISTORY OF FILM SCHOLARSHIP

All historians operate within general cultural contexts that influence their research. Historians are also affected by the more specific context provided by the particular branch of history within which they work. Contemporary historians of ancient Greece add their efforts to a tradition of scholarship centuries old, while investigators of twentieth-century European political history study phenomena themselves within living memory. Few fields of historical research are as recent in their development as film history. The vast majority of books and scholarly articles on American film history have been written since 1960; most of them during the last decade. To be sure, some important works appeared prior to 1960 in the United States—Terry Ramsaye's *A Million and One Nights,* Lewis Jacobs' *The Rise of the American Film,* and Benjamin Hampton's *History of the American Film Industry,* to name three notable examples—but film history as a distinctive field of scholarly inquiry is barely twenty years old.

To the film historian working in the latter part of the twentieth century, the new-fledged status of the discipline presents him or her with a significant problem historians in older fields do not have: the lack of preceding analyses. Film historians hoping to build upon existing research nearly always discover the hoped-for prior work of film history to be slight and often unreliable.

There are several reasons for the embryonic status of film history as a field of scholarship; most obvious among them is the youth of its object of study. The cinematic apparatus (camera, film, projector) did not appear until the mid-1890s, and it was several years after that before films were shown commercially. Hence we might expect to find a "generation lag" of twenty years or so between the innovation of cinematic technology and historical study of the artistic, economic, and social results of its use. The teaching of film courses in colleges and universities and the recognition of the value of film as an area of "serious" academic research had to wait for the concept of "culture" to change from one that excluded film and other popular artistic and recreational activities to one that could accommodate their study. As intellectual historian Henry May has pointed out in *The End of American Innocence,* to the generation of American academics, critics, pundits, and other intellectuals who encountered film in its first decades, the term "culture" meant:

> not so much a way of describing how people behaved as an idea of how they *ought*
> to behave and did not. More specifically, culture in America meant a particular part
> of the heritage from the European past, including polite manners, respect for tradi-
> tional learning, appreciation of the arts, and above all an informed and devoted
> love of standard literature.[1] (Emphasis added)

While some (social reformer Jane Addams, for example) spoke of the potentiality of the cinema to dispense values, most of the "custodians of culture" regarded film, at best, as a mass diversion like roller skating and hence nonculture, or, at worst, as an enemy of culture that reduced *Hamlet* to twelve silent minutes of wild gesticulation. As the movies in America developed into a multimillion dollar industry, their very popularity militated against their being considered "serious" cultural contributions by most academics: How could anything turned out on an assembly line by former furriers with an audience made up of the uneducated masses be considered "art," according to any "serious" cultural standards? Film might be studied (and was with great frequency from 1908 on) to assess its social effects (presumed to be deleterious in most cases) upon criminal behavior or the sexual mores of youth, but as a phenomenon worthy of study in its own right film was seen as having little place within a university.

At the same time that intellectuals were guarding, to use Matthew Arnold's definition of culture, "the best that has been thought and said" from dilution, American and European anthropologists were expanding the use of the term "culture" to mean a *description* of a particular way of life or the meanings and values that inform the actions of a group of people. This anthropological sense of culture extended the arena of cultural activity to be studied in industrialized societies from the very limited realm of the social and economic elite to encompass many other questions of taste, values, and social activities among all classes.

By the 1960s, American scholars in speech, art, English, history, foreign languages, and sociology were conducting and publishing investigations of cultural phenomena, which would have been heaped with scorn and ridicule by their academic colleagues only a few decades before. "Popular culture" courses appeared in the curricula of many American colleges and universities, doctorates were awarded for dissertations on "hard-boiled" detective novels and western pulp fiction, and journals devoted exclusively to popular culture were launched. This movement toward investigating previously ignored aspects of culture accelerated during the late 1960s into early 1970s, as universities added programs in Women's Studies, Black Studies, Latino Studies, and Southern Studies.

Cinema studies took hold and flourished in this time of expanding cultural studies. The respectability of film as an academic area was enhanced by the fact that by the 1960s in the United States film no longer functioned as *the* American popular entertainment form, having been recently supplanted by television. With television viewing becoming a daily habit in millions of American households, fewer alarms were raised over the negative social effects of movie-going and more concern was expressed over the effects that televised violence and advertising had on children. An influx of European films by Bergman, Fellini, Rossellini, and others into America after World War II helped to raise the cultural status of film in the eyes of serious analysts. Auteurist critics argued that these directors were artists. Cinema studies also took root in departments of speech and mass communication, where the research and teaching of film seemed a logical extension of work already being done in rhetorical criticism, journalism, broadcasting, and media theory and history. Moreover, the 1950s and 1960s saw a proliferation of courses in film production, brought about by the development and improvement of cheaper and simpler filmmaking equipment, particularly in 8mm and super-8mm gauges. At some colleges "film appreciation" courses began as complements to course work being offered in filmmaking. English departments used film adaptations of famous novels and plays as a means of teaching literature.

It is quite probable that cinema studies was the fastest growing academic discipline in American universities between 1965 and 1975. In 1967 some 200 colleges offered courses in film. Ten years later the number had passed 1000, an increase of more than 500 percent. In 1978 the American Film Institute counted nearly 4200 separate courses in film studies being offered in American colleges, and nearly 150 schools offered degrees in film.

This boom in film study gave rise to a huge demand for film scholarship—particularly scholarship that could be used as textbook material in film classes. The most sought-after type of film history book was the general, introductory text: the overview history of American or world cinema from the 1890s to the present. This type of book was well suited for use in "Introduction to Film History" or "American Film History." Such survey works do exist in all branches of history. However, historians in other areas are able to construct their "overviews" on the basis of an accumulated mass of original research reported in journal articles, monographs, case studies, and specialized book-length works built up over a period of decades, if not centuries. Film history's recent admission to the academy meant there existed no such reservoir of basic research—only a few seminal studies and a handful of historical surveys. It is not surprising that American film histories, no matter how old, were reprinted in paperback and pressed into service as textbooks: Terry Ramsaye's *A Million and One Nights* (1926) appeared in a paperback edition in 1965, Benjamin Hampton's *A History of the Movies* (1931) was renamed *History of the American Film Industry* for its paperback printing in 1970, and Lewis Jacobs' *The Rise of the American Film* (1939) was brought out in a new edition in 1968. None of the authors was a trained historian; none of the works meant to be measured against rigorous standards of historical scholarship.

A new generation of survey histories born of the film studies boom has now replaced these pioneering works. Today's student of film history can choose from a dozen histories of American and world cinema, with more coming out every year. Most of them represent advances over older works—inaccuracies have been corrected and new research has been incorporated. Most contemporary writers of film history textbooks would not claim that their works are definitive studies, however. They would be the first to admit that their books represent not so much *the* history of the cinema, but what, at present, we *think* we know about how the cinema developed historically. They would even acknowledge that, because of the spectacular growth of film as an academic discipline, the demand for film history books has far outrun the pace of original research in film history. The fact that so much in film history remains to be done means that ours is a tremendously exciting field to work in and read about. As students of film history quickly learn, however, the technological nature of film itself creates a further set of serious research constraints.

FILMIC EVIDENCE

Each type of historical inquiry has its own special evidentiary problems, that is, problems arising from the nature and scope of the extant evidence relevant to the object of historical study. While the historian's work is far more than merely the collection and presentation of such data, the historical artifacts available to him or her does influence which historical problems get investigated and which remain hidden in the shadows of historical inattention. In a sense, what we can know of the past is limited to the historical traces of it that exist in the present.

The primary documents for many types of film history are, of course, the tens of thousands of individual motion pictures made since the invention of cinema in the 1890s. Unfortunately, however, most of the films produced no longer exist—in any form. We estimate that nearly half of the theatrical-length motion pictures made in the United States are lost forever. Consider the enormity of this loss for the historical study of the cinema. It is difficult to construct even a hypothetical analogy on the same scale in another branch of history. To do so we would have to propose, for example: What if two-thirds of all the paintings done in the twentieth century were destroyed, and most of the remaining one-third were saved through happenstance rather than systematic preservation?

The reasons for this irrecoverable loss are technological and economic. Motion picture film is made up of three parts: (1) a light-sensitive emulsion that records and holds the photographic impression, (2) a base on which the emulsion is spread, and (3) a binder to hold the former to the latter. Film base must be transparent, flexible, strong, and have a surface texture able to be coated with emulsion. Between 1888 and 1951, the material best meeting these requirements was cellulose nitrate, a substance derived from animal tissue (first developed in 1868 as a replacement for ivory billiard balls). However, in addition to those qualities that make cellulose nitrate an excellent base for motion photography, it also has properties making it a film historian's nightmare. Chemically, nitrate stock is a third cousin to gun cotton, a powerful explosive. It cannot be made chemically stable. Stored even under the best of conditions, nitrate film will self-destruct usually within fifty years. Technically, what happens is that cellulose nitrate begins to oxidize, releasing nitrogen oxide. The surface of the film first becomes sticky, then, with further deterioration, the emulsion separates from the base. If the film is stored in a sealed container, gases build up that enter into combination with the binder releasing acid. The image in the emulsion fades and eventually the base itself is eaten away, leaving only a pile of brown dust. To make matters worse, as this deterioration occurs, the film becomes increasingly explosive. If the gases released by oxidation build up, spontaneous combustion can occur. Even if this does not happen, the flash point of the brown powder residue is lower than that of newsprint. Since cellulose nitrate contains its own oxidant, it doesn't need air to burn. Once it is ignited, it is extremely difficult to extinguish.[2]

As early exhibitors discovered, sometimes with disastrous results, even brand new nitrate film stock is subject to explosion and fire. Considering the use of open-flame lamps to illuminate early film projectors, it is surprising more people were not killed. Obviously if the cinema was to become a mass entertainment industry, the movie-going public had to be protected against theater fires due to nitrate film combustion. So projectors were placed in lead-lined booths and projector design was improved to assure the public that movie theaters were safe.

The volatility of nitrate film stock created problems for producers as well. There was little incentive to store prints of films more than six months or so—after their economic potential had been exhausted. A few cans of film in a theater were dangerous enough, but thousands of warehoused reels constituted a veritable ammunitions depot. After the distribution runs, some producers stored films in concrete buildings with "blow-off" roofs carefully isolated from other structures. That way if the film did explode and burn, at least it would do minimal damage to facilities. Many Hollywood producers found it easier and less expensive simply to dump prints in the Pacific Ocean, after preserving one "master" copy of each film. It is not that the Hollywood executives were callous philistines. Until television began to run old Hollywood movies in the mid-1950s, the value of a film at the end of its distribution run was seen as zero. Before the advent of videotape local television news shows were not saved for the same reason.

Much of the world's film heritage was obliterated between 1896 and 1951. Shown here is an employee of the Douglas Fairbanks Studio destroying nitrate film to help recover silver (1922).

The National Center for Film and Video Preservation

Viewed from the perspective of the film historian, however, what occurred between 1896 and 1951 was the obliteration of much of the world's film heritage. Whereas had our books, music, or paintings been threatened there would have been a public outcry, hardly a thought was given to preserving films. In large measure, what militated against film preservation throughout the world, and certainly in the United States, was precisely what kept it for so many years out of universities: its status as "cheap" entertainment for the masses, as a cultural product with no more serious value than a side-show or picture postcard.

With profits the motive, it is not too surprising that the first preservation effort in the United States had nothing to do with film art, but rather to protect its economic value as a product: copyright. In 1894 there were no motion picture provisions in copyright law—its authors could hardly have foreseen the invention of this new technology nor the industry that was to grow from its exploitation. Nevertheless, Edison laboratory assistant W. K. L. Dickson needed some means to protect from unauthorized duplication the films he was making at the Edison works in Orange, New Jersey. Hoping to have his works protected under a section of the law dealing with still photographs, Dickson prepared copies of his films on paper and submitted these to the Library of Congress. Other producers followed suit, and so between 1894 and 1912, more than 5500 "paper-prints" were deposited. In 1912 the submission of paper-prints ended when motion pictures were added to the copyright law. Only a written description was needed for registration. For forty years, the rolls of paper lay forgotten in the bowels of the Library of Congress while all the celluloid prints of most of the films depicted in the paper-prints disappeared. In 1952 a team of archivists, led by Kemp Niver, developed a process for preserving and creating viewable positive films from the paper-prints, and the tedious task of rehabilitating the largest cache of early American films began. In all, some 3050 titles were saved.

Unfortunately, however, for every "paper-prints" victory in the battle for film preservation there have been many more setbacks. Only about 75 of the over 500 films made by the pioneer French director of fantasies, Georges Méliès, are known to have survived. Entire bodies of cinematic work, particularly of directors, producers, writers and actors of the silent era, have vanished. Film historian Kevin Brownlow sums up the problem this way in his *The Parade's Gone By*:

> Archives are short of space and desperately short of money. They do their best to preserve films of accepted importance and films by well-known directors. But they cannot gamble. They cannot afford to waste space or risk funds on unknown films by unknown directors.[3]

As Brownlow goes on to point out, even the works of critically acclaimed directors have disappeared. Almost all of the silent films directed by William Wellman (who later directed *Public Enemy*, *A Star Is Born*, and *The Ox-Bow Incident*) are lost. Among the "lost films" archivist Gary Carey mentioned in his book of that title are four silent films directed by Joseph von Sternberg (who later made *The Blue Angel, Blonde Venus,* and *Morocco*); four of the nine silent American films directed by the great Swedish director Victor Sjostrom, including one with Greta Garbo; all but two of the many films directed by Cecil B. DeMille's brother William, a major directorial talent in his own right; and *The Patriot,* a 1928 film starring German emigré actor Emil Janning, of whose performance the *New York Herald Tribune* said, "one of the greatest in the history of stage or screen, . . . [which] places him as the outstanding actor in any current form of dramatic art."[4]

Perhaps the most devastating nitrate film tragedy occurred in Sweden in 1941. Since its founding in 1907, the film production company Svenksa has dominated the Swedish film industry. It produced all the films of the two noted silent film directors, Mauritz Stiller and Victor Sjostrom, and, more recently, those of Ingmar Bergman. Until 1941 all the Svenska negatives had been carefully preserved, and because of the preeminent position of the company, Sweden, alone among film-producing countries, could boast that its entire filmic heritage was intact. In September 1941, Svenska archive was torn apart by a violent explosion. Two people were killed, and the negatives of 95 percent of all films produced in Sweden in the preceding thirty-four years were destroyed in a few minutes.[5]

The major technological problems in black-and-white film preservation, and the volatility and disintegration of nitrate stock were solved finally in 1951 when, after decades of research and experimentation, a satisfactory substitute film base was developed. Acetate stock, still used today, is chemically stable, nonflammable, and will not disintegrate.

As film has grown in stature as an art form and academic discipline since the 1950s, so has the concern that as many films as possible be saved. Today most countries with a tradition of domestic film production have some agency charged with collecting and preserving films and other materials relating to that nation's film history. Every year archivists discover lost films in attics, basements, warehouses, and among private collections, and transfer the images from deteriorating nitrate to acetate. However, no major film-producing country has as yet devoted the resources necessary to finance a complete nitrate-to-acetate transferral program. The Library of Congress has some 80 million feet of nitrate film—the equivalent of 13,300 feature films—yet to be put on acetate stock. At its current rate of transfer, it will take Great Britain's National Film Archives sixty years to make acetate prints of its nitrate. But, of course, in sixty years there will be few if any images left on the nitrate to copy. Tens of thousands of film prints rot away in France, Italy, Germany, and other countries because of inadequate funding for preservation.

The film archivist, then, is placed in the difficult position of having to decide through the allocation of scarce preservation funds which pieces of film-historical evidence will survive and which will be forever lost. Should first priority be given to those nitrate films most in danger of deterioration? Should the films of established directors be preserved or an effort made to resurrect the work of critically overlooked filmmakers? Could the film historian benefit most from the preservation of what were regarded as the "best" films of a particular period or should the archivist save a representative sample of work? Obviously each decision means that some films are condemned to oblivion, some possibly vital pieces of historical evidence irretrievably lost.

Unfortunately, nitrate deterioration is not the only serious technological obstacle to film preservation and the researching of film history. It is difficult to properly hear early sound films since the necessary projection equipment is not available. Almost all the color films produced since the 1950s are subject to color fading that can render them in only a few decades pale ghosts compared to their original hues. Martin Scorcese's *Raging Bull* (1980) was shot in black and white to avoid this problem. Theatrical and television prints of *Rebel Without a Cause*, *Tom Jones*, and *Once Upon a Time in the West*, to name but a few of the more notable examples, look like the paintings of an artist whose palette was limited to pastels. According to Eileen Bowser, film curator at the Museum of Modern Art, color fading is the most serious technological problem in film preservation. Several solutions are being investigated: more stable color dyes, electronic reenhancement of faded images, and even the use of laser holography, but at present all archivists can do is store their color prints in freezers to slow fading and hope an economically feasible remedy is discovered before it is too late.[6]

The details of film preservation—locating nitrate prints, storing them properly, transferring nitrate to acetate stock, and dealing with color fading—are the concern primarily of the archivist rather than the historian. However, while the archivist's problems might end with the successful preservation of a film, the issues the historian must face in dealing with it as a historical artifact have just begun. Even before a historian can view an old film, he or she must, of course, determine whether it has been preserved, and if so, where. This is by no means a simple task. There presently exists no catalog of nitrate films held by film archives that have been transferred to safety film, nor a list of films awaiting transfer. Even if the particular title being sought is American, the search cannot be limited to American archives. Since film was from the beginning an international business, a print of an American film could have easily wound up in Lisbon, Moscow, or Buenos Aires. Although there is an international organization of film archives (FIAF: Federation International des Archives du Film), most of its members do not publish a catalog of their complete holdings; many publish no catalog at all. Hence, a historian must contact dozens of archives in as many countries, realizing all along there is a good chance the film for which he or she searches does not exist in any form in any archive.

Let us assume (for the sake of our discussion) that you can locate the film you need to view at an archive, that the film has been transferred to acetate and can be projected, and further that you have the financial resources to go to the archive (most archival prints must be viewed on the premises). You view the print, take copious notes, but then the question arises: What have you just seen? Have you seen the only version of the film or merely one of two or three different versions?

Textual variation (several versions of a single film) is not just a concern in isolated instances, but a pervasive problem in film history. Multiple versions of a film might have been prepared *intentionally* by a studio or distributor: to circumvent varying censorship standards, to please foreign audiences, or to provide exhibitors and/or television stations with a choice of running times, to name but a few motivations. Once the print left the producer (particularly if it was a silent film), it might have been reedited, shortened, or otherwise altered at any of a number of points. For example, *The Joyless Street*, a 1925 German film directed by G. W. Pabst and starring Greta Garbo and Asta Nielsen, depicted the effects of post–World War I inflation on two German women. The film was released in many European countries and in the United States, but judging from contemporaneous reviews, it is clear that almost every country saw a different version of the film, largely because of censorship regulations. In 1935, when Greta Garbo had achieved stardom, the film was re-released in the United States. Assuming that audiences would be drawn to *Joyless Street* only to see what Garbo looked like a decade earlier, distributors excised Asta Nielsen's role entirely—nearly 40 percent of the original film. It is this mutilated 1935 version that is still being rented as "Pabst's *Joyless Street*" by a major distributor of films to college cinema classes and television stations. While *Joyless Street* suffered more extensive mutilation than most films of its day, deletions, reediting, and multiple versions of films are problems film historians encounter very frequently.

One of the most troublesome instances of textual variation in film history concerns the 1903 American film *Life of an American Fireman*. This film, made by Edwin S. Porter for the Edison Company, is lauded by many film historians because it purportedly contains the "first" use of editing to tell a story. This evaluation is based on one scene in the film in which a woman and her child are rescued from a burning building by a fireman. Porter, we are told, used "cross-cutting" (cutting between two simultaneous events occurring in different locales) to create suspense. Shots of a woman and child awaiting rescue in a second-story bedroom are intercut with shots of firemen outside the house rushing to save them. The initial analyses of *Life of an American Fireman* (by Terry Ramsaye and Lewis Jacobs in the 1920s and 1930s, respectively) were done from an Edison catalog description and photographs, for the film was "lost." Claims of complex editing seemed to be supported when in 1948 a print, discovered by archivists at the Museum of Modern Art, was found to contain nine shots in the rescue scene. Bolstered by the "proof" from the newly found print, historians confidently proclaimed Porter's prescience as an editor in *Life of an American Fireman*.

In the course of restoring the paper prints, however, archivists at the Library of Congress discovered a second version of the film. In that version the crucial scene contains only three shots and none of the cross-cutting of the Museum of Modern Art print. In fact, in the Library of Congress version there is an overlap in the action between shots in the scene: The action is viewed first from within the burning building, *then* repeated from a camera position outside.

Still most film historians continued to base their appraisals of Porter's work on the Museum of Modern Art print. That version enabled them to value Porter as the "grandfather" of the narrative editing style, which, further developed by D. W. Griffith and others, has come to be the dominant use of editing in narrative films. The repetition of action in the Library of Congress version makes it difficult to fit the film into this scheme of evolutionary editing progress. However, in 1977 after closely examining both prints, Porter's career, and the popular entertainment context in which he worked, film historian Charles Musser (a student at the time he conducted his research) concluded:

> Today it should be clear that the Library of Congress paper-print is internally consistent, is consistent with Porter's own development as a filmmaker and consistent with the development of international cinema during the 1901–1903 period. The [Museum of Modern Art] version is a re-edited version, probably for release sometime after 1910.[7]

Using the Library of Congress print as his basis, Musser constructs an interpretation of the film almost antithetical with that of most other historians. The editing style of *Life of an American Fireman* does not anticipate "modern" editing techniques of Griffith and Hollywood, but looks backward to the style of magic lantern shows of the late nineteenth century—a style in which repeated narrative action was the rule not the exception. Musser's contention is that the cinema did not develop simply and directly but by fits and starts. Some methods of structuring films became part of standard cinema practice; others, represented by *Life of an American Fireman*, were tried but not continued.

Musser's work raises important questions for film history, and will raise questions in your mind when reading a survey history or film historical article. With so few early films extant and accessible to historians, it is often vitally important to know which print of a given film the historian is using. When was it made? By whom? Who saw it? What other versions exist? How do the variations differ? Has the historian actually seen the film he or she discusses or have scripts, catalog descriptions, reviews, or the analyses of other historians been substituted? Keep in mind that textual variation is not a problem limited to the dark days of the cinema's beginnings. *Grease* was cut by several minutes after its first theatrical run so that its "rating" could be changed from "R" to "PG." Movies shown on television are frequently altered to fit a particular time slot or to remove "objectionable" material.

Some types of film historical research, such as Musser's work on the editing strategy and narrative patterns in *Life of an American Fireman*, demand the detailed analysis of specific films. This is true particularly with regard to aesthetic film history: the study of camera movement, composition, lighting, performance, sound, or color. In a few cases, historians have tried to "reconstruct" lost films by verbal or visual accounts of films from frame enlargements, production stills, inter-title lists, censorship notes, or scripts. For example, Herman G. Weinberg has produced a pictorial reconstruction of Erich von Stroheim's lost two-part work, *The Wedding March* (1926), from stills. Swedish filmmaker and historian Gosta Werner put together verbal descriptions of thirty-one early works of Mauritz Stiller, all of which had been destroyed in the 1941 Svenska fire. Obviously, however, neither the use of stills nor the "reconstruction" of films through written accounts can replace the film itself as historical evidence. Verbal descriptions can merely suggest the way a shot might have looked. Still photographs cannot represent camera movement or editing. There is the further problem that often when stills are used to "illustrate" a film, we are not told whether the photograph is a *production still* or a *frame enlargement*. While a frame enlargement is a photograph actually made from a frame of the film, a production still is a photograph shot by a still photographer usually after a shot was recorded by the movie camera. Hence, production stills can give us an idea of what a particular *set* looked like, but they are of questionable value otherwise in that they were not a part of the film itself. In brief, if the object of film historical research is a question concerning a film, or group of films, or even an element of cinematic style, the historian must depend upon films as primary documents.

THE OBJECT OF FILM HISTORICAL RESEARCH

The extent to which filmic source problems complicate the study of the cinema's past depends on how we define the object of film history—in other words, what exactly is the historian studying when he or she studies *film* history? To some film historians, film history is the study of *films*. For example, John Fell entitled his recent survey of world film history *A History of Films*. He acknowledges in the Introduction the limitation this view imposed upon his work: "Because of the decision to concentrate on film texts, the book sacrifices attention that might otherwise have been directed toward the many social, political, and economic contexts from which films have emerged."[8] Film history certainly includes the study of individual films: the ways in which cinematic technique and technology has been used by different filmmakers at different times in different places. However, film history is considerably more complex (as Fell recognizes) than just the phrase "history of films" would imply.

First, what is a film? *Citizen Kane*, for example, is often treated by film critics and historians as a work of art, a milestone in the history of American cinema as art form. To its studio, RKO, however, *Citizen Kane* was primarily an economic product: one unit of their annual output, a capital outlay that had to be recouped at the box office. When the film was released in 1941, many commentators read *Citizen Kane* as a social statement—a thinly disguised account of the life of newspaper magnate William Randolph Hearst and a sermon on the corrupting effects of material and political power. *Citizen Kane* might also be regarded as an illustration of "state-of-the-art" in Hollywood movie technology, with its use of deep-focus photography and elaborate special effects. Which of these definitions of *Citizen Kane* as historical artifact is correct? Clearly, *Citizen Kane* is at one and the same time an artwork, an economic product, a social statement, and use of technology.

Even if all these aspects of individual films are taken into account, however, film history is more than just the history of individual films. Films do not just appear; they are produced and consumed within specific historical contexts. For example, since 1894 American films have been produced and exhibited primarily by entrepreneurs. A large economic institution has been established for which films are a means of generating profits. Any historical analysis of the American cinema would be woefully incomplete without consideration of the movies as an economic enterprise. Film or the cinema is more than any one thing, certainly more than a collection of individual films; it is a set of complex, interactive systems of human communication, business practice, social interaction, artistic possibilities, and technology. Hence, any definition of film history must recognize that the development of the cinema involves changes in a film *as* a specific technology, film *as* an industry, film *as* a system of visual and auditory representation, and film *as* a social institution.

In this book we have divided the field of film history into four major areas, representing the major avenues of film historical investigation to date. In Part Two we will examine these areas in considerably more detail, but we will briefly review them here to give you some idea of the range of topics that might be included within our definition of film history.

Aesthetic film history deals with the history of the cinema as an art form. Obviously the broadness or narrowness of this area of film history depends on one's notion of what constitutes "art" and "aesthetics." To some film historians aesthetic film history involves the identification, description, and interpretation of the masterpieces of filmic art.[9] We prefer to define the aesthetic history of the cinema much more generally to include the study of all the ways film technology has been used to give sensory (aesthetic) pleasure to and create meaning for audiences since the beginnings of the movies. Thus aesthetic film history would not only include the study of directors, styles of filmmaking, and artistic movements in the cinema, but a consideration of why some aesthetic uses of the cinema (narrative uses, for example) have been predominant in film history while others have been used less frequently.

Technological film history involves the study of the origins and development of the technology that makes possible the creation and presentation of movies. Film is inseparable from a specific and fairly complex technology. Without film stock, processing equipment, cameras, lenses, and projection apparatus there would be no cinema. How did this technology come to be? Why did changes in cinematic technology occur (such as synchronous sound, more versatile film stocks, color processes, wide-screen, and others) and why did they appear at specific historical moments? How did the technological state of cinema at any given time condition the ways in which the movies could be used as art form, economic product, and communications medium? These are some of the questions technological film history seeks to answer.

Economic film history, in its simplest sense, concerns who pays for movies to be made, how, and why. The relative technological sophistication of the movies has always rendered them a costly means of communication. A feature film (*Heaven's Gate,* for example) can cost over $40,000,000, and even a student film shot in 8mm film can run into the hundreds of dollars. Hence, every film emerges from an economic context: Stock must be purchased, equipment bought or rented, processing paid for, prints made, projectors obtained, and so on. As noted earlier, the movies in America have been a commercial enterprise since their inception—so successful a business that in the 1920s the motion picture industry was one of the fifty largest in the country. Much of American economic film history has examined the operation of the large and complex businesses set up to produce, distribute, and exhibit films—what we have come to refer to as "Hollywood."

Social film history, in its crudest sense, is concerned principally with three questions: (1) Who made films and why? (2) Who saw films, how and why? (3) What was seen, how and why?[10] Clearly, social film history covers a lot of ground, from questions of who makes what decisions at the studio to the social functions served by move-going. Much social film historical research has dealt with individual film content as a reflection of social values and attitudes. We turn to a discussion of these and other important issues in Chapter 7.

NONFILMIC EVIDENCE

Just as the study of film history is multifaceted, the data of film history are numerous and diverse. It is true that for one narrow form of film historical inquiry prints of films are the only valid data. However, for broader (and more interesting) questions, we think, nonfilmic materials prove invaluable. For certain investigations, film viewing is really an inappropriate research method. To give but one example of studying films without the need to see them, let us say you are interested in the general area of the economic power of Hollywood in the 1920s—particularly the relationship between Hollywood and Broadway. From a review of contemporaneous movie trade papers (*Variety* or *Moving Picture World*), some historians contend that during the 1920s Hollywood became increasingly reliant upon buying rights to stage plays as a source of movie screenplays (written materials upon which films are based). Specifically, one could ask: To what extent were U.S. movies of the 1920s based on plays, and did this reliance increase as the decade progressed? One could begin to answer this question without seeing a single film. The *American Film Institute Catalogue* for the 1920s, found in most college libraries, provides a list of all the films made in the

United States between 1921 and 1930, complete with cast lists, credits, and property sources. You could compare reliance upon stage property by year, studio, and type of film (westerns versus comedies). Please note, however, that conducting this research task depends on the existence and reliability of a special type of resource: the *American Film Institute Catalogue*. A similar question about industrial practices in the 1930s would prove extremely difficult to answer, precisely because at present only two decades of the catalog have been published—the 1920s and the 1960s.

We raise this particular example of using nonfilmic sources in the study of film history to point out both that these sources are available (and, we think, underutilized), and that the cataloging of national cinema production is far from complete. Where production indexes, such as the AFI catalogs, do exist, they provide an invaluable resource for the film historian and student of film history that can in some instances, at least, compensate for the loss or inaccessibility of film prints. With them, we can conduct quantitative studies of production trends that are otherwise impossible. Used in conjunction with other nonfilmic sources, the catalogs open up whole new areas for film historical investigation.

Given the paucity of extant film titles and the incomplete status of film cataloging, some film historians see the scope of "answerable" film historical questions to be extremely limited—not only because of the preceding two factors but also because of what they perceive to be the inadequacy of other nonfilmic sources. We are much more optimistic about the use of nonfilmic sources in certain types of film historical investigations. For example, let's examine an area where substantial nonfilmic sources do exist: film industrial history. Filmic sources are of limited usefulness in this type of research. The viewing of a given film might give the historian some information as to its status as an economic commodity: its "production values," use or absence of certain stars, or others who worked on that particular picture, but viewing will reveal little about the businesses that produced, distributed, and/or exhibited it. Films themselves tell us next to nothing about modes of production, organization structures, market situations, management decision making, or labor relations, just as close examination of a bar of soap would reveal little data in the study of the personal hygiene industry.

The major problem some historians see in using these nonfilmic materials is that they do not exist with the same objectivity and irrefutability as the primary documents of aesthetic film history: the films themselves. This dichotomy between "objective" filmic sources and hopelessly tainted corporate records or trade papers is a false one; the problem of textual variation means that the evidentiary status of archival film prints is often far from clear-cut. As in any branch of historical research, what we have are not "good" data and "bad" data, but sources of varying degrees of mediation and complexity.

Two of the most important sources for the historical study of the film industry are corporate records and industry trade papers. Access to corporate records has been a particularly vexing problem in conducting American studio histories; the companies involved (for example, Paramount, Warner Bros., and Columbia) were and continue to be businesses, not libraries. They do not seek, nor desire to handle, scholarly inquiries as an archive would. However, during the past decade, the situation has gotten much better. For example, Richard Schickel and other historians have been allowed access to Disney Studio records. In 1968, United Artists donated all their papers (5000 cubic feet) concerning film distribution from the founding of the company in 1919 to its sale to other parties in 1951 to the University of Wisconsin (Madison) Center for Film & Theatre Research. The papers of the Edison Company are available to scholars at the Edison National Historical Site in West Orange, New Jersey. Crates of Biograph Company records were discovered a few years ago in a bank basement, and have since been made available to historians at the Museum of Modern Art.

Not all corporate records are private; some are public information, such as annual statements, reports to stockholders, and other types of financial data required by the Securities and Exchange Commission. Other documents have become public record as a result of the many litigations or government investigations involving film industry corporations and individuals. Patent disputes, anti-trust actions, contested copyrights, and other civil court cases have made literally thousands of pages of corporate documents part of trial transcripts. Granted, this information is often not easy to locate, nor is it indexed for the convenience of the film scholar. Unlike private company records, however, court transcripts and governmental records are open to anyone who takes the trouble to find them. Certainly, the legal documents serve the interests of one party or the other, and are thus far from impartial. However, their usefulness to film history is not intrinsic to the documents themselves, but dependent on the nature of the historical question posed and the skill of the investigator in weighing and analyzing the data. While not exactly corporate records, testimony given before Congressional Committees investigating the motion picture industry often provides insights into industry practices and the industry's justification for them. Since the 1910s scores of hearing on the U.S. film industry were held by committees of the United States Senate and House. In all, thousands of pages of testimony were compiled. Some of these pages are only marginally related to the trade practices under examination, but the testimony is open to public scrutiny and, unlike most court records, available on microfilm to students and historians throughout the United States.

Since the first commerical exploitations of cinematic technology in the United States during the 1890s, economic, social, technological, and even some aesthetic developments in film have been covered in various entertainment trade newspapers. Theatrical trade papers such as the *New York Dramatic Mirror* and the *New York Clipper* first noticed early photoplays because of the use of motion pictures in vaudeville theaters (c. 1896). When *Variety*, the premiere American show business publication, began publication in 1905, it immediately commenced covering the movies—along with the legitimate theater, circus, vaudeville, and burlesque. As the movies became an autonomous entertainment form with its own exhibition outlets (c. 1906), and as the size of the industry increased dramatically, *Moving Picture World* (1907) was begun to service the motion picture industry exclusively. It was later joined by others: *Motion Picture Herald*, *Film Daily*, and *Photoplay* (the last is a cross between a trade paper and a fan magazine).

The trades are in themselves no substitute for corporate records, but they are valuable tools of the film historian. They are probably the most accessible source of institutional data we have: *Variety* (1905–present), *Moving Picture World* (1907–1927), and *Motion Picture Herald* (1915–1950) are all now available to university libraries on microfilm. Being contemporaneous with the events they report, they provide a sort of baseline chronology for institutional history. They are important sources of statements by industry leaders and frequently record the production plans of the studios. Since the trades were published for people working in film, they also cover events outside the industry proper that might be of interest or concern to it: developments in related industries, national or state legislative actions affecting film, patent disputes, and technological developments. Like any historical document, they are not to be trusted implicitly, but neither should they be ignored.

No one who has undertaken extensive film historical research can deny there exist serious materials-related problems in our field—problems the reader of film histories would do well to keep in mind. By now you should have surmised also that a tremendous amount of film historical scholarship remains to be done using those sources immediately available to the scholar. Furthermore, the absence or inaccessibility of traditional sources of data should be an invitation to the historian to look for evidence in unusual, if not exotic, places.

One of the most fascinating, and, for the historian, exciting aspects of film viewed historically is the extent to which film as a system of aesthetic, social, technological, and economic relationships intersects with so many different aspects of various national cultures since the 1890s. These multiple points of intersection mean that film also fits into other types of historical inquiry and that we can draw upon the methods and materials of those fields. As a leisure activity, film-going is part of recreation history; as an industry, it enters business history; as buildings, movies theaters interest the architectural historian; as a facet of city life, the movies command the attention of the urban historian.

We are also encouraged by the greater availability of films made possible by recent developments in media technology. Video cassettes and discs have lowered the cost of obtaining copies of films from several thousand dollars (in 16mm film versions) to as low as $15 (for some films on video disc). The number of titles available in these new formats increases every year. Film availability is also increased by the expansion of programming services offered by cable television systems. In some markets it is now possible to subscribe to several "no cuts/no commercials" movie channels (Home Box Office, for example), several independent commercial "super-stations," which rely heavily on feature films, in addition to the full complement of local commercial and public stations. This explosion in video programming will not solve filmic resource problems for the film historian, but it will facilitate certain types of film historical research.

So, rather than spend our time crying over jellied nitrate, we prefer to emphasize the research opportunities open to the film historian. Even with the evidentiary problems the field faces, there are more than enough researchable topics in film history to keep scholars busy for the foreseeable future. As we shall see in Chapter 4, a great deal of basic film historical research remains to be done using materials available at the local level.

NOTES

1. Henry May, *The End of American Innocence* (New York: Knopf, 1959), p. 30.
2. Ralph N. Sargent, ed., *Preserving the Moving Image* (Corporation for Public Broadcasting and NEA, n.p., 1974).
3. Kevin Brownlow, *The Parade's Gone By* (New York: Ballantine Books, 1968), p. 179.
4. Gary Carey, *Lost Films* (Greenwich, Conn.: New York Graphic Society, 1970), p. 72.
5. Gosta Werner, "A Method of Constructing Lost Films," *Cinema Journal* 14 (Winter 1974–75): 11–15.
6. Color fading is discussed by Bill O'Connell in "Fade Out," *Film Comment* (September–October 1979): 11–18; and in "Technology: The Arts," by Sol Manna, *Omni* (June 1981): 30, 148.
7. Charles Musser, "The Early Cinema of Edwin Porter," *Cinema Journal* XIX (Fall 1979): 1–35.
8. John L. Fell, *A History of Films* (New York: Holt, Rinehart and Winston, 1979), p. viii.
9. See, for example, Gerald Mast, "Film History and Film Histories," *Quarterly Review of Film Studies* I (August 1976): 297–314.
10. Ian Jarvie, *Sociology of the Movies* (New York: Basic Books, 1970), p. 14.

3

Reading
Film History

As Chapter 1 pointed out, the writing of history is not the passive transmission of facts, but an active process of judgment—a confrontation between the historian and his or her material. Similarly the reading of history, in this case film history, should not be thought of as mere reception, but rather as skeptical questioning—a confrontation between reader and historical argument. This chapter discusses some of the issues involved in reading film history, issues that pertain mostly to general survey works, but that are applicable to more specific studies as well. The chapter concludes with a case study of early film historical writing, relating the general historiographic concerns discussed in Chapter 1 and the specifics of film historical writing examined in Chapter 2.

FILM HISTORY AS NARRATIVE

Many historical analyses and almost all survey histories of film are couched in *narrative* terms. Film history thus becomes a story to be told by the film historian. David Bordwell and Kristin Thompson define narrative as "a chain of events in cause-effect relationships occurring in time....A narrative begins with one situation; a series of changes occurs according to a pattern of causes and effects; finally, a new situation arises which brings about the end of the narrative."[1] We have become so accustomed to relating to history as a story (the two words are related etymologically) that they are sometimes used interchangeably. Arthur Knight, for example, announces in the Introduction to his film history, *The Liveliest Art*, "Since the story I elected to tell is of the development of an art, I had to forego much of the chatty gossip about personalities or behind the camera maneuverings that so often pass for film history." Thomas Bohn and Richard Stromgren's *Light and Shadow: A History of Motion Pictures* "tells an integrated story of those experiences which influenced artistic expression . . . and those which influenced the advancement of an industry."[2] Most survey film histories, whether they announce the fact explicitly or not, attempt to "tell the story" of the movies. The story might be "about" the cinema as art form, industry, cultural product, and/or technology, but is usually a story that begins with the invention of the cinematic apparatus and ends with the present.

Organizing historical arguments as narratives (a chronological arrangement of events in a cause-effect relationship) is an accepted and frequently illuminating historical strategy. Because so much of film history is written exclusively as narrative, however, it should be pointed out that the qualities that make for a good story are not necessarily those that make for good history. Difficulties arise in the writing of film history when the conventions of traditional fictional narrative are allowed to take precedence over solid historical analysis, and in the reading of film history when we allow our expectations for a good story to take precedence over our expectation that the historian will present us with a convincing argument. Clearly, when we read a spy novel or watch a Hollywood film, we expect more than just a "chronological arrangement of events in cause-effect relationship." We expect to find characters who act and who are acted upon, a plot with a definite beginning, middle, and ending, and the resolution of all the questions or mysteries the story poses. We do not expect to find gaps in or doubts about character motivations or cause-effect relationships, nor do we have reason to question how the storyteller knows what is being related to us or if he or she is reliable. As readers of film history, as opposed to readers of fictional stories, we should always be aware that narrative structures are imposed on historical phenomena by the historian. The data of film history do not conveniently form themselves into a traditional narrative, with a neat beginning, middle, and end—all ready-made to please and excite us.

Traditional fictional narratives often revolve around struggles between one set of characters, with which the reader clearly is meant to sympathize, and another, which is cast as villainous or undeserving of "living happily ever after." Film history is sometimes related as a story containing such heroes and villains. Aesthetic film history is particularly subject to the danger of confusing narrative character depiction with historical interpretation of the individual's role in historical events. In American film history, where the filmmaker usually works within the context of a large economic institution, it is easy to view the filmmaker as a romantic artist who confronts the philistinism of insensitive, greedy movie moguls. For example, Lewis Jacobs analyzes D. W. Griffith's desire to make longer films in the following way:

> Now Griffith began to chafe under the arbitrary limitation of a picture to one reel. One reel was hardly adequate to unfold a complete story; the limitation hindered development, curtailed incidents, and proved a general barrier to the choice of deeper themes. . . . But just as Porter in 1903 had had to convince his doubting employers that the public would sit through a picture a full reel in length, Griffith now had to struggle with Biograph's reluctance to lengthening films to two reels.[3]

All too frequently, the transformation of historical personae into narrative characters glosses over complex problems of historical causality. Certainly, individuals sometimes act in ways that produce significant historical consequences. In film history they might invent devices, make business decisions, or direct films that affect the course of film history, but individuals do not operate outside of historical contexts. In an institution as large and complex as the American cinema, innovation of whatever kind almost always occurs as a response to a set of economic, aesthetic, technological, or cultural forces far larger than the actions of one person. Hence, to say of Edwin S. Porter, as does Lewis Jacobs, that as "the father of the story film" he "transformed motion picture art"[4] does not explain very much about why the narrative film became predominant in the United States. It does, however, simplify the "telling of the story" of early American film history.

One reason for the prevalence of the reduction of historical change to the genius of individuals in early American film history is that the work of some directors has survived the ravages of nitrate disintegration while most, if not all, of the films of some of their contemporaries have not. Thanks in large measure to the preservation efforts of the Library of Congress, many of Griffith's early works are extant, as are all of his later feature films. Most of Griffith's fellow directors of the early period were not nearly so lucky. We will never be able to compare Griffith's early work adequately with that of his peers—J. Searle Dawley, Sidney Olcott, or George Loane Tucker, for example—because not enough of their films survived to enable us to do so. Griffith was a very important figure in the aesthetic history of the American cinema. He was acknowledged as such by commentators at the time. However, assessments of the enormity of his role (such as Arthur Knight's: "[He] took the raw elements of movie making as they had evolved up to that time and, singlehanded, wrought from them a medium more intimate than theatre, more vivid than literature, more affecting than poetry") must be viewed in light of the paucity of extant films directed by others against whose work this and other panygerics can be measured.[5]

Traditional fictional narratives ask us to "suspend our disbelief," to take for granted the "truth" of the story being told us and the narrator's knowledge of the events being related. Our attention is directed into the world of the story and away from how that story is being told and by whom. When reading history we cannot afford to be seduced by the story being told as history so that we neglect to ask those historiographic questions the fictional storyteller can so neatly avoid. A historian certainly has the right to relate historical events as a narrative, but as readers of history we have the corresponding right to stop him or her at every turn and ask, "On what grounds is this narrative sequence based?" Even if the relationship depicted between two events makes narrative sense, we must also ask, "Is it supported by historical evidence?"

Survey narrative histories of film present the reader with a serious obstacle to getting at the historical arguments behind their narratives. In many of them, the quantity and quality of evidence used as the foundation of the historical narrative are difficult to determine from the text itself or from references in footnotes and bibliographies. One standard criterion for judging the merits of any historical argument is the extent to which its conclusions are supported by relevant evidence. The absence of footnotes and detailed bibliographic references in survey film histories frequently makes it impossible to trace conclusions back to their evidentiary sources. Compounding this problem is the fact that, unlike survey works in other historical disciplines, survey film histories are not based on mountains of more narrowly focused books, specialized monographs, journal articles, and other pieces of primary research, which have been accumulated, scrutinized, and critiqued over a period of years if not decades.

As an academic discipline, film history is still in its infancy, and the amount of primary research produced thus far is tiny compared to other branches of history. Some of the conclusions presented in a survey of European political history, for example, might well be the result of the application of the principle of noncontradiction (discussed in Chapter 1) to primary research conducted by others. In other words, the survey historian has presented as a conclusion an interpretation that has been confirmed by several historians from differing philosophical orientations having studied the same phenomenon and *not* having disagreed on the issue in question. This is all too rarely the case in film history, however—nor are most survey histories of the cinema based on extensive and detailed primary research conducted by the author. To be sure, most authors of survey film historical works engage in some new research, but all too often they rely on other survey works for their interpretations of many film historical phenomena—survey works that are themselves based on still other survey works. Lack of supporting documentation and the narrative form of survey histories frequently give untested generalizations the undeserved status of accepted historical "fact." Thus it is not surprising to find that much recently published primary research revises or refutes the conclusions offered in survey histories.

There are some film historians who would agree with the preceding criticisms of the sometimes cavalier manner with which problems of evidence and explanation are treated in survey histories, but who would argue for a distinction between narrative or descriptive film history and interpretive or critical film history. They see the former as the establishment of a well-founded chronological account of "what happened when" in film history, and the latter as the subsidiary task of the application of explanatory models to this chronology. Establishing what happened, they would argue, must take precedence over and can proceed apart from individual interpretation. It is difficult, however, to see how film history can be divided neatly between establishing "what happened" on the one hand and "why it happened" on the other. The two are necessarily part of the same enterprise. The explanatory model being used in the narrating of film historical events might be implicit and hence difficult to specify precisely, but the very selection of which events are worthy of being chronicled and the ordering of those events into a narrative sequence are both acts of interpretation.

READING FILM HISTORIES

Becoming a discriminating reader of film historical works is first a matter of attitude and expectation. The film historian is not presenting the indisputable truth and the only possible interpretation of the facts, but an argument as to how a particular event *might* have happened and the *possible* consequences following therefrom. Any time we pick up a work of film history we are in effect asking the author to convince us of the validity of his or her argument. Hence as readers we should approach the work not as passive receptors but as skeptical questioners, persuaded of the author's interpretation only after a thorough scrutiny of its merits.

A profitable reading of history requires us to read closely and well. Particularly in reading survey film histories, it is sometimes necessary to "de-narrativize" the work, to pull apart the threads of the story and see if the study makes historical and logical as well as narrative sense. Narrative is not the only or necessarily the most appropriate mode of film historical explanation. The narrative mode's central concern—What finally happened?—necessarily emphasizes a limited set of characters and events as they develop over time and can restrict consideration of the complexities of a historical phenomenon.

For many years social and physical scientists have used a nonnarrative format for the presentation of research—a format also found in the presentation of some primary film historical research. Basically this format includes (1) statement of the problem investigated, (2) review of pertinent literature dealing with that problem, (3) posing of the specific research question answered or hypothesis tested, (4) discussion of the method used, (5) presentation of the data generated by the study, (6) conclusions derived from the data, and (7) suggestions for further research that have arisen from the study. This nonnarrative mode of historical writing opens to scrutiny the nature and extent of background research that has been done in preparation for conducting a specific study, the method employed in that study, the sources used, and the validity of the conclusions based on those sources. Rather than presenting history as a preknown and closed story to be related, it reveals history to be an ongoing process of question framing, data collection, theory building, and argumentation.

READING AS QUESTIONING

In short, getting the most from reading film history is a matter of asking the right questions. Here are some questions one might ask of any film historical work.

1. *To what extent does the author define the nature and scope of the study?*   Every historical work is "about" something, and none can be about everything. The subject matter of the work should be defined in such a way that the reader knows the specific project being undertaken and the specific historical question(s) being asked. Furthermore, the reader has a right to ask how certain limits to the study were decided upon, particularly chronological and geographical ones. Every branch of historical inquiry must deal with the issue of periodization: the division of history into smaller units of time—eras, epochs, periods, or ages. By western custom, historical time is divided into years, decades, and centuries, but for most historical purposes these divisions are arbitrary.

Historical phenomena usually do not conveniently coincide with a ten- or one hundred-year chunk of time. A work entitled "The American Cinema of the 1920s," for example, should demonstrate that there is some relevant reason for beginning this investigation in 1920 and ending it in 1930, rather than, say, 1914 and 1927. In fact, a much stronger case can be made for the latter set of dates as markers of a distinct "period" in American film history. World War I, which had a tremendous impact on the American film industry, began in 1914. This year also roughly marks the establishment of the feature-length film as the standard for the industry. The year 1927 marks the beginning of the end of the silent film era with the commercial success of the feature-length sound film. Furthermore, what might be a relevant segment of time with respect to one aspect of film history might not be relevant to another. For example, 1927 is clearly a watershed date for technological film history in the United States. In terms of the representation of social issues, however, the silent films of 1926 have more in common with the sound films of the early 1930s than do the latter with those films made after 1934—the year in which self-censorship began to be more rigidly enforced by the Production Code Administration.

2. *How does the historian analyze historical change, and what assumptions underlie these explanations?*   All historians explain change in some manner, and usually there is a pattern to arguments within a particular work. Regardless of the model from which the film historian works there will be certain assumptions underlying explanations of historical change. To give but one example, which will be expanded upon in Chapter 7, the pioneer social film historian, Siegfried Kracauer, argues that changes in the style and content of German films between 1919 and 1933 resulted from changes in the psychological disposition of the German people. As German hopes and fears modulated during that turbulent period, films changed to reflect "those deep layers of collective mentality

which extend more or less below the dimension of consciousness."[6] Two of the many assumptions implicit in his thesis are (1) that groups of people can be said to have a "collective mentality," and (2) that historians can identify the hopes and fears of an entire nation and thus speak of "the German people" in any meaningful way. To his credit, Kracauer lays out his method rather explicitly. In most film histories the explanatory mechanisms being used are presented much less directly and must be teased out by the perspicacious reader.

3. *How does the historian analyze historical stasis and what assumptions underlie these explanations?*   The massive changes that have occurred in the cinema since its initial development in the late nineteenth century disguise the fact that some aspects of film history have remained remarkably resistant to change for long periods. Just as the historian is obliged to analyze change, so must he or she account for why things do not change. Explaining stasis is a particular concern if one adopts the systemic view of cinema outlined in the previous chapters. Assuming that the cinema is a complex entity composed of interactive elements, how can one account for change in one element but stasis in others, when logically we would expect that if change occurs in one part of the system, the entire system is altered as a consequence? It might be that changes in other elements of the system in fact occurred, but are not apparent upon cursory examination. It could also be that the rate of change differs among elements of the system, that the elements are not directly connected to one another but are uneven in their historical development. Or it might be the case that some elements of the cinematic system are capable of "absorbing" the consequences of change in others. For example, David Bordwell, Janet Staiger, and Kristin Thompson argue that although the style of Hollywood films was modified somewhat between the 1920s and 1960, it has not changed radically—this despite changes in film technology, audience, and economic structure.[7] They and other film historians are presently engaged in an analysis of this apparent historical equilibrium in the face of significant change.

4. *Does the historian's presentation of conclusions and generalizations make logical sense?*   History is a form of argument. It makes a claim upon belief and supports this claim with a reason or reasons. Any time an argument contains the words *hence, thus, it follows that,* or *consequently,* its author is making a conclusion based on reasons given previously. As philosopher Monroe Beardsley has noted, "Whenever we are asked to agree to a certain statement because we already agree to another statement—when, in short, someone is trying to convince us of something—we must always raise the question *whether the reason is such that we ought to be convinced*"[8] (italics in text). As previously pointed out, it is frequently difficult to see the relationship between generalizations and evidence in survey film histories because of the paucity of documentation; however, the reader can ask in many cases whether or not a conclusion logically follows from one presented previously. Another way of asking this question is: Can an equally logical alternative conclusion be fashioned from the same material?

5. *What are the sources of data used for the study?*   Unfortunately, at present this question applies more to narrowly focused book-length works and journal articles than to most survey film histories, since many of the latter do not cite the sources used to support a particular generalization. Historians usually discriminate between *primary* and *secondary* sources. Primary sources are taken to mean those produced as a part or result of the event under study; secondary sources are commentaries on or later reports of that

event. Such a distinction is useful, but it should not blind us to the fact that not even the "most" primary evidence comes to the historian "pure." All our information about the past is filtered or mediated in various ways—certainly by the passage of time, and usually by someone's consciousness. The reader has a right to expect that the historian has used the "best" or least mediated sources of data available, and further, that he or she has brought all the available, relevant data to bear upon the investigation at hand. Whether or not "best evidence" was used in a particular account is often difficult for the reader to determine, but a close examination of the data sources cited is helpful in comparing historical accounts.[9]

The constant reiteration of the Chaser Theory provides a good example of why it is dangerous to accept at face value unsupported conclusions in survey histories of film. The vast majority of American film historians argue that although movies were popular attractions in vaudeville theaters when first introduced in 1896, audiences soon tired of seeing simple films of objects in motion. Within only a few years, it is contended, audiences were so bored with the movies presented in vaudeville theaters that the principal use for films became that of a "chaser": an act so boring that it drove patrons from the theater at the end of the program. Despite the fact that this argument appears in film histories from the 1920s to the present, it is largely unsupported by the evidence, and obscures rather than illuminates the early problems of film exhibition. An examination of extant vaudeville manager's reports and the theatrical trade press of the period between 1896 and 1903 reveals that while the novelty of the cinema did wear off after some months, films never sank to a level of ubiquitous disdain. In fact, when films could be made of important news events, the movies were often elevated to a place at the "top of the bill." It is because of the reliance of survey histories upon other survey histories that this simplistic historical generalization has circulated for half a century.[9]

6. *Does the evidence cited support the interpretation being presented?* As anyone who has done research knows, inclusion of a footnote or reference to a piece of evidence does not in itself lend credence to a historical argument. As historian David Fischer puts it, ". . . Every fact in history is an answer to a question, and that evidence which is useful and true and sufficient in answer to question B may be false and useless in answer to question A. A historian must not merely get the facts right. He [or she] must get the right facts right."[10] For example, in his book, *The Dream That Kicks: The Prehistory and Early Years of Cinema in Britain,* Michael Chanan quotes a reminiscence of an early exhibitor of films in English music halls in support of his contention that some music hall performers resented the intrusion of a mechanical novelty on the music hall stage.

> At the time. . . we showed [films] from behind through a transparent screen . . .
> which was thoroughly damped with water and glycerine. . . . I remember. . .getting
> fearfully ticked off by Marie Lloyd [a popular music hall performer], who was in the
> turn following us, as we wetted the stage rather badly, to which she took strong and
> forcible objection, particularly as far as language was concerned.

To this Chanan adds: "Notice here, incidentally, that film, within two years had been promoted to a billing second only to the leading stage artistes."[11] Chanan might quite justifiably use this recollection to support (1) that films were shown in music halls, (2) that in some music halls they were projected through translucent screens, and (3) that at least one music hall performer took umbrage at having to follow the movies and the mess their exhibition apparently made when projected in this manner. Note, however, that there is no justification for the further use Chanan makes of this reference—that "within two years [film] had been promoted to a billing second only to the leading stage artistes." The quotation indicates that, on this occasion, at least, the movies directly preceded Marie Lloyd sequentially *on the program,* but it in no way indicates the movies' relative programmatic importance, their *billing.* In fact, music hall, like American vaudeville, did not arrange acts in ascending order of importance or popularity on the program, although the "star" usually did appear at or toward the end of the program. How popular or important movies were as music hall turns at this time cannot be deduced from the evidence Chanan cites.

Conspicuously absent from the preceding list of questions is one raised initially in Chapter 1: How has the historian's culture and his or her place in it conditioned the writing of a particular film historical work? This question is set apart and left until last for two reasons. First, the questions discussed earlier in this chapter, including those dealing with narrative histories, usually can be answered through an examination of the work itself. A close reading will go a long way toward revealing how the film historian has used evidence, what causal mechanisms he or she sees in operation, and the philosophical orientation of the work. The relationship of the film historian to his or her culture, on the other hand, necessarily carries the reader outside the work. Also, examining the role of culture in the writing of film history is less straightforward and more complex. Culture influences the writing of history not only at the level of articulated positions but also at that of presumptions, emphases, and omissions. The following case study shows how two influential film historical works might be "opened up" and their cultural determinations read out.

CASE STUDY: THE FIRST AMERICAN FILM HISTORIANS

The history of the writing of film history in the United States began with two works: Robert Grau's *Theatre of Science* (1914) and Terry Ramsaye's *A Million and One Nights* (1926). These works interest us today not only because they were "firsts," but because subsequent film histories have relied greatly on them for their analyses of the origins and early development of American film. Grau and Ramsaye not only established the relevant "facts" of film history, but by what they chose to include *and* exclude, and by the emphasis they placed on certain events, films, and persons, they helped to determine the range of film historical subject matter for historians who wrote after them.

What Grau and Ramsaye saw as constituting film history was influenced by the historical contexts in which each work was written and published. To read either historian today is to read a work wrenched out of one set of historical circumstances and shoved awkwardly into our own. What will be attempted here is an "archeology" of the contexts out of which the two works emerged, to borrow a term and an approach from French historian Michel Foucault.[12] Specifically, the two works will be placed within their larger *discursive* contexts: within the larger body of thought and writing (the discourse) on the subjects Grau and Ramsaye dealt with in their histories.

At the time they wrote, Grau and Ramsaye knew of no other film histories to which they could relate their efforts (except that Ramsaye, working a few years later, did have Grau). Similarly, their readers received these works not so much as film histories, a species of discourse they had never encountered, but as works on show business, art, technology, and success. Hence it is within the discursive space created by these topics that *Theatre of Science* and *A Million and One Nights* were produced and consumed. Film history was for both authors and their readers the point at which these traditional discourses converged. Also to be considered are the circumstances surrounding the publication of these books, since the economic context of book publishing had much to do with the way these works were written and presented to the public.

Overview

Before writing on film Robert Grau had been a theatrical agent and personal manager of opera and theater stars. In 1910 he turned to free-lance journalism, producing articles on various aspects of show business for the trade and general press. In one year, 1915, Grau claimed to have published 500 articles.[13]

In *Theatre of Science* Grau focused on the contributions individuals had made to "the general progress in filmdom." He included in this category the inventors of the cinematic apparatus itself, film directors, actors, and writers, and especially film entrepreneurs. Many of the chapters are personality profiles and personal histories. We learn that Marcus Loew's success could be attributed to a "dominating yet ingratiating personality" and that David Horsley's rise to prominence in film production "was accomplished as a result of adamantine persistency in the fact of never ceasing disappointments."[14] The book is sprinkled with excerpts from letters written to Grau by these persons themselves, detailing their achievements.

Basically, *Theatre of Science* gives us history as the result of herculean acts by great individuals. To Grau, film history was the inevitable progression toward perfection of the cinematic art, guided from one stage of development to the next by a few people who had the foresight to see that film would one day eclipse the stage as a dramatic medium, an intuitive knowledge of public taste, and the perseverance to see their projects through to fruition. In Grau's account their efforts were invariably rewarded by economic success.

While personality characteristics figure greatly in Grau's analysis of the progression of film history, negative attributes such as greed, acquisitiveness, deceit, or selfishness are almost totally missing from his descriptions of the geniuses of film history. At the time Grau wrote, the movie industry was locked in a prolonged and bitter economic struggle between the Motion Picture Patents

Company, the old guard film companies led by Edison and the Biograph Company, and the "independents," an assortment of producers, distributors, and exhibitors, led by Carl Laemmle and William Fox. Grau refused to take sides in this crucial issue or to impune the motives of either group. All contenders, he asserted, performed "constructive pioneer work in the development of the motion picture."[15]

Terry Ramsaye began his professional life as a newspaper reporter. When Grau's *Theatre of Science* was published in 1914, Ramsaye was an editor of serialized stories for the *Chicago Tribune.* Between 1915 and 1917 Ramsaye served as director of publicity for the Mutual Film Company, the first of several such positions he held with various film companies. In 1921, at the behest of editor James Quirk, Ramsaye began a long-running series of historical articles on the motion picture for *Photoplay* magazine. These articles, revised and expanded, were published as *A Million and One Nights* by Simon and Schuster in 1926.

In the Preface to his book, Ramsaye asserted a rigorous objectivity: "Within the domain of the motion picture I have neither friendships nor enmities of sufficient weight to influence the telling of this story." His stance was that of a journalist; his aim was "to cover the birth of a new art—the motion pictures."[16] Unlike Grau, Ramsaye went to considerable trouble to track down not only the testimony of important individuals, but documentary evidence as well: personal correspondence, corporate records, and court cases. Ramsaye took his title from the story of Scheherezade, the maiden of Arabian legend who nightly postponed her execution by beguiling the king with a different story. Like her, Ramsaye is a storyteller, the eighty-one chapters of his book relating "tales," which together form the history of the movies in America.

The heroes of his tales are for the most part technological and industrial giants: Eadweard Muybridge, E. J. Marey, Thomas Armat, Jesse Lasky, Carl Laemmle, William Fox, and especially Thomas Edison. The flyleaf contains Edison's endorsement and his signature; the frontispiece bears his portrait. The chapter on Edison's early experimentation with moving pictures is entitled, "In the House of the Wizard." Edison emerges from Ramsaye's work as the most brilliant person of his age, a tireless inventor who finally realized the "wish of the race": motion pictures. Ramsaye even seconded Edison's insistence (long since legally denied) that the right to exploit motion picture technology was his and his alone.[17] Ramsaye, like Grau, clearly subscribed to what has been called the "great man" theory of history: the belief that history is "made" by the inspired acts of outstanding individuals, whose genius transcends the normal constraints of historical context.

To Ramsaye, the cinema's historical significance lay in its being a new and unique art form: "For the first time in the history of the world, . . . an art has sprouted, grown up, and blossomed in so brief a time that one person might stand by and see it happen." Furthermore, Ramsaye sees the history of the movies as art and its history as industrial product to be aspects of the same story: "All of the arts and all the industries are products of the same forces." This compression of art, industry, and technology into a single phenomenon helps to explain the fact that while Ramsaye announces his book as a history of an art, he spends the first 300 of his 833 pages discussing the history of movie technology prior to 1896.

There are differences between the two works. Ramsaye's is more comprehensive. Grau states at the beginning of *Theatre of Science* that he will skip over the better-known aspects of film history to bring to light other factors that also deserve credit. Both, however, share some basic ideas about the nature of film and film history.

1. The aesthetic, technological, and industrial history of the movies are not seen as separate issues but as inseparable parts of the same phenomenon. Hence, inventor, entrepreneur, and filmmaker are given equal stature and treatment.

2. Film is first and foremost a popular art form, and the aesthetic quality of a given film is seen as directly proportional to its audience appeal.

3. Film history is the story of the steady, inevitable progress toward technological and aesthetic perfection.

4. This progress is achieved through the discoveries and innovations of outstanding individuals.

5. This concentration on "great men" excludes other causal factors (economic, social, aesthetic) from their interpretations of film history.

Film History and Popular Discourse on Technology

The placement of these film historical works into a larger context might begin by examining the general discourse on technology of the late nineteenth and early twentieth centuries. This discourse is characterized by an idolization of the machine and the belief that the marvels achievable by technology were limitless. By 1900 the railroad, interchangeable parts, and developments in communication had helped to transform America from an agrarian to an industrialized society. Despite severe financial crises (the panic of 1863 and the recession of 1893), social dislocation, and violent labor disputes (the Haymarket Riot and the Pullman Strike, to name but two), the machine was admired, celebrated, and revered. Seldom was technological change seen as the root of social trauma. Much more frequently it was regarded as the solution to social, economic, and moral problems. The popular discourse on technology, says historian John Kasson, shows a belief that "the course of technology was ... bringing in sight a world civilization of reduced labor and enriched leisure, health and longevity, abundance, peace, and human brotherhood." The "overriding paradox" of this age, he says, was a consistently laudatory discourse on technology at a time of constant social disorder.

Popular journals such as *Scientific American* were established to chronicle technological progress. Elaborate expositions allowed the public to gawk at the latest wonders of the machine age. Given this discursive context, it is hardly surprising that Grau and Ramsaye made technology a central part of the history of motion picture art. Neither saw anything incongruous in an art work (a film) emanating from a machine. They regaled the inventor as an artist, and the invention as the producer of art. Nor did the cinema's blatant appeal to mass taste (Ramsaye called it "adolescent" taste) seem to be inconsistent with the cinema's role as *the* art form of the twentieth century. Their view of movie technology as democratic art—the "Theatre of Science," Grau calls it—is an expression of an aesthetics of technological progress to be found in the more general popular discourse of the time. Here we find the machine regarded not only as a utilitarian problem-solver, but quite literally as a wonder to behold, as an aesthetic experience. As the *Scientific American* put it in 1849, "Inventions are the poetry of physical science and inventors are poets."[19] The nineteenth-century view of the machine as art was fed by an American distrust of the "fine arts," which were regarded in popular discourse as European (and, hence, non-American), elitist, and of no practical value. Not only could a huge steam engine induce aesthetic rapture, it *did something*—it ran other machines, provided jobs, and produced goods and services. To Ramsaye, movie technology takes the age-old dream of high-art—the exact rendering of reality—and fulfills it more perfectly than could the most schooled painter. The same technology then makes this aesthetic miracle available to millions of people simultaneously, while preserving that experience for all time. The inventor becomes the artist of the twentieth century.

By the time Grau and Ramsaye wrote their film histories, popular accounts of a technological breakthrough fit a well-established pattern. Each new invention was seen as moving society one rung higher on the ladder of technological progress. The "new" invention had to be larger, more complex, more awe-inspiring than those it superceded. Grau and Ramsaye's treatment of motion picture art fit squarely into this "onward and upward" schema of technological progress. At the exhibition of the Vitascope projector at Koster and Bial's Music Hall, Ramsaye reported, the "amusement world was agog with speculation about the invention."

Viewing the introduction of the movies in the 1890s from the perspective of a decade or two later, however, both men saw the initial success of projected movies as merely the embryonic stage of motion picture progress. In the first few years of the use of movies in vaudeville theaters, filmmakers developed a repertoire of subjects appealing to a variety of audience interests. Audiences enjoyed films of vaudeville performers, vignettes from stage plays, travel films, cinematic portraits of political leaders, and "home movies" of their own cities and towns. To Grau and Ramsaye, however, these documentary subjects were simplistic and primitive. Following a brief flurry of interest, Ramsaye argued, the movies declined to the level of "chaser."[20]

Ramsaye and Grau looked for new and improved movies with "potentialities of screen art" to revitalize the medium and new artists to put cinematic pigment to canvas. They found such an aesthetic hero in Georges Méliès, a French magician turned filmmaker. Méliès specialized in elaborate trick films in which devils, witches, imaginary creatures, and scantily clad young women levitated, multiplied, and then disappeared in puffs of smoke. Méliès used both stage and movie technology to achieve his mysterious effects. To Ramsaye, Méliès's films represented a milestone along the road of cinematic progress because he exploited the technological capacities of the cinema.

> In his efforts to mystify and startle his audiences Méliès evolved the fade-out, the overlap dissolve, the double-exposure and life expedients which have become commonplaces of camera practise [sic] since. . . . For the first time ideas for the use of the camera as an instrument of expression, rather than of mere recording, were being born.[21]

While Méliès represented to Ramsaye a techno-aesthetic advancement, Méliès's work remained fatally flawed. It could not evolve further because of his adherence to aesthetic conventions derived from the hopelessly low-tech theater. Méliès used editing only to tie large segments of his films together. The space of a Méliès film was stage-space in which characters entered from the wings, and which was observed from a camera positioned as a theater spectator seated in the fourth row. When a closer view of a trick was demanded, Méliès moved his figures toward the camera, rather than moving the camera closer to them. In *Marvellous Méliès*, Paul Hammond has argued that, given the effects Méliès wanted to achieve in his films, narrative editing and other devices would have been unnecessary, even counterproductive.[22]

To Ramsaye, further cinematic progress required yet another innovator, this time in the person of Edwin S. Porter, the Edison-employed director of *The Great Train Robbery* and *Life of an American Fireman*. What Porter did to make him a cinematic hero in Ramsaye's eyes was not just to tell a story on the screen, but to make a cinematic device, editing, central to the process of cinematic storytelling. Porter's *Life of an American Fireman* was, to Ramsaye, a "gripping masterpiece. . .[that] swept the motion picture industry." Porter's next story film, *The Great Train Robbery*, confirmed his pioneering status by becoming a "boxoffice knockout."[23] As Charles Musser has pointed out, the editing strategies in Porter's films look backwards to the conventions of magic lanternry as much as they look forward to later Hollywood techniques. To Ramsaye, however, Porter's work was a giant leap toward cinematic perfection.

Technology and Success

In addition to being an aesthetic phenomenon and regarded as evidence of America's steady progress toward political, social, and economic perfection, technology also plays a central role in the public discourse on business success during the early twentieth century. As John Cawelti has noted in his book *Apostles of the Self-Made Man*, one American boast of the era was that the United States was the "land of opportunity" where any child could grow up to become President or the head of a large corporation. The epitome of success was the entrepreneur who achieved economic wealth by taking advantage of the opportunities offered by the industrial age.

Successful entrepreneurs were seen as forming an American aristocracy, an elite based not on birth or inherited wealth but on a combination of traditional values (frugality, hard work, and piety) and those demanded by the competitive world of industrial enterprise (self-confidence, initiative, and determination). The businessperson's striving for success, says Cawelti, was seen in the public discourse of the day as "the indispensable ingredient of human progress."[24] Technology came to be viewed in this context as an important avenue to business success. In the machine age would success not surely come to the inventor of a better machine? The flood of patents issued in the decades around the turn of the century testifies to the belief among thousands of Americans that invention held the key to their success.

The great example of success achieved through invention was, of course, Thomas Edison. By the time Grau and Ramsaye wrote, Edison had been for decades the most celebrated American of his age. The public image of Edison was that of the inexhaustible genius, whose demeanor was still that of the folksy midwesterner. His inventions were practical ones in which middle-class Americans could see immediate and beneficial application: the electric light, the phonograph, the mimeograph machine, the ticker-tape machine, and, of course, the motion picture camera. His productivity engendered the notion that there were no limits to his inventive capacity. Edison seemed to be pushing America toward technological utopia single-handedly. Between 1880 and 1920 no person in the world was so well known or revered. He was feted by every American president from Hayes to Coolidge and received by European monarchs and heads of state. He won every scientific award and medal then given. A man in North Carolina wagered with a friend that a letter bearing only Edison's picture for an address would be delivered to Edison. It was.

There were, however, several aspects of Edison's personality and activities that were conspicuous by their absence from his image in public discourse. Despite the huge sums of money Edison's laboratory generated through its inventions, Edison paid his workers poorly. When he needed university-trained personnel, he hired them from among recent immigrants who willingly accepted substandard pay. The idea of a labor union organizing his operation was so anathema to Edison that when in 1903 his workers did strike for higher wages, he used Pinkerton detectives to break the strike. The Edison facilities in and around West Orange, New Jersey, produced pollution so foul that in 1889 civic groups were able to secure 1500 names on a protest petition. Edison hired a private detective to pay off local public officials so that his property taxes could be kept at a fraction of their assessed value.[25]

While Grau's treatment of Edison is laudatory but slight, Ramsaye perpetu-
ated and amplified upon the popular image of Edison as the kindly, homespun
wizard of technology. His lionization of Edison served several functions. First,
Edison provided Ramsaye with a "great man" to whom the origins of modern
motion picture technology could be assigned. The "birth" of the cinema was
auspicious, indeed, if its "father" was none other than the most respected inventor of his age. Second, Edison's involvement in the invention of the motion picture linked the movies to a larger tradition of American technological progress.
The connection of the movies with Edison associated the movies with his other
inventions, particularly the phonograph and electric light, that were viewed as
benefitting the entire human race. Because of Edison's public image as the self-
taught farm boy, the elevation of Edison to the status of father of the movies
rendered the cinema a democratic, American technology, and, by extension, a
democratic art form. "Every motion picture machine, every motion picture enterprise, every motion picture personality, screen star or magnate of the screen
theatre, can be traced to some connection growing out of the little black box
that Edison dubbed the Kinetoscope," wrote Ramsaye. "This is one of the
absolute facts of the history of the motion picture."[26]

In *A Million and One Nights*, Edison's role is much more than that of
historical personage whose activities are recounted by Ramsaye. Edison and his
public image helped to sell the book as well as provide material for its contents.
As has been noted, Edison's endorsement adorned the flyleaf and his portrait
was displayed in the frontispiece. His involvement in the project did not end
there, however. The first edition of the book, published in 1926 by Simon and
Schuster, was limited to a few hundred copies, each signed not only by Ramsaye but by Edison as well. As early as 1921, five years before its publication,
Ramsaye asked Edison to review drafts of his manuscript and make comments
in the margins. According to Ramsaye, he relied heavily on these notes and
Edison's responses to letters of inquiry.[27]

Recent scholarship has indicated that Edison's role in the invention of cinema technology was much more limited than what Grau and Ramsaye indicated.
In *The Edison Motion Picture Myth*, Gordon Hendricks argued persuasively
that Edison had relatively little to do with the invention of the Kinetograph
camera, the first movie camera, patented in 1891. Most of the work was done
by an Edison assistant, W. K. L. Dickson. The first successful motion picture
projector used in America was invented by two Washington, D.C., men,
Thomas Armat and Francis Jenkins. They were persuaded to allow their device
to be manufactured and marketed under Edison's name because of the enormous publicity value attached to it. Yet when the Vitascope, as it was called,
was unveiled to the press on April 3, 1896, at Edison's laboratory, Edison
touted the device as his own. In the Koster and Bial program for the April 23
debut, the Vitascope was hailed as "Thomas A. Edison's latest marvel."
Edison's own papers show that, in fact, he had little interest in the movies, either as an invention or as a business venture, being much more concerned with
other, more lucrative projects.

Film History and Subscription Publishing

These revelations are not to say that Ramsaye is guilty of some sort of breach of historical ethics in his connection with Edison or that his treatment of him was a willful misrepresentation or distortion of fact. The role of Edison in *A Million and One Nights* must be understood (1) in the context of the popular discourse on Edison, technology, success, and art at the time; and (2) in the context of book publishing in the 1910s and 1920s. In 1914 or 1926 there were no college courses in film history to guarantee sales for a history of the cinema. The very notion of a book-length history of film would have seemed daring and risky to a publisher. The imprimatur of Edison's name no doubt helped to reduce this risk and make of the work a type of discourse more familiar to both publishers and prospective buyers.

The "great man" theory of history is to be found not only in Ramsaye's treatment of Edison, but throughout Grau's work as well. One reason for this historical perspective is, no doubt, that it was common to historical writing as a whole at that time, particularly among histories intended for popular consumption. As we have seen, technology was viewed as the work of one great inventor superseding that of another, forming a chain of technological progress. In the case of both Grau and Ramsaye, however, it was important that each author cultivate the good will of the then still-living historical personages about whom they wrote. In Grau's case it was absolutely essential that he do so; otherwise, his book would never have been published.

From correspondence discovered among the papers of early film distributor George Kleine, it is now apparent that *Theatre of Science* was published by subscription. Although almost never used today, subscription publishing was a common mode of book marketing at the time Grau wrote. Basically, subscription books were those for which a market was created, often prior to publication, by selling advance orders on the basis of a brochure or saleman's pitch. Subscription publishing reduced the risk taken by the publisher and facilitated the production of expensive works and those for which there was thought to be a relatively small market. Subscriptions were sold by traveling salesmen or, as in the case of Grau, by the author himself.

Grau sought orders for his yet-to-be-published book from the film luminaries about whom he wrote. He frequently combined requests for information on the history of film with requests for subscription. Kleine responded to several such letters in the following manner:

> I confess that I would take greater personal interest in your book if every letter did not contain some reference to a subscription blank. My attitude towards your book is one of interest and I am inclined whenever they are ready to buy a copy, but, the purchase of a book should not be injected in some way into every letter that passes.[28]

Although Grau claimed that his treatment of Kleine would in no way be affected by the number of copies he agreed to buy, he said he planned to include an entire chapter on Kleine and display his photograph prominently. To Kleine's refusal to cooperate, Grau responded, "Perhaps, Mr. Kleine, if the matter was put to you in an advertising way you would resent it less...," meaning that Kleine might look upon the purchase of copies of the book as grateful compensation to one who had provided him with free advertising of considerable value. Kleine still did not respond. As a token of what he could do for Kleine in his book, Grau informed Kleine of his intention to attend the opening of Kleine's new movie theater in New York, promising "to send out more published matter on this than anyone in America."[29] Finally, after a barrage of subscription requests over the spring and summer of 1914, Kleine agreed to buy one copy of the book. *Theatre of Science* does contain a photograph of Kleine, among dozens of others, but rather than one full chapter on Kleine's career, there are only a few paragraphs.

Ramsaye's book was not sold entirely by subscription; however, subscriptions were almost certainly sought from the film community for the expensive, autographed first edition of *A Million and One Nights*. Following the publication of his film history in 1926, Ramsaye did produce a subscription work on film. *The Famous Two Hundred of the Motion Picture* was a limited-edition, Moroccan leather-bound volume containing "accurate biographies" and five-by-seven photographs of the 200 most influential persons in the history of the cinema. A prospectus informed the chosen 200 that "a proportionate share of the expense of distributing free copies to leading newspapers and libraries and the cost of printing the book is being charged to those who are presented in its pages, though failure to subscribe will not keep any of the two hundred persons from being included in the book."[30]

Clearly, then, the economic context in which both books were published influenced what Grau and Ramsaye saw as the subject matter of film history. At issue here is not how many pages each film pioneer received, but the need—in Grau's case, the necessity—of conceiving of film history in terms of the exploits of great individuals. Both discursive and economic contexts influence the writing of film history not so much at the level of the truth or falsity of an account of a specific historical event, but at the more general and equally important level of selection and interpretation of those events.

Conclusions

The pioneering nature of their work, the popular audience for which they aimed, and the ways in which their books were marketed and sold all combine to make Robert Grau and Terry Ramsaye convenient (one is tempted to think too convenient) illustrations of the influence of cultural and economic forces on the writing of film history. It would be wrong to suppose that just because film history is now an "academic" as well as a popular discourse, because the boundaries between film history and press agentry now seem clearer, that these forces are less relevant today than they were a half-century ago. No film historian stands outside his or her culture or economic system.

The emergence of film history as an academic discipline since the 1960s has made the economics of book and journal publishing more, not less, of a factor in determining what film historical topics are investigated and how they are presented to the reader. Many books of film history published over the past fifteen years (this one included) have been designed and marketed principally as college textbooks. Sales in bookstores have been considered incidental to the vastly larger sales resulting from the adoption of the book as a textbook in some of the thousands of film history courses offered by colleges all over the country.

As Chapter 2 pointed out, one of the pressures placed on an author by publishing companies is that the work be turned out reasonably quickly, since there can be a delay of as much as eighteen months between the completion of the manuscript and its publication as a book. The need for speed oftentimes overrides the need for a reconsideration of the unquestioned reiteration of generalizations from yet other secondary sources—as was seen in the case of the Chaser Theory. In the name of "readability," footnote citations are frequently dropped from survey works designed for use as textbooks in favor of a more general bibliographic list at the end of the chapter or even the entire work, making it difficult if not impossible for the reader to scrutinize the evidentiary basis for the author's conclusions. At its worst, the desire to sell as many copies of a survey textbook as possible to the largest market (students in introductory film classes) reduces film history to an unproblematic story and the reading of such works to a passive consumption. Even university presses, which exist to publish works of scholarly merit rather than to make a profit, are not immune from economic pressures. Increases in publishing costs, a shrinking library market, and decreases or elimination of university subsidies have caused some academic presses to give priority to scholarly works with more general appeal. Potentially important works directed toward a limited academic audience have greater difficulty finding their way onto a publisher's list today than ever before. These remarks are not intended as an inclusive indictment of all film history publishing methods, but rather is a reminder that all works in film history are published within economic contexts that have influenced their production and consumption.

One example of the subtle yet powerful cultural biases at work in the contemporary writing of world film history is pointed out by British film historian Roy Armes. There is, he says, a distinct western orientation not only in the writing of world film histories in general, but also in cinema histories of nonwestern countries. Because until fairly recently film production has been centered in America and western Europe, film historians have interpreted film history to mean filmmaking history. Many countries in Latin America, Africa, and Asia have had little in the way of indigenous film production—in many cases precisely because the importation of American and European films and distribution control by foreign firms made local production unfeasible. Thus these countries are seen as having a film history only to the extent that they have had a history of film production. What goes unwritten and unexamined is the history of filmic reception in the Third World and the tremendous cultural impact made by decades of viewing only films produced by "foreigners."[31]

Finally, every reader of a film historical work comes to that reading experience with a set of norms and expectations derived largely from the surrounding culture. Based on their experiences in high school, many college students regard the study of history as the memorization of facts—facts already determined and codified by history professors and the textbooks they write. Both professors and textbooks are placed in a position of knowledge and power. The student regards his or her role as that of receiving that knowledge but rarely as questioning it and almost never as contributing to it. The first three chapters of this book have asked the reader to challenge these assumptions about film history by regarding history as an ongoing process of confrontation between the historian and the materials of the past and by regarding works of historical writing as arguments to be read carefully and questioned by the reader. Chapter 8 takes this challenge one step further by suggesting that the consumer of film historical writing might become the producer of it as well.

NOTES

1. David Bordwell and Kristin Thompson, *Film Art: An Introduction* (Reading, Mass.: Addison-Wesley, 1979), p. 50.

2. Arthur Knight, *The Liveliest Art* (New York: New American Library, 1959), p. v; and Thomas Bohn and Richard Stromgren, *Light and Shadow: A History of Motion Pictures* (Port Washington, N.Y.: Alfred Pub. Co., 1975), p. xv. The examination of historical works as narratives is by no means limited to film histories. In his influential study of nineteenth-century European historical works, Hayden White treats "the historical work as what it most manifestly is: a verbal structure in the form of narrative prose discourse." See his *Metahistory: The Historical Imagination in Nineteenth-Century Europe* (Baltimore: Johns Hopkins University Press, 1973).

3. Lewis Jacobs, *The Rise of the American Film* (New York: Teachers College Press, 1939), pp. 112–113.

4. Ibid., pp. 35–36.

5. Knight, *The Liveliest Art*, p. 31.

6. Siegfried Kracauer, *From Caligari to Hitler* (Princeton, N.J.: Princeton Univ. Press, 1947), p. 6.

7. David Bordwell, Janet Staiger, and Kristin Thompson, *The Classical Hollywood Cinema: Film Style and Mode of Production to 1960* (London: Routledge and Kegan Paul, 1985).

8. Monroe Beardsley, *Thinking Straight* (Englewood Cliffs, N.J.: Prentice-Hall, 1970), p. 11. Beardsley's is a good introduction to the logic of discourse in general.

Others include: Steven Baker, *The Elements of Logic* (New York: McGraw-Hill, 1965); Stuart Chase, *Guide to Straight Thinking* (New York: Harper and Row, 1962); and Howard Kahane, *Logic and Contemporary Rhetoric* (Belmont, Calif.: Wadsworth, 1976).

9. For a discussion of the Chaser Theory, see Robert C. Allen, *Vaudeville and Film 1895–1915: A Study in Media Interaction* (New York: Arno Press, 1980); and "Contra the Chaser Theory," *Wide Angle* 3 (Spring 1979): 4–11.

10. David H. Fischer, *Historians' Fallacies: Toward a Logic of Historical Thought* (New York: Harper and Row, 1970), p. 62.

11. Michael Chanan, *The Dream That Kicks: The Prehistory and Early Years of Cinema in Britain* (London: Routledge, Kegan Paul, 1980), p. 132.

12. In *The Order of Things* (New York: Random House, 1970) Foucault embarks on an archeology of the history of science—not a study of science as it progressed through time, but an examination of the level of largely unconscious "rules" that governed what could be said and written about science at a particular point in time. Foucault explains:

I should like to know whether the subjects [authors] responsible for scientific discourse are not determined in their situation, their function, their perceptive capacity, and their practical possibilities by conditions that dominate and even overwhelm them. In short, I tried to explore scientific discourse not from the point of view of the individuals who are speaking, nor from the point of view of the formal structure of what they are saying, but from the point of view of the rules that come into play in the very existence of such discourse; what conditions did Linnaeus . . . have to fulfill, not to make his discourse coherent and true in general, but to give it at the time when it was written and accepted, value and practical application as scientific discourse. . . (p. xiv).

13. Grau to George Kleine, May 3, 1915, George Kleine Collection, Manuscripts Division, Library of Congress. (Hereafter referred to as "Kleine Collection.")

14. Robert Grau, *Theatre of Science* (New York: Broadway Pub. Co, 1914), pp. 11, 19, 35.

15. Ibid., pp. 111–112.

16. Terry Ramsaye, *A Million and One Nights* (New York: Simon and Schuster, 1926), pp. vi, xi.

17. Ibid., p. 113.

18. John Kasson, *Civilizing the Machine: Technology and Republican Values in America 1776–1900* (New York: Grossman, 1976), p. 185.

19. "The Poetry of Discovery," *Scientific American* 5 (1849): 77; quoted in Kasson, *Civilizing the Machine*, p. 147.

20. Ramsaye, *A Million and One Nights*, p. 394.

21. Ibid.

22. Paul Hammond, *Marvellous Méliès* (New York: St. Martins, 1975).

23. Ramsaye, *A Million and One Nights*, pp. 414, 416, 418.

24. John Cawelti, *Apostles of the Self-Made Man* (Chicago: Univ. of Chicago Press, 1965), pp. 2–4, 171–187.

25. Robert Conot, *A Streak of Luck* (New York: Seaview Books, 1979), pp. 113, 186, 284, 387–414.

26. Ramsaye, *A Million and One Nights*, pp. 72–73.

27. M. Lincoln Schuster to George Kleine, April 5, 1926, Kleine Collection; and Ramsaye, *A Million and One Nights*, p. 68.

28. Subscription publishing is discussed in John Tebbel, *A History of Book Publishing in the United States*, Vol. II (New York: R. R. Bowker, 1975), p. 511; and Grau to Kleine, February 16, 1914, Kleine Collection.

29. Grau to Kleine, February 25, 1914 and April 4, 1914, Kleine Collection.

30. Brochure for *The Famous Two Hundred of the Motion Picture*, n.d., Kleine Collection.

31. Roy Armes, ed., "The Possibility of a History of World Cinema," in *Problems of Film History* (London: BFI, 1981), pp. 7–24.

PART TWO

Traditional Approaches to Film History

4

Aesthetic
Film History

"Primarily the motion picture is a great popular art and, as such, concerns the art student first." These words of Iris Barry from her 1939 Preface to Lewis Jacobs's *The Rise of the American Film* are echoed forty-five years later by Gerald Mast in his best-selling film history, *A Short History of the Movies:* "The history of the movies is, first of all, the history of a new art."[1] Most of our encounters with film history—whether in college courses or through books —are with the history of film as an art form. Aesthetic film history is the predominant form of film history and has been so since the beginnings of film study in the United States and Europe. However, what constitutes the history of film as art is a subject of profound philosophical and historiographic disagreement among film historians. This chapter first discusses the *masterpiece tradition* in aesthetic film history, the major approach to the history of film as art through the 1960s. Then a reformulation of aesthetic film history is suggested, based on more recent developments in film theory and criticism.

THE MASTERPIECE TRADITION IN AESTHETIC
FILM HISTORY

To many film historians, aesthetic film history means the identification and evaluation of the great cinematic art works of the past. In a 1976 essay Gerald Mast stated, "The historical question which has been asked most frequently about the history of the cinema may be stated thusly: What are the significant works of the cinema art?" Mast then outlined the several assumptions underlying this approach. The job of the historian, he asserted, is the examination and evaluation of films of the past according to some criteria of aesthetic excellence or significance. The data for this type of historical analysis are primarily, if not exclusively, the films themselves. To Mast, the aesthetic film historian is not concerned with the circumstances of the film's production or reception; for his or her purposes "however the work got to be what it is, it is what it is." According to Mast, the reliance on filmic documentation in this type of aesthetic film history offers an evidentiary advantage over other forms of film historical research in that a film made in 1930 is the same today as it was then. Films are not products of the filmmaker's faulty memory or open to contradiction or dispute as are other pieces of evidence; "they simply are."[2]

It would be unfair to infer from this essay that Mast and other film historians of what is being called the *masterpiece tradition* completely disregard nonaesthetic factors in film history, but for them economic, technological, and cultural aspects of film history are subordinate to the establishment of a canon of enduring cinematic classics. Also, implicit in Mast's remarks is the notion that the subject of aesthetic film history is limited to only those films that are true works of art. Part of the job of the film historian, according to this view, is winnowing out the chaff that forms the largest portion of cinematic output of any given period from the few masterpieces worthy of historical treatment.

Film History and Film Theory

On what grounds are some films elevated to the status of "art," while others are consigned to aesthetic and historical oblivion? In Chapter 1 film history was distinguished from film theory, the latter being the making of general propositions about the nature and functions of cinema. Theorists and historians generally ask different sorts of questions about film. In the case of aesthetic film history, however, it is necessary to reexamine this relationship, since, in many cases, the film historian's theoretical orientation (what constitutes cinematic art) conditions the selection of films for historical analysis.

Until the 1960s, film theory could be divided into two major schools of thought: what Dudley Andrew has called *formativist* and *realist*. (As Chapter 1 pointed out, this is *not* Realism as a philosophy of science and history.) Both begin with the observation that the cinema, more than any other art form, has the power to render accurate, life-like representations of places, people, and objects: visible, everyday reality.

Formative theorists (Hugo Munsterberg, Sergei Eisenstein, and Rudolph Arnheim, among others) argued, however, that so long as the cinema did nothing more than record the visible world, it could never aspire to the level of art. The formativists maintained that in order to become art, the cinema must go beyond mere mechanical reproduction. Film, they said, should not copy reality, but change it so that it is distinct from nature or visible reality. The photographic image recorded on motion picture film was, for the formativists, the raw material of filmic art. The work of art itself emerged from the manipulation of the image through the use of the unique properties of the cinematic medium. In his book, *Film as Art*, Rudolph Arnheim even catalogued the ways in which film could be made different from reality and invested the aesthetic opportunities of film in those limitations. To formativists, art begins with nature but is the product of the artist's personal expression of it through the formal properties of the artistic medium—in the case of cinema, editing, camera work, sound, and mise-en-scene (the organization of elements within the frame). Hence, a formative-based aesthetic history of the cinema would single out those works that exploit the medium's potential for artistic manipulation of reality, those films and filmmakers that demonstrate film's capacity to go beyond recording.

Chapters 2 and 3 considered some of the ways in which some film historians have dealt with the early years of film history. It is now possible to see in these interpretations (and those of other film historians) the influence of a formative approach to film art. In Jacobs, Ramsaye, Knight, and most other American film histories, the path of development of film art was seen as moving away from the Lumieres' mechanical reproduction of objects in motion and toward the exploration of the ways in which the cinema could alter "reality" through editing, optical effects (stop-motion photography, superimposition), camera movement, or mise-en-scene.

The key formal device in this early period (pre–1912), according to formative historians, was editing, for it was through editing that time and space could be detached from their logical relationships in the "real world" and made to serve the artistic demands of the artist. The meaning of any image or sequence of images could be made subordinate to the will of the filmmaker. Films were described as "cinematic" or "uncinematic" according to the degree to which editing and other devices were manipulated—the degree to which the film's pull toward reality was "overcome" by the expressive potential of the cinema to transform the reality into something else. To A. R. Fulton, *The Great Train Robbery* was "the first really cinematic film." To Alan Casty, Méliès was a historically significant filmmaker because he "provides the first real examples of the film's ability to surmount space and time, to manipulate physical reality with great freedom, to control it...." Jacobs entitled his chapter on Porter, "Art: Edwin S. Porter and the Editing Principle." "Almost all motion picture developments since Porter's discovery spring from the principles of editing," said Jacobs, "which is the basis of motion picture artistry."[3]

Another formative influence on film history comes from the formativist emphasis on the uniqueness of each art form. A painting is "artistic" when it creatively utilizes those properties exclusive to it. Musical art is produced by the manipulation of pitch, timbre, melody, and harmony; art in painting through color, line, and texture. It follows, then, that if film is also an art form, it must have its own set of "peculiarities" that set it apart from all other means of artistic expression. For if film only imitates other art forms—painting or theater, for example—it cannot, by this reasoning, become an art form in its own right. Hence, to some film historians, early films are historically significant to the extent that they reveal differences between the capabilities of film and those of other art forms. As we have seen, Méliès's fatal aesthetic flaw to some was his theatricality; Porter's greatest achievement was his break with, in Knight's words, "stage forms and stage techniques." In *A History of the Cinema From its Origins to 1970*, Eric Rhode distinguishes between film as play, which is merely derivative of stage techniques, and film as art, which calls attention to the unique capabilities of the cinematic medium.[4]

Realism (the Bazinian Variety)

In the 1930s and 1940s, a theoretical challenge to formativism emerged. *Realism*, as it came to be called, has been less influential on the writing of film history in general, although central to the theory and history of documentary filmmaking. Realism deserves brief mention, at least, because of the historical implications of the writings of one of its chief proponents, French critic and theorist André Bazin. While formative theorists found the heart of film aesthetics to lie in the ways in which cinema could be made to differ from reality, Bazin resolutely insisted that film art depended on the exploitation of the close connection between the filmic image and that which it represents—not on the denial of this relationship. "Cinema," he wrote, "attains its fullness in being the art of the real." Unlike painted images, filmic images are read as "real" because they are produced by the dispassionate and objective mechanism of the camera, rather than the imagination and interpretation of the artist. "All the arts," wrote Bazin, "are based upon the presence of man, only photography [and, by extension, the cinema] derives an advantage from his absence.[5]

In a famous essay entitled (in its English translation) "The Myth of Total Cinema," Bazin argued that the cinema was the product of an age-old dream: the complete representation of reality, or, as Bazin put it, "a re-creation of the world in its own image, an image unburdened by the freedom of interpretation of the artist or the irreversibility of time."[6] Asking the cinema to undo the effects of time—to defeat death, as it were—is giving it an impossible task. This Bazin realized; hence his use of the term "myth" to describe the cinema's relationship to this unattainable yet tantalizing hope. No filmmaker can ever fulfill the human desire for a "total cinema"; yet, said Bazin, filmmakers can exploit this special relationship cinema has with reality thus bringing us closer to its ultimate purpose. Bazin even noted specific cinematic techniques that seemed to him to foster realist cinema: deep focus photography and the long take, in particular.

For Bazin film history is a process of organic evolution: the gradual realization of the age-old "myth" of complete representation—what Bazin called the myth of "total cinema." This basic psychological need takes precedence as a historical force in film history over scientific experimentation, economics, or cultural factors. The technological history of cinema, for example, becomes a steady progress toward greater and greater realism as each technological advancement (color, sound, wide-screen) produces a closer connection between the cinematic image and the world it strives to represent. Like the work of formativist film historians, Bazin's essays are written from a masterpiece perspective, although the films that mark turning points in film history for Bazin are those most faithful to his conception of reality-representation rather than those that foreground the cinema's formal attributes. What sets Bazin apart from the masterpiece tradition, however, is his evolutionary schema of historical change and his view that cinema is a unique recording medium first and an art form second.

THE MASTERPIECE TRADITION AND THE AUTEUR THEORY

Since the Romantics, mainstream aesthetic theory in the west has reserved a central place for the artist. The art work has frequently been seen not only as the exemplum of formal properties but also as the embodiment of artistic vision and expressivity. This *artist-centered* aesthetic rendered as history becomes the examination of individual art works as they reflect the genius of the person who made them. Masterpieces are, literally, works created by the "masters." Artist-centered aesthetics has exerted enormous influence upon the researching and teaching of art, theater, literary, and, as you might guess, film history. In the Preface to his *A Short History of the Movies* Gerald Mast proclaims:

> A study of eighty-years of film history has led this author to make one basic assumption: no great film has ever been made without the vision and unifying intelligence of a single mind to create and control the whole film. Just as there is only one poet per pen, one painter per canvas, there can be only one creator of a movie.[7]

Mast's statement is predicated upon the *auteur theory*: an artist-centered critical and theoretical formulation first proposed by a small group of French critics and filmmakers in the mid-1950s and then strongly embraced by many English and American academics in the following decades. By the end of the 1960s "auteurism" had become the basis of the first self-conscious and fully articulated theory of film history to emerge from the young discipline of cinema studies.

The auteur theory grew out of the frustrations experienced by a group of film critics and would-be filmmakers (François Truffaut, Jacques Rivette, and Jean-Luc Godard, among others) centered in Paris in the 1950s. They were angered by a critical establishment in France that lauded a film's fidelity to a screenplay or novel and regarded the film director as merely a translator of material from the verbal medium to the cinematic. For this view Truffaut and

company substituted a notion of personal cinema—a cinema in which the director, not the screenwriter, could be seen as the controlling force behind the film.
Truffaut's notion of cinema art reflected his own desire to open up the stultified
French film industry to allow young filmmakers like himself and his friends the
opportunity to make low-budget feature films of personal artistic expression. In
essays and film reviews in the film journal *Cahiers du Cinema,* Truffaut set
forth the major tenets of *la politique des auteurs:* the centrality of the director in
the creation of film art, and the paramount importance of personal expression
as a criterion for critical evaluation of films.[8]

In the United States auteurism was championed most strongly by critic
Andrew Sarris. In "Toward a Theory of Film History," the introductory essay
in his 1968 book *The American Cinema,* Sarris presented auteurism as an *historical* method particularly suited to the Amercian cinema. Sarris asked how
one might begin the task of studying American film history, given the thousands of films turned out by Hollywood over the past half-century. As a first
step, he suggested giving priority to the works of true film auteurs: those directors who have imposed the stamp of their personality on their films. The history
of the Amercian cinema that follows in Sarris's book is a rank-ordering of those
American directors who have been the true authors of their works, despite their
having to work within a production situation (the Hollywood studio system)
that militated against the expression of a single intelligence and imagination in
films.

Most directors, said Sarris, have allowed their artistic vision to be dulled by
the demands of the studios, constraints imposed by scripts they did not write or
supervise, actors, cameramen, and writers assigned to them by producers, and
the limitations of various film genres (westerns, gangster films, musicals) within
which most directors were forced to work. A few notable exceptions have been
able to overcome these impediments and express a consistent style and world
view through all their works. Fourteen directors (Ford, Hitchcock, Hawks, and
Welles, among them) comprised Sarris's "pantheon" of auteurs who have "transcended their technical problems with a personal vision of the world." Twenty
other directors fell into a slightly lower category "either because of a fragmenta-
tion of their personal vision or because of disruptive career problems."[9]

Most American film histories written between 1965 and 1980 either take an
explicitly auteurist position or show its influence. Mast's indebtness to the
auteur theory has already been noted. Casty begins his history by stating "at the
core [of film history] is the single filmmaker. . . . The history of the film must be
the story of filmmakers and their works." Robinson declares in his Preface, "It
is true that in the end what will count is the dominating artistic personality of
the author of any film. . . ." And, more recently, Jack Ellis announces the orientation of his history as follows: "Exceptions aside, if personal vision is assumed
to be the primary prerequisite for the creation of a work of art, as it will be in
this book, the case for the director's ascendancy is a strong one."[10] While all of

these works do take other factors into account, they are devoted largely to an analysis and evaluation of the works of great directors. In other words, they are masterpiece histories.

Historical Context and Change in the Masterpiece Approach

To most film historians of the masterpiece tradition, the historical context out of which a film emerges is less important than its enduring values as a work of art. To repeat Mast's declaration, "The sole fact that concerns the [aesthetic] historian. . . . is that however the work got to be what it is, it is what it is." Indeed, the very term "masterpiece" implies not the historical specificity of a work but its timelessness. The true work of cinematic art transcends its own time and "speaks to us" here and now. As Sarris puts it, "Old movies come out of their historical contexts, but they must be judged ultimately in the realm of now."[11] Because aesthetic timelessness holds a higher value to masterpiece historians than historical context, they have not been particularly concerned with developing models that would account for historical changes in film art. As Mast has pointed out, both Knight and Casty see the historical development of film art as an organic process of evolution. One aesthetic development provides the impetus for the next as the aesthetic potential of the medium is realized by one filmmaker after another. To Casty, this evolution is dialectical: the silent period is marked by formative concerns (editing, abstraction), the early sound period by realism, and today's films represent a synthesis of these two extremes.[12]

To both Mast and Sarris, industry, culture, and technology have influenced the history of film as art, but the determining factor in aesthetic film history has been, in Mast's words, "the great film minds." Because they believe film art depends on the vision and skills of great artists, Sarris and Mast see film history not as evolutionary or dialectical but rather episodic. To paraphrase Sarris, the cinema rises and falls in relation to the artists involved at any given time. This belief is expressed in the very organization of Sarris's *The American Cinema.* The chapters are arranged not chronologically but according to the aesthetic quality of the directors discussed, and the arrangement of directoral essays within each chapter is alphabetical.

To sum up, the masterpiece approach is based on the following assumptions:

1. Film history is primarily the study of the cinema as art form. Other concerns—economic, technological, cultural—are secondary to this study.

2. The subject matter of aesthetic film history is the individual work of cinematic art: the film itself or the personal vision of the artist, which can be determined from a viewing of his or her films.

3. For the most part, the meaning of a film and its aesthetic significance transcend that film's historical context. Thus, unlike personal memoirs or other nonfilmic evidence, a film is an objective historical "fact."

4. Most films fall outside the scope of aesthetic film history, since only a small percentage of all the films ever made can be considered great works of art.

5. The primary task of the film historian is the critical evaluation of films.

6. Historical change in film art is seen either as an internal process of evolution or as a result of artistic genius, rather than caused by factors external to the creative process.

Critique of the Masterpiece Approach

Bolstered by the impact of auteurism on film studies during the formative decade of that discipline's development, the masterpiece orientation toward film history remains an influential model for how film history classes and textbooks should be organized. However, in film study, as in other disciplines that examine forms of cultural production, the basic assumptions of the masterpiece approach to art are increasingly being challenged. One of the first to come under attack was the notion, shared by many historians of the masterpiece school, that the meaning and aesthetic qualities of a work of art are historically transcendent—according to Mast, the historian viewing *The Birth of a Nation* today is able to "see" the same film that was screened initially in 1915. The issue here is not that raised in Chapter 2 of textual variation, but rather whether meaning in art (and, indeed, the more general reception of the work by its readers) is in some way bound by the time period and culture of the person viewing that work.

As early as 1940 historian George Boas suggested that the meaning of a work of art is not entirely inherent in it but changes with the background and perspective of the viewer. Taking for his test one of the most revered works of western art, Da Vinci's *The Mona Lisa,* Boas discovered that for 300 years (from the time of the painting's completion in 1506 until the early nineteenth century), *The Mona Lisa* was admired, but principally for the accurate depiction of its ostensible subject matter: the young wife of a wealthy Italian banker. It was not until the early 1800s that the work was seen to have any of the mysterious qualities we associate with it today. In other words, it took three centuries for "the Mona Lisa smile" to have any meaning. More recently, "reception-oriented" literary theorists, such as Wolfgang Iser and H. R. Jauss, have emphasized the active role of the reader in constructing meaning from any aesthetic experience. For Iser and Jauss, literary history is not a history of "works," but the history of their "realization" by readers and critics, whose readings and responses are themselves historically conditioned.

This notion of art (or film) history as a history of aesthetic reception raises a corollary challenge to the timelessness of the masterpiece approach: If a reader or viewer's understanding of a work is conditioned by historical circumstance, are not the criteria by which masterpieces are chosen themselves subject to historical change? Iser and Jauss, among others, would contend that aesthetic value judgments derive their authority not from timeless features of texts but from critical consensus of the moment (although that "moment" may last for decades). That there is no unchanging and unanimously agreed upon set of aesthetic criteria by which film historians make aesthetic and historical judgments can be seen clearly in aesthetic film historical writing. The radical change in critical fashion that accompanied the academic acceptance of auteurism in the 1960s also changed the subject matter of film history. Such directors as Sam Fuller, Douglas Sirk, Budd Boetticher, and Howard Hawks, who had been either ignored or scorned by earlier American film critics and historians, suddenly became what American film history was "all about."[13]

Given the change over time of aesthetic values and the differences in taste among film historians of the same generation, some scholars have questioned the masterpiece tradition's limitation of the subject matter of film history to only those works that are deemed to be art by the critic/historian. As British film scholar Edward Buscombe has noted,

> Even the lowest, most despised products [films] are made with some kind of art. Do they not share the same language as the acknowledged masterpieces; do they not tell a story, try to affect the spectator's emotions? They may do it more or less effectively, but isn't this a difference of degree, not of kind?[14]

Buscombe also points out another potential problem with the masterpiece approach: its tendency to hold aesthetic aspects of the cinema apart from all others, particularly economic. Mast's contention that for the aesthetic film historian what matters is the "however the work got to be what it is, it is what it is" is seen by Buscombe as symptomatic of the absolute split some scholars assume to exist between art and industry—a split inherited by film historians from the masterpiece tradition in other art forms, where economic and technology perhaps have had less to do with aesthetic change than in film history. Buscombe argues that the history of the cinema as an art form cannot be viewed as autonomous from the history of cinema as economic product and technological apparatus. For purposes of critical analysis it might be possible to regard cinema art as a realm of autonomous activity, but, Buscombe says, it is difficult to see how the *history* of cinema art, whether American or Soviet, can be studied apart from the substantial economic institution needed to support the production of most kinds of films.

Certainly the fact that since its invention the cinema in American and most other countries has been used principally as a commercial entertainment form has affected the subject matter of films, the development of cinematic styles, and other aesthetic considerations. This is an important point to Buscombe and to some other contemporary film historians because their interest in aesthetic film history lies in *explanation*. Why, for example, did certain aesthetic styles emerge at particular times and not at others? Why did particular film-makers make the aesthetic choices they did and how were these choices circumscribed by the economic, social, and technological context they found themselves in? How might a work have been read at a particular period and would these readings have differed according to gender or class? These issues do not concern Mast and other historians of the masterpiece tradition nearly to the same degree. Their major concern is with *explication* of selected works of the cinema's past: why certain films deserve to be called "art" and others do not. Buscombe would attempt to deal with the historical specificity of a given film, while Mast would search out those films whose aesthetic significance extends, he felt, far beyond their own time.

In short, some film scholars of the past decade have concluded that the masterpiece tradition in aesthetic film history has backed itself into an awkward historiographic corner. Having as its goal aesthetic evaluation, the masterpiece approach devalues context in historical analysis. Moreover, attributing "art" in the cinema to the evolution of form or the personal vision of the artist short-circuits further discussion of other possible causal factors in film history. The isolation of aesthetics from other aspects of cinema inhibits or precludes examination of non-aesthetic forces that might shape the aesthetic uses of cinema at any given moment. We are left, Buscombe and others would say, with a brand of film history that is not very *historical*—that is merely film criticism and aesthetic evaluation applied to films in chronological order.

SEMIOTICS AND FILM HISTORY

Although the masterpiece approach to aesthetic film history is still very much in evidence in books on film history, its entire project—the description and evaluation of the great works of cinema art—has been called into question by the application of a new aesthetic theory to film. *Semiotics* or *semiology* (literally the scientific study of signs) endeavors to understand how meaning is achieved in various forms of visual and auditory representation. What is the process, it asks, by which we understand a painting, know to stop at a traffic sign, derive pleasure from a circus act, or interpret cinematic images and sounds? As we shall see, semiotics is not a theory of film *history* per se, but its acceptance as a theory of film in general among film scholars over the past decade has far-reaching implications for film history.

Semiotics began as the application of the principles of structural linguistics to phenomena that fall outside the realm of linguistics proper. Semiotics brought together developments in several fields: logic (the work of American philosopher Charles Sanders Peirce), linguistics (Ferdinand de Saussure), anthropology (Claude Levi-Strauss), and literary theory (the Prague School critics of the 1920s and 1930s), all of which focused on the human capacity to conceptualize and articulate the world through a variety of media: verbal language, gesture, sound, stories, clothes, and pictoral representation, among others.

Semiotics has examined phenomena that appear to be obvious and simple in their operation (photography, the language of the novel) and has shown them to be the products of complex sets of rules and conventions. Similarly it has dealt with phenomena that appear to be if not random at least rule-less (table manners, wrestling matches, circus acts), and has shown them to be rule-governed as well. The question anthropologist Claude Levi-Strauss asked of primitive myths can be seen as the question semiology asks in general: "Whether the different aspects of social life (including even art and religion) cannot only be studied by methods of, and with the help of concepts similiar to those employed in linguistics, but also whether they do not constitute phenomena whose inmost nature is the same as that of language."[15]

In other words, semiotics asks what aspects of social life are rule-governed systems? It was Saussure who discovered that although a verbal language with its thousands of words and seemingly infinite combinatory possibilities would at first appear to defy any attempt to express it as a set of rules, it, in fact, produces meaning on the basis of a finite number of rules or codes. These rules must necessarily pre-exist any particular utterance; we can speak only because we already "know" the rules.

Semiotics was first applied to film in the 1960s by French scholar Christian Metz. Film semiotics has sought to explain how meaning is embodied in a film and how that meaning is communicated to an audience. A semiotician might attempt to determine the variety of ways meaning could be created through film lighting or assess the function lighting plays in a given film. Among Metz's early semiological investigations of the cinema was a typology of the various combinatory possibilities of shots and sequences of shots in a film and the types of filmic "punctuation" (the straight cut, dissolve, wipe) that could be used to connect them.[16]

A full discussion of film semiotics and its considerable impact on film studies as a whole is not possible here. Furthermore, film semiotics is not a monolithic method nor have its emphases remained constant since its introduction in the early 1970s. Increasingly semiotics has been merged with other theoretical approaches—Marxism and psychoanalysis, in particular. Thus the discussion here will be limited to the overall project of semiotics and to its several and important consequences for the *historical* study of film art.

First, the concern of semiotics in general is not so much with a specific instance of a type of phenomenon (a poem, a tribal myth, a speech) as with the system of principles, conventions, or codes that govern any particular instance. As linguist Charles C. Fries has said of the Saussurian view of linguistics, semiotics moves away from an "item-centered" view of the world, and toward a "relational" or "structural" one.[17] For the historical study of film art, this interest in structure or system means a shift in the subject of film history. The individual film is still important, but equally so is the set of principles and conventions that a film shares with other films of the same style, period, or genre. In the early days of film semiotics, for example, Metz suggested that a history of cinematic style might begin by comparing the frequency with which various films from different nations and time periods use particular shot combinations. A construction that is "typical" of the films of one era might be extremely rare in the films of another.[18]

Regarding a film as a system of conventions and codes means deemphasizing the role of the artist in film history to some degree. At the very least it forces the artist to share the stage of film history with less personal forces. Film semioticians would admit that film is different from verbal language in that the former has no set of hard and fast "rules" by which cinematic meaning is created. In film, to use Metz's terms, grammar and syntax are the same. However, they would stress that no filmmaker, no matter how skillful a craftsperson, operates outside of the constraints imposed by precedent, convention, and audience expectation. Furthermore, the ultimate project of film semiotics goes beyond the individual film, beyond the individual artist, even beyond the realm of cinema itself. For the semiotician film is but one form of signification among many. To be sure, film has its own particularities as a producer of meaning, but semiotics seeks to explain the process of signification (the production of meaning) in general, regardless of the form that signification takes.[19]

An aesthetic film history based on semiotics would see as its subject matter the totality of ways in which meaning and pleasure have been produced in films and not only those few films that other historians have elevated to the status of art. It could be said, in fact, that a semiotics-based film history would not be an "aesthetic" film history at all, insofar as semiotics regards traditional distinctions between "art" and "non-art" as inappropriate to its project of understanding how meaning is generated. At the very least we can say that in semiotics the line between "artworks" and other films is much more blurred (if recognizable at all) than any masterpiece historian could accept.[20]

TOWARD A REFORMULATION OF AESTHETIC FILM HISTORY

The impact of semiotics on film theory and criticism has been deep and far-reaching, but to date has been less strongly felt in film history. Neither semiotics nor structural linguistics, on which it is based, is a historical theory.[21] Semiotics might explain how editing functions in a given film or map out the signifying potential that editing has made available to all filmmakers throughout film history, but it cannot without reference to some other explanatory model tell us *why* editing came to be used in a particular way at a particular time, or why some uses of editing became dominant and others marginal in western filmmaking practice. In other words, there is no well-formulated "semiotic film history" to present as an alternative to the traditional masterpiece approach. Furthermore, it would be simplistic to represent the debate over aesthetic film history in dichotomous terms: masterpiece historians vs. semioticians. However, it is possible to see the masterpiece and semiotic positions as two fundamentally different sets of concerns and emphases, which, in turn, suggest divergent historical orientations. The contributions made by semiotics to film criticism and theory might form a starting point for a reformulation of the types of questions aesthetic film history can and should ask.

Semiotic's shift in critical focus—from film as static object to film as a set of relationships, both internally (an individual film as a system of relationships among codes) and externally (the relationships among films)—suggests a corresponding redefinition of aesthetic film history as the history of the production of meaning in the cinema, or, put in semiotic terminology, the history of signifying practices. Rather than asking, Which films are art? we might instead ask: How and why have the elements of film form (lighting, editing, camera movement) been used in particular films at particular points in film history? How and why have some styles become normative for long periods of film history (the Hollywood "style," for example), while others have flourished for only brief periods (German Expressionism, French Impressionism) or have been idiosyncratic (the "personal" style of Méliès or Dreyer)? What have certain cinematic devices meant to audiences at various points in film history (high-contrast lighting or the jump cut, for example), and how was this meaning created? Such a redefinition of aesthetic film history lays aside matters of taste and evaluation. Rather than endowing selected works with timeless artistic value, the history of film as signifying practice attempts to understand any use of cinematic form in its historical specificity and complexity.

Kristin Thompson has developed a "neo-formalist" approach to film criticism, applying to film principles of literary criticism articulated by so-called formalist critics in the 1920s. Formalism, although based to a large degree on the pioneering work of Saussure in linguistics, differs from semiotics in maintaining the distinction between aesthetic and nonaesthetic uses of language and in concentrating upon art's ability to alter our perceptions as well as create meaning. The differences between neo-formalism and film semiotics as critical systems are less important to a discussion of aesthetic film history than is Thompson's suggestion that every film is situated in and depends on a network of relationships with other systems of art and meaning production. Thompson calls these relationships "background sets." To her, a film is an "open system" produced and consumed in constant interaction with other systems. A film at once invokes other systems and constitutes a unique organization of elements from those systems. The reader of that film understands it in terms of the conventions and norms derived from those systems or backgrounds. Thus, says Thompson, "the formalist critic must remain grounded in history." The formalist interest in the aesthetic context within which a work is produced and consumed is echoed in the reception theory of Iser and Jauss. Jauss speaks of the "horizon of expectations" against which each new work is positioned by its readers and critics.[22]

Relating the historicized aesthetic theories of Thompson and Jauss to the Realist historical framework suggested in Chapter 1, we might recast the "background sets" she speaks of as aesthetic *generative mechanisms*, the interaction of which determines how a given film is structured and how it is read by audiences at any given time. The aesthetic film historian's task then becomes the identification of these generative mechanisms and explanation of their interaction. Understanding a film *historically* would mean understanding it as a specific conjuncture of backgrounds or generative mechanisms. Every film, even the most routine formula picture, is historically unique in that it represents a particular ordering of elements. Yet this uniqueness does not mean that the historian must regard each film as an inexplicable historical accident; what differs from film to film is the individual arrangement of elements and not the system of elements itself. We find many of the same generative mechanisms at work in seemingly very different films.

Both the concept of backgrounds and its parallel in response theory, the horizon of expectations, provide a framework for understanding the forces at work in the reception of a given film at a given time within a given culture. To return to Jauss for a moment, the horizon of expectations represents "the sum total of reactions, prejudgments, verbal and other behavior that greet a work upon its appearance." A given work might so fulfill its expectations that it easily blends into its background, but such a work risks being perceived as so undifferentiated as to be "boring." Works that stand out more sharply from their horizons create what Jauss calls an "aesthetic distance," in response to which an audience might alter its horizon so that the work is accepted, or, in more extreme cases, reject the work as "unreadable."

There is yet another possibility, however; the work might split its audience into those who accept it and those who reject it. Thus, to Jauss, understanding the history of a particular work entails grasping its use of previous strategies, the horizon of expectations against which it is read, the articulated response the work engendered, its subsequent assimilation into or distancing from the reader's horizon, and the textual changes brought about in other texts of the same form or genre by the resultant feedback process among readers, authors, and cultural institutions. Jauss is careful to qualify what he means by reconstructing the horizon of expectations against which a work is received. Such a project is *not* an attempt to somehow "crawl into the minds" of past audiences. The historically specific conditions under which a given work is produced and consumed are only partially objectifiable by the historian, since this horizon was not fully conscious to or articulated by historical readers. Individual differences in decoding among audience members are inaccessible to the historian, but the more general horizons which all members of an audience group have at their disposal are not.[23]

What, specifically, are these backgrounds or generative mechanisms that interact to determine how a given film sounds and looks and how an audience reads what is presented on the screen? The project of identifying and explaining the operation of the factors responsible for filmic signification and audience response at a given moment in the past is only now beginning. What is offered here is not an exhaustive catalog but a preliminary mapping out of some of the more important factors.

Style

Cinematic style may be defined as the systematic use of specific cinematic techniques characterizing a given film or group of films. Using this notion of style, the historian can specify normative aesthetic practice at a given point in the past. This historically defined stylistic norm can serve as the background or horizon against which any individual cinematic work can be examined.

The predominant filmic style of cinema in the west since the 1910s has been called the classical Hollywood narrative style. This term designates a particular pattern of organization of filmic elements whose overall function is to tell a particular kind of story in a particular way. The story the Hollywood film relates involves a continuous cause-effect chain, motivated by the desires or needs of individual characters and usually resolved by the fulfillment of those desires or needs. Nothing is introduced into the story that will distract us from this sequence of narrative events, and the story ends only when the initial question posed by the film's narrative has been answered. (Will the farmers win out over the ranchers? Will Dorothy make it back to Kansas? Can Sam Spade solve the case of the Maltese Falcon?)

All filmic elements in the classical Hollywood cinema serve the narrative and are subordinate to it. Editing, mise-en-scene, lighting, camera movement, and acting all work together to create a transparency of style so that the viewer attends to the story being told and not to the manner of its telling. Spatial relations, for example, must be kept clear from shot to shot so that the viewer is never in doubt as to his or her relationship to the action. The passage of story time is manipulated through editing, so that narratively insignificant events can be eliminated. The close-up serves to concentrate viewer attention on dialogue, through which much of the narrative is conveyed, and in many instances the background in a close-up will be rendered out of focus, to prevent the viewer's eye from wandering from the narratively significant part of the image. Camera movement is usually unobtrusive and frequently "motivated" by the movement of a character (the camera pans to follow a walking character, for example). The formal system created by these and other formal devices constitutes a "zero point of cinematic style" in that they are used only to serve the needs of the narrative and remain themselves "invisible."[24]

The historical import of the classical Hollywood style lies in the fact that by the late 1920s, Hollywood style had become accepted in most of the world as *the* style of narrative filmmaking. Other styles were forced into the stylistic shadow of Hollywood and judged according to the standard it set. For the film historian, the Hollywood style provides an historically definable benchmark, an aesthetic frame of reference in relation to which other styles can be assessed and films and filmmakers within it positioned.

A consideration of "Third World Cinema" illustrates the usefulness of historically specifiable stylistic models in understanding aesthetic film history. Until after World War II, most countries in Latin America and Africa had little or no tradition of indigenous filmmaking. Their film industries were controlled by American or European firms and their movie screens were dominated by Hollywood-style films. Since the 1950s, a growing number of filmmakers in Third World countries have attempted to fashion a style of cinema capable of addressing local political and cultural issues. The cinematic results have been stylistically varied, but in all cases of what is called Third World Cinema the starting point has been a critique of the Hollywood cinema.

To such filmmakers and theorists as Fernando Solanas, Octavio Gettino, Miquel Littin, Ousmene Sembene, and others, Hollywood cinema represented film as commodity, a product fabricated some place far away and sold to consumers in the form of a pleasant, inconsequental, escapist experience. Even where Hollywood films dealt with "social" issues, these films were unable to conceive of these issues except as problems to be faced, and eventually overcome, by individual characters. The stylistic transparency of the Hollywood style prevented films from raising the issue of their own status as cultural or aesthetic objects, for to do so would have been to undermine the primacy of the narrative. Hollywood films, the critique continues, never encourage their audiences to think of them as films or to question their relationship to the events on the screen.

The response encouraged by a Hollywood film is passivity: everything the audience needs to see and hear is laid out unproblematically via the Hollywood style; there is no "work" involved in reading *Jaws* or *E.T.* Finally, by answering all the narrative questions it poses, the Hollywood film isolates the film viewing experience from the "real" world of the viewer. No matter how absorbing or disturbing the film, its style always announces it as "just" a film.

It is difficult to read a Third World film such as Solanas and Gettino's *La Hora de los Hornos* (*The Hour of the Furnaces*) except as a reaction against Hollywood style and the approach to film production and consumption it represents. The three-part, four-hour film is "about" Argentine politics, culture, and economics, and their domination by foreign interests, but it is equally about filmmaking and the possibility of using film as a political and cultural weapon. Whereas Hollywood films are stylistically invisible, *La Hora de los Hornos* constantly reminds the viewer of its status as a film through direct address, the interruption of shots by mottos and legends printed on the screen, and a collage of various cinematic styles.

Whereas the Hollywood film is a commodity that encourages audience passivity, Solanas and Gettino have conceived of their film as a *film act* that forces the audience to think about both the reality of the film and the reality the film depicts. Several times during the film a legend appears on the screen asking the projectionist to stop the screening and the audience to discuss what they have seen. Thus while the commodity nature of the Hollywood film dictates that each screening of it should be the same (so that every customer "buys" the same product), every screening of *La Hora de los Hornos* is different. To Solanas and Gettino, "this means that the result of each projection act will depend on those who organize it, on those who participate in it, and on the time and place; the possibility of introducing variations, additions, and changes is unlimited." Finally, whereas the Hollywood film is a self-contained, autonomous aesthetic object, *La Hora de los Hornos* is left open-ended so that changes might be made or additional material added as a result of audience discussions. As the closing titles announce, ". . . it opens out to you so that you can continue it." There is no narrative resolution, no sense that the film can answer the questions it raises, no "aesthetic satisfaction" as a result of seeing *La Hora de los Hornos*.[25]

Ironically, no matter how far away from the tenets of Hollywood style Third World filmmakers may wish to take their films (*La Hora de los Hornos* represents a position nearly 180 degrees away), they cannot escape its effects. One historical consequence of the dominance of the Hollywood style over international filmmaking has been the establishment of a set of audience expectations with regard to what a film is "supposed" to look like and what the experience of viewing a film "should" be like, not only in America and Europe, but in the countries of the Third World as well. Thus a filmmaker whose film departs too radically from "ordinary" filmmaking practice (read: Hollywood style) risks alienating the audience to the extent that the political effectivity of the film is negated. Realizing this, some Third World filmmakers have fashioned styles that retain some of the characteristics of Hollywood films (a closed narrative form, individual characters) while modifying others to fit their specific aesthetic and political aims.

In addition to using the classical Hollywood style as an historical benchmark to which other stylistic systems might be compared, the film historian must also examine the historical origins and development of Hollywood style itself. One reason for the longevity of the Hollywood style of cinema has been its resilience; it has accommodated itself to economic changes, technological revolutions, influences from other stylistic systems, and the individual aesthetic demands of thousands of filmmakers over a half a century. How, we might ask, have these accommodations been made? What has constituted "standard" Hollywood practice at a given point in film history and where have the limits of acceptable practice been set? What possibilities for variation within Hollywood style have existed and how have they been manifested in individual films? What has been the effect on the Hollywood style of technological change—sound, color, wide-screen, and so on?

In short, if the concept of the Hollywood film is to be at all historically useful, it must be understood not as a static, rigid entity, but as a set of practices *with* a history. Nothing about cinema technology as it was invented in the 1890s "predestined" it to be used primarily as a story-telling medium. The first movie audiences saw and apparently enjoyed a variety of film styles: travelogues, newsreels, community "home movies," trick films, scenes excerpted from popular stage plays, as well as narrative films. One of the most complex and challenging questions in the history of film style is how the Hollywood style developed out of this multiplicity of competing uses of cinema technology and rapidly established itself as "normal" filmmaking practice.

As was discussed previously, many survey histories of American film have regarded the Hollywood style as somehow the inevitable fulfillment of the cinema's storytelling potential. However, as the case of *Life of An American Fireman* (discussed in Chapter 2) points out, the ascendancy of the narrative film was neither inevitable nor a straightforward process. The preliminary findings of a number of recent investigations (and at this stage in aesthetic film history they can only be preliminary) suggest that the style of silent film storytelling that eventually developed into the Hollywood style emerged over a period of a decade or more as a response to economic forces (the need to produce a consistently marketable product on a regular schedule), audience expectations, and the aesthetic models provided by other art forms and entertainment media.[26]

Intertextual Backgrounds

The classical Hollywood film style constitutes an aesthetic system that can be used (or reacted against) by filmmakers. For audiences, it represents an important part of their horizon of expectations, establishing what a fictional film is "supposed" to look and sound like. The classical Hollywood narrative style is by no means the only aesthetic system at work in a Hollywood film, either at the level of production (coding) or consumption (decoding). A Hollywood film might use conventions or codes derived from or make reference to many other textual systems, making that film a sort of intertextual intersection: the point of convergence for a number of signifying practices.

The other textual systems involved in the production of filmic meaning stand out most clearly in the film parody, where aspects of texts well known to the audience are invoked for comic effect (Mel Brooks's satire of Hitchcock in *High Anxiety*, for example, in which specific shots from Hitchcock films—the opening shot from *Psycho*, among them—are lampooned). But every Hollywood film is to some degree an intertextual network, relying on patterns of meaning already existing in other films, and other art forms. These patterns of meaning are historically determined; conventions in other art forms change over time, just as do conventions in the cinema. Hence, understanding how a particular film derives meaning involves understanding the use it makes of other textual systems at a particular point in time.

We might divide these other textual systems into three categories: *filmic,* *nonfilmic,* and *extra-filmic*—the first two of which would be included in aesthetic film history, broadly defined. A filmic intertext would be the use by a film of elements from other films (everything from a reference to another single film to the use of conventions drawn from an entire genre of films: the western, science-fiction film, or musical). A nonfilmic intertext would involve the use of conventions or codes from other art forms or systems of representation (painting, theater, literature, fashion, graphics, photography). The third category of intertext, the extra-filmic, would include film's use of signifying practices that are clearly nonaesthetic in nature: law, biology, business, politics, etc. Analysis of the use of these textual systems in a film would be more the province of social film history than of aesthetic film history.[27] The filmic and nonfilmic intertextual networks formed by even the most standard studio product could be quite extensive; after all, the production of meaning in any text is a complex process. A run-of-the-mill gangster film from the 1930s might involve conventions derived from the gangster-film genre in general, the detective novel, the iconography of Los Angeles, fashion, and American slang of the 1930s, among others. Even publicity material on a film or its star becomes an intertext—as is clear from the case study on stardom in Chapter 7.

The intertextual system that has received the most scholarly attention in film studies is genre. Basically, genre study asks two questions: What does it mean to say that a film is a musical, western, or horror film? and How can we explain the fact that while the topics available to filmmakers are virtually limitless, the same types (genres) of films are made over and over again without, it seems, exhausting audience interest in them?

Traditionally, film genres have been defined on the basis of recurrent characters, themes, settings, plots, and iconography: A western is a film containing settlers and cowboys, desert, the one-street town, and confrontations between the forces of civilization and those of the wilderness. As Andrew Tudor points out, definitions of genre derived from films alone are inevitably somewhat circular: "Western" traits are gleaned from films the analyst has already defined as westerns. Tudor suggests that to call a film a western or a musical is not only to say that the film contains certain traits, but also that the film would be recognized as such by film audiences. The very notion of genre depends on common agreement as to what constitutes a western or a gangster film. "Genre," he says, "is what we collectively believe it to be."[28] Put in terms we have been using in this chapter, genre forms an important intertextual background set that generates definite audience expectations. The spontaneous singing and dancing of the musical is accepted and, indeed, anticipated as a generic convention of the musical film by its audience.

Generic conventions operate both as aesthetic constraints and sources of meaning. Once a set of generic conventions has been invoked in a film—Indians appear along the horizon line, or a trolley car becomes a stage for a musical number—the expectations generated by those conventions also come into play. These conventions then serve as parameters within which other aspects of the film are "expected" to fall: character depiction, setting, dramatic conflict, narrative progression. The risk in violating these parameters, of course, is of thwarting the expectations of the audience. On the other hand, generic conventions become a sort of aesthetic framework of preexisting meaning that a film can establish quite economically. To signify "western," a film need only open with a long-shot of a lone horseman galloping across a vast expanse of prairie. This single shot is sufficient to "plug in" the film to a vast and complex intertextual network: that of the "western." No exposition is needed to establish who the settlers are, why livestock are being driven across open countryside, what the functions of the saloon are, or why the protagonist rides into the sunset at the end of the film.

Modes of Production

The categories "Hollywood," "avant-garde," and "documentary" refer to stylistic differences among films, but also to differences among them in terms of the contexts of their making, in their modes of production. The term "mode of production" here means the overall structure of production organization of a film: the reasons for the making of the film, division of production tasks, technology employed, and delegation of responsibility and control, and criteria for evaluating the finished film. Each mode of production produces its own set of production practices: normative conceptions of how a particular kind of film "should" look and sound. These norms exercise considerable yet subtle force in artistic decision making.

There are at least three basic modes of production.

1. The *individual* film production mode describes the production situation in which a single person is entirely or primarily responsible for production. The avant-garde or experimental film is frequently made by an individual.

2. The *collective* mode involves several people sharing equally in the production process. Specific tasks are delegated in this mode, but decision making is shared among the participants. The Cine Liberacion collective in Argentina, among whose members are Solanas and Gettino, exemplifies the collective mode. Every member of the crew is capable of operating every piece of equipment, and production decisions are made by the entire group.

3. The *studio* mode of production is by far the most complex of the three. Its purpose is not the production of a single film but the mass production of many films. While profit may or may not be the primary motive for filmmaking in the individual and collective modes, it is certainly profit which forms the basis for the studio mode of production. The studio mode is characterized by a hierarchical organization, extensive division of labor, and standardized production practices.[29]

Just as styles and intertexts have histories, so do modes of production. In her 1981 dissertation, Janet Staiger examines the history of the Hollywood studio system, and concludes that it was developed, in part at least, out of the need to regularize film production on a large scale and thereby to maximize profits for the owners of the production company. In short, the studio system was the Hollywood equivalent of the Detroit assembly line, which developed at roughly the same time. The production process was segmented into distinct tasks and labor divided so that each worker had responsibility for only one task or set of tasks: scriptwriting, continuity, set construction, camera operation, lighting, processing, editing, titling, etc. Decisions as to which projects to produce and which workers would be assigned to them (including actors and directors) were made by management, and their decisions implemented by employees further down the hierarchy.

Although the studio mode of production was but one of several competing systems of production organization in the 1910s, it quickly became the industry standard. Its development was, according to Staiger, more influential on American film style than any single film or director. As she points out, however, it would be simplistic to infer that economic considerations alone "caused" the studio system, which in turn "caused" the development of the classical Hollywood style, which in turn "caused" the production of films as identical as so many pieces of chewing gum.

In the first place, the studio system was by no means the cheapest method of film production. Producing "invisible" editing in a Hollywood feature required the work of an editor, assistant editor, writer, and an elaborate system of production record keeping—all so that shots would fit together smoothly and the illusion of continuous space maintained. In this case and in other instances of Hollywood production practice, achieving a particular "look" in films took precedence over keeping costs low. Furthermore, while the consumer expects each pack of a particular brand of chewing gum to be identical, the movie audience expects each film made by the same studio to be different. Hence, the pressure for regularity and standardization in the Hollywood system must be considered in relation to the countervailing pressure for differentiation among films.[30]

Authorship

The auteur approach to film criticism sparked a controversy, still debated in some circles, over who should receive credit for the artistic achievements in Hollywood films. Truffaut and later Sarris argued that in true cinema art the director's vision showed through. This claim prompted other critics to assert, equally vociferously, that a case for authorship could be made for the scriptwriter, producer, star, and even the cameraman. In a reformulation of aesthetic film history, the question, Who has made cinema art? might be recast as Why and how have films looked and sounded the way they have? Such a question is historical rather than evaluative and recognizes that the forces responsible for the particular qualities of any given film are multiple and both personal and impersonal. To be sure, a close reading of the films of Hawks, Ford, and Hitchcock shows them to bear a distinguishing signature, but their films also reveal the "marks" of studio, Hollywood style, and genre.

In its need to discover the unifying traits among the films of a Hollywood director, to attribute meaning to the work (conscious or unconscious) of the director, even the more critically sophisticated variety of auteurism necessarily dismissed other sources of meaning as "noise." As Peter Wollen said in *Signs and Meanings in the Cinema*, "What the *auteur* theory does is to take a group of films—the work of one director—and analyse their structure. Everything irrelevant to this, everything non-pertinent, is considered logically secondary, contingent, to be discarded."[31] The key word here is "nonpertinent," for while non-auteur sources of meaning might be "nonpertinent" to the critic determined to discover authorship, there is no logical or historiographic reason why they should be "nonpertinent" to the aesthetic film historian.

Almost from its inception, auteurism deflected attention away from actual production practices. Rather than raise the thorny issue of how much control a director had and where that control was exercised, auteur critics insisted that their concern was with the author as critical construct, author as pattern of meaning inferred from the texts that bore his or her name and not the historical personage of the director at all. This closing off of the auteur enterprise from history might have been logically necessary to protect auteurism as a critical system, but it is both unnecessary and counterproductive when applied to film history. Once the presumption that the auteur is the ultimate source of meaning in his or her films is removed, we can then ask quite valid historical questions that auteurism cannot ask. How are production decisions made in various modes of production? What are the constraining forces in any individual's role in the filmmaking process? What are the accepted limits of aesthetic innovation at a given time within a given style and how are these limits arrived at? How is authorship in the cinema perceived by audiences at a given time?

As one step in historicizing the concept of authorship in the cinema, we might borrow a distinction made by formalist critic Boris Tomasevskij between authors with biographies and authors without biographies. Most popular culture products are produced by authors "without biographies" in the sense that to their audiences they are anonymous. Their names signify nothing beyond the credit line at the beginning of their films; they have no persona outside of their films. *Knowing* that a film was directed by Joseph Pevney or Gregory La Cava makes no difference in decoding his work. Even in the case of most American directors whom critics have designated as auteurs, recognizing them as such is, to use Peter Wollen's terms, an act of "decypherment" or "decryptment," of discovering and, indeed, constructing authors from their films alone.

There are other authors, however, including filmmakers, who are known not only as credit lines on their films, but also as public figures. The "facts" of their lives, their production practices, and their pronouncements are conveyed to the public via journalists, reviewers, their own publicists, advertising materials for their films, memoirs, and, most recently, television talk shows. Their resulting "biographical legends," to use Tomasevskij's phrase, become an important historical background for reading their films, and, in fact, frequently become inscribed in their films as well.[32] This inscription might take the form of stylistic flourishes that call attention to the "author" of the film. We tend to associate these authorial inscriptions with the European "art" cinema (the metaphysical ruminations of Bergman's characters, or the grotesqueries of Fellini), but they also appear in the work of some Hollywood directors (the stylistic excess of Orson Welles, for example).

Reference to authorship might also be more literal, as when films are publicized as being "autobiographical," when the film is about the process of filmmaking, or when the director becomes a character in his or her own or another director's films. The historical significance of Alfred Hitchcock's brief appearances in his own films is that they make reference to a biographical legend that at once informs and is informed by his films. The genre Hitchcock frequently worked in, the suspense film, lent to his biographical legend a penchant for the macabre; while his whimsical cameos evoked another side of his persona—his sense of humor. Hitchcock's biographical legend was so strong that he could endow "authorship" on texts he played no part in creating: anthologies of "mystery" short stories, and the long-running television series of the 1950s and 1960s, *Alfred Hitchcock Presents*, the vast majority of whose episodes Hitchcock only "introduced."

The biographical legend of a filmmaker is important to the film historian for several reasons. First, it might help us to understand the production practices embraced by the filmmaker, since the biographical legend, especially the public pronouncements of the filmmaker, helps establish the relationship between the filmmaker and the dominant practices of the mode of production in which he or she works. Second, the biographical legend can condition the reception of a given film, influencing how it "should" be read. Both of these aspects of authorship will be examined further in the case study for this chapter.

Aesthetic Discourse on the Cinema

As we have seen, a portion of any historical audience's horizon of expectations is generated by films themselves. The audience's prior viewing experience has led its members to expect certain qualities from a western, musical, or documentary. By the early 1930s, it is safe to say, American film audiences regarded the classical Hollywood style not merely as one set of conventions among many, but as "normal" film style in relation to which other styles represented greater or lesser deviation. Other expectations derive from a more general discourse about the cinema contained in a variety of sources. The overriding paradox of the Hollywood studio mode of production was the need, on the one hand, of standardizing its product, and, on the other, of differentiating each film made from every other film, so that the audience could be enticed to pay to see it. The function of film advertising during the studio era was to make each film appear to be in some way special and thus a unique film-viewing experience. To be sure, audiences quickly learned to discount the superlatives used to describe films in movie trailers, posters, lobby cards, and newspaper advertisements, but advertising discourse on the cinema did help to condition audience expectations and to establish the terms by which a film would be judged. Advertising could also help to position a film in an intertextual network by associating or comparing it with other films, as in "Not since *Psycho*..." or "If you liked *Gone with the Wind*...."

Since the 1890s innumerable critical evaluations have been made of specific films in newspapers, all manner of magazines, books, and now, on television. In 1929, *Film Daily Yearbook* identified 326 American newspapers employing someone designated as "film critic." Whether this critical discourse on the cinema has affected movie-going behavior to any appreciable degree is difficult to determine. Certainly no movie reviewer has ever had the power to "kill" a picture in the way, it is said, certain theater critics can ruin a Broadway play's chances for commercial success. It is also dangerous to assert a correlation between critical judgment and "public taste," there being many examples in film history of films despised by the critical establishment but loved by enough movie-goers to make them commercial "hits."

A study of the critical discourse on the cinema at a particular point in film history is valuable to the film historian in that, like advertising discourse, it tends to establish the critical vocabulary and frames of reference used not only by reviewers, but by film audiences as well. To borrow a term from mass communication research, critical discourse on the cinema has had an "agenda-setting" function in aesthetic film history; that is, it has not told audiences what to think so much as it has told them what to think *about*. Critical discourse also helps the historian to establish the normative limits of the dominant style of cinema at a given point in the past. These limits are exposed when critics are confronted with a film that is "different," that doesn't fit neatly into the customary frames of reference of standard critical discourse.

As we shall see in the case study for this chapter, in some films these differences are such that the film can still be pulled into the discursive field, and, in fact, may be perceived as an artistic innovation because it sets itself apart from "ordinary movies." In other cases, however, the film so violates normative stylistic standards that it cannot be dealt with by the prevailing critical discourse and is either rejected or simply ignored. Thus, negative film reviews are sometimes more useful to the film historian in understanding the aesthetic context in which films were received than are laudatory ones, and silences sometimes speak more loudly than choruses of praise.

Noël Carroll has gone so far as to argue that all film theories (and, hence, theories of film history) that attempt to locate "art" in some inherent property of the work itself are misguided. Adapting what is called the "institutional theory of art" to film history, Carroll holds that a film becomes the object of aesthetic film history only if it has been nominated as an artwork by reviewers, critics, and others who form part of the "institution" of film art. The work is "aesthetic" because it has been seen as having some relationship to larger traditions of art. A work might be regarded as a repetition of previous tendencies, an amplification of those trends, or a repudiation of them—in any case, it occupies some position relative to previous works. However, "if, at any given point in history, the object cannot be connected with the tradition by means of these kinds of interpretations, it is not art."[33]

CASE STUDY: THE BACKGROUND OF *SUNRISE*

In 1972 the British film magazine *Sight and Sound* conducted a world-wide poll of film critics to determine the great film masterpieces of all time. Only five silent films placed among the twenty "greatest" works of the cinema. One of them was F. W. Murnau's *Sunrise* (1927). Fifteen years before the *Sight and Sound* poll, *Cahiers du Cinema* had named *Sunrise* "the single greatest masterwork in the history of the cinema." *Sunrise* seems stubbornly to refuse historical categorization. Although based on a German short story and directed, written, and designed by Germans, *Sunrise* was filmed in Hollywood and financed by the William Fox Company. Stylistically, the film seems to stand apart from other works of its time (both German and American), particularly in its use of moving camera. The shot depicting a trolley ride from country to city—for which an elaborate forced-perspective set was especially constructed—is one of the most famous in film history. Sarris, who includes Murnau in his pantheon of auteurs, calls the trolley scene from *Sunrise* "one of the most lyrical passages in world cinema."

Except in two respects the film is regarded by most film critics and historians as standing outside of aesthetic film history, as a sort of fortuitous historical accident by which the resources of Hollywood were put, for once, at the service of a great film artist. *Sunrise* is seen as marking the apex of Murnau's brief career (barely ten years) and the end of the silent era. The most expensive silent film made by Fox, *Sunrise* failed even to recoup its costs, and Murnau's next two films for Fox were both compromised by studio interference. Thereafter, Murnau made only one more film, *Tabu*, co-directed with documentary filmmaker Robert Flaherty. Murnau was killed in an automobile accident in March 1931 at the age of forty-three. When *Sunrise* made its New York debut in September 1927, it shared the bill with a Fox-Movietone synchronous-sound newsreel of Mussolini. Fox's plans for sound motion pictures were sufficiently advanced by the time of the production of *Sunrise* so that prints of the film were prepared with a synchronous music and effects track, making the film a curious technological hybrid: not silent, but not quite "sound." Historically, the film comes to represent the premature and artificial end to a directorial career just reaching its peak and, in retrospect, a fitting monument to the aesthetic possibilities of the silent film.

Sunrise, then, would seem to present us with a film that cannot or will not be historicized. Dudley Andrew has said of it that "as a film aspiring to the claims of 'high art' it resists all critical [and, by extension, historical] schemas which might sap whatever it is which makes it outstanding."[34] However, aesthetic film history need not mean the critical impoverishment of a cinematic text by reducing it to a simple set of historically determined signifiers or by forcing it into rigid historical categories. By the same token, no film, no matter how far its aesthetic reverberations carry beyond its own time, is without a history and a position within history—or, more accurately, positions within histo-

The forced-perspective "city" set constructed especially for *Sunrise* is one of the most famous in film history.

The Museum of Modern Art/Film Stills Archive

ries. By examining some of the aesthetic backgrounds of *Sunrise* along the lines suggested in this chapter, our understanding of the film becomes richer, not poorer.

The Biographical Legend of Murnau

There can be no doubt that F. W. Murnau was an artist "with a biography" at the time of the production of *Sunrise*. When Murnau arrived in New York from Germany in July 1926, he was feted by his new employer, William Fox, at a banquet at the Ritz Carlton, attended by one hundred members of Manhattan society and broadcast to thousands of others over radio station WNYC. The *Moving Picture World* correspondent covering the event remarked of Fox: "It was a proud night for him. He realizes the move on which he is embarking will have a tremendous influence on pictures as an international art." *Motion Picture Classic* wrote

> Highly paid editorial writers, justices, admirals, generals, professors, bankers—all fared forth to pay homage to one of the greatest (if not the greatest) pictures of the screen [Murnau's *The Last Laugh*, which had been seen in the United States in 1925]. It was a tribute to an artist and his art that representative men from various walks of life responded with such deep regard and enthusiasm.[35]

Murnau was well known to the Hollywood establishment, film critics, and many movie-goers long before he ever stepped foot in the United States, thanks largely to the critical acclaim afforded *The Last Laugh* and *Faust* (released in the United States in January 1925 and December 1926, respectively). Such was their critical success that few filmmakers have ever enjoyed the critical reputation that F. W. Murnau found bestowed upon himself when he arrived in the United States in the summer of 1926. According to his biographer, Fox believed Murnau to be "the genius of his age," and *The Last Laugh* "the greatest motion picture of all time."[36]

In America, neither Murnau nor his films were regarded in aesthetic isolation, but rather as part of a larger cinematic phenomenon, the German cinema. In American discourse on the cinema of this period, the term "German cinema" meant much more than just the country of origin, but rather came to stand for a particular type of film marked more by its perceived difference from the standard Hollywood product than by any consistent set of stylistic traits. By direct reference or association, Murnau was situated in American discourse as a *German* director. To understand what this label meant, we must examine what the German cinema had come to signify in general in the 1920s.

First, however, it should be made clear that aesthetic discourse on the cinema in America in the 1920s was not a static or uniform body of thought, constituting a single "view" or "perception." In fact, as we shall see, changes in this discourse around 1927 might well have affected how *Sunrise* was critically received. At any given time critical opinions differ. Some American critics and commentators saw German films as the only true example of cinema art in the world; others were much less enthusiastic. What establishes the discursive context of *Sunrise* is not only or even primarily the consensus view of the film itself, Murnau, or German cinema in general, but rather the frames of reference within which these issues are discussed. We might ask: Which aspects of German cinema or Murnau's work within it are seen as pertinent and which not? And what is the aesthetic agenda on which the German cinema is to be included? Two critics might hold antithetical views regarding the relative aesthetic merits of a film, and yet both serve to define the same terms by which this debate is conducted.

The German Film in American Critical Discourse

It is possible to begin our discussion of American discourse on German films of the 1920s with a statement of consensus: Between 1921 and 1927 German films imported into the United States were regarded as significantly different from Hollywood films particularly in their aspirations toward or achievement of the status of "artwork." As early as 1921, the movie trade press discussed a "foreign invasion" of American screens by German films. In relation to the total number of films released, the actual number of German films imported into the United States in the early 1920s was inconsequential; however, some in Hollywood believed German films to be a threat to the American film industry and pressured Congress for protectionist tariffs.

The German films received attention in the movie trade press in part because they were products of a recent military adversary, but in larger measure because their effect on aesthetic discourse was enormously disproportional to their number. Beginning with Ernst Lubistch's *Passion* (originally titled *Dubarry*) in 1920, and continuing through *The Cabinet of Dr. Caligari* (1921), *Anne Boleyn* (originally titled *Deception*, 1921), *Gypsy Blood* (originally titled *Carmen*, 1921), *The Golem* (1921), *Siegfried* (1925), *The Last Laugh* (1925), *Variety* (1926), *Faust* (1926), and *Metropolis* (1927)—one German film after another played to rave reviews in New York.

The film critic for the *New York Globe* even suggested that cries for import controls were motivated not by economic fears but by the desire to keep the American public from seeing artistic films Hollywood was unwilling or unable to make. *Passion* was hailed as "one of the pre-eminent motion pictures of the present cinematographic age." *The Cabinet of Dr. Caligari* was seen as marking an epoch in film history. *The Last Laugh* was called by several critics the best movie ever made and was voted best picture of the year by *Motion Picture Classic* in 1925. The critic for the *New Republic* called *Variety* "a perfectly coordinated work of art." And in 1926 *Film Yearbook*'s poll of over 200 screen

critics from across the country named *Variety* best film over such American pictures as *Ben Hur, Beau Geste,* and *What Price Glory?*[37]

Something in the German films was obviously viewed as "aesthetic," but
what was it? In America the term "German cinema" came to mark out an aesthetic space, if you will, somewhere outside the normative boundaries of conventional Hollywood style. At issue was how far outside, and whether this aesthetic distance from the Hollywood cinema constituted a positive or negative
aesthetic difference. Discussions of individual films tended to be framed by
three aesthetic criteria, each having both a positive and a negative dimension:
spectacular/excessive, complex/elitist, and artistic/self-indulgent. The closer
the individual film came to being described by the first term in each pair, the
more its difference from Hollywood films was regarded as "innovative" and
hence positive. A film defined by the latter terms, however, was seen as too different and hence "strange."

Interestingly, it was not *The Cabinet of Dr. Caligari* that first sparked critical interest in the German cinema, but the historical pageant films of Ernst
Lubitsch, three of which opened in New York between December 1920 and May
1921. *Passion,* Lubitsch's French Revolution epic, was the first major German
production to play in the United States after the end of World War I. *Passion,
The Golem,* and *Siegfried* were lauded by American critics for their attention to
historical detail and high production values. Particularly during the period
from 1921 to 1925, these qualities were regarded by American reviewers as
spectacular rather than merely showy. Massive crowd scenes and elaborate studio sets were seen as being in the service of "art," as raising the tone of the cinema to a level seldom aspired to in Hollywood.[38]

German films made explicit reference to established works of art and, by
association, asked to be read themselves as artworks. The first German work to
be so regarded in the United States was *The Cabinet of Dr. Caligari,* which took
the critical establishment by storm in the spring of 1921. Since the publication
of Siegfried Kracauer's *From Caligari to Hitler* in 1947, much has been made of
the "expressionistic" qualities of *The Cabinet of Dr. Caligari:* its distorted mise-
en-scene, intensified and stylized acting, and macabre plot. At the time of its release, few American critics placed the film within the expressionist camp, but
while they disagreed as to which school of art it resembled, they agreed that it
was "artistic." It was called "cubistic" by many, "post-impressionist" by others;
and it was compared to the works of Poe, Baudelaire, and even surrealist
Marcel Duchamp.

The Cabinet of Dr. Caligari was seen as appealing especially to a "high-
brow" audience, but the film was also seen as being not so different from
Hollywood films as to represent totally foreign aesthetic values. The *New York
Times* critic was quick to point out that one need not be an art historian to enjoy
the film: The art of *Caligari* was couched in a "coherent, logical, a genuine and
legitimate thriller." In other words, the film transcended the aesthetic boundaries of the Hollywood cinema, but could be pulled back within the discursive

field by virtue of its being, "a feast for those who want their fiction strong and straight." Directed toward prospective exhibitors, advertisements for the film in *Moving Picture World* played down its stylistic innovation, presenting it instead as "a mystery story that holds the public in suspense every minute . . . [and] a bizarre picture with a real trick ending that brings a laugh."[39]

The need to position German films within a context of other works of art can perhaps best be seen in the critical discussion of Fritz Lang's *Siegfried*. Titles at the beginning of the film alerted the audience that the film was *not* based on Wagner's opera, but rather on ancient Germanic myths, the Niebelungen Sagas. Nevertheless, American critics insisted upon foregrounding this operatic intertext, sometimes to the exclusion of all other aspects of the film.[40]

In speaking of *The Cabinet of Dr. Caligari, Siegfried*, and *Faust*, the historical spectacles of Lubitsch, and other German films, American critics frequently pointed out that they appealed to a "discriminating" and "intelligent" audience, and by doing so chastised Hollywood producers for ignoring the audience for cinema art in their pursuit of maximum profits. Lubitsch's *Anne Boleyn*, one critic said, was "for those who want genuine realism and can do without simpering heroines, pretty heroes, mechanical plots, and sentimental happy endings." *Faust* stood apart from Hollywood product in that "not in a single instance has any one connected with this picture bowed to the usual commercial conventionalities." *Variety* was "utterly devoid of the pale, peurilities and sterile conventions that cabin and confine the cinema." *Nation* critic Evelyn Gerstein left no doubt that the issue was profits versus art. "Hollywood lives for money and sex," she said, while the Germans "experiment in film art."[41]

According to the terms of general aesthetic discourse of the 1920s, where the critic found art he or she must also have found an artist. One of the difficulties in discovering "art" among the works of the Hollywood cinema was that demands of the classical Hollywood style left little room for stylistic flourishes that could be seen as signs of artistic intervention. These signs of intervention were abundantly clear in German films, however, and they were usually ascribed to the artistic vision of the director. German directors were discussed as artists and compared with artists from other media in ways few Hollywood directors—with the exception of D. W. Griffith—ever were. German directors were compared to painters and musicians and their works were regarded as expressions of artistic vision rather than industrial imperatives. Writing in *New Republic*, Gilbert Seldes asserted that German films were marked by a "unity of intention" that was frequently lacking in Hollywood films.[42]

German Directors and the "Highly Artistic Picture"

As early as 1923, Hollywood studios began luring German filmmakers to the United States. Ernst Lubitsch was the first to come, followed by Ludwig Berger, Paul Leni, E. A. Dupont, and, of course, F. W. Murnau. But why did Hollywood go to the trouble and expense of importing these filmmakers and what did the studios expect from them? Certainly, with German films regarded in the critical discourse as the *sine qua non* of cinema art and with German directors viewed as the repositories of their underlying artistic vision, it can be safely said that Hollywood expected the immigrant directors to produce "art." But was that all they expected? And, if so, of what value was "art" to Hollywood in the 1920s?

The American box-office record of German films was mixed. No doubt Hollywood's interest in German films was first peaked by the critical *and* financial success of Lubitsch's *Passion* in 1921. It reportedly earned its importer $2 million. Other German films also did well, particularly in New York theaters. *Deception*, *The Cabinet of Dr. Caligari*, and *Variety* all broke one-day attendance records at their respective Manhattan theaters. Critical success by no means assured profits, however. Whereas *The Last Laugh* was universally acclaimed by critics, economically it was, in the words of *Motion Picture Classic*, "destined to become the worst flop in history.... Theater owners refuse to play it at any price, and in numerous instances... [it] has been withdrawn from

The "highly artistic picture," *The Cabinet of Dr. Caligari* asked to be read as art.

the theater after playing one day."[43] Thus the importation of German directors would appear to have been a doubtful strategy for increasing studio profits.

There is evidence, however, that the studios financed some films in order to enhance their prestige, and, by doing so, create an image of themselves as not only businesses but as producers of popular art. The economic prospects of these "highly artistic pictures," as they were called, were less important than the public relations value inherent in them. As *Moving Picture World* said of these pictures in 1927, "They are made to satisfy the comparatively limited number who appreciate the best, and produced in the hope that they will help to give tone to the general product through satisfying the minority demand."

The "highly artistic picture" served several functions for the studios. First, as the preceding comment points out, these films were meant to appeal to a "high-brow" audience, those patrons in New York, for example, who made *The Cabinet of Dr. Caligari, Passion,* and *Variety* so successful there. Furthermore, it was hoped that the prestige picture would elevate the "tone" of the entire studio release schedule.

The concept of the release schedule deserves a brief explanation. In the 1920s, Hollywood executives rarely thought in terms of a single work; each film was regarded as one component of the year's total output, a portion of the yearly production budget. Within this yearly schedule, the studios grouped films within three or more categories according to their relative importance and expense. The top group, "specials" some studios called them, featured the studio's leading stars and directors and received the largest production budgets. These films were frequently based on popular novels or stage plays, for whose screen rights the studio had paid thousands, if not tens of thousands of dollars. Next came the feature pictures, a studio's bread-and-butter releases, using contract players and directors, based on original screenplays or adapted from magazine stories, and receiving smaller production budgets. Finally came the category which Universal studio called the "thrill drama": the cheapest of a studio's feature releases, often including the bulk of its western films—in the case of Universal a genre that comprised 45 percent of the studio's total feature film output.[44] While the major Hollywood studios (Paramount, MGM, Fox, Universal, Warner Bros., Producers' Distributing Organization, and First National) were each producing thirty-five to seventy films per year in the mid-1920s, it was the top 20 percent of their schedule—the specials—that received a lion's share of budget, attention, and advertising. It was into this category that the "highly artistic picture" fell.

The desire among the Hollywood studios to include prestige pictures among their specials was probably motivated by more than merely the need any industry has to be perceived as a beneficent member of the community. Beginning in 1921, Hollywood was shaken by a series of morals scandals involving top stars and directors. Religious and civic groups pressed for federal censorship of films and Congressional investigations were threatened. Furthermore, in the early 1920s, the Federal Trade Commission began an investigation of possible monopolistic business practices by the Hollywood studios. Thus, while there is no direct evidence, it is possible that the studios used prestige pictures to demonstrate that they were more than venders of entertainment for the masses but were also patrons of the highest cinematic art.

Murnau and the Fox Strategy

William Fox's decision to hire F. W. Murnau and to give him virtually carte blanche in the production of *Sunrise* involved much more than the addition of one more "highly artistic picture" to the 1927–1928 Fox schedule. Fox used Murnau's considerable biographical legend as part of a carefully orchestrated plan to elevate the status of his studio to that of preeminence in the motion picture industry. In the mid-1920s, Fox occupied, along with First National and Warner Bros., a middle echelon within the film industry both in terms of economic power and product prestige. (*Prestige* can be defined as the extent to which the films of a studio are perceived to be of "quality" in the critical discourse of the period.) In the mid-1920s Fox was known as a producer of unpretentious, "folksy" pictures, not highly regarded by critics but for the most part popular with the mass audience. Examining the "Best Films" of *Film Yearbook* and *Photoplay* for 1925, for example, we find that of 184 "best" pictures cited by 104 different critics, only 9 were Fox titles; in both lists the films of Paramount and MGM predominate.

In 1925, however, William Fox launched one of the greatest expansion plans in the history of the motion picture industry. The plan eventually collapsed with the stock market crash of 1929, but just before his downfall Fox controlled the production of Fox and MGM studios, Loew's Theatres, Fox's own large theater chain, one-third interest in First National Theatres, British Gaumont, and assorted other holdings.[45] The Fox drive for economic power in the late 1920s was paralleled by attempts to enhance the prestige of Fox productions, and it is in this context that Murnau's hiring and his production of *Sunrise* must be viewed. Fox anticipated that Murnau's production of the highly artistic picture would bolster his studio's "special" films category. Unless the specials could attract greater critical attention, Fox would never have the prestige to match his hoped-for economic status.

Hiring the "genius of this age" was but one aspect of the plan to improve the position of Fox films in critical discourse. In 1925 Fox began buying the film rights to popular stage plays to use as the basis for what he was now calling "Fox Giant Specials." Among the fifteen films in this category for the 1926–1927 season were nine adaptations of stage plays, including *What Price Glory?* the 1924 smash Broadway hit for which Fox paid $100,000. By basing his "Giant Specials" on successful stage plays Fox hoped to give these films a built-in critical recognition factor (a prominent intertext, to use the language of this chapter) and a source of public appeal that would compensate for the absence of many "stars" among Fox's actor corps. Neither the plays nor the films based on them were aesthetically ambitious, but Fox did give them careful production attention and large production budgets.

A case in point is *Seventh Heaven*, released in May 1927 while *Sunrise* was being edited. Like *What Price Glory?* the film *Seventh Heaven* was based on a successful stage play (704 performances on Broadway), assigned one of the top Fox directors (Frank Borzage), and given what was for Fox a huge budget ($1.3 million). The film was a critical *and* a box-office triumph. With the dual success of *Seventh Heaven*, Fox's bid for prestige began to be taken seriously. The lead article of the Hollywood section of *Moving Picture World* for May 14, 1927, noted "One does not have to travel very far in these parts to hear that not only is Fox product... many times better than it ever has been, but that Fox artistry and quality are second to no contemporary."[46]

Much was expected of Murnau and of *Sunrise*. The quintessential film artist and representative of the great German school of cinema was to have as his patron Hollywood's most ambitious mogul. *Sunrise* would be the fulfillment of Fox's commitment to film art, which had already been presaged by *What Price Glory?* and *Seventh Heaven*. The *New York Times'* film critic concluded his review of Murnau's *Faust* in December 1926 by saying, "While gazing upon this delicate and easy-flowing masterpiece, one is impelled to wonder what Mr. Murnau's next film will be like."[47]

The Discourse on *Sunrise*

There are signs that the discursive context in which *Sunrise* was received in the fall of 1927 was different from that for earlier German films. The terms of the discussion of German films and directors were the same, but increasingly what had once been positively regarded as spectacle came to be viewed as excess; the artistic complexity of the German style became a sign of elitist as opposed to popular art; and the German director began to be seen by some as a prima donna. In short, while the objects of critical discourse—German cinema and directors—changed little during the mid-1920s, what they signified within this discourse does seem to have altered considerably and rather quickly by late 1927.

In announcing Fox's decision to hire Murnau in early 1926, *Moving Picture World* saw Fox as giving the German director an opportunity "to put... subjective thought on the screen, to open up the mind, the heart, the soul." Less than one year later (April 1927), however, the paper's leading critic, E. Winthrop Sargeant, chastised his fellow reviewers for thinking that "nothing is good, unless it be a handful of UFA's," referring to the huge German production company for which most of the German film "artists" had worked. A few months later, James Quirk, editor of *Photoplay*, the most respected and influential of the Hollywood fan magazines, derided the "pseudo-intellectuals" who reserved their praise for foreign works while dismissing American films.

This does not mean that in 1927 the discourse on Murnau, his films, and the production of *Sunrise* suddenly became hostile, but there was a marked change from the unanimous adulation that characterized references to him only a short time before. A critical backlash seems to have developed against German films and filmmakers, and even Murnau was not immune. Whereas his *Faust* had been called by the *New York Times* critic a "radiant jewel" and "as far removed from the ordinary picture as a Tintoretto painting," *Tartuffe* (released in the United States during the summer of 1927) was called "heavy and primitive" by the same reviewer. *Moving Picture World* said the film did not even equal American filmmaking standards.[48]

Reports on the production of *Sunrise* focused on the film's costs and "unusualness." The trade press frequently mentioned the elaborate sets constructed at Murnau's insistence and the added expense these sets entailed. Even before *Sunrise* had been edited, reports began to circulate in the trade press emphasizing what we might call the film's "otherness." What had been seen but a year before as the possibility of aesthetic synthesis among individual artistic expression, German sensibilities, and Hollywood know-how now began to be spoken of as unnecessary extravagance, and speculation was raised that the end result

F. W. Murnau on location while directing the elaborate production, *Sunrise.*

The Museum of Modern Art/Film Stills Archive

would be as much anomaly as artwork. In February 1927, *Variety* reported that to date the costs of *Sunrise* had reached $1,200,000. On March 5, the Hollywood columns of *Moving Picture World* noted that "reports and photographs filtering through from Hollywood indicate that the distinguished German director has created an unusual picture." Possibly fearing that preliminary reports would emphasize the film's circumvention of certain conventions of Hollywood style (its elaborate moving-camera sequences and stylized acting, for example), Murnau asked that the studio release no publicity material on the film until it was ready for release. He even went so far as to request that no one outside the production team be allowed to view rushes of the film until it had been edited. Murnau's secretiveness no doubt reinforced suspicions that *Sunrise* would be unusual.

What is important to note here is that this "otherness" was spoken of as difference and strangeness rather than progress and innovation. Perhaps most telling is William Fox's own public statement issued one month before the premiere of *Sunrise*, denying rumors that the film was in any way bizarre or that Murnau had been unnecessarily extravagant in its production. This statement was necessary, said Fox, "because of the exotic and sometimes freakish character of the majority of foreign films which have been shown in this country." Then, as if trying to squeeze *Sunrise* into the Fox prestige-film mold of stage and literary adaptations, Fox reminded the exhibitor-readers of *Moving Picture World* that *Sunrise* was based on a "well-known" story.[49]

The Fox statement is strong evidence of a discursive shift toward the negative poles of the terms by which German cinema had been discussed throughout the 1920s: elitism, excess, and self-indulgence. Whereas Fox publicists had boasted of the high production budgets of *What Price Glory?* and *Seventh Heaven*, and commentators had interpreted these budgets as evidence of Fox's commitment to "quality" pictures, Fox himself found it necessary to fend off charges of extravagance in the production of *Sunrise*. His remarks can be seen as a fairly desperate attempt to pull *Sunrise* (not yet seen but object of discourse, nevertheless) back within the limits of aesthetic acceptability. The term "desperate" is appropriate because by distancing *Sunrise* from the "freakish" and "exotic" majority of foreign films seen in the United States, Fox attempted to sever Murnau's connection with the very aesthetic tradition of which he had been foremost representative but a few years earlier: the German cinema. Whereas Fox had emphasized Murnau's uniqueness as a cinema artist when he brought him to the United States, he now stressed the similarity of his forthcoming film to the less self-consciously artistic stage adaptations that had produced both critical recognition *and* economic success for his studio.

The initial response to the German cinema and changes in this response by 1927, Murnau's biographical legend, and Fox's attempts to boost the prestige of his studio together help to form the discursive background against which *Sunrise* was read in the fall of 1927. Discourse on the film itself can now be seen as an attempt to position *Sunrise* within some familiar discursive space. What

Sunrise "meant" in 1927 was contingent upon the assessment of what the film was "like." Fox had tried to make a place for *Sunrise* within the discursive boundaries of the Hollywood cinema. Certainly the film bears some marks of a Hollywood studio production. Its stars, George O'Brien and Janet Gaynor were Fox contract players. Its narrative concerns—the illicit lust for a "vamp" almost bringing an otherwise "good" man to murder his wife, and the pastoral life of the country set against the excitement of the city—locate *Sunrise* within familiar American literary and cinematic traditions of the 1920s. However, the style of *Sunrise*, with its forced-perspective sets, probing camera, compositional precision, use of off-screen space, vaguely European decor, and "expressionistic" acting render the film unreadable as just another Hollywood film.[50]

Had *Sunrise* been made in Germany by UFA, it might not have been received more favorably in the United States, but it almost certainly would have been less problematic to position within American aesthetic discourse. However, as a Hollywood film, made by Fox Studios, directed by a German artist, narratively conventional but stylistically self-conscious—*Sunrise* presented critics and audiences with too many contradictions. As Steven Lipkin has pointed out, even the Fox publicity department found it difficult to "say" anything about the film itself; advertising focused on the reputation of its stars and director instead.

The positive reviews of the film contained equivocations and uncertainties. *New York Times* film critic Mordaunt Hall, who had nothing but praise for *Faust* and *The Last Laugh*, said of *Sunrise* that Murnau had once again shown himself to be an "artist in cinema studies," but also pointed out that the film had cost a "staggering" amount of money and that its "exotic" style was a "mixture of Russian gloom and Berlin brightness." Other critics commented positively on camera work in *Sunrise* but derided its artificiality. To many contemporary reviewers, however, the unconventional style of *Sunrise* was ostentatious rather than innovative, and its visual flourishes were an attempt to gloss over a weak, sentimental story. Calling actor George O'Brien "the Golem's little boy," *Photoplay* called the film, "The sort of picture that fools the high-brows into hollering 'Art!' Swell trick photography and fancy effects, but boiled down, no story interest and only stilted mannered acting."[51]

Poorly promoted, released amidst the hoopla of *The Jazz Singer* and misteamed with Fox's Movietone newreel, *Sunrise* had no chance at the box office. Although Fox had signed Murnau to a five-year contract before the release of *Sunrise*, the film's ambivalent critical response and poor exhibition record soon made it clear it would not serve as a model for future Fox "highly artistic pictures." *What Price Glory?* and *Seventh Heaven* represented an alternative route to studio prestige: the well-produced but aesthetically less-ambitious adaptation of proven stage and literary successes.

This discussion of the discursive backgrounds of *Sunrise* has not been an attempt to force a complex work into a place in film history so that it can be explained away and all its aesthetic complexities simplistically accounted for.

So long as it is shown to audiences *Sunrise* will no doubt continue to fascinate most viewers and enthrall many. This case study has demonstrated, however, that neither films nor aesthetic discourse about films exist outside of history. *Sunrise*, Murnau, and the German cinema in general had meaning in the United States as elements of a larger discourse about movies, art, artists, entertainment, and business. Furthermore, like the words of a verbal language, Murnau and his work "meant" something only by virtue of their positions within an aesthetic system of similarity and difference. *Sunrise* was difficult for contemporaneous critics and audiences to read because its position within this system was ambiguous.

The backgrounds discussed here are only the most immediate to an understanding of *Sunrise*'s position(s) within history. This brief sketch of Fox's situation in the 1920s leads naturally (but for immediate purposes here, impossibly) to a consideration of Hollywood production, distribution, and exhibition practices and industrial organization as they compare to those Murnau left in Berlin. Murnau's work and that of other German film "artists" can be positioned not only in relation to Hollywood style, but also in relation to more conventional German films and other art cinema movements of the period: Soviet cinema, French impressionism, and both European and American avant-gardes.

Finally, relating *Sunrise* to William Fox's ambitious economic plans suggests that even in the case of the most conspicuously "aesthetic" film, nonaesthetic contexts must eventually be taken into account. Aesthetic film history is not autonomous from economic, technological, and social histories, it merely marks out one set of generative mechanisms.

CONCLUSIONS

The discussion of the backgrounds, horizons, or, to put them in Realist terms, generative mechanisms in aesthetic film history has not been intended as an exhaustive catalog of all the factors responsible for how films have looked and sounded throughout film history. Rather the terrain of film history has been only partially mapped out and only the most prominent features of the aesthetic history of the American commercial cinema noted. For other national cinemas and for other modes of production—Soviet cinema of the 1920s or documentary filmmaking, for example—other features of the aesthetic landscape will need to be added or features only sketched in here drawn in bolder relief.

This chapter has demonstrated the relationship between film theory and film history, particularly aesthetic film history, and, by doing so, has suggested that a change in theoretical orientation can produce a change in what is seen as constituting the "history" of the cinema. By redefining aesthetic film history as the history of film as signifying practices and historically specific confrontations between audiences and films rather than the history of art films, the object of aesthetic film history becomes all films and not just that small, changing body of films designated as "classics." Furthermore, this redefinition requires that the film historian regard any film as occupying a position within history, and not as merely illustrative of a set of timeless aesthetic values. Any given film represents the convergence of a number of historical forces: individual and institutional, filmic and nonfilmic. These forces (or backgrounds or generative mechanisms) are also *historical* in the sense that they have histories—histories that are also the province of the aesthetic film historian.

In this chapter the lines separating aesthetic film history from social, economic, or technological history have not been clearly drawn. This was by design. Far too often in the past the history of film as art has been assumed to have little or no relationship to other aspects of film history. Style, mode of production, intertexts, and authorship represent basic categories of generative mechanisms that help explain how films looked and sounded at a particular point in film history. Clearly these mechanisms operate within larger contexts, however, and their individual histories involve both aesthetic and non-aesthetic factors. Understanding the historical development of the Hollywood mode of production requires a consideration of the economic functions it performed. Every film decoding operation involves the use of codes that are cultural as well as aesthetic. The definition of style at any point in film history presumes a particular level of technological development. In the following three chapters the examination of the generative mechanisms of film history is continued and extended to include the economic, technological, and social contexts in which films have been made and received.

NOTES

1. Iris Barry, "Preface" to Lewis Jacobs' *The Rise of the American Film* (New York: Teachers College Press, 1939), p. xix; and Gerald Mast, *A Short History of the Movies* (Indianapolis: Bobbs-Merrill, 1981), p. 10.

2. Gerald Mast, "Film History and Film Histories," *Quarterly Review of Film Studies* 1 (August 1976): 297–314.

3. A. R. Fulton, *Motion Pictures: The Development of an Art from Silent Film to the Age of Television* (Norman: University of Oklahoma Press, 1960), p. 45; Alan Casty, *Development of the Film: An Interpretive History* (New York: Harcourt Brace Jovanovich, 1973), p. 6; and Jacobs, *Rise of the American Film*, p. 35. See also, David Robinson, *The History of World Cinema* (New York: Stein and Day, 1973), p. 37.

4. Eric Rhode, *A History of the Cinema From its Origins to 1970* (New York: Hill and Wang, 1976), p. 30.

5. André Bazin, *What Is Cinema?*, Vol. I, Hugh Gray, ed. (Berkeley: Univ. of California Press, 1971), p. 13. See also, Dudley Andrew, *Major Film Theories* (New York: Oxford University Press, 1976), Chapter Six; and Dudley Andrew, *André Bazin* (New York: Oxford University Press, 1978).

6. Ibid., p. 21.

7. Mast, *Short History of the Movies*, p. 3.

8. The seminal statement of the auteur theory came in Truffaut's "Un Certaine Tendence du Cinema Francais," *Cahiers du Cinema* 31 (January 1954): 15–29, trans. in *Movies and Methods*, Bill Nichols, ed. (Berkeley: University of California Press, 1976), pp. 224–236. The economic and aesthetic contexts of the auteur theory are discussed in John Hess, "La Politique des Auteurs: World View as Aesthetic," *Jump Cut* 1 (May–June 1974); and Steven N. Lipkin, "The Film Criticism of Francois Truffaut: A Contextual Analysis," Ph.D. dissertation, University of Iowa, 1977.

9. Andrew Sarris, *The American Cinema* (New York: Dutton, 1968), pp. 39, 83.

10. Casty, *Development of the Film*, p. viii; Robinson, *History of World Cinema*, p. xiv; and Jack Ellis, *History of Film* (Englewood Cliffs, N.J.: Prentice-Hall, 1979), p. 6.

11. Mast, "Film History and Film Histories," p. 299; and Sarris, *American Cinema*, p. 25.

12. Mast, "Film History and Film Histories," p. 302.

13. George Boas, "*The Mona Lisa* in the History of Taste," *Journal of the History of Ideas* 1 (April 1940): 207–224; Wolfgang Iser, *The Act of Reading* (Baltimore: Johns Hopkins University Press, 1978); and Hans Robert Jauss, *Toward an Aesthetic of Reception*, Timothy Bahti, trans. (Minneapolis: University of Minnesota Press, 1982).

14. Edward Buscombe, "Notes on Columbia Picture Corp. 1926–41," *Screen* 16 (Autumn 1975): 65–82.

15. Claude Levi-Strauss, *Structural Anthropology* (London: Penguin Books, 1972), p. 62.

16. Andrew, *Major Film Theories*, p. 217; and Christian Metz, *Film Language: A Semiotics of the Cinema* (New York: Oxford University Press, 1974), especially Chapter Five: "Problems of Denotation in the Fiction Film."

17. Charles C. Fries, *Linguistics and Reading* (New York: Holt, Rinehart and Winston, 1964), p. 64.

18. Metz, *Film Language*, p. 179.

19. Stephen Heath, "Introduction: Questions of Emphasis," *Screen* 14 (Spring/Summer 1973): 10. This double issue of *Screen* is devoted to semiotics and the work of Metz in particular.

20. Metz, *Film Language*, p. 83.

21. As Keat and Urry put it, "Generally, structuralists are anti-causal and anti-historical in their methodological pronouncements." *Social Theory as Science* (London: Routledge and Kegan Paul, 1975), p. 75.

22. Kristin Thompson, *Ivan the Terrible: A Neo-Formalist Analysis* (Princeton, N.J.: Princeton University Press, 1981), pp. 14–18. A similar approach is taken by David Bordwell in *The Films of Carl Dreyer* (Berkeley: University of California Press, 1981); and Hans Robert Jauss, *Aesthetic Experience and Literary Hermeneutics* (Minneapolis: University of Minnesota Press, 1982), p. xii.

23. Jauss, *Toward an Aesthetic of Reception*.

24. For a discussion of the classical Hollywood narrative style, see David Bordwell and Kristin Thompson, "Space and Narrative in the Films of Ozu," *Screen* 17 (Summer

1976): 41–73; Bordwell, *The Films of Carl Theodor Dreyer*, pp. 25–38; David Bordwell, Janet Staiger, and Kristin Thompson, *The Classical Hollywood Cinema: Film Style and Mode of Production to 1960* (London: Routledge and Kegan Paul, 1985); Noel Burch, *Theory of Film Practice* (New York: Praeger, 1973), p. 11; and Edward Branigan, "The Space of Equinox Flower," *Screen* 17 (Summer 1976): 74–105.

25. Fernando Solanas and Octavio Gettino, "Towards a Third Cinema," in *Movies and Methods*, Bill Nichols, ed. (Berkeley: University of California Press, 1976), p. 63.

26. See, for example, Noel Burch, "Porter or Ambivalence," *Screen* 19 (Winter 1978/79): 91–105; Charles Musser, "The Early Cinema of Edwin S. Porter," *Cinema Journal* 19 (Fall 1979); and Robert C. Allen, "Film History: The Narrow Discourse," *1977 Film Studies Annual Annual*, pp. 9–16.

27. These categories are adapted from those used by Jane Feuer in her discussion of intertextuality in the Hollywood musical. See "The Hollywood Musical: The Aesthetics of Spectator Involvement in an Entertainment Form," Ph.D. dissertation, University of Iowa, 1978, pp. 179–236.

28. Andrew Tudor, *Theories of Film* (New York: Viking, 1973), pp. 131–137.

29. David Bordwell and Kristin Thompson, *Film Art: An Introduction* (Reading, Mass.: Addison-Wesley, 1979), p. 8.

30. Janet Staiger, "The Hollywood Mode of Production: The Construction of Divided Labor in the Film Industry," Ph.D. dissertation, University of Wisconsin, 1981; and "Dividing Labor for Production Control: Thomas Ince and the Rise of the Studio System," *Cinema Journal* 18 (Spring 1979): 25.

31. Peter Wollen, *Signs and Meaning in the Cinema*, 2nd. ed. (Bloomington: Indiana University Press, 1972), p. 104.

32. Boris Tomasevskij, "Literature and Biography," in *Readings in Russian Poetics: Formalist and Structuralist Views*, Ladislav Matejka and Krystyna Pomorska, eds. (Ann Arbor: Michigan Slavic Publications, 1978), pp. 47–55. David Bordwell adapts Tomasevskij's notion of authorship in *The Films of Carl Dreyer*, pp. 5–10.

33. Noël Carroll, "Film History and Film Theory: An Outline for an Institutional Theory of Film," *Film Reader* 4 (1982): 81–96.

34. Dudley Andrew, "Introduction," *Quarterly Review of Film Studies* 2 (August 1977): vi; and Sarris, *American Cinema*, pp. 68–69. See also, Lotte Eisner, *Murnau* (Berkeley: University of California Press, 1973), pp. 167–195.

35. *Moving Picture World*, July 17, 1926, p. 51; and *Motion Picture Classic*, September 1926, p. 3.

36. *Motion Picture Classic*, October 1925, p. 25; and *New York Times*, December 7, 1926, p. 21. See also, Robert C. Allen, "William Fox Presents *Sunrise*," *Quarterly Review of Film Studies* 2 (August 1977): 327–338; Steven Lipkin, "*Sunrise*: A Film Meets Its Public," *Quarterly Review of Film Studies* 2 (August 1977): 339–358; and Gordon Allvine, *The Greatest Fox of Them All* (New York: Lyle Stuart, 1969), p. 98.

37. Quoted in "The Menace of German Films," *Literary Digest*, May 14, 1921, p. 28; *New York Times*, December 13, 1920, p. 19; *Current Opinion*, June 1921, p. 786; *New York Times*, March 20, 1921, VI:2; *New Republic*, February 25, 1925, p. 19; Lipkin, *Sunrise*, p. 341; *New Republic*, July 28, 1926, p. 280; and *Film Daily Yearbook 1927*, p. 16.

38. *New York Times*, December 13, 1920, p. 19; June 20, 1921, p. 17; and April 24, 1925, p. 17.

39. See Siegfried Kracauer, *From Caligari to Hitler* (Princeton, N.J.: Princeton University Press, 1947), pp. 61–76; *New York Times*, March 20, 1921, VI:2; April 4, 1921, p. 18; *Current Opinion*, June 1921, p. 786; and *Moving Picture World*, April 23, 1921, pp. 785, 787.

40. See *Literary Digest*, September 26, 1925, pp. 27–28. For a summary of critical responses, see also, *New York Times*, August 24, 1925, p. 17; and *Nation*, September 16, 1925, p. 311.

41. *New York Times*, April 18, 1921, p. 8; December 7, 1926, p. 21; *New Republic*, July 28, 1926, p. 280; and *Nation*, March 23, 1927, p. 324.

42. *New Republic*, May 27, 1925, pp. 19–20. See also, *New Republic*, July 28, 1926, p. 280; *Nation*, September 16, 1925, p. 311; and *Moving Picture World*, July 31, 1926, p. 277.

43. *Literary Digest*, May 14, 1921, p. 28; *Moving Picture World*, May 7, 1921, p. 31; May 14, 1921, p. 119; April 23, 1921, p. 852; *Film Daily Yearbook 1927*, p. 22; and *Motion Picture Classic*, October 1925, p. 25.

44. *Moving Picture World*, April 23, 1927, p. 719; and March 26, 1927, p. 376.

45. *Film Daily Yearbook*, 1927, p. 741; *Moving Picture World*, April 2, 1927, p. 267; June 25, 1927, p. 589; "The Case of Mr. Fox," *Fortune* (May 1930): 49; and Allvine, *The Greatest Fox*, pp. 12, 105–112, 157.

46. Robert McLaughlin, *Broadway and Hollywood* (New York: Arno Press, 1974), pp. 52–80; *Moving Picture World*, January 2, 1926, p. 5; April 3, 1926, p. 332; May 21, 1927, p. 192; May 28, 1927, p. 289; and May 14, 1927, p. 92.

47. *New York Times*, December 7, 1926, p. 21; and *Moving Picture World*, July 23, 1927, p. 244.

48. *Moving Picture World*, January 2, 1926, p. 69; July 17, 1926, p. 151; *Photoplay*, November 1927, p. 27; and *Moving Picture World*, September 3, 1927.

49. See, for example, *Moving Picture World*, December 4, 1926. *Motion Picture Classic* quoted in Lipkin, *Sunrise*, pp. 342–43; *Moving Picture World*, March 5, 1927, p. 35; *Variety*, March 27, 1927, p. 4; and *Moving Picture World*, August 6, 1927, p. 402.

50. For discussion of the style of *Sunrise*, see Alexandre Astruc, "Fire and Ice," *Cahiers du Cinema in English* 1 (January 1966): 70; Robin Wood, "On *Sunrise*," *Film Comment* (May–June 1976): 10–19; Mary Ann Doane, "Desire in *Sunrise*," *Film Reader II* (1978); and Dudley Andrew, "The Gravity of *Sunrise*," *Quarterly Review of Film Studies* 2 (August 1977): 356–379.

51. *New York Times*, December 24, 1927, p. 15; *New Republic*, October 26, 1927, pp. 263–264; and *The Arts*, November 1927, p. 283. See also, *Literary Digest*, December 3, 1927, p. 29; and *Photoplay*, December 1927, p. 53.

5

Technological
Film History

Cinema depends on machines. However, we forget the fundamental technological basis of the cinema as we sit in a darkened movie theater, engrossed in the story effortlessly unrolling before us on the screen. It is only when something goes wrong—the projector bulb burns out, the image loses focus, the volume is set too high or too low—that the technological complexity of the cinema is foregrounded. For a few moments (until the problem is corrected for us) we confront some of the difficulties encountered in the latter decades of the 1890s by the many American and European tinkerers, inventors, and scientists who sought a way of producing life-like projected images that gave the appearance of natural movement. By the early 1890s the three machines required for this task had been assembled: the motion picture camera, through which individual photographs could be taken in rapid succession; the printer, which converted the exposed film to positive images; and the projector, which, reversing the process of the camera, fed the positive print past a lens and light source, projecting the resulting image on a screen. To this basic triad has been added a vast array of devices, from special equipment to move the camera through space, to "special effects" printing, to new projection systems. With these subsequent technological developments have come new possibilities in filmmaking: sound, color, wide-screen, and "3-D," among others.

All art forms and communications media have a technological history. Western painting could hardly be discussed without reference to the development of oil paints, nor modern theater without reference to the development of electrical stage illumination. It is possible, however, to conceive of poetry, theater, rhetoric, or painting with all or most of its technological augmentation stripped away and yet still be left with something recognizable as a poem or a play. In fact, some artists choose to dispense with the technological trappings of their medium—minimalist painters or performance artists, for example. The filmmaker, by comparison, cannot escape the relatively high degree of technological complexity that is a prerequisite to the production of any film. While the cinema is by no means unique in having a technological history, its inescapable dependence on a set of complex machines, themselves dependent on a particular formation in the history of optics, chemistry, and machine tooling, gives the study of technology a prominent place in film history.

The basic task of the historian of cinema technology is the examination of circumstances surrounding the initial development of the cinematic apparatus (camera, printer, projector) and those attending the subsequent alterations, modifications, and extensions. This does not mean merely cataloging inventions in historical sequence; machines do not invent themselves. The technological history of the cinema necessarily must also entail how particular pieces of technology came to be developed at a particular time, their relationship to the existing state of technology, the extent and nature of their use, and the consequence of that use—whether foreseen or unforeseen. Cinema has developed from a specific technological basis that has been changing since the 1890s. Not so obvious is how and why this original technology and the alterations to it came about. Answering these questions presupposes some theory of technological change. This chapter examines the major theories of technological change that have been applied to the history of the cinema, again emphasizing their application to the history of American cinema.

THE "GREAT MAN" THEORY AND TECHNOLOGICAL DETERMINATION

The first place one might think to look for the impetus behind technological change in cinema is in the laboratory itself, that is, the inventor who transforms an idea into apparatus. As we have seen in Chapter 3, the image of the solitary inventor crying "Eureka" in the wee hours of the morning has been a particularly appealing one, combining as it does an ethos of individual achievement with technological progress, relatable in terms of high drama, exciting enough to match the stories produced in Hollywood. Technological history is thus often portrayed as an evolutionary chain of technological success stories centering on the "breakthroughs" of individual inventors. The inventor supervises the birth of the appropriate technological change and nurtures it to maturity. This new technological state of affairs gives rise to new problems, needs, and/or opportunities, which provide the starting point for yet another technical genius. Such a schema carries with it its own criterion for historical significance: Only those inventors and inventions that move the cinema onward toward its present state of technological sophistication are fit subjects for technological film history. History is constructed backwards from the present—tracing the evolutionary chain of events and great individuals that recede from today to the nineteenth century and beyond. With this chain in mind it becomes possible to recognize certain elements of technological change that cannot be accommodated by it as missteps and/or anachronisms—Smell-O-Vision in the 1950s or Edison's attempts at synchronous sound in 1912, for example.

We have deliberately outlined this "great man" theory of technological change in its most simplistic and least tenable form in order to carry its underlying precepts to their logical conclusions. "Great man" accounts of the technological history of the American cinema vary considerably in detail and complexity—from the rather simplistic (and in light of its method of publication, probably necessary) hero-worship of Grau, to the painstaking descriptions of the invention of early cinematic apparatus in Gordon Hendricks's work. However, so long as one holds that the ultimate "cause" of technological change is the genius of a few individuals, then there is not much else in the way of historical explanation that need be said. The task of the technological historian is limited to (1) separating the important technological advancements from the unimportant, (2) identifying the person(s) responsible for those advancements, (3) relating a narrative of their success, and, in doing so, (4) awarding them their proper place in the history of the cinema. Hence, for example, Hendricks's exhaustive examination of every scrap of documentation relating to the invention of the first working motion picture camera, the Kinetograph, is done in order to establish that it is not Thomas Edison who deserves credit for this achievement, but in fact his laboratory assistant, W. K. L. Dickson.

Certainly, the history of technological change in the cinema involves individuals whose training, skills, aptitudes, and, finally, achievements single them out for special consideration by the historian. To deny that Thomas Edison, W. K. L. Dickson, Lee de Forest, Theodore Case, or Herbert Kalmus played a part in the technological history of the cinema is not only shortsighted but historically unsupportable. However, by foregrounding the role of the individual in technological change, the "great man" theory excludes or greatly reduces consideration of other factors. The shortcomings of such a theory are, in fact, highlighted by the ongoing debate over who actually "invented" the movies. Since the 1920s claims of primacy have been made for inventors in the United States, England, France, Germany, and the Soviet Union: Thomas Edison, W. K. L. Dickson, Gray and Otway Latham, Jean LeRoy, William Friese-Green, Jules Marey, and Max Skladonowski, among others. What this historical hairsplitting ignores is the larger historical questions of what caused this flurry of research in the 1880s and 1890s, what is the context in which these inventors labored, and why a few machines received widespread commercial exploitation, while others—just as "technologically advanced"—were hardly used outside the laboratory. The historical context of technological change in the cinema is not limited to the laboratory, and it is this larger context that the "great man" theory fails to take into account.

The "great man" approach to technological change concentrates on the steps leading to a major breakthrough and on the individual responsible for it. Other film historians have concentrated on what they see as the determining effect of these technical breakthroughs themselves on the future course of film history, shifting the focus from person to machine and from invention to the aesthetic consequence of that invention. Such historians might be called technological determinists, in that they presume, as Raymond Williams notes, that

> new technologies are discovered by an essentially internal process of research and development, which then sets the conditions for social change and progress. The effects of the technologies, whether direct or indirect, foreseen or unforeseen, are, as it were, the rest of history.[1]

According to this view, film history becomes (1) inventions, plus (2) the consequences that follow from their availability.

The thrust of technological determinism can be clearly seen in this forceful comment by an historian of film technology, Raymond Fielding

> All my work as an historian, at least in recent years, has proceeded from the premise that the history of the motion picture—as an art form, as a medium of communication, and as an industry—has been determined principally by technological innovations and considerations. . . . The contribution of a Porter, Ince, and Griffith followed as much from the availability of portable cameras, larger magazines, interchangeable lens, and improved emulsions as it did from their individual artistic vision and talent.[2]

To Fielding, then, each technological advancement contains within it a certain potential that is then realized by perceptive filmmakers, but what they can achieve artistically is already established by the technological parameters available to them. It is but a short step from this view to the assigning of artistic merit to those filmmakers perspicacious enough to understand the full implication of a new technology. Hence even in a nontechnologically oriented work such as Jacobs' *The Rise of the American Film*, one can see traces of technological determinism in, for example, his assessment of Walt Disney. Jacobs argues that during the 1930s Disney functioned as the consummate filmmaker because his studio completely exploited all the technological potential then available to the filmmaker, including color and sound. Disney possessed a "technical dexterity and remarkable command of the medium [that] gives all his efforts a brilliancy of rendition that makes even the least of them dazzling."[3]

To Jacobs and other film historians the "great man" theory and technological determinism coalesce. The great inventors are celebrated for contributing to technological advancement of the cinema, and then another set of great individuals take the stage of film history—those who saw the possibilities inherent in technological change and came closest to "fulfilling the promise" in that potential. The technological advancement itself determines the nature of that artistic fulfillment. Once the promise of a particular device has been fulfilled, history awaits yet another great individual to push film technology one step higher on the evolutionary ladder.

As with the "great man" theory of invention, technological determinism contains within it a kernel of unarguable fact: The state of technology at any given moment in film history imposes certain limits on film production. It marks out what is possible and feasible and thus makes more probable certain types of films and less probable or even impossible other types. Robert Altman's *Nashville* presupposes a state of sophistication in the field of sound recording and reproduction that had only been obtained by the 1960s. The difficulties of maintaining synchronous sound via the 1913 Edison Kinetophone system made it highly unlikely that it would be used to produce feature length films on a mass scale. However, the simple availability of technology does not in itself determine filmmaking practice, nor does it necessarily specify a general direction for artistic innovation. For example, lightweight, portable 16mm filmmaking equipment was "available" to Hollywood in the 1950s and 1960s, but did not find its way into use in Hollywood. Nothing inherent in basic film technology predisposes the cinema to the production of narrative films, or, indeed, to the use of editing to tell a story, and yet since 1908 the predominant form of commercial cinema in Europe and America has been a narrative form based in part on a particular style of editing.

THE ECONOMICS OF TECHNICAL CHANGE

The work of Hendricks and other "great man" historians (even Ramsaye) does help to provide a sense of the immediate context of technological change in the cinema. It is useful to know the specific technical obstacles that had to be overcome and the struggles among individual inventors to receive the acclaim we traditionally afford to the inventor who comes up with a solution "first." Similarly the research of more technological deterministic historians like Fielding provides invaluable information on the state of technical possibilities at a given moment, which nontechnically minded film historians ignore at their peril. However, the limitations of both approaches are apparent even at the pre–cinematic stage of film history (why had Edison put Dickson to work on the Kinetograph in the first place?), and become even more glaring as one moves into the industrial era of American film history.

By the 1920s technological change in the motion picture industry was by and large part of a much larger industrial process. Even when technological innovation in the cinema originated outside the Hollywood studio itself (as was the case with much of the early work on synchronous sound), it came from companies in related industries (electronics, radio), not "lone wolf" individual inventors. In short, as the American cinema took on the characteristics of a mature capitalist industry—that is to say, a collection of firms, each trying to generate maximum long-run profits—technological change became largely a matter of economic decision making.

One approach to technological change that takes into account the larger economic context can be adapted to the technological history of the cinema from the field of industrial economics. Economic historians have developed a collection of sophisticated tools to analyze the behavior of corporations, one subset of which addresses questions of technological change. This approach, labeled the "theory of technological change," presumes that companies, over the long run, act in such a way as to make the highest possible profit (defined as the residual share after a firm has paid all costs of capital [interest], land [rent], and labor services [wages]). Technological change is one means of achieving that end. This chapter shall discuss this approach in some detail, as it is an important step in placing technological change in the cinema in a wider context.

The first steps in the economic analysis of a particular technological change involve establishing the basic structure of the industry under consideration, and the industry's closest competitors in the years prior to that technological change. In the case of the movies the latter might include vaudeville, popular music, phonograph records, live theater, television, and/or other leisure-time industries—depending on the time frame of the study. Having set forth this industrial context, the historian can move on to consider the three stages in the introduction of any new product or process, in other words, the technological change itself. The first of these stages is the *development of the invention* necessary for effecting the introduction of a new product or process. Economist Edwin Mansfield has defined an invention as "a prescription for a new product or process that was not obvious to one skilled in the relevant art at the time the idea was generated."[4] Usually the invention is not a single idea, but rather a system of concepts linked together. Certainly this was the case for most inventions in motion picture technology—color and sound being the most striking examples.

Once the system of inventions is initially adopted for practical use, it becomes an *innovation.* The innovation stage of technological change involves a firm altering its past methods of production, distribution, and/or marketing because it has determined that the adoption of the invention will result in greater long-term profits. Obviously, firms generate or are presented with many new inventions only a few of which ever reach the innovation stage. The decision to innovate is made only after the expected profits from the invention have been compared to those from alternative inventions and from continuing to employ existing products and processes. An invention does not have to be developed by the industry that ultimately adopts it. The inventor and innovator might be the same corporation (or individual), but in modern industrial practice they rarely are.

For any motion picture company, the process of innovation involves a large number of variables. The firm must have the necessary talent to organize and effect the change. The company must weigh the costs of acquiring new long-term debt, and making adjustments in production, distribution, and exhibition against anticipated revenue. It must also formulate marketing strategies to generate that revenue at the box office. Finally there is the factor of risk. Timing is crucial in innovation. A firm must decide to wait and gather more information about the technological potential and public acceptance of an innovation or gain the competitive leverage of being first on the market with the new product or process. Firms with a significant degree of economic power can afford to be cautious, for they possess the resources to make up for lost advantages.

The process of *diffusion* begins once the technology begins to receive widespread use within an industry. Again central to decision making during this stage is ranking all various investment policies open to the firm, including adopting the new technology. An investment rarely requires a quantum change in production, distribution, or exhibition. The firm continually must decide how and when to alter the speed of the transformation as new information is acquired. Simultaneously it can seek to alter and/or "improve" the invention to adapt it to the firm's particular needs. Early versions of an invention often possess serious technological and marketing disadvantages. Hence modifications at this stage may turn out to be more significant than the initial invention system itself. The diffusion process also involves a reallocation of resources. New plant, equipment, and labor replace those in current use. For example, workers with required new skills are hired. Since buildings and large-scale apparatus once in place become relatively inflexible, changes here take place largely through the construction of new plant and equipment.

The rate of diffusion is directly related to the perceived profitability of the new product or process. Three considerations are crucial. First, what is the nature of the potential profits relative to those earned by the next best investment possibility? The greater the difference, all other things being equal, the faster the rate of diffusion. Second, the greater the financial investment required, the slower the diffusion, unless potential profits loom very, very large. Finally, the rate of diffusion depends on the degree of success of the marketing strategy the firm adopts. The company's owners/managers must seek that avenue best able to convince customers to purchase the new product in large numbers.

CASE STUDY: THE COMING OF SOUND—AN ANALYSIS OF TECHNOLOGICAL CHANGE

The preceding framework—invention, innovation, and diffusion—provides the historian with a powerful, basic methodology by which to analyze the introduction of any technology. For the film industry, this would include any improvements in the camera, printer, or projector, as well as alterations in all three, such as the addition of a color, 3-D, or wide-screen process. One such fundamental benchmark in cinema history was the coming of sound to the American film industry during the late 1920s, and the resulting adoption of sound by all other film industries in the world.

Traditional accounts of the coming of sound to Hollywood stem from two sources: Benjamin Hampton's *History of the American Film Industry* and Lewis Jacobs' *The Rise of the American Film*.[5] Hampton presented the hypothesis that because the U.S. film industry had reached a steady-state, no-growth equilibrium, it was "ready" for sound. He offered no reasons why the industry was "ready" at that point and not before. Hampton then went on to describe how Warner Bros., alone, agreed to experiment with a sound system tendered by the American Telephone & Telegraph Corporation. Almost magically, the tiny Warners became a profit-making colossus on the strength of a single hit film, *The Jazz Singer* (1927), featuring America's most popular vaudeville/musical star, Al Jolson. But why Warner Bros.? Hampton provided no systematic answer. Lewis Jacobs did: Warner Bros. introduced talkies because it feared bankruptcy. The larger film industry concerns, Paramount and Loew's (parent company for MGM), shunned and at times actively opposed Warners' efforts. Again only because of *The Jazz Singer*, did Paramount and Loew's convert to sound. For Hampton and Jacobs the analysis is reduced to a David-and-Goliath narrative featuring the heroics of the Warner brothers.

Such an analysis fails to examine the complexity of the transformation. What firm or firms supplied the equipment and why? Didn't giants Paramount and Loew's eventually switch over to sound, and also generate huge profits? From our short local analysis of the changeover in Milwaukee, we are certainly skeptical about the ability of one film, *The Jazz Singer*, to alter the course of history. Were the vaudeville shorts, so popular in Milwaukee, used elsewhere? What was the timing of the sound transformation?

Using the theory of technological change, it is possible to analyze systematically the American film industry's conversion to sound in terms of the desire of the motion picture companies and the suppliers of the necessary inventions to maximize their long-run profits. The data for this study come from court records, motion picture trade papers, and corporate records.

The history of the invention phase of sound motion pictures begins even before the commercial introduction of the movies. In 1895 Edison's laboratory demonstrated a system for synchronous-sound motion pictures, but neither Edison nor his army of assistants could solve the vexing problems involved in the synchronization of sound and image. Ten years later, with the movies now a profitable and popular entertainment industry, dozens of would-be millionaires took up sound experimentation where Edison had left off. None, however, solved the fundamental problems of synchronization and amplification.[6] Typical was the experience of a French company headed by Leon Gaumont. In 1905, Gaumont recorded popular American vaudeville stars using his Chronophone sound system and presented the resulting short films in U.S. vaudeville theaters. Technologically, the Chronophone was quite simple. A motion picture projector was linked by a series of cables to two phonographs positioned near the screen. Unfortunately the system frequently lapsed out of synchronization, and the primitive amplification system Gaumont employed emitted only muted and tinny approximations of the recorded performances. The Chronophone failed to attract large audiences on a sustained basis, and the scheme was finally dropped.[7]

In 1913 Edison boldly announced his laboratory had perfected a superior sound motion picture system. To its credit Edison's corporate laboratory had augmented the sensitivity of the recording microphone, increased power for amplification, and structurally improved the linkage between the phonograph and projector. Consequently the Edison Company was able to persuade the powerful Keith-Albee vaudeville circuit to try out the Kinetophone in four New York City theaters. On February 13, 1913, the premiere took place, with four entertaining shorts, including a lecturer smashing plates and "singing" (off-key) to demonstrate the tone and volume of the Edison device. However, after two week's run, it was clear to all involved that Edison Labs had not overcome problems of synchronization and amplification. Projectionists frequently failed to maintain the delicate balance necessary to preserve synchronized speech, nor could the Kinetophone eliminate the metallic sounds associated with the acoustical (pre-electronic) phonographs of that time. After several months of attempted innovation, Edison and the Keith-Albee vaudeville chain abandoned sound movies completely. Edison's withdrawal signaled the end to a decade of frustrated efforts by scores of other inventors/entrepreneurs.[8]

Work continued, however, among a handful of scientists who were attempting to develop a complete alternative to phonograph-linked systems through recording sounds directly on motion picture film, thus solving the problem of maintaining synchronization. In 1923 noted radio pioneer, Lee de Forest, demonstrated his Phonofilm system for the press. De Forest, not backed by a large corporation, tried to market his invention using only his own limited resources, and nearly went bankrupt funding a distribution network. Moreover, to raise backing he mortgaged his patents, and thus slowly lost control of that vital resource.[9] Technically, De Forest's system was hampered by an inadequate amplification apparatus.

Indeed it took the scientists and resources of the world's largest company, American Telephone & Telegraph (hereafter AT&T) more than ten years to perfect a satisfactory sound-on-film system. Working through its manufacturing subsidiary, Western Electric, AT&T engaged in sound-recording research because it desired sensitive apparatus by which to record and test the quality of long distance telephone transmission. Western Electric experimented with both traditional phonograph sound-on-disc and sound-on-film, and by 1922 they had developed a much improved loudspeaker, microphone, and turntable drive shaft. Labeled "electronic sound," these inventions produced a volume and tone far superior to then conventional "acoustical" recording. In 1923 AT&T pondered how best to create a profit from these remarkable inventions. An electronic phonograph seemed an obvious possibility, but so did motion pictures with sound. To kick off a sales campaign, AT&T created several experimental short films, and began to approach members of the U.S. film industry.[10]

AT&T would eventually link up with Warner Bros., and later the Fox Film Corporation. In 1924 Warners was a small but growing motion picture enterprise that lacked the corporate muscle to challenge such industry giants as Paramount and Loew's. Warners sought help from Wall Street and eventually formed a liaison with a Wall Street investment banking house, Goldman Sachs. Quickly Warners and Goldman Sachs formulated a long-range plan to try to vault that movie company into a position equal to Paramount. Goldman Sachs established a $3 million-dollar revolving credit account with a consortium of banks to finance "prestige" big-budget feature films, and then floated a $4 million-dollar loan to improve studio facilities, acquire a small theater chain, and create a world-wide network for distribution. As part of the master design for expansion, Warners purchased a Los Angeles radio station. Through these radio dealings, Warners learned of AT&T's new sound recording technology. Needing all the comparative advantage it could muster, Warners incorporated the new technology into its plans for growth. The firm would continue to produce silent films, but, in addition, create more sales by recording the most popular vaudeville acts and offering them to exhibitors as low-priced substitutes for the stage shows then presented in all the best theaters in the United States. Moreover, recordings of the orchestral accompaniments for silent features would enable theater owners to save the considerable expense of paying a permanent group of 25 to 100 unionized musicians.[11]

It would take four years before Warners would reap substantial rewards from its scheme to market movies with sound. Paramount and Loew's expressed initial skepticism: "Talkies" had failed consistently for twenty years, why would they succeed now? Consequently, on June 25, 1925, AT&T gladly signed an agreement with "small-time" Warner Bros. calling for an undefined period of joint experimentation. Western Electric would supply the engineers and equipment, Warners the technicians and studio space. In the meantime Warners continued to supervise the other phases of expansion. By the end of the year the company had begun to produce its most expensive feature films to date, and had purchased a laboratory for film processing, more foreign distribution outlets, and a second radio station. Not surprisingly, Warners recorded a million-dollar loss in its annual report issued in March 1926. Historians have read this red ink as a sign of impending bankruptcy. In fact, Warner Bros., with Goldman Sachs' backing, had intentionally imposed a short-term loss to help construct the proper basis for greater profits in the future.[12]

By the spring of 1926 experiments with sound were going so well that all parties agreed to a permanent, long-term contract. Warners formed the Vitaphone Corporation to contract for and develop sound motion pictures. In turn

Western Electric granted Vitaphone an exclusive license, and agreed to manufacture the necessary apparatus. As the motion picture trade papers announced the new alliance, Warner shifted its strategy for innovation into high gear. It signed up stars from vaudeville, Broadway, and even the Metropolitan Opera. In addition, Vitaphone acquired the services of the New York Philharmonic to record the "incidental" musical music for silent films. Warner Bros. could now tender an exhibitor the most popular musical/vaudeville artists, albeit in the form of motion picture recordings.[13]

Warners opened the 1926–1927 movie season with its first Vitaphone show. Eight "Vitaphone preludes" replaced a typical theater's stage show. Initially, on that August evening in New York, the audience saw and heard film industry czar, Will Hays, congratulate Warners and AT&T for their pioneering achievement. The stage "illusion" was complete; Hays bowed at the end, anticipating the audience's applause. The New York Philharmonic followed with the "Overture" from Tannhauser. Conductor Henry Hadley also bowed as if "on stage." The six recordings that followed consisted of performances by op-

Jack Warner (right) with his less famous but more powerful older brother, Harry M. Warner, in 1945.

Quigley Photographic Archive, Georgetown University Library

eratic and concert stars. Only Roy Smeck, a vaudeville comic and musician, broke the serious tone of the evening. Warner Bros. remained cautious. No one could object to technological change that brought classical music to greater numbers of people. Vitaphone continued to make steady advances throughout the fall and winter months. The *Don Juan* program opened in Atlantic City, Chicago, and St. Louis. In October, Warners premiered a second package of shorts with the silent feature film, *The Better 'Ole*, at the Colony Theater in New York. These shorts, however, were directed at popular tastes. The five acts, which would have cost over $40,000 per week if presented live, included top vaudeville attractions, George Jessel and Al Jolson. The motion picture trade paper *Variety* predicted a bright future for an invention which could place that much high price vaudeville talent in a single theater.[14]

The central problem for Warners now became how best to develop the *long-run* profit potential for motion pictures with sound. As a first step in that direction Warner Bros. initiated an all-out sales campaign to convince exhibitors to install reproducing sound equipment. By April 1927 100 U.S. theaters could play Vitaphone shorts. However, AT&T, dissatisfied with what they perceived as slow progress on Warners' part, began to harass Vitaphone sales efforts at every turn. Eventually AT&T terminated the April 1926 agreement, paid Warners $1,300,000, and issued Vitaphone a *nonexclusive* license for sound. Warners had lost important leverage, but was now free to resume its slow and steady path for growth, including the innovation of motion pictures with sound. Vitaphone stepped up production of vaudeville shorts to five per week. A new package of a silent film with these shorts opened monthly, and previous packages, having completed initial long runs, moved to smaller markets and opened at popular prices.[15]

In addition, Vitaphone formulated plans for the following movie season, which began in September 1927. Feature films would contain "Vitaphoned" sequences. The initial effort, *The Jazz Singer*, filmed on Warners' newly completed Hollywood sound stage, premiered in October, but it was the inexpensive shorts (average cost about $15,000) that would provide Warners with a least cost method by which to experiment. Vitaphone first would try a new formula for motion pictures with sound as a short, and if response seemed positive, the programming innovation would become part of Warners' "Vitaphoned" features. For example, on December 4, 1928, Warners presented a ten-minute comedy short, *My Wife's Gone Away*, its first all-talkie story film. Later that month *Solomon's Children* opened; this all-talkie narrative film lasted nearly thirty minutes. (Both these shorts, usually ignored by the New York critical establishment, drew pointed praise in the *New York Times*.)[16]

Based on three years of growth and experimentation, financial success did come almost "overnight" during the spring of 1928. *The Jazz Singer* (and its accompanying sound shorts) gradually emerged as the 1927–1928 movie season's most popular box-office attraction. In medium-sized U.S. cities especially, where silent films rarely evoked enough drawing power to stay for more than one week, *The Jazz Singer* package was held over for weeks, even months. In Charlotte, North Carolina; Columbus, Ohio; Reading, Pennsylvania; Seattle, Washington; and Baltimore, Maryland, *The Jazz Singer* continued to attract larger and larger crowds the longer it remained. Fortunately, Warners had the trained staff and sound stages to "instantly" react to this demand for talkies. Its experiments with vaudeville shorts guaranteed that. In fact, Warners' first all-talkie length film, *Lights of New York*, originated as a short subject, and was simply "stretched" to feature film length. Within one year, Warners' innovation of sound earned millions of dollars in profits. By 1930, the firm reached the zenith of the American film industry, in size and profitability, to rank along side Paramount and Loew's.[17]

This is the point at which most historical analyses of the introduction of sound cease. However, Warner Bros. was not the only innovator of sound, nor was AT&T the sole developer of a system for sound recording. Simultaneous

Left to right: Albert Warner (brother to Jack and Harry), exhibitor Moe Mark, Harry M. Warner, and exhibitor Moe Silvers pose before entering the premiere of *Lights of New York*, Warners' first all-talkie length film.

Quigley Photographic Archive, Georgetown University Library

with Warners' activities were the effects of the Fox Film Corporation, in particular its subsidiary Fox-Case. The inventions of the Fox system were based on the work of inventor Theodore W. Case and his laboratory. In 1917 this independently wealthy, Yale-trained physicist directed the creation of the Thalofide Cell, a highly improved vacuum tube. Spurred on by rival Lee de Forest's announcement of the Phonofilm, Case Labs turned all efforts to integrating the Thalofide Cell into a sound-on-film recording system. By 1923 Case could boast of an improved microphone, recording apparatus, and amplifier. Two years later, after learning of the AT&T–Warner Bros. alliance, Case tried to locate a motion picture concern to market Case Labs' sound system. Only by turning all rights over to Fox Film (predecessor to today's Twentieth Century-Fox) could Case contract an outlet. Fox, then a secondary member of the U.S. film industry behind Paramount and Loew's, was primarily interested in producing more "big-budget" silent films and expanding its chain of theaters. Moreover, initially, the movie company had to expend resources defending the fragile patent position inherited from Case, and contracting to use AT&T's superior amplification system.[18]

After the inauspicious beginning, Fox was at last ready to assault the marketplace. At first Fox tried to imitate Warners, and created popular vaudeville performances. Vitaphone commenced operations in June 1926; four months later, Fox recorded its first sound short. Production continued on an irregular basis throughout the winter. Then on February 24, 1927, in an attempt to seize the public relations rostrum from Warners, Fox staged a widely publicized press demonstration of the newly christened Movietone system. At 10:00 A.M. fifty reporters and photographers entered the Fox studio near New York's Times Square, and were filmed using the miracle of Movietone. Four hours later these representatives of the U.S. and foreign press corps saw and heard themselves as part of a special private screening. In addition, Fox presented several vaudeville sound shorts: a banjo and piano act, a comedy sketch, and three songs by a popular cabaret performer.

The demonstration worked! Favorable commentary flowed in from all sides. By then, however, Warners had cornered the market for vaudeville shorts by signing exclusive contracts with the most popular performers. Fox needed an alternative cost-effective marketing strategy. Fox reconsidered an earlier plan: newsreels with sound. Then it could provide a unique, economically viable alternative to Warners' presentations. Fox could cheaply move into a heretofore unoccupied portion of the market for motion picture entertainment. Furthermore, sound newsreels would provide a logical method by which Fox could gradually perfect necessary new techniques of camerawork and editing, and test the market at minimal cost.[19]

Fox moved quickly. On April 30, 1927, Fox Movietone News premiered at New York City's largest theater, the Roxy. Lasting only four minutes, patrons saw and heard cadets march at the United States Military Academy. Despite limited publicity compared to the February press showing, this earliest Movietone newsreel drew an enthusiastic response from motion picture trade papers and New York-based motion picture reviewers. Soon after, Fox seized on one of the most important symbolic news events of the 1920s. At 8:00 A.M. on May 20, 1927, Charles Lindbergh departed for Paris. That evening Fox Movietone News presented footage of the takeoff, with sound, to a packed house (6200 persons) at the Roxy theater. The throng stood and cheered for nearly ten minutes. The press saluted this new motion picture marvel and noted how it had brought alive the heroics of the "Lone Eagle." In June, Lindbergh returned to a tumultuous welcome in New York City and Washington, D.C. Again Movietone News camera operators recorded portions of those celebrations on film, and Fox Film distributed a ten-minute Movietone newsfilm to the few theaters equipped for sound.

The Fox system seemed to be heading down a propitious path. Quickly Fox Film wired all theaters in its growing chain. Movietone camera operators scattered to all parts of the globe. They recorded heroics of other aviators, harmonica contests, beauty pageants, and sporting events, as well as the earliest sound film statements by public figures such as Italian dictator Benuto Mussolini and Arctic explorer Admiral Richard Byrd. Newspaper columnists, educators, and other opinion leaders hailed these latter short subjects for their educational value. In addition Fox established a regular pattern for release of Movietone newsreels: one ten-minute reel per week. It also hired on a permanent staff of camera operators and laboratory employees, and developed a world-wide network of stringers.[20]

Warners was still ahead of Fox when the spring of 1928 arrived and talkies became the newest fad of the 1920s, but Fox continued to move quickly. Before 1928 Fox-Case had released only one silent feature film with a recorded score, *Sunrise*. Boldly, Fox declared that *all* future products would be completely "Movietoned." Fox could film and record out-of-doors where Warners' disc system required studio conditions. Fox even made enough money from its sound newsreels to offer Warners a challenge in the arena of vaudeville shorts. By 1929, based on its successful innovation of sound through newsreels, and its expanded network of distribution and exhibition outlets, Fox Film neared the peak of the U.S. film industry, a climb only rivaled by the other innovator of sound, Warner Bros. The innovation stage for sound was now finished.[21]

Here the analysis of technological change should proceed to the diffusion phase. For brevity's sake, we will provide only a summary of that analysis. At first the largest firms, Paramount and Loew's, were very skeptical. They had the most to lose. Quietly they studied the efforts of Warners and Fox. When long-run profits seemed assured, both signed with Western Electric (on May 11, 1928). Once the decision was made, the actual switchover occurred rapidly and smoothly. The giant firms had learned a great deal from Warners and Fox, and had formulated elaborate contingency plans. Moreover, profits proved so much greater than expected that no time was lost fueling a maximum effort. Within fifteen months (by September 1929) the full transformation to sound had been completed. Hollywood would subsequently only produce talkies. The result was greater profits than any time in industry history. AT&T prospered because of royalties; the large theater circuits (which were wired for sound first) grew stronger; and Paramount and Loew's, joined by Warner Bros., Fox, and the Radio Corporation of America-sponsored Radio-Keith Orpheum, now formed the U.S. film industry's "Big-Five" companies. This corporate structure, shaped by technological change, would remain intact until the 1950s.

RETHINKING THE ECONOMICS OF TECHNOLOGICAL CHANGE

This brief case study illustrates the cogency of the economic theory of technological change in specifying some of the most important factors involved in technological change in the capitalist film industries. The primacy given long-term profitability as a determining factor by this approach seems justified in light of (1) the size and complexity of the American film industry by the 1920s, and (2) the relative cost of even the most basic film technology.

Individuals still have a role to play in the historical analyses generated by this approach, but the great men of previous accounts (Edison, Gaumont, Case, de Forest, the Warners and others) should be seen as operating within constraints defined by economic forces. De Forest's failure to innovate the phono-phone sound system was based to some degree on unsatisfactory amplification but also his inability to compete in a technological marketplace dominated by powerful corporations. The Warner brothers emerged not as free-wheeling moguls heroically saving their company from bankruptcy, but as able administrators of a corporate enterprise, obeying the demands of a pregiven economic system. By defining technological change as a tripartite process—invention, innovation, and diffusion—the economic theory of technological change broadens the scope of historical analysis to include not just the historical moment of technological discovery but the events leading up to and following from it as well.

The effectiveness of the economic theory of technological change is greatest when applied to commercial filmmaking in capitalist economies. It is here that the fundamental axiom of the approach—that firms take whatever measures necessary to assure the greatest long-term profitability—is most clearly in operation. However, if the danger of reductionism is to be avoided, even in such "classic" cases as the advent of sound, several complicating factors must be kept in mind.

First, some technological change originates in institutions for which profitability (in a strictly economic sense) is not a motivation; the primary modern example being the state. As we shall see in the case study in Chapter 9, the invention and innovation of certain pieces of technology necessary for what was to become cinema verité filmmaking resulted from certain military needs during and immediately following World War II. This is not to say that the technological interests of the government and those of private industry are necessarily distinct. One of the primary justifications for the American space program has been the adoption of many of its inventions by private corporations—from the silicon chip to freeze-dried food. In fact, the historian of technological change must always keep in mind that the introduction of a new product or process can have uses and consequences not intended or foreseen by those responsible for it. For example, the original Edison phonograph, patented in 1878, was developed as a business dictating device, and it took nearly a decade for it to be used for popular entertainment.

Furthermore, economic decision making does not occur in a vacuum; corporations operate within societies, and are subject to accepted norms and values when making any decision, including those having to do with technological change. Thus interacting with the economics of technological change is what we might call a sociology of technological change. In the realm of consumer goods and services (of which the movies are a part) in capitalist societies, the "marketability" of a new product or process is another way of describing the perceived social utility of that product or process. Would people in 1927 spend their money and time attending sound films rather than or in addition to listening to the radio, attending sporting events, or buying phonograph records? In other words, is there a social need for the new technology? Some would argue that technological change in capitalist economies is not only a response to a perceived social need, but is also the manufacture of a perceived need through advertising, which can then be conveniently "met" by the new product or service. It is in this context that the more general discourse on technology at any particular historical moment becomes important.

As pointed out in Chapter 3, the American fascination with technology around the turn of the century certainly conditioned the public response to the movies, not to mention subsequent historical discourse on the movies. If part of technological change is the production of ideas (recalling Mansfield's definition of invention), then we need to include in the notion of technological change the production of ideas about technology and technological change itself.

A French scholar, Jean-Louis Comolli, has tried to do this. Writing from an avowedly Marxist perspective, Comolli calls for analysis of technological change in a broad context.[22] For his wider perspective Comolli identifies the interaction of two types of social forces—the ideological and economic. Cinema is the mutual reinforcement of an ideological demand "to see life as it is" with the economic forces of profit maximization. For the ideological component Comolli argues that machines of cinema (projectors, lens, cameras, and so on) are not neutral objects meant to reflect a true view of the world. No, inventors and innovators of all forms of technology, including the cinema, have created machines in terms of how they knew and understood the world. That is, technology change was (and is) influenced by the ideas and beliefs about the world and how it works.

For Comolli technological film history (indeed all types of film history) is dialectical in form. Rather than a single linear progression, history is a plural series with neither origin nor end. An ongoing process, history has a plurality of beginnings, a series of points which may even be contradictory. It is not possible to single out one event or one "invention." For example, Comolli "deconstructs" the origin of the cinema into a scattered series of events that go back many centuries. According to him, all necessary knowledge for cinema was available some fifty years before the actual films were presented The pressure to display cinema in the 1890s came about because of the confluence of ideological demands to (1) represent life in a certain way, and (2) economically exploit that power of vision. The knowledge of technology was available before capitalists found a social demand to convert that knowledge into profits.

For Comolli change in capitalist cultures is measured in the Marxist terms of an unrelenting class struggle. This includes technological innovation and diffusion. Comolli rejects analysis based on evolutionary change, but instead seizes on those breaks or discontinuities in the innovation of new technologies. Such a view sees gaps, not the stages of a smooth evolution. For example, certain lens provide the ability to capture several planes of action, the arena of deep space. Filmmakers during the first decade of this century made use of this technique. With the coming of the factory-line Hollywood style, little deep space was utilized in films of the 1920s and 1930s. Only later were *Citizen Kane*, and other films of the early 1940s, hailed for their vibrant use of deep space. It is such gaps in the use of technology which Comolli finds at the core of technical change.

Comolli also downplays the role of the individual in the process of technical change. Individuals exist only in relation to ideology. Ideology is complex, coherent, and logical systems of images, ideas, beliefs, and actions by which and through which people live their daily lives. Cinema plays an important role in this representational system through which people encounter and deal with the material reality of their existence. For Comolli technology functions along with other institutions to link members of a society in a particular set of relationships. Technology is produced by and functions in an ideology. Consequently it has not ever been "neutral"—but neither is it determined forever by its past or present functions, for as social relations change, so do peoples' relationship with technology.

Comolli argues that cinema came about as people attempted to compensate for limitation of the human eye. The camera—first through still photography and then cinema—can be more objective and scientific. In the late nineteenth century cinema seemed to be human vision perfected. This belief was part of a larger system of beliefs that shaped the technological development of the cinema. The rhetoric by which great men were credited with the invention of the cinema lays bare this system of belief. For example, Edison was a wizard who created modern miracles. He was able to use science to "improve" the way we could see. This scientific rendering was argued to be far superior to drawing, painting, sculpture, or human sight. The late nineteenth century belief was that science (here invention) had improved the human condition, but "science" for Comolli has always been part of the web of ideas and beliefs of how people know the world. Science adapted to capitalist needs. It didn't make the world necessarily better, only different. Historians should seek to understand this difference.

Edward Branigan provides a useful example of how Comolli, the historian, might deal with one particular "chunk" of the history of one particular technological change, the coming of color. With improvements in the camera, lighting equipment, and laboratory processing, it became possible in 1936 to make color films using lighting levels extremely close to the common black and white standards. Three years later, the Technicolor Corporation introduced a faster film stock that made possible further improvements. This meant that color could finally achieve techniques which until then were the province of black and white photography. Images could be softer, shadows better retained, and close-ups could be more precise. In sum, the result was that color became less garish and more natural.[23]

For Comolli this change would be seen as an illustration of technology acting to reinvest "realism" into color cinematography. Technological change, in this case, was responding to an ideological demand for "realism." The film industry could now achieve effects that black and white had built up as a preferable set of conventions. Technological change was pursued in order to achieve a certain use of visual codes. Color was not only more scientifically accurate, but it also was able to "repeat" the dominant forms of the culture. In this sense ideological historians argue the coming of color does not begin with the Technicolor Corporation or even hand tinting of early silent films. The coming of color begins with the Renaissance's interest in color and linear perspective. One must understand the use of color in other forms of communication and art before one can study the coming of color to film.

In sum, for Comolli technological transformation is important in the writing of film history only insofar as it can be related to ideological and economic change. Despite its importance and considerable explanatory power, however, Comolli's work, still in progress we should note, does contain several weaknesses in its present form. He seems to want to make "ideology" do more than it can. In its somewhat vague, undefined state, Comolli uses ideology to sweep all Western civilization into one concept. There are few specific classes or institutions to be analyzed. There are even fewer examples of specific historical analysis. Technology and ideology, unfortunately, seem to have become abstract, ahistorical concepts. Furthermore, Comolli's work, so far, suffers from inadequate evidence. He constantly criticizes the work of others, yet he takes up their terms, concepts, and even historical data. If Comolli is to truly overhaul technological film history, he cannot let others set the agenda, since the acceptance of concepts and data necessarily leads to acceptance of fundamental assumptions. Comolli has provided a strong beginning for the reexamination of technological film; however, much fundamental work remains to be done.

NOTES

1. Raymond Williams, *Television: Technology and Cultural Form* (New York: Schocken, 1975), p. 13.

2. Raymond Fielding, "The Technological Antecedants of the Coming of Sound: An Introduction," in *Sound and the Cinema*, Evan W. Cameran, ed. (Pleasantville, N.Y.: Redgrave, 1980), p. 2.

3. Lewis Jacobs, *The Rise of the American Film* (New York: Teachers College Press, 1939), p. 505.

4. Edwin Mansfield, *The Economics of Technological Change* (New York: W. W. Norton, 1968), p. 50.

5. Benjamin B. Hampton, *History of the American Film Industry* (New York: Covici Friede, 1931), and Jacobs, *Rise of the American Film*. Both continue to provide the basis for textbook accounts of the coming of sound.

6. It should be noted that there were experiments in which actors stood behind the screen and provided "voices" for characters in silent films. Required naturalism, i.e., synchronization, doomed all such efforts. Live music provided no such barriers, and became a part of silent film presentation by the end of the first decade of the twentieth century.

7. Gordon Hendricks, *The Kinetoscope* (New York: Beginning of the Film, 1966), pp. 90–92, 119–125; *Moving Picture World*, November 30, 1908, p. 342: *Moving Picture World*, May 1, 1909, p. 558; *Moving Picture World*, March 27, 1909, p. 362; and *Moving Picture World*, June 28, 1913, p. 1348.

8. *New York Times*, January 4, 1913, p. 7; *Moving Picture World*, June 28, 1913, p. 1347; *New York Times*, March 9, 1930, ix, p. 6; *Moving Picture World*, February 22, 1913, p. 758; *Moving Picture World*, March 19, 1913, p. 1318; *New York Times*, February 18, 1913, p. 3; *Variety*, March 21, 1913, p. 1; *New York Times*, April 18, 1913, p. 1; *New York Times*, May 6, 1913, p. 20; and *New York Times*, January 21, 1914, p. 1.

9. Lee De Forest, *Father of Radio: The Autobiography of Lee De Forest* (Chicago: Wilcox and Follett, 1950), pp. 358–400; *General Talking Pictures Corporation v. American Telephone and Telegraph Co. et al.*, 18 F. Supp. 650 (1937), Louis B. Hoffman deposition, pp. 1–4, Findings of Facts, pp. 1–4, and M. A. Schlesinger deposition, pp. 1–3; *New York Times*, September 24, 1922, II, p. 1; *Variety*, February 25, 1925, p. 23; *Variety*, March 18, 1925, p. 43; *Variety*, September 2, 1926, p. 25; and *Variety*, May 19, 1926, pp. 5, 22.

10. *General Talking Pictures Corporation et al. v. American Telephone and Telegraph Company et al.*, 18 F. Supp. 650 (1937), Record, pp. 2488–2508; and Frank H. Lovette and Stanley Watkins, "Twenty Years of Talking Movies," *Bell Telephone Magazine* (Summer 1946): 84–95.

11. *Koplar (Scharaf et al., Interveners)* v. *Warner Bros. Pictures, Inc. et al.*, 19 F. Supp. 173 (1937), Record, pp. 283–330, 353–363, 390–400, 1101–1111; *Variety*, February 4, 1925, p. 23; *Moving Picture World*, May 2, 1925, p. 25; *Moving Picture World*, September 5, 1925, p. 74; *Variety*, August 26, 1925, p. 21; *Variety*, September 23, 1925, p. 36; *Variety*, December 2, 1925, p. 36; and *Variety*, December 16, 1925, p. 7.

12. *Koplar*, 19 F. Supp. 173, Record, pp. 402–420; *General Talking Pictures*, 18 F. Supp. 650, Record, Exhibit 6; U.S. Federal Communication Commission, *Telephone Investigation Exhibits* (Pursuant to Public Resolution No. 8, 74th Congress, 1936–37, Exhibit 1606); *Moving Picture World*, January 9, 1926, p. 161; *Variety*, April 14, 1926, p. 23; *Moving Picture World*, May 1, 1926, p. 44; and *Moving Picture World*, September 18, 1926, p. 173.

13. U.S. Congress, House, Committee on Patents, *Pooling of Patents*. Hearings before the Committee on Patents, House of Representatives, on H.R. 4523, 74th Congress, 1st Session, 1935, pp. 1242–1261; F.C.C., *Telephone Exhibits*, Exhibits 1605 and 1606; *Koplar*, 19 F. Supp. 173, Record, pp. 446–54; *Variety*, November 17, 1926, p. 5; *Variety*, April 28, 1926, p. 36; *Moving Picture World*, June 5, 1926, p. 1; *Variety*, September 15, 1926, p. 5; and *Variety*, August 11, 1926, pp. 4–5.

14. *Variety*, August 11, 1926, p. 11; *Moving Picture World*, August 14, 1926, p. 1; *New York Times*, August 8, 1926, II, p. 6; *Koplar*, 19 F. Supp. 650, Record, pp. 1128–1130; *Moving Picture World*, September 18, 1926, p. 4; *Variety*, September 8, 1926, p. 1; *Moving Picture World*, September 25, 1926, p. 200; *New York Times*, October 8, 1926, p. 23; and *Moving Picture World*, October 16, 1926, p. 1.

15. *Koplar*, 19 F. Supp. 173, pp. 455–565; *General Talking Pictures*, 18 F. Supp. 650, Exhibit B; F.C.C., *Telephone Exhibits*, Exhibit 1606 and 1609; and Congress, *Pooling of Patents*, pp. 1302–1351.

16. F.C.C., *Telephone Exhibits*, Exhibits 1605 and 1606; *Variety*, May 4, 1927, p. 1; *Moving Picture World*, May 2, 1927, p. 793; *Moving Picture World*, May 28, 1927, p. 253; *Variety*, August 10, 1927, p. 9; *Moving Picture World*, August 20, 1927, p. 506; and *Variety*, September 7, 1927, p. 11.

17. *Variety*, October 12, 1927, pp. 7, 11, 16; *Variety*, October 19, 1927, pp. 21, 25; *Variety*, November 30, 1927, p. 5; *Variety*, December 7, 1927, p. 36; *Variety*, March 21, 1928, p. 44; *Variety*, February 1, 1928, p. 18; *Variety*, April 4, 1928, p. 40; and *Variety*, April 18, 1928, p. 46.

18. T. W. Case, "Thalofide Cell—A New Photo-Electric Substance," *The Physical Review*, XV, Series II No. 4 (April, 1920): 289–292; Lee De Forest, "Journal Notebook," Volume 21–22, 1923–24, Lee De Forest Collection, Library of Congress Manuscript Collection, Washington, D.C.; Earl I. Sponable, "Historical Development of Sound Films," *Journal of the Society of Motion Picture Engineers* 48 (April 1948): 286–299; and *Paramount Publix Corporation* v. *American Tri-Ergon Corporation*, 294 U.S. 464 (1935), Record, pp. 410–412.

19. U.S. Congress, *Pooling of Patents*, pp. 1670–1672; *Moving Picture World*, February 19, 1927, p. 1; *Moving Picture World*, February 26, 1927, pp. 622, 677; *Variety*, March 2, 1927, p. 10; *Variety*, April 6, 1927, p. 54; *Variety*, April 13, 1927, p. 9; and *Variety*, May 4, 1927, p. 4.

20. *Variety*, May 4, 1927, p. 27; *Variety*, May 25, 1927, pp. 9, 18; *Variety*, June 15, 1927, p. 28; *Moving Picture World*, May 28, 1927, p. 248; *Variety*, June 29, 1927, p. 11; *Variety*, August 17, 1927, p. 12; *Variety*, September 21, 1927, pp. 1, 20, 23; *Variety*, November 30, 1927, pp. 18–19; and *Moving Picture World*, December 3, 1927, pp. 12–13.

21. *Electrical Research Products, Inc.* v. *Vitaphone Corporation*, 171 A. 738 (1934), Affidavit of John E. Otterson; *Variety*, May 16, 1928, passim; *Variety*, August 22, 1928, p. 28; *Variety*, September 26, 1928, p. 17; *Variety*, March 20, 1929, p. 7; "An Analysis of Fox Theatres Corporation, August 2, 1929," pp. 1–2, Fox Folder 19, Bache-Halsey Stuart Library, Chicago, Illinois; and *Variety*, November 28, 1928, p. 19.

22. Jean-Louis Comolli, "Technique et ideologie," six parts in *Cahiers du Cinema* no. 229 (May–June 1971): 4–21; no. 230 (July 1971): 51–57; no. 231 (August–September 1971): 42–49; nos. 234–35 (December–January 1971–1972): 94–100; and no. 241 (September–October 1972): 20–24.

23. Edward Brannigan, "Color and Cinema: Problems in the Writing of History," *Film Reader* 4 (1979): 16–34.

6

Economic
Film History

As seen in the last chapter, questions of technical change in movie history have been inexorably intertwined with economic forces. When anyone raises the issue of business arrangements in film's past, the image of Hollywood and its riches quickly comes to mind: swimming pools, starlets, and multimillion dollar deals. Certainly few doubt that the American film industry has functioned as a business—albeit a nontraditional one with its production of value from sight, sound, and story. Consumers paid for, and then hopefully received, a pleasurable experience. Somehow the movie was created; somehow it got to one's local moviehouse or television screen. But who owned the movie companies? How were films distributed—then exhibited? And what effect did all this have on the development of motion picture history? This chapter will seek to develop ways to better understand how motion pictures—as a business and economic institution—operated in the history of cinema.

First, some definitions must be laid out. The movie business has always included three basic sectors: (1) production, (2) distribution, and (3) exhibition. Initially a motion picture must be created. Production has taken place in Hollywood proper as well as other southern California hamlets: Culver City (MGM), Universal City (Universal), and Burbank (Warner Bros.), all suburbs of Los Angeles. Indeed, during the 1930s few feature films made in the United States were shot outside a "Hollywood" studio. In recent years American filmmakers have created films throughout the world, but usually for Hollywood-based companies. These giant corporations (Warners, Twentieth Century-Fox, Paramount, Columbia et al.) have also handled the distribution (wholesaling) of films. That is, they have made copies of the film, and scheduled bookings into theaters, all for a fee. Finally, we locate the exhibitors—the owners and operators of motion picture theaters. In special buildings, some elaborately decorated (the "movie palace"), exhibitors offered images and sounds, usually constructed to tell a story, for a fee.

This process of production, distribution, and exhibition has represented a basic descriptive model of the business of film since the turn of the century. All movie industries since then have devised ways to handle these three fundamental tasks. The historian then should ask: How, when, where, and why were motion pictures produced, distributed, and exhibited? For example, until 1948 the famous Hollywood production companies, the Warners and Paramounts, produced, distributed, *and* exhibited motion pictures. This representation in all three functions is called *vertical integration*. Sometimes a different name labeled separate functions. Loew's, Inc., a distribution and exhibition firm, owned Metro-Goldwyn-Mayer, its far more famous production arm. We must not confuse the use of different names with the position of ownership and control.

But why study the economic history of Hollywood? Or any film industry? Doesn't all this take the fun out of the study of film history? We argue that first we should recognize how important economic empires like Hollywood have been in the development of film in the Western world. This influence and power has been felt not only in the United States, but in every country of the world as well. Second, no national cinema, however large or small, has escaped the need for the enormous costs associated with production, distribution, and exhibition. A requirement for large amounts of money has always been tied to the expensive technology and scarce talent necessary in the movie business. Simply compare moviemaking to the production of poetry, or the performance of dance. The latter can be accomplished for a relatively small investment whereas in 1980 the *average* Hollywood feature film required $25 million at the box office *just* to break even. That is, at least 10 million people in 1980 had to pay $2.50 to view an average Hollywood feature before any investor saw one dollar in return. The importance of the business of film has been with us (in Europe and the United States at least) since film production and exhibition first became widespread phenomena. Since film has always been a relatively costly form of expression—increasingly more so with each passing decade—the economic history of film must be considered as one important part of any complete historical analysis of film.

It must be stressed that no film has ever been created outside of an economic context. It is not necessary to think of *The Godfather, Jaws,* or *Star Wars* to be reminded of the importance of film economics. For example, all so-called "alternative" practices, be they labeled amateur, independent, documentary, or avant-garde, have their economic component. For every Hollywood corporation that has had to seek out funds through major U.S. banks, there have been dozens of "independent" filmmakers who have competed for money from the

American Film Institute, a state Arts Board, the National Endowment for the Arts, the Ford Foundation, and/or simply a rich patron. Our point is simply that a sizable amount of money has had to come from somewhere. Economic constraints have played an important role in the film activity in all nations, even though they might not have had a U.S.-style Hollywood factory system. Simply put, not all countries of the world have organized moviemaking and exhibition in terms of the profit motive as we have in the United States. For example, in the USSR since 1922 the central government has controlled film production, distribution, and exhibition. Thus the state allocated goods and services to film and away from food, steel, or some other industry. The cost was always there for basic apparatus and its use, as it was in the United States and Western Europe.

If the economic history of film is important, why then has so little systematic analysis been set forth? This seems particularly unexpected for the U.S. film industry, the most powerful and influential in cinema's past. For one thing, an unfortunate consequence of the aesthetic orientation of film writing and study has been to downplay the economic aspect of film study. With film being taught as part of an art or literature curriculum, there existed no impetus to understand an industrial component, any more than there had been in a traditional study of dance, music, or poetry. Analysis of a Bergman or Fellini film did not seem to call for probing economic considerations. Since film has suffered from categorization as a "low" art form, many writers, including most film historians, wished to nudge film into a higher category with other more "respectable" forms. We trust the study of film has now transcended its original unidimensional aesthetic categorization, and should be considered an important form of expression in our modern world.

An equally compelling reason for the dearth of economic film history has been a paucity of data. If no records of the past survived, how could there be a history—in whatever form? Until the past decade, movie companies regularly buried or burned their financial records. Recently there has been a significant reversal in this trend. In the United States, the United Artists collection at the University of Wisconsin in Madison, the Warner Bros. collections at Princeton University and the University of Southern California, and the RKO collection, also at the University of Southern California have opened during the past decade. Only a lack of training in historiographic practices can now prevent film historians from reevaluating the impact and importance of the changing U.S. film industry.

Hence the study of film economics stands ready to take its proper place as a necessary component for a complete understanding of film's past. With a shortage of reliable research in this area, it is most important that researchers familiarize themselves with the various approaches available. At least two such methods compete for our attention. Since the selection of an appropriate method for the question raised *determines* the form and scope of the analysis, it is important to examine both.

Before doing so, however, it is useful to note the unsystematic way traditional film historians have treated questions of film economics. Again and again one encounters the "great man" theory. For example, one sort of person formed, shaped, designed, and ran Hollywood: the all-powerful movie mogul, usually characterized as a crude, ambitious, cigar-chomping little man who controlled the destiny of millions of American movie-goers from his tiny East European mind. From movies (*The Godfather*) and books (*King Cohn*) we have been told that these men (always men) continually used hunches and intuition to run the movie industry, completely removed from the "normal" world of labor, capital, governmental restraints, and accountants. The "great man" theory places all decision-making power in the hands of a few "far-sighted" individuals, those who were able to transcend the traditional bounds of economic constraints the rest of us experience. This approach does not stress historical analysis, but a form of biographical narrative. However sophisticated, the "great man" theory tries to remove the movies from the realm of "ordinary" economic activity. It mystifies the interplay of economic forces, simplifies all questions into examinations of personal decision-making processes of one person, and deflects us from any complex understanding of business practice. In contrast, the two approaches considered in this chapter serve to shift the discussion from the individual genius to a system of business operations, and the effects of supply and demand.

Throughout Western culture most people use the terms *economics* and *business* interchangeably, but for the economic historian the difference is vital. On one hand, a business is an organization set up to make money by selling a product and/or service. When a person goes to business school, he or she learns techniques of management, finance, accounting, and marketing. Students master the practical skills necessary to steer a corporation, partnership, or small enterprise toward larger and larger profits. Economists, on the other hand, investigate the processes that households, businesses, and governments employ to produce and allocate goods and services. They construct models to understand why and how economic institutions operate and affect lives. Historians of film are interested in two aspects of economic history. Overall they try to position film in the economy of a nation or region. Specifically they seek an understanding of the development of a particular collection of businesses—an industry. That is, they analyze the changes in the behavior of a set of firms producing, distributing, and exhibiting one particular product—motion pictures.

THE MARXIST CRITIQUE

The first approach grows out of action to challenge past social and economic practice. For example, one group of radical historians, utilizing the social theories of Karl Marx, observes the profit-seeking sector of any capitalist economy with a jaundiced eye. Why should we accept a business system in which a handful of corporations hold the majority of power? Why do a small number of corporations in each industry continually receive three-quarters of all profits? Why does there seem no end to constant ups and downs in the business cycle? Marxist economists argue that such characteristics of modern capitalist economies have not been created accidentally, but have emerged as the logical end products of all such capitalist economic systems. In consequence, it would not be surprising that eight corporations have dominated trade in American movies for more than sixty years. Millions of people have seen Hollywood films while only a handful of men have controlled production distribution, exhibition, and profits.

Marxist economists not only attack the U.S. economy; they offer a radical critique of all economic systems built on the profit motive and wealth accumulation. The U.S. economy of the twentieth century, they argue, can best be understood as one historical epoch in a process by which capitalism will destroy itself and eventually lead to a world of workers'-controlled economies. In twentieth-century America, the owners of giant corporations and equally large financial institutions have formed a "ruling class" through domination over the nation's wealth and power. The majority of citizens (as workers) continue to "own" only their own labor, and consequently have been exploited by this "ruling" class. As the elite has sought greater wealth, it has exploited more and more people. In the process it has drawn natural resources from Third World countries, leaving their citizens poorer. The economy has played the boom/bust cycles that leave workers ever more impoverished, racked by inflation, recession, and an inability to accumulate wealth. Within individual industries, a few firms, controlled by the "ruling" class, collude to extract all possible profits and gainfully exploit consumers as well as workers.

Taken as a whole, economic forces form what Karl Marx called the economic *base* (infrastructure). Upon this base, during every period of human history, has emerged a *superstructure:* certain forms of law and politics, and a government whose essential function has been to legitimate and forcefully support the power of the "ruling" class. The superstructure has involved more than this, however. Specific forms of "social consciousness" have been developed, political, religious, ethical, and aesthetic, which Marxism has designated as *ideology*. Here is where motion pictures fit in the Marxist critique. The function of ideology has been to legitimatize the power of the "ruling" class. So films strongly tend to reaffirm (not challenge) the dominant ideas and beliefs of a society, those ideas and beliefs of the "ruling" class.[1]

Using this type of Marxist approach, Thomas Guback has created an analysis of the American film industry's dependence on trade with European nations. In *The International Film Industry: Western Europe and America Since 1945*, Guback analyzed relations between Hollywood and European film industries since World War II.[2] Exploitation of European markets ("economic imperialism") by Hollywood has had, Guback argued, significant effects on film industries on both sides of the Atlantic. He finds a case of economic exploitation of the weak (the European film industries) by the strong (the U.S. film industry in the twentieth century).

Guback proceeds from an analysis of the economic base of European–American trade in motion pictures to one of the ideological effects on the motion pictures produced. First looking at the economic base, he finds that, with the direct assistance of the U.S. government, the giant Hollywood corporations (Twentieth Century-Fox, Warner Bros., Paramount, RKO, Loew's) formed a cartel after World War II to coordinate economic action in Western Europe. This institution, the Motion Picture Export Association, secured a trade situation in which Hollywood was "free" to extract all possible profits, regardless of the consequences. In a most fascinating chapter, Guback describes how the U.S. film industry and U.S. Defense Department cooperated to take over film exhibition in West Germany after World War II by claiming to employ Hollywood feature films to "reeducate" the German population.

In the final part of *The International Film Industry*, Guback tries to explain how this one-sided economic exchange affected "what was ultimately shown on the screen." He finds that Hollywood's exploitation resulted in a "homogenized" product which "blurred differences vital to the essence" of national cultures. Most 1960s European and American films presented "dehumanized characters" and "deflected audience's attention away from reality." Such productions bombarded audiences with synthetic images. Shallow, cardboard characters polluted the screen, camouflaged by vivid colors, panoramic vistas, and a "slick" bland style. Since capitalist filmmaking created such inadequate films, Guback pleads for greater economic independence and cultural integrity. Guback artfully summarizes his position on film as an economic, social, and cultural institution this way:

> Because film is an art which portrays man's interpretation of life, it is imperative that contrasting perspectives be given the opportunity to exist and develop. The movement toward oligopoly and monopoly in American industry in general is now spreading elsewhere, paralleling American expansion. While this might spell efficiency in economic terms through the elimination of duplication, with fewer producers serving larger markets, it is to be avoided in the field of culture. It would be a pity to have but one control overall printing presses in a nation—or in the world. The same can be said for film production and distribution. Yet this is coming about in the world of the West.[3]

Guback then utilizes his analysis to press for social change, a new type of filmmaking practice.

Needless to say, such a radical approach has its detractors. Many rightly object to a simple straightforward economic determinism. How, they ask, does one move directly from economic analysis to questions of ideological formation? But in fact the virtues and possibilities of the Marxist economic approach to cinema history have not been fully realized, in part, because the goal in the past has been to link the analysis to a particular film, or set of films. This can best be illustrated by closely examining the now classic Marxist analysis of *Young Mr. Lincoln* by a collective from the influential French publication, *Cahiers du Cinema*.[4] The analysis of the film tells us a great deal about how film functioned as a part of U.S. superstructure during the 1930s. It is clearly an advance over earlier ways to develop a Marxist critical methodology. Yet in this essay only three pages (of forty-four) were used to analyze the relationship of the economic base to the film industry to that particular film. Historians cannot be satisfied with the simple assertion that Hollywood represented a typical capitalistic production system, and leave it at that. How did it relate to other industries? How did it maintain its power?

A case study helps reveal methods of understanding the answer to these and other important questions. How did Hollywood survive the Great Depression? Did it receive help, like other industries, from the U.S. federal government? Through the writings of James O'Connor and Paul Sweezy, Marxist economists have worked out an explicit theory for how governments and oligopolies (like the U.S. film industry in 1933) interact.[5] In "advanced capitalism" the "ruling" class fashions a government to enforce a set of property relations that function in the best interest of that class. So big government becomes an ally to big business. Regulation of industry, however well-intended, exists only to benefit the large corporations. There might be a short-term struggle, even a setback or two, but over the long haul, the powerful few in all industries, including motion pictures, work in tandem with governments on all levels to help politicians and the owners of wealth maintain their power. We can see how this interaction worked through a close examination of the interaction of the National Recovery Administration and the U.S. film industry during the Great Depression of the 1930s.

The National Industrial Recovery Act became law on June 16, 1933. Title I established the National Recovery Administration (NRA) to institute and supervise codes to promote fair competition and hence prosperity in all U.S. industries.[6] In exchange for accepting a government-mandated code, an industry would become exempt from prosecution under existing anti-trust laws. Historians continue to debate whether the NRA had any effect in helping the United States emerge from the Great Depression. Using a Marxist approach, historians argue that the NRA generously aided all industries, including the U.S. film industry. Specifically, through the NRA the U.S. federal government openly sanctioned the exploitive behavior of the giant corporations. Instead of "informal" collusion, which had existed since the mid-1920s, open and explicit collusion and exploitation took place, freed by the NRA law from the threat of any anti-trust action.[7]

For the film industry the NRA guaranteed that the Paramounts and Foxes could use almost any method to ride through the Depression. No one would go out of business. Losses were minimized while the Hollywood giants made sure no one took over their economic turf. Although the NRA expired in 1935, the large Hollywood corporations had in two years strengthened their economic muscle to the point to be able to press their advantage for nearly two more decades. Not surprisingly, like many federal government programs viewed from a Marxist perspective, the NRA seemed to fail at its appointed task. The United States did not emerge from the Great Depression until the onset of World War II.

The NRA enabled the U.S. motion picture industry as well as other large U.S. industries to survive and even prosper during an economic downturn. The film industry was even stronger than the critics of *Cahiers du Cinema* have suggested. This NRA case study suggests further questions. For example, did the changing role of government influence specific films? Certainly many film historians argue it did. This study of the film industry—and economic history in general—can provide a critic of films with an important component of his or her analysis. Economic analysis is vital for a complete understanding of a radical critique of film and its function in society.[8]

INDUSTRIAL ANALYSIS

A second approach, industrial analysis, tries to analyze only a set of institutions, business enterprises (usually corporations), that desire to maximize profits. An industry is simply a collection of similar businesses. The industrial analyst only seeks to understand economic variables, leaving questions of sociology and ideology to others. This is both a strength and weakness. On the plus side, industrial analysis does provide a powerful tool to analyze the behavior of corporations in our modern world. On the negative side, industrial analysis is limited to economic terms.

How does the industrial historian go about analyzing a single industry? A useful model—structure, conduct, and performance—is schematized in Fig. 6.1. Starting at the base with *performance*, industrial analysts attempt to establish the qualities a society seems to want from a particular industry. Criteria usually include some combination of a desire for fair and efficient utilization of scarce inputs, and an equitable distribution of the final products. It is very difficult to delineate the values a society truly embraces in practice. For example, few Americans have ever agreed on the necessity of unfettered access to the channels of film production, distribution, and exhibition. Some place high value on free access to the media; others argue that in certain cases the rights of certain parties are far more important (for example, to achieve a fair trial or conduct proper national security).

The industrial analyst defines performance criteria *only* in economic terms. He or she cannot tell us what is best, only force us to make explicit our goals and values. For example, industrial analysis reminds us that under the present system every time we go to the movies we "vote" our preferences, and this leads to the numerous sequels in popular filmmaking. We are all familiar with the 1970s science fiction film onrush sparked by *Star Wars*. But was such imitation progress? Or the best use of scarce filmmaking dollars? Judgment always plays a role in history. This is as true for the economic approach as well as any other. Scholars are familiar with the American film industry's defenders ("the industry gives the people what they want") and detractors ("a few corporations decide that audiences will see the same genres over and over again"). Which position should one adopt? Or is there a third or fourth alternative that is preferable? The reader

Figure 6.1   A Model for Industrial Analysis: Structure, Conduct, and Performance*

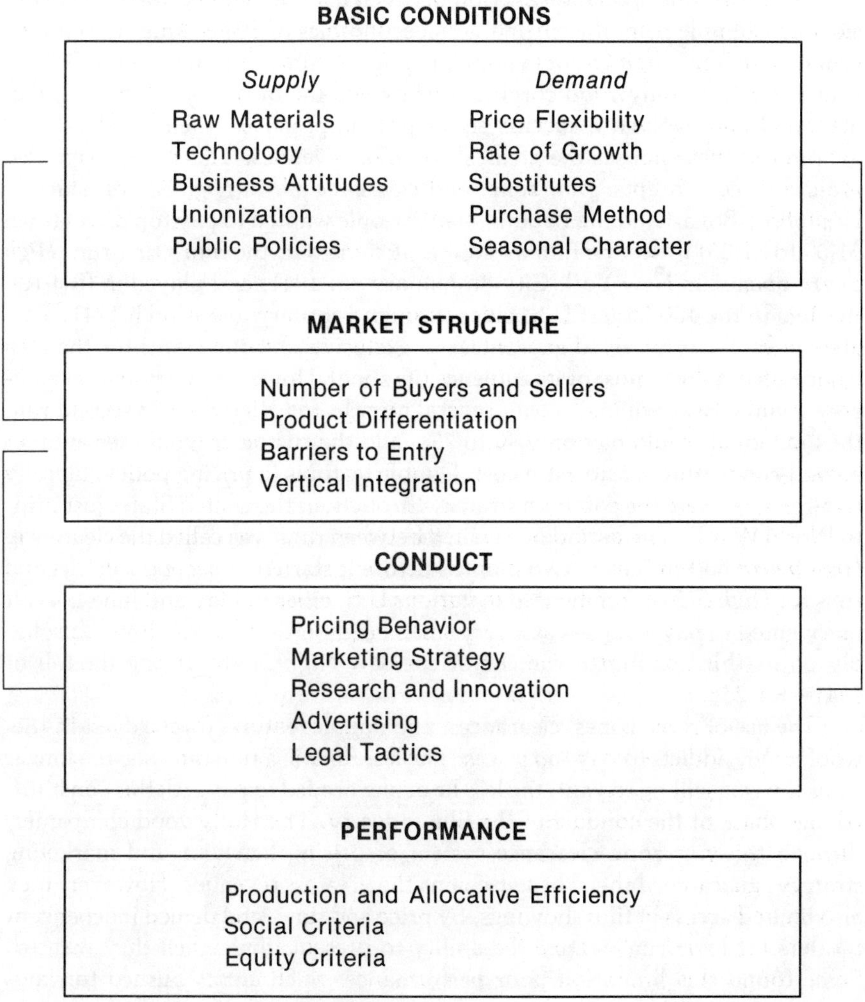

BASIC CONDITIONS

Supply	*Demand*
Raw Materials	Price Flexibility
Technology	Rate of Growth
Business Attitudes	Substitutes
Unionization	Purchase Method
Public Policies	Seasonal Character

MARKET STRUCTURE

Number of Buyers and Sellers
Product Differentiation
Barriers to Entry
Vertical Integration

CONDUCT

Pricing Behavior
Marketing Strategy
Research and Innovation
Advertising
Legal Tactics

PERFORMANCE

Production and Allocative Efficiency
Social Criteria
Equity Criteria

*Adapted from Frederick Scherer, *Industrial Market Structure and Economic Performance*, 2nd edition (Chicago: Rand McNally, 1980), p. 4.

should think through these important questions as he or she considers questions of economic performance, past and present.

Industry performance cannot properly be studied in a vacuum. We must understand how corporations actually have acted. That is, how have they conducted themselves in economic terms? *Conduct* is considered observable economic behavior. For example, we might ask: How have film corporations established prices for their products or services? Why did a movie show cost 10¢ in 1910, and $5.00 seventy years later? Such questions concern conduct and do not ask whether 10¢ or $5.00 was a fair or reasonable price, the latter being a question falling under the economic performance category.

To clarify this crucial distinction between *conduct* and *performance*, consider an example from the cinema-going economics of 1940s America centered around one film, *High Sierra* (a popular gangster film released in 1941). By that year the major Hollywood corporations owned the most important U.S. theaters and had evolved a specific set of pricing practices (their conduct) that guaranteed these houses the greatest share of revenues. This system centered around three concepts: *run, zone,* and *clearance.* With *High Sierra,* starring Humphrey Bogart and Ida Lupino, many people wanted to pay top prices (then $1.00 to $1.25) to see the film as soon as it came out, the film's first run. *High Sierra* opened in New York City on January 25, 1941, and played in first-run theaters in the 100 largest U.S. cities through February and March 1941. Theaters in each city received guarantees to exclusive first-run status for the area from which it drew most of its audience (its zone). However, if a potential audience member was willing to wait several months for *High Sierra*'s second run, the individual would pay only 40 to 75¢, and the customer would see another second-run feature for no extra cost. Double features (a pricing policy, literally two-for-one) were the common strategy throughout the United States just prior to World War II. The period one waited between runs was called the clearance. *High Sierra* had to "clear" two months before it started its second run. Second runs for *High Sierra* commenced in various U.S. cities in May and June 1941. If one wanted to pay even less at a very small neighborhood movie house, probably on its third or fourth run, he or she saw *High Sierra* during the fall of 1941—for 25¢.

The use of runs, zones, clearances, and double features forced dyed-in-the-wool movie addicts to pay top prices. The less fanatic a film fan was, the longer he or she was willing to wait, the less he or she needed to pay. All this constituted one phase of the conduct of the film industry. The Hollywood companies, through this run–zone–clearance system of pricing behavior and marketing strategy, guaranteed their theater chains the greatest revenues. However, they also limited access of film showings, by price and time, and denied independent theaters (of low "run" status) the ability to present films when they wanted. Some found this limitation poor performance. Such critics pushed for laws against certain types of conduct.

They could seek to change structure as well, for corporate conduct, industrial analysis posits, in turn depends on the *structure* of the industry (see Fig. 6.1). The structure of an industry embraces the number and relative size distribution of all companies involved in an industry. For a movie industry this includes firms in production, distribution, and exhibition.

For our purposes we can isolate three types of market structure: monopoly, oligopoly, and competition. In a monopoly, a single firm dominates the market. Natural gas, electric, and telephone utilities provide familiar examples. Competition, at the other extreme, describes a situation in which there exist numerous small firms, selling essentially the same product. In twentieth-century America there have been precious few examples—perhaps the market for wheat or potatoes. Finally, an oligopoly is a structure dominated by a few firms, usually less than ten. In the 1970s everyone knew of the three American car manufacturers (General Motors, Chrysler, and Ford), and the three television networks (CBS, ABC, and NBC). For the U.S. film industry much has been written about the movie oligopoly, the control by the five majors: Paramount, Twentieth Century-Fox, Warner Bros., Loew's, and (until 1955) Radio-Keith-Orpheum (RKO). Such a structure was considered so evil that the U.S. Supreme Court sought to rearrange it in 1948 as part of *U.S.* v. *Paramount Pictures et al.*

The final step in our paradigm, illustrated in Fig. 6.1, argues that market structure, in turn, is influenced by *basic conditions* of the *supply* of inputs to, and the nature of the *demand* for, the industry's product. On the supply side for the U.S. film industry, basic conditions have included the cost, availability, and unionization of talented performers and skilled technicians, the utilization of sets and studios, and the innovation of new technology. On the demand side, the industrial analyst investigates how sensitive consumer behavior has been to changes in price, location, and the availability to close leisure-time substitutes. For example, how did the emergence of television decrease the demand for movie screenings in conventional theaters? Most historians point to the reduced attendance at conventional theaters as proof of television's devastating effect. But what about the drive-ins that grew up at the same time television spread across the United States? And how should we factor in "attendance" for movies shown on television? Such questions force us to investigate the reasons for the demand for movies, and focus in on issues of marketing, seasonality, and method of purchase.

In Michael Conant's study of the aforementioned anti-trust case, *U.S.* v. *Paramount et al.* (1948), we find a well-wrought example of how an industrial economist analyzes governmental attempts to alter the structure, conduct, and performance in the U.S. motion picture industry.[9] During the late 1930s, deciding that the NRA hadn't worked, President Franklin D. Roosevelt's administration began to attack oligopolies in order to help pull the United States out of a prolonged economic depression. The film industry proved to be an attractive visible target. In 1938 the Justice Department sued the Hollywood oligopolies to procure "better" performance. Conant lays out the government's objections by citing two sets of statistics: (1) less than 5 percent of America's feature films came from independent, non-oligopolistic producers; and (2) the oligopolists collected 94 percent of all revenues from movie distribution in the United States.

Conant locates the source of the oligopoly's power in their ownership of the bulk of the first-run theaters in America's 100 largest cities. Customers viewing first-run shows poured money directly into the hands of Paramount et al. Since the oligopolists successfully utilized their control of production, distribution, and exhibition to erect formidable barriers to entry, no one could break into their production of profits. All noncooperative exhibitors, relegated to fourth-, fifth-, or sixth-run status, complained bitterly (and correctly) about limited access to the movie business. A second group worried about how good it was for a handful of corporations to provide the majority of entertainment fare for millions of American children. Should eight corporate boards decide the entertainment agenda for a nation? (This same charge was leveled against the three television networks during the 1960s and 1970s.)

The U.S. Justice Department assaulted this rigid oligopolistic structure in 1938. Ten years later the U.S. Supreme Court ruled that the Hollywood oligopolists must sell their theaters—a structural remedy. In addition, the eight had to dismantle their restrictive run–zone–clearance system—a conduct remedy. From a vantage point a decade later Conant examines the ramifications of these judgments on economic performance. His overall evaluation of the Supreme Court's actions is positive. In sum he argues:

> The *Paramount* decrees have destroyed the nationwide combination that controlled the motion picture industry. . . . The bottleneck in the flow of films created by the majors' near monopoly of first-run theatres was broken. Large numbers of subsequent-run theatres received earlier access to films, and were relieved of the oppressive restrictions. . . .[10]

He goes on to add that the general public benefited from greater access to film screenings, and new independent theater owners and independent producers could enter the industry, not faced with unsurmountable barriers to entry.

In sum, Michael Conant researched and wrote a detailed industrial analysis of the anti-trust suits of the U.S. federal government against the American film industry. His work offers a classic example of the power of the industrial analysis paradigm. Nearly all histories of the U.S. film industry during its golden age originate with Conant. Text after text repeats his descriptions of Hollywood's power and practice during the 1930s and 1940s. Yet industrial analysis applies to more than the 1930s oligopoly. The framework—structure, conduct, and performance—provides the historian with a powerful and subtle methodology by which to analyze questions in the history of a film industry. Logically, if we know so much about the U.S. industry after 1930, we might ask how such a powerful oligopoly came into place. How did the movie industry evolve—from its origins in "peep shows" to the picture-palaces of the "Roaring Twenties"? How did the industry's structure and conduct change during the first two decades of the twentieth century? We will utilize the economic theory of industrial analysis to answer these questions, thereby formulating a clear, concise, logical explanation of the formation of the U.S. film industry.

THE FORMATION OF THE U.S. FILM INDUSTRY

At first, numerous small enterprises made up the structure of the American film industry. Industry conduct was competitive, almost cut-throat. Yet within a decade an oligopoly was in place. Initially a handful of corporations sought dominance through control over patents. That effort failed. A more subtle system of control replaced it. This second (and successful) oligopolistic thrust coalesced around (1) the star system, (2) national (and international) distribution, and (3) the run-zone-clearance system of exhibition. Within a decade less than ten firms constituted the American film industry's market *structure*, and dictated its *conduct*. It is the process of change—from competition to control by a few—that we wish to analyze in the following case study.

CASE STUDY: THE FORMATION OF THE U.S. FILM INDUSTRY

Our study begins with the invention of cinema. The first projected motion picture was commercially exhibited in the United States in New York City in 1896. With this exchange of money for visual pleasure, we have the basis for an industry. The structure and conduct of the industry was quite different from what we know about how Hollywood functioned during the 1930s. Competition prevailed. Here we specifically define competition as the following:

1. Interchangeable products
2. Smallness of buyers and sellers relative to the whole market
3. Absence of artificial restraints
4. Mobility of resources.[11]

By interchangeable products we mean that all sellers offer units very similar to all others. Buyers have little reason to prefer one to another. Second, each buyer and seller must be so small in relation to the entire market that it cannot influence the price of inputs, or the output of the goods produced or sold. So, on the seller's side, if one manufacturer drops out, there should be no significant change in the prevailing price or total quantity offered. Most consumers are usually in this position with respect to most items they purchase. No person, as an individual, has an impact on the price of bread, meat, milk, or safety pins.

Our main point here is that competition demands the "insignificance" of any one buyer or seller, and the presence of products which differ very little.

To meet the third criterion, no artificial constraints can exist. Prices for all inputs (including labor) must be free to move wherever they are pulled by changing conditions of supply and demand. For example, there can be no laws fixing prices, nor cartels setting prices. Mobility of all goods, services, and resources must be the norm. No barriers can constrain new competitors. The highest bidder must be able to secure goods and services. These four criteria furnish a logical starting place for our industrial history. This detailed concept of competition establishes a "norm" against which we can examine precisely how and why competition broke down.

In the first years of the U.S. movie industry there existed a state of relatively free competition. There were lots of small producers, many of which went out of business. Three (Edison, Biograph, and Vitagraph) received the most publicity, but a glance at records from the times indicates many more made an attempt. In Chicago, for example, Essanay, Selig, and a score of smaller companies set up shop. Historian Kathleen Karr has observed:

> There were dozens of . . . attempts to establish off-the-beaten-track film companies, from the Prudential Film Corporation of Worcester, Massachusetts; to the western company of Méliès Star Films which operated out of San Antonio, Texas between 1909 and 1911; to the Japanese–American Film Company which made films for the ethnic market in California to 1914; to the United States Motion Picture Corporation of Wilkes-Barre, Pennsylvania. . . .[12]

Historians have traditionally chosen to remember only those concerns that produced "great" films, and/or survived. Economic historians cannot forget those that failed, both aesthetically and economically, at a time when the necessary requisites for production seem to have been only a camera and money to buy film.

For distribution, numerous small concerns quickly arose, usually located in major metropolitan areas. Indeed, at this level films were marketed not by story or star, but by the foot. By 1904 formal wholesalers—film exchanges—appeared. All evidence indicates the battle for profits was intense. We also note that initially production and distribution were often collapsed into single companies, a policy that was the norm until 1904. Vitagraph, Biograph, and Selig, for example, all provided full service, films, projectors, and projectionists to vaudeville theaters.

The exhibition sector was also comprised of dozens of small enterprises retailing "movies" as a novelty. The rapid rise of nickelodeons points up how easy it was to enter the exhibition side of the industry. Numerous biographies indicate how easily later movie moguls entered the exhibition business. The experience of the Warner brothers and Adolph Zukor testifies to the competitive nature of exhibition. Each was able to enter this industrial arena with assets of a few thousand dollars and no connections or special training. Certainly the length of the nickelodeon era has been exaggerated, but all evidence does indicate that up to 1908 only "social respectability" prevented anyone from becoming a movie exhibitor. Patent problems caused little problem for exhibitors, nor was the equipment expensive. For example, an adequate projector could be had for less than $150. Indeed, even in the field of vaudeville exhibition where the operating company was significantly larger, none proved powerful enough to exert any extraordinary power over the market.

Overall there existed precious few artificial restraints to free entry and exit of resources. Control of patents, always a concern, never presented an insurmountable hurdle in cinema's early years. (Edison had begun trying to enforce a patent monopoly in 1897, and did succeed in winning one lower court case which was overturned six months later.) No intervention by government existed in the form of special tariffs or taxes. Likewise there seems to have been highly mobile resources. Equipment was cheap, as was labor. Profits accumulated rapidly, and many sought to climb this new ladder toward riches. The few who made it big have been eulogized by traditional historians. We should recognize that many others did well and moved on, while others failed and left the business. With so many small firms, it is not surprising that historians have judged this a particularly difficult period to research. A veritable flood of small businesses came and went. Yet it must have been an ideal age in a "performance" sense, for never has it been as easy to "break into" the movies: no domination by a few firms, no unions, no governmental restrictions, and no expensive stars or sets.[13]

This era of competition did not last into the second decade of this century. In 1908, ten leading producers and equipment makers combined to form the Motion Picture Patents Company (MPPC). Why? Because as a cartel (compare the OPEC oil producers), the MPPC could set prices and quantity, and create additional profits by virtue of its economic size and position. Indeed an oligopolist would seek ways to protect its position and thwart the entry of competitors. That is, members of a cartel seek to break down assumptions #3 and #4 of our definition of competition. All firms desire additional profits as well as the security of an oligopolistic position. Yet it demands skill to maintain such an exalted position.

The MPPC utilized a classic strategy to obtain and secure its monopoly position: the pooling and control of patents. Only firms licensed by the MPPC could produce "legal" motion pictures. Eastman Kodak agreed to supply film stock only to MPPC members or their licensees. Most importantly, the MPPC extracted three types of royalties: (1) to be able to manufacture projectors a firm had to pay the MPPC five dollars per machine; (2) to use these projectors exhibitors paid two dollars per week; and (3) producers of motion pictures contributed one-half cent per foot for film stock. To enforce these fees and keep a steady flow of royalties coming in, the Patents Trust "certified" distributors. An approved distributor could only handle MPPC films, and tender them to licensed exhibitors. Quite early on, the MPPC leaders realized that additional controls on the distribution of film would better guarantee its dictums. So, a little more than twelve months after its formation (in 1910), the patents trust organized its own distribution arm, America's first nation-wide network. With the formation of this General Film Company, nearly all existing distributors were acquired, or driven out of business. Consequently, at first there seemed no stopping the establishment of, in effect, *one* movie company for the whole United States.

Yet this embryonic monopoly failed—and very quietly, we must add. Why? Some historians argue that the members of the cartel proved too greedy, and stupidly fought amongst themselves rather than work to maintain their advantage. Other analysts point to the "great man" (usually William Fox or Carl Laemmle, founder of Universal) who struggled, sometimes alone, against the patents monopoly. But were these independents successful only because they had geniuses at the helm? We point to factors rather than stupidity or simple greatness. First, the members of the Trust were joined, as we noted earlier, in a "shot-gun" wedding, consummated only after years of competition. Some adhered strictly to MPPC policy. Many, like Sigmund Lubin, chafed under the restrictions and cooperated less frequently. All seemed to have one pet complaint. For example, Vitagraph wanted to move onto longer films while those who serviced vaudeville theaters had no use for features, and wanted to stand pat with one- or two-reelers.

From outside the film industry came two more contributing factors. In 1912 newly inaugurated president, Woodrow Wilson, broke with his predecessor, William Howard Taft, and instituted an era of trust busting. MPPC lawyers agreed that antitrust suits could successfully enjoin the bulk of the trust's monopolistic restrictions. Thus after 1912 the MPPC became reticent to exercise sanctions against those who broke restrictive agreements. In this new political and industrial climate independent distributors were able to convince exhibitors to show their films. One potent weapon had been removed from the MPPC's arsenal. Furthermore, these same distributors could acquire films of all types, increasingly from European sources. Producers from Europe, for example, rushed to supply independent distributors in the United States. By 1914 the days of the Patents Trust were numbered.[14]

During this same period, other film industry enterprises, epitomized by Famous Players-Lasky (later Paramount), innovated a more flexible way to monopolize the U.S. movie industry. Subtle but basic, a new strategy grappled with all four parts of the definition of competition we outlined earlier. By 1921 a small number of firms, headed by Famous Players-Lasky, had become so large they controlled nearly 50 percent of the market (Assumption 2 is broken) by producing feature length films with stars (Assumption 1 is violated). Consequently they could erect barriers to entry and monopolize necessary resources in the form of first-run theaters and stars (Assumptions 3 and 4 are broken). In short, the U.S. film industry brought forth a three-part method to gain and secure its monopolistic position by (1) differentiating its products, (2) controlling film distribution on first a national, then international, level, and (3) dominating exhibition through ownership of a small number of first-run theaters in the United States. Through changes in all three branches of the film industry—production, distribution, and exhibition—a handful of firms established oligopoly positions far more powerful than the members of the Patents Trust ever achieved. No one person thought up the complete strategy one day; rather, as soon as it was perceived that an innovation was successful, firms rushed to initiate that business tool. In the end, Famous Players achieved the most power, not always by being first, but by being shrewd enough to mold a system for monopolization and then use it to squeeze out all possible extra profits.

For film production the new oligopolists differentiated their products. Gone were the days of films being sold by the foot. Each motion picture became a unique product because of traits that could be advertised, including stars and particular genres. Early producers (including the MPPC) had not capitalized on performers' drawing power, often keeping players' names secret. Gradually, however, movie firms began to differentiate their products using the star sys-

Motion Picture Patents Company (MPPC) pioneer Thomas Edison stands with Adolph Zukor, the leader of Famous Players (1926).

Quigley Photographic Archive, Georgetown University Library

tem. Mary Pickford may have been the most famous early star. Her fans loved her and thus she ascended the salary scale:

Rung 1 (1909)—$100/week

Rung 2 (1915)—$2000/week

Rung 3 (1916)—$7000/week

Rung 4 (1917)—$15,000/week

Rung 5 (1919)—own company: United Artists

In the latter portion of her rise, Famous Players willingly paid "Little Mary" such enormous sums because her presence promised huge box office grosses. In economic terms Famous Players differentiated its products with its stars, and specific stories written for them. Studios inked stars to exclusive, long-run contracts so that the player could not seek a higher salary from a rival company. This legal maneuver insured that vital resources would remain immobile, thus breaking Component 4 in our definition of competition. Through advertising of the star's presence, a film could become a unique product. The more popular the star, the more revenue the film earned. Studios regularly issued feature-length attractions with stars, constructed elaborate advertising campaigns upon release, and repeated gigantic profits. Famous Players, true to its name, raided the legitimate stage for potential kings and queens of the screen. Other studios attempted to create indigenous stars by testing potential luminaries in cheaper productions or shorts. Fans may not have known they were going to see a certain studio's product, but they would stand in line for hours to see a vehicle with Mary Pickford or Douglas Fairbanks.[15]

The second part of the new oligopolistic strategy focused on national, and later, world-wide distribution. Economists have long recognized that when operations of distribution reach a certain threshold, average costs per unit produced cease to rise, then level off and begin to fall. Adam Smith, the founder of modern economics, pointed out more than 300 years ago the various cost advantages of the division and specialization of labor. For example, in movie distribution we can point to cost savings through division and specialization in advertising, sales promotion, and service. The large concerns could use these savings to acquire more popular stars. After twelve producers and numerous regional distributors united to form Famous Players-Lasky in 1916, few competitors could match Famous Players' cost efficiency. Such cost savings also helped to block the emergence of serious competition. It was only logical then for film companies to extend their sales territory to include the entire world. The cost of the film was already in hand; the revenues from world-wide rental far exceeded the publicity and advertising costs and the amortization of a set of offices. By 1925 the U.S. film industry exported its product throughout the world.

The exports to Europe, for example, generated more than one-quarter of the revenue for a 1920s Hollywood feature film. In 1925, one-third of foreign take was generated from theaters in Great Britain. In that particular market Hollywood had captured nearly 95 percent of revenues. The case in France was nearly the same. In that country more than three-quarters of the dollars flowed to Hollywood. Even in what would seem to be quite a different culture, Japan, Hollywood achieved nearly an equal share to the native industry.[16]

Finally, industry members learned that it was not necessary to own all exhibition outlets to gain a measure of economic power in exhibition. The major exhibition chains helped establish the restrictive run–zone–clearance system of exhibition discussed earlier in this chapter. Furthermore chains consolidated. By 1930, for example, renamed Paramount controlled nearly 1000 theaters. (There were more than 20,000 theaters showing movies in the United States at this time.) Over two million people attended a Paramount theater each day. Circuits garnered power by owning only those profitable theaters that presented hit movies first in the larger metropolitan areas.[17]

During the late 1910s and early 1920s many U.S. movie companies attempted to innovate these methods. In 1917 a consortium of theater owners, understanding they controlled some of the finer first-run houses in their respective communities, banded together to form a production company and an international distribution network known as First National. In 1919 there was also another kind of reaction. Mary Pickford, Douglas Fairbanks, Charlie Chaplin, and noted director D. W. Griffith attempted to cash in on their "star power" by creating their own distribution company, called United Artists. During the 1920s United Artists added a small theater circuit. There were many mergers and consolidations and so by 1930 five corporations held dominion over the U.S. film industry: Loew's, Inc., Radio-Keith-Orpheum (RKO), Warner Bros., Fox (later Twentieth Century-Fox) and Paramount. Each of the "Big Five" owned production facilities in California, a world-wide distribution network, and a sizable theater chain. Three other smaller companies ("Little Three") maintained production units, and world-wide distribution, but owned few theaters: Columbia, United Artists, and Universal. For the next two decades the "Big Five" and "Little Three" dominated U.S. movie production, distribution, and exhibition. They generated most of the major motion pictures, featuring the best known stars. Through their distribution networks nearly all U.S. film rentals came to them. In exhibition the "Big Five" operated more than three-quarters of the most profitable movie houses in the United States.

Famous Players, and its seven allies, had led the way in the transformation of the U.S. movie industry into a smooth-running, profitable trust. The "Big Five" succeeded where the MPPC failed. Gone were the days of easy entry into the movie business. Artificial restraints loomed everywhere. Giant companies colluded to keep out the competition. The products featured unique stars, controlled through contractual involuntary servitude to one studio. This was the industrial framework which the U.S. Supreme Court judged restrictive and unfair in 1948. Structurally the film industry consisted of too few firms whose conduct only served to remind all who looked closely that they were quite willing to take full advantage of their oligopolistic, vertically integrated status.

CONCLUSIONS

This short discussion on the economic formation of the American industry illustrates the power of industrial analysis. This paradigm enables us to understand how the U.S. film industry moved from a competitive situation to an oligopolistic structure. Stars guaranteed that each feature film could be sold individually with a high demand and low risk. International distribution generated huge-scale economies and cost savings. Ownership of first-run theaters in major cities tendered economic power in the exhibition sector. This era of monopoly continued until 1948, a period which encompasses Hollywood's Golden Age.

As powerful as we find industrial analysis, we must admit it has a significant drawback. This approach forces our analysis away from aesthetic questions by providing too narrow a perspective for many historians for it deals only with the economics "half" of any consideration of a socioeconomic perspective. Even so, a Marxist historian would have little trouble with our economic analysis in this chapter, provided it was seen as simply a first step. Our analysis of how Hollywood developed its concentration of power through cost advantages, distribution in other countries, and the maintenance of the oligopoly by restraint of trade are perfectly consistent with "advanced capitalism." The crucial difference comes with disagreement over the proper use for the knowledge. A Marxist would see such characteristics as signs of a fundamental flaw in the economic system, correctable only by revolutionary action. Industrial analysis assumes capitalism requires smaller, more marginal changes to improve industry performance. Radical change would rarely be necessary.

NOTES

1. The field of radical economics is undergoing a fundamental challenge and rethinking at the time this essay is written. Antony Cutler, Barry Hindess, Paul Hirst, and Athar Hussain, for example, in their *Marx's Capital and Capitalism Today* (London: Routledge & Kegan Paul, 1977) find traditional Marxist economic analysis wanting. Still, as the methods of Marxist economic analysis undergo important transformations—possibly even a complete restructuring—radical historians studying film industries continue to employ the classical model.
2. Thomas H. Guback, *The International Film Industry: Western Europe and America Since 1945* (Bloomington: Indiana University Press, 1969).
3. Ibid., p. 203.

4. Editors of *Cahiers du Cinema*, "John Ford's *Young Mr. Lincoln*," *Screen* 13, No. 3 (Autumn 1972): 5–43.

5. James O'Connor, *The Fiscal Crisis of the State* (New York: St. Martin's Press, 1973); and Paul M. Sweezy, *The Theory of Capitalist Development* (New York: Monthly Review Press, 1970).

6. Other titles covered labor, permitting employees to organize and bargain collectively, outlawing company unions, and stipulating maximum hours and minimum wages.

7. Bernard Bellush, *The Failure of the NRA* (New York: W. W. Norton, 1975); and Ellis W. Hawley, *The New Deal and the Problem of Monopoly* (Princeton, N.J.: Princeton University Press, 1966).

8. See Douglas Gomery, "Hollywood, the National Recovery Administration, and the Question of Monopoly Power," *Journal of the University Film Association* XXXI, No. 2 (Spring 1979): 47–52 for the details of the argument as well as supporting evidence.

9. Michael Conant, *Antitrust in the Motion Picture Industry* (Berkeley: University of California Press, 1960).

10. Ibid., pp. 218–219.

11. This is a commonly accepted definition. See, for example, Richard H. Leftwich, *The Price System and Resource Allocation* (Hinsdale, Illinois: The Dryden Press, 1970), pp. 103–114.

12. Kathleen Karr, "Hooray for Providence, Wilkes Barre, Saranac Lake—and Hollywood," in *The American Film Heritage* (Washington, D.C.: Acropolis Books, 1972), pp. 104–106.

13. Benjamin B. Hampton, *A History of the Movies* (New York: Covici Friede, 1931), pp. 3–63; Robert C. Allen, *Vaudeville and Film 1895–1915: A Study in Media Interaction* (New York: Arno, 1980), pp. 23–260; and William M. Seabury, *The Public and the Motion Picture* (New York: The Macmillan Co., 1926), pp. 8–18.

14. *United States* v. *Motion Picture Patents Company*, 225 F. 800 (E.D. Pa., 1915), Record, pp. 23–30, 1067–1121, 1567–1580 and 3160–3175; Ralph Cassady, Jr., "Monopoly in Motion Picture Production and Distribution, 1908–1915," *Southern California Law Review* (Summer 1959): 327–390; F. L. Vaughan, *Economics of Our Patent System* (New York: The Macmillan Company, 1926), pp. 53–59, 106–109; and Hampton, *History of the Movies*, pp. 64–82.

15. United States Federal Trade Commission, *Annual Reports of 1923, 1924, 1925, 1926 and 1927* (Washington, D.C.: USGPO, 1924, 1925, 1926, 1927 and 1928); Tino Balio, "Stars in Business: The Founding of United Artists," in *The American Film Industry*, Tino Balio, ed. (Madison: The University of Wisconsin Press, 1976), pp. 135–152; and Hampton, *History of the Movies*, pp. 121–169.

16. Thomas Guback, "Hollywood's International Market," in *The American Film Industry*, Tino Balio, ed. (Madison: The University of Wisconsin Press, 1976), pp. 387–394; Sidney R. Kent, "Distributing the Product," in *The Story of Films*, Joseph P. Kennedy, ed. (Chicago: A. W. Shaw, 1927), pp. 203–210; and Janet Staiger and Douglas Gomery, "The History of World Cinema; Models for Economic Analysis," *Film Reader* 4 (Spring 1979): 35–44.

17. For details on the changes in exhibition, see Ben M. Hall, *The Best Remaining Seats* (New York: Bramhall House, 1961); Douglas Gomery, "The Growth of Movie Monopolies: The Case of Balaban & Katz," *Wide Angle*, vol. 3, no. 1 (1979): 54–63; and Douglas Gomery, "The Movies Become Big Business: Publix Theatres and the Chain Store Strategy," *Cinema Journal*, 18, no. 2 (Spring 1979): 26–40.

7

Social
Film History

In 1909 theater critic Walter Eaton wrote:

> When you reflect that in New York City alone, on a Sunday 500,000 people go to
> the moving picture shows, a majority of them perhaps children . . . you cannot dis-
> miss canned drama with a shrug of contempt. . . . Ten million people attended pro-
> fessional baseball games in America in 1908. Four million people attend moving
> picture theatres, it is said, every day. . . . Here is an industry to be controlled, an in-
> fluence to be reckoned with.[1]

Ever since films were first shown to an audience, the cinema has been a social phenomenon. And for almost as long as audiences have been seeing films,
journalists, ministers, reformers, social scientists, and historians have been
commenting on the unique place held by the movies in the lives of tens of millions of Americans. What were the movies "doing" to all those viewers while
they sat transfixed by the realistic, larger-than-life images on the screen? In 1910
Harvard psychologist Hugo Munsterberg, author of one of the earliest aesthetic
treatises on film, warned of the power of the movies to break down "normal
resistance" to pernicious ideas in the minds of young people. "The possibilities
of psychical infection and destruction," he wrote, "cannot be overlooked."[2] To
continue Munsterberg's suggestive metaphor, others have attempted to view
the movies not as a source of social infection, but rather as symptomatic of the
psychic condition of society. The immense popularity of the movies (annual
attendance in 1941 in the United States topped 2.8 billion, while the total popu-

lation numbered but 132 million) has prompted the belief among many social scientists and historians that the movies somehow reflect the desires, needs, fears, and aspirations of a society at a given time. This chapter will suggest the types of questions that, taken together, constitute the area of social film historical investigation. In doing so it will also consider the range of approaches that have been used in dealing with these questions, both in standard survey histories of American cinema and in more recent research as well.

In *Movies and Society*, Ian Jarvie suggests four questions to be considered by a *sociology* of film:

1. Who makes movies and why?
2. Who sees films, how and why?
3. What is seen, how and why?
4. How do films get evaluated, by whom and why?[3]

As was suggested in Chapter 2, a definition of social film history might begin by casting these sociological questions in the past tense: Who *made* films and why? and so forth. Jarvie's questions highlight the social components of the cinema, while the shift to the past tense recognizes the different time frames dealt with by sociologists and social historians, respectively. At the outset we should keep in mind a point made in Chapter 1 regarding methods available to the scientist (in this case, the social scientist) and those available to the historian. In some kinds of sociological research, the investigator can present a hypothesis and then construct an experimental situation in an attempt to validate it. The historian, on the other hand, works within a much more circumscribed universe, both in the sense that historical data cannot be "produced" as a result of historical investigation, and in the sense that scientific experimentation is not a research avenue open to the historian.

WHO MADE FILMS AND WHY?
A SOCIAL HISTORY OF FILM PRODUCTION

Chapter 4 discussed the relevance of production practices to the style and meaning of the films produced as a result of those practices. The making of films also has a social dimension for several reasons. Filmmakers are members of society, and, as such, are no less subject to social pressures and norms than anyone else. Furthermore, all filmmaking occurs within some social context. Especially in the United States, but typically in all film-producing countries, films are rarely the product of a single person, but usually represent the work of a group organized for the purpose of making films—a studio, company, university, collective, or government agency.[4]

While every filmmaking practice has a social history, Hollywood suggests itself as a logical focus for this type of research. Not only did the Hollywood studio system establish a widely imitated model for filmmaking, Hollywood also represents the most complex social organization ever established for the purpose of making movies. Among survey histories of American cinema, the general question, Who made American movies and why? is of particular concern to the authors of the three most socially-oriented works: Lewis Jacobs' *The Rise of the American Film*, Garth Jowett's *Film: the Democratic Art*, and Robert Sklar's *Movie-Made America*. Sklar suggests that a starting point for understanding who made the movies is recognition of the fact that almost all of the original Hollywood movie moguls (Adolph Zukor, Jesse Lasky, Marcus Loew, Carl Laemmle, among others) were first- or second-generation Jewish immigrants, and hence did not share the ethnic or religious backgrounds either of their audiences or of the leaders of other cultural and business institutions in America.[5]

As Sklar would acknowledge, however, the social history of "who made the movies" extends far beyond the ethnicity of some studio executives. A comprehensive social history of Hollywood would at least include an examination of (1) the organizational structure of the studios, (2) the recruitment of personnel, (3) the division of labor within each studio, (4) the roles played by various participants in the film production process, (5) the star system, (6) the immediate social context outside the studio (the Hollywood community), and (7) public discourse on Hollywood and the film industry.

As you might guess, such an inclusive social history of Hollywood has yet to be attempted, although scholars have addressed themselves to some of the constituent elements of such a history. Most of the histories of individual Hollywood studios are implicitly informed by the "great man" theory of history and concentrate on the idiosyncracies of their executives: Louis B. Mayer and Irving Thalberg (MGM), the Warner brothers (Warner Bros.), and Harry Cohn (Columbia). These works are also limited by the degree of access their authors were granted to studio records—records that might reveal the organizational structure and decision-making patterns within a studio at a given time. An exception to both the "great man" approach and to the lack of studio documentation is Tino Balio's *United Artists: The Company Built by the Stars*, a business rather than social history of the studio founded by D. W. Griffith, Mary Pickford, Douglas Fairbanks, and Charlie Chaplin.[6]

In *Image and Influence*, Andrew Tudor suggests as a starting point for a sociology of filmmaking the investigation of the movie-making community *as if* it constituted a distinctive society, with its own organizational structure, hierarchies, goals, and problems. To a limited degree two works have taken this approach: Leo Rosten's *Hollywood: The Movie Colony, the Movie Makers*, and Hortense Powdermaker's *Hollywood: The Dream Factory*. Powdermaker, an anthropologist, assumed for the purposes of her study that Hollywood was as appropriate a subject for anthropological study as Navajo Indian society or the Troribund Islanders. Both books provide interesting "snapshot" glimpses of life in Hollywood in the 1940s.[7] Several other studies have used the production case study as a means of grasping the social factors in filmmaking: Lillian Ross's

Picture, Donald Knox's *The Magic Factory: How MGM Made "An American in Paris,"* and Dore Schary's *Case History of a Movie,* among others.[8] All of these works are useful to the film historian as raw materials from which more general theories of social interaction in film production might be developed. Their usefulness is obviously limited, however, in that they are sociological (in some cases merely journalistic) in orientation, not historical. They offer a picture "in the present tense" of some aspects of Hollywood as a social system or of the role played by participants in the making of a film, but the studies are much less useful in explaining how the organizational structure of the studio developed and changed.

Integral to the notion of Hollywood as society has been the "star" phenomenon—that curious transformation of an employee into a saleable commodity, of an actor into an icon. An understanding of the historical development of the star system is crucial not only to the study of the studio system, but of the relationship between films and audiences. As Tudor points out, "The relatively fixed persona of a star, created though the movies themselves and through the publicity machine, was a central element in audience involvement."[9] The star phenomenon will be discussed in some detail in the case study for this chapter.

WHO SAW FILMS, HOW AND WHY?
THE HISTORY OF MOVIE-GOING

In sociological terms, the movie audience is an "unstructured group." That is, unlike more formalized social groups (political parties, religious denominations, college fraternities) the unstructured group has "no social organization, no body of custom and tradition, no established set of rules or rituals, no organized group of sentiments, no structure of status roles, and no established leadership."[10] Hence the "audience" for movies in any sociological or historical sense is really only an abstraction generated by the researcher, since the unstructured group that we refer to as the movie audience is constantly being constituted, dissolved, and reconstituted with each film-going experience. There are no membership cards issued to participants of the movie-going audience, no computerized list of the names and addresses of the faithful. The vast popularity of the movies in America during the past eight decades (an average of three trips to the movies each week per household in 1930) might lead us to equate the movie audience with American society. How convenient it would be if the considerable demographic and sociological data we have on American society as a whole could be applied with equal validity to the movie-going public. However, as the local exhibition project in Chapter 8 makes clear, patterns of movie-going have varied historically according to region, social class, income, age, and ethnicity. We are only now beginning to determine who saw films in a particular locale at a particular point in film history, and we know even less about how patterns have varied historically from country to country.

Related to the question of who saw films is the issue of how they were seen. The experience of viewing a film in a dank, store-front nickelodeon is as different from the viewing situation provided by the picture palace as it is from that found in the sterile multiplex cinemas of the contemporary, suburban shopping center. Also, as the Balaban and Katz project in Chapter 8 demonstrates, in the case of first-run theaters in the 1920s the experience of "going to the movies" and "watching a film" were by no means synonymous. The movie-going experience included the architecture and furnishings of the building itself, an elaborate stage show, the newsreel, a program of shorts, *and* the feature film. It could well be that for many patrons in the 1920s which feature film happened to be playing made little difference.

Finally, a history of film audiences must address why people went to the movies. In answering this question the history of movie-going should be examined alongside that of other leisure-time activities. For example, patterns of movie-going clearly changed with the development of television as a commercial mass entertainment medium in the 1950s. For many people movie-going ceased being a habitual activity and became instead a less frequent but more carefully planned outing. "Going to the movies" became "going to see a film." Jarvie suggests that a sociology of film-going might ask why people go the cinema rather than to any other social institution of entertainment. What are the social attractions, advantages, and functions of the cinema?

Once again, sociologists have the advantage of being able to generate data in an attempt to answer these questions. Although the social historian cannot poll movie audiences from the 1930s, he or she can make use of sociological, statistical, marketing, and demographic data collected at that time. Such sources can provide the historian with evidence that is otherwise unobtainable, but the quality of these data as historical evidence depends on the rigor with which the original studies were conducted, their ostensible purpose, and the questions the historian asks of the data. The more the historian knows about how, where, when, why, and by whom the original data were collected, the more valuable they are likely to be as historical evidence. In short, understanding why people have gone to the movies can be approached by the historian only indirectly: by examining the leisure activities available to a particular social group at a particular time, contemporaneous accounts of film-going in newspapers, memoirs, fiction, and research data gathered at the time.

WHAT HAS BEEN SEEN, HOW AND WHY?
THE HISTORY OF FILM AS CULTURAL DOCUMENT

The popularity of film as a mass entertainment medium has prompted both film and social historians to regard the movies as a unique source of insight into national cultures. It is indeed tempting to look back on the 1920s or 1930s when movie attendance in the United States was as high as 75 million movie-goers each week and see films of these eras as reflections of the values and beliefs of a society, exponents of American culture, or windows into the national psyche. The objection that films are merely a means of "escape" for audiences is not a cogent one. Even if we assume that films have functioned as vehicles of escape from everyday woes, we must also assume that they have represented an escape *into something*. Audiences have made active choices to "escape" into the movies rather than into some other form of entertainment or recreation. Furthermore, however indirectly and obliquely, movies are social representations. That is, they derive their images and sounds, themes and stories ultimately from their social environment. In fictional films, characters are given attitudes, gestures, sentiments, motivations, and appearances that are, in part at least, based on social roles and on general notions about how a policeman, factory worker, debutante, mother, or husband is "supposed" to act.

The overall question, What has been seen, how and why? has been the one most frequently asked in social film history for several decades now. Hence a considerable portion of this chapter is devoted to a discussion of the major approaches taken thus far to the issue of how film might be used as a social–historical document. Relating the social structure of a given time and place to the representation of that structure in film is one of the most tantalizing yet vexing tasks faced by the entire field of film historical study.

"Image" Studies

It is obvious that the fictive world of the Hollywood movie is not inhabited by a randomly selected cross-section of contemporary society. Some groups within society appear with disproportional frequency while others are underrepresented or entirely absent. It has also long been apparent that different social groups are represented differently on the screen. Examining how various social groups within society have been depicted in the films of a particular era has formed the focus of a significant body of film historical research. At issue is not how an individual film represents a particular ethnic or demographic group, but whether there is a pattern of screen images among films, if these images change over time, and how this change comes about.

In *From Reverence to Rape*, Molly Haskell advances the thesis that American movies have functioned to perpetuate "the big lie": the assumption of the basic inferiority of women. Calling the film industry "the propaganda arm of the American Dream machine," she argues that images of women in American films have embodied a central dichotomy: While female characters have frequently been depicted as more resourceful, intelligent, and capable than their male counterparts, they are forced by the end of the film's narrative to submit to men or be subjugated by them. These "myths of subjection and sacrifice" were necessary, says Haskell, because "audiences for the most part were not interested in seeing, and Hollywood was not interested in sponsoring, a smart ambitious woman as a popular heroine. A woman who could compete and conceivably win in a man's world would defy emotional gravity, would go against the grain of prevailing notions about the male sex." To Haskell, screen images of women reflect in a fairly straightforward manner prevailing male attitudes toward women in society as a whole. Stereotypes of women's roles existed on the screen because these stereotypes existed in society.[11]

The assumption that cinematic stereotypes reflect stereotypic attitudes within society underlies several works that examine the image of blacks in American cinema. For example, in *To Find an Image: Black Films from Uncle Tom to Super-Fly*, James P. Murray argues that films reflect "what people think of themselves in relation to the world." In much of the literature on black screen images the concern is expressed that stereotypic images affected as well as reflected public attitudes toward blacks. The effect of Hollywood's representation of blacks, says Murray, was to reinforce the notion among both blacks and whites that "it was whites, not blacks, who were significant" in American society.[12]

Most of the studies of women and blacks in films emphasize the analysis of films themselves. Since filmic images are assumed to be reflections of prevailing social norms, changes in representations are attributed to changes in public sentiment. Thomas Cripps's *Slow Fade to Black* examines the external pressures at work behind the representations of blacks in American films between 1896 and 1942. Cripps presumes that "popular art is an expression of deep seated values and attitudes," but he does not see the screen image of blacks as being the automatic reflection of these values. Rather he examines how control over the production of filmic images was established and maintained by non-blacks (the "Hollywood" industry), and how the forces in control responded to pressures from audiences and other groups. The image of blacks in films changed markedly after 1942, he argues, not because of a massive shift in public sentiment, but because Hollywood finally began to yield to continuing pressure from civil rights groups.[13]

How Films Reflect Society: Kracauer and the German Cinema

All of the studies of the "image" of particular social groups raise the larger question of what films "say" about society. In other words, how can films be said to be cultural artifacts? Since this issue underlies all works that in some way ask What is seen, how and why, it needs to be discussed in some detail. The seminal historical account of the relationship between film and society is Siegfried Kracauer's 1947 book *From Caligari to Hitler*. Kracauer's conclusions have found their way into numerous survey histories of world cinema and his method has served as the basis for other historical studies. In *From Caligari to Hitler*, Kracauer's analysis of German films between the end of World War I and the rise of Hitler, he argued that films provide uniquely accurate reflections of the inner workings of a society at a given point in the past—a notion that has formed the basis for numerous books, theses, and scholarly and popular articles.[14]

Kracauer's thesis is that "through an analysis of the German films deep psychological dispositions predominant in Germany from 1918 to 1933 can be exposed—dispositions which influenced the course of events during that time and which will have to be reckoned with in the post–Hitler era." According to Kracauer, the films of a nation "reflect its mentality" more directly than any other artistic medium for two reasons. First, films are a collective rather than an individual enterprise. As such they tend to be immune from "arbitrary handling of screen material" and "individual peculiarities." Second, since films are made for mass audiences, motifs within popular movies can be seen as satisfying "mass desires." In other words, the biasing effects of film production are inhibited through the group nature of filmmaking, while audience feedback and the assumption that commercial producers always aim at attracting the largest possible audience assure the accurate reflection of a society's "mental climate."

To Kracauer all films are not equally reflective of the "inner life" of a nation. The most popular films of an era are "particularly suggestive of mass desires," but a sample limited to only the biggest box-office hits would preclude the discovery of important "motifs" that recur in many slightly less successful films. Kracauer explains: "What counts is not so much the statistically measurable popularity of films as the popularity of their pictorial and narrative motifs. Persistent reiteration of these motifs marks them as outward projections of inner urges." In all, Kracauer examines approximately 100 films, which he sees as containing these motifs, out of the more than 1000 feature films made in Germany between 1919 and 1933.

What films reflect about society, says Kracauer, "are not so much explicit credos as psychological dispositions—those deep layers of collective mentality which extend more or less below the dimension of consciousness." In his book, Kracauer proceeds chronologically, extracting important recurrent motifs—the choice between tyranny and chaos, the futility of rebellion, the immaturity and impotence of the middle-class male—contained in the narrative patterns, mise-en-scene, characterizations, and composition of the films he analyzes. These motifs are indications, says Kracauer, of the psycho-social traumas of the post–World War I period and, as the 1920s progress, indications of the German people's unconscious disposition to accept authoritarian rule as the only viable solution to the nation's problems.[15]

The motifs in the films are reflective of the state of mind of not only individual film audiences but the entire society, as terms such as "inner life," "psychological disposition," and "collective mentality" would suggest. Kracauer's justification of this attribution can be stated in the form of a syllogism:

1. Cinema audiences in Germany in the 1920s were predominantly middle-class.
2. Middle-class values and attitudes pervaded all of German society.

Therefore:

3. Recurrent screen motifs reflect the needs and fears of the entire nation.

Despite Kracauer's generalization to the whole of German society, his focus remains on the middle class and on the possibility that filmic motifs might provide clues toward understanding the bourgeoisie's capitulation to and, to some extent, endorsement of Hitler in the early 1930s. The German films of the 1920s are to Kracauer outward projections of the "overwhelming compulsions" that determined the behavior of the middle class—compulsions that led it to scorn any connection with anti-fascist movements, with which its practical interests actually lay. Films become for Kracauer evidence of a "secret history" of the period, one which cannot be understood on the basis of observable social "facts" alone.

Kracauer's method, terminology, and implicit theoretical stance tie his project in *From Caligari to Hitler* to a larger movement in social and social-historical analysis that originated in Germany in the 1920s. The "Frankfurt School" is a term used to designate the overall social theory of a group of intellectuals, among them Max Horkheimer, Frederich Pollock, Theodor Adorno, Erich Fromm, Herbert Marcuse, and Leo Lowenthall, associated with the Institute for Social Research, founded in Frankfurt in 1923. Although their approaches differed in many respects, the Frankfurt School members shared an orientation toward social analysis derived from Marx and a focus on the relationship between the individual and the social totality informed by Freud. As we shall see shortly, in its attempts to integrate Marx and Freud, the Frankfurt School's work prefigures that of *Screen* and *Cahiers du Cinéma* several decades later.

Although Kracauer was never formally associated with the Institute nor with the later work of its members, who were (like Kracauer) forced to emigrate in the early 1930s, he both influenced and was influenced by the "critical theory" developed by the Frankfurt School. Of central concern to the Frankfurt School were the social effects of modern industrial capitalism in the Western world in general and Germany in particular. As Germany developed rapidly toward monopoly capitalism after World War I, the plight of the working class deteriorated badly throughout the 1920s: unemployment rose, wages dropped, and inflation in the early 1920s devastated many. Yet despite the stage being set for decisive revolutionary action, it did not materialize. The economic and social status quo were maintained, and, in 1933, any hopes for restructuring German society along socialist lines were dashed by the *election* of the Nazis to power. Now intellectuals in exile (as was Kracauer), the Frankfurt School group addressed themselves to issues surrounding the rise of fascism: the manipulation of public opinion, and the acquiescence of large portions of the German population to an anti-democratic, militarist regime.

An early sociological treatise by Kracauer, *The Clerks* (1929) formed an important background for the analysis of the social dimensions of capitalism and fascism by Horkheimer and others of the Frankfurt group in the 1930s. One of the first serious studies of the effects of modern industrial practices on white-collar workers, *The Clerks* argued that the introduction of "scientific" management practices to German industry in the 1920s had resulted in the status degradation of clerical workers. Much of their decision-making power removed and many of their traditional tasks now performed by machines, the working conditions of white-collar workers were in many instances virtually indistinguishable from those of blue-collar workers. Why, then, Kracauer asked, did these white-collar workers consistently refuse to side with working-class political parties? Why, instead, did they deliver their votes in the early 1930s to the fascists?

Kracauer interviewed white-collar workers and discovered that while they were objectively aligned with the proletariat in terms of their position within the production process, they were psychologically separated from ordinary workers to a far greater degree. White-collar workers, he found, clung to their few remaining opportunities to exercise authority over their subordinates—to play the "little master" both in the work place and in their homes. The distinctions between themselves and the "working man" had to be maintained psychically, even if the economic and social bases for these distinctions had all but disappeared. The metaphor Kracauer used in describing the psychological state of the white-collar worker in Germany in the 1920s was the "cycling mentality": "with their backs they stoop; with their feet they tread hard."[16]

Writing from the post–World War II perspective of 1947, Kracauer expands upon this thesis in *From Caligari to Hitler*, drawing indirectly upon subsequent analyses of Weimar society by such proponents of "critical theory" as Horkheimer, Fromm, and Franz Neumann. The subtitle of *From Caligari to Hitler* is "A Psychological History of the German Film," and what Kracauer sees these films reflecting about German society is, in fact, a psychological malaise on a mass scale. "The German soul," he says, "is haunted by the alternative images of tyrannic rule and instinct-governed chaos, threatened by doom on either side, tossed about in gloomy space like the phantom ship in *Nosferatu*" (Murnau's 1922 version of the Dracula story). The motifs contained in the films not only mirrored mass psychological states, contends Kracauer, they actually anticipated what was to befall German society: "It all was as it had been on the screen. The dark premonitions of a final doom were also fulfilled."[17]

Kracauer's status as a German emigre infuses his work with a compelling passion, and few who have seen the films Kracauer discusses can fail to be struck by what is in some cases their bizarre narratives and haunting imagery. At the very least *From Caligari to Hitler* elevated film to a new level of importance as historical document and raised the possibility that film might be the object of serious academic study. Viewed within the context of the Frankfurt School tradition of social analysis, however, *From Caligari to Hitler* does not evince the same degree of concern for theoretical grounding as do mainstream works of "critical theory."

In attempting to establish the mechanisms by which economic, social, and psychological realms were interconnected, the Frankfurt School continually wrestled with, adapted, modified, and argued among themselves about the psychoanalytic theories of Freud and his interpreters and with the relationship of psychoanalysis to Marxism. "Critical theory" recognized that, in Horkheimer's words, society is translated by the individual into "the language of the unconscious," but also recognized the need to specify how this process of translation occurs. In *From Caligari to Hitler*, however, the notion that films reflect "collective predispositions," "inner urges," and "psychological tendencies" is an unexplored premise without grounding in any particular psychological theory. Although he sometimes uses a film-as-dream metaphor, Kraucauer avoids specifically Freudian terminology. Phrases such as "collective predisposition" and "German soul" have a faintly Jungian ring to them, but any connection to Jung's theories of archetypes or racial unconscious is left unpursued.

Kracauer's influence on subsequent social film history has been more inspirational than methodological. Of the two works that follow most closely in the Kracauerian tradition, one puts even less stress on psychological theory than does Kracauer, while the other cites Kracauer only as a negative precedent. Andrew Bergman places his *We're in the Money* squarely in the tradition of *From Caligari to Hitler*, but he faults Kracauer for his "unsupported Jungian premise." Rather than propose an alternative theory to explain the social–psychology of the cinema, however, Bergman avoids the issue entirely by maintaining:

> It is impossible to say with any certainty that a straight line can be drawn from films to popular thought. "Popular thought" is too private, too diverse, too affected by regional differences. But merely taking the intellectual history of the films by themselves provides the richest of sources for studying various of the tensions and assumptions of the period.

Films, he says, are "myths," representations of "things lost and things desired." These formulations, however, while clearly containing a psychological component, are not more precise than Kracauer's.

In *Cinema and Society* Paul Monaco foregrounds the psychological aspects of film history in his study of German and French films of the 1920s. "Movies," he says, "find their relationship to society in oblique symbolism. The most fruitful source of insight into an individual's latent concern is the dream. One of the most striking characteristics of film is its kinship to the dream." Extrapolating from Freudian dream theory, Monaco sets out to demonstrate that the most popular films of the two countries reveal differences between their "group minds." Monaco does not confront Kracauer directly until the final page of the book, and here only to establish his work as a negative precedent:

> This study does not want to fall into the errors of one of its predecessors: *From Caligari to Hitler* by Siegfried Kracauer. Kracauer produced an intriguing account of Weimar cinema that read too much out of the films through hindsight. It began with a perception of Hitlerian Germany (unfortunately not a very profound one) and then attempted to tack a number of filmic themes together and find them all pointing to Hitler's ascension to power in 1933.[18]

The Empiricist Critique of Kracauer

Kracauer shared with the Frankfurt School a distrust of empiricist methods, believing that the quantitative analysis of "facts" yielded only superficial interpretations of that portion of social reality easily measured. Hence Kracauer's assertion that his object of study was a body of motifs, not merely the plots of the most popular films. For Kracauer and for critical theory, art constituted a "code language for processes taking place in society" that had to be deciphered by the analyst but which was irreducible to a set of statistics. However, Kracauer's vague criteria for determining which films contained these "pictorial and narrative motifs" and what constituted "persistent reiteration" of them combined with his unsubstantiated claim that these motifs "pervaded films of all levels" left his work open to methodological question, particularly by empiricist historians and sociologists. Several critics have commented on the vulnerability of Kracauer's method to charges of the *post hoc ergo propter hoc* fallacy of historical reasoning: the idea that because event *B* happened after event *A*, the former occurred as a result of the latter.[19] Writing after World War II and in the wake of Hitler's destruction of German society, Kracauer proceeds backwards from effect to presumed cause, from the historical fact of Hitler's rise to power in 1933 to the positing of the cause for his success as the psychological predisposition of the German people to acquiesce to authoritarianism. Therefore, certain recurrent motifs in German film of the period immediately preceding Hitler's ascension appear as reflections of this mass-psychological malaise and as anticipatory of what turned out to be social–historical events. Historian William Aydelotte would contend that all historical generalizations are by their very nature quantitative. Such terms as "typical," "representative," "widespread," and "recurrent" (generalities Kracauer is prone to use) are quantitative statements whether or not figures are presented to support them. As a social researcher working in Germany in the 1920s Kracauer was certainly in a good position to survey German film output, but Aydelotte would point out that even the best-intentioned scholars tend to remember those examples among numerous data that support their pet hypotheses.[20]

The Empiricist Alternative: Content Analysis

The empiricist alternative to Kracauer's method of assessing the historical relationship between film and society would be *content analysis*. Drawn from mass communication research, content analysis is a method for making quantitative inferences about unobservable aspects of a particular source on the basis of a body of messages from that source. In this case the messages are films and the source is society, or at least that portion of society that constitutes the movie audience. Wishing to understand something about the "national mood," or "public sentiment" during some period in the past—a phenomenon that cannot be gauged directly—the content analyst examines messages (films) that can be regarded as the expressions of audiences who paid to see them.

The rationale for assuming the source of filmic messages to be the movie audience is that in capitalist countries film producers desire to make as much money as possible from each film released. Hence films are made for as wide an audience as possible. The audience votes, in effect, for various types of films with their box-office dollars. Storylines, characters, settings, themes, actors that prove popular are recycled into subsequent films; failures disappear from the screen. According to this logic, popular entertainment films are not so much the result of personal artistic expression or manipulation by producers as they are the medium through which society communicates with itself.

The content analyst first defines the range of texts—in this case, films—to be included in the study (the *population*), then selects a sample of those texts for analysis. The decision as to which films are actually to be examined depends in part on how the analyst believes films reflect society. If the assumption is made that films reflect society equally, then a *random* sample is called for (each film in the population having an equal chance of being included in the sample). If, on the other hand, the analyst holds that some films by virtue of their popularity are more reflective than others, then the sample would be limited to only box-office hits.

Once the films in the sample have been examined they must be reduced to data—usually quantifiable data. In doing so the analyst must have some notion of how beliefs, attitudes, or norms are actually reflected in a film. In other words, what in a film *says* something about the culture out of which it comes and *how* does it say it? Kracauer, Bergman, and Monaco would all contend that films are the indirect expression of society's fears, aspirations, and preoccupations. Like dreams, they would argue, films deal with potentially threatening concerns by disguising them. Put in social–scientific terms, they have examined the *latent* content of the films: those layers of possible meaning that lie below the surface of a text, what the text *connotes* rather than *denotes.* Most content analysts, however, concentrate on the *manifest* level of content in a text: its literal, surface meaning. In the case of feature films, the manifest content would include the socioeconomic status of characters, their articulated sentiments, plot developments, setting, and ostensible themes.

There are two basic reasons content analysts limit filmic content to the manifest level. In keeping with the tenets of the scientific method, the content analyst wants to keep the interpretation of data as "objective" a process as possible and conversely wants to eliminate wherever possible subjective (and hence possible idiosyncratic) readings. That *The Cabinet of Dr. Caligari* is "about" German society's tragic choice between tyranny and chaos is a debatable subjective interpretation; that the film contains a psychiatrist, petty government officials, and a somnambulist, and is set in a mental institution, a fair ground, and a German city is a much more objective assessment upon which almost all readers would agree. Also, most content analysts would hold that data must be analyzed *quantitatively* and that only those units of content that can be counted should be included. Where Kracauer argued that the statistically measurable popularity of motifs should not be the only analytic criterion, content analysts would maintain that it is the only testable and hence valid criterion.

The tradition of quantitative content analysis of motion pictures in the United States began in the 1930s as part of a large-scale project financed by the Payne Fund to assess the effect of the movies on the beliefs and conduct of movie audiences. Among the most rigorously "scientific" of the content analyses of this period was Dorothy B. Jones's "Quantitative Analysis of Motion Picture Content," produced for the Office of War Information in 1942. Jones examined 100 Hollywood feature films released between April 1941 and February 1942 to determine the demographic characteristics (age, economic class, marital status) of leading characters, the "wants" of these characters, and how these desires were fulfilled or denied. She discovered, for example, that most characters desired romantic love above all else (68.1%) and that while films held ideal marriage to be of paramount importance in their characters' lives, the films studied rarely depicted the lives of heroes and heroines beyond the marriage ceremony. Jones was also careful to note that quantitative content analysis could deal with only some aspects of movie content—that is, only those superficial aspects that could be counted. Other, potentially important features of the movie viewing experience could not be so rigidly quantified, she admitted.[21]

Jones's warning regarding the limits of quantitative content analysis raises a more general issue pertaining to any attempt to read movies as reflections or indices of societal beliefs or values. In speaking of the relationship between literature and social reality, Wolfgang Iser insists that the critic (or, in this case, the historian) maintain the distinction between fiction and "real life" that the reader does as a matter of course. As readers, we do not relate to characters, ideas, situations, and events in a fictive narrative in the same way we relate to people, ideas, situations, and events in our everyday lives. By its inherent "falseness" the fictional narrative creates a distance between itself and the real world—a distance that forms the basis for the aesthetic pleasure we experience from a novel or film. During the reading process, we might accept the world of the novel *as if it were real* but, under ordinary circumstances, we do not mistake that world for one that *is* real.

Furthermore, a fictional text does not represent the transferral intact of values and beliefs from the experiential world of the reader to that of the text. The fictional text selects from among the variety of situations, values, beliefs, and norms to be found in any given culture and then combines these selected aspects of the social structure in such a way that they *appear* to be interrelated. In doing so, however, the text wrenches these values and conventions out of their ordinary contexts and strips them of their applications. Fictional language, says Iser, "depragmatizes the conventions it has selected," and in the process calls those conventions we take for granted to our attention. Thus it is dangerous to presume that the values displayed within a film or novel correspond in some direct way to the operation of those values within their "real" contexts.[21] Films are certainly cultural documents, but what they *document* is the complex relationship among reader, fictional text, author, and culture.

The Psychology of Film Viewing

Understanding the relationship between image and viewer—a thorny problem both for Kracauer and the Frankfurt School tradition of social research out of which he comes—reenters the social film history debate in the 1970s. Much of contemporary film theory, particularly that originating in England and France, has concerned itself with the nature of the image/viewer exchange, drawing upon semiotics, Marxism, and psychoanalysis to explain, in the language of Jarvie's question, "What is seen, how and why?" A full discussion of this project, to which the journal *Screen* was devoted between 1973 and 1982, is not possible here. However, a brief consideration of how the social–psychology of the cinema has been addressed by contemporary film theorists seems called for—if only to point out that the issues raised first by Kracauer are still high on the agenda of film studies.

The work of French psychoanalyst Jacques Lacan has been extremely influential on recent attempts to understand what happens when one watches a film. Lacan's theories of psychoanalysis represent a rereading of Freud in light of the developments in structural linguistics discussed in Chapter 1. Lacan is particularly concerned with the role language, in its broadest meaning of a structured system of symbolic representations, has in the development of the individual personality. Taking an extreme conventionalist position, Lacan argues that there is no thought, no knowledge either of ourselves or of the world around us that exists outside of language. Language literally re-produces reality. The act of becoming a distinct individual to Lacan is the act of being inserted into a preexisting network of symbols (the *symbolic*), of being positioned by society and language in a system of similarity and difference. We are defined in terms of social and linguistic relationships: "the son of . . . ," "I," "Mary Smith." The young child has no choice but to submit to society and the web of language which at the same time ensnares and defines him or her.

In Lacan's work concern for the crucial role played by language and society in constructing the person as a "subject" in the social order is laid over the Freudian emphasis on the young child's psycho–sexual development, particularly the necessity of the child's resolving the Oedipal complex. Prior to its access to language, says Lacan, the child views the world around it as belonging to or being an extension of its own self. This relationship of unity Lacan calls the *imaginary*. The infant is the center of an undifferentiated world that it controls and possesses, a world that revolves around the source of its nourishment and care—the mother. With the movement from the realm of the imaginary to the realm of the symbolic, the infant becomes a fragmented subject and the possibility of "having" the mother is lost forever. Of course, it is only by means of the symbolic that the child becomes an individual person—the ultimate Catch-22. This original desire (to sexually possess the mother) and the lack produced as a result of its inevitable nonfulfillment do not disappear with the entry of the child into society. Rather, they remain as elements of the unconscious, but are repressed and then expressed through language in disguised forms.[23]

Films, then, become one vehicle for the displaced expression of the language of the unconscious. To Lacanian film theorists, however, films are not isolated texts to be read by the analyst for the unconscious imagery they might contain. Rather the *act* of film viewing is seen as an illustration of how the cinema "constructs" the viewer as a subject.

A key work in Lacanian film analysis is Colin McCabe's "Theory and Film: Principles of Realism and Pleasure," published in *Screen* in 1976.[24] In it McCabe begins with the Lacanian notion that "as speaking subjects we constantly oscillate between the symbolic and the imaginary—constantly imagining ourselves granting some full meaning to the words we speak, and constantly being surprised to find them determined by relations outside our control." This oscillation between the imaginary (the innately narcissistic notion that we construct the world and impose meaning upon it) and that of the symbolic (the painful recognition of a world that exists independent of our consciousness) McCabe finds expressed in the style of the classical Hollywood narrative film. The dominant mode of vision in a Hollywood film can be called imaginary, says McCabe, in that it positions the viewer at a point of omniscience.

The Hollywood style works to show us all that we need and want to know: the world of the film is arranged for the purpose of our being able to see it from an "all-seeing" point of view. This imaginary mode of seeing alternates with what McCabe calls "the look," the shot taken from the point of view of a character in the film. The look threatens the dominance of the omniscient mode of seeing by reminding us that "the object we are looking at [another character] offers a position from which we can be looked at." Our position is exposed by the gaze of another. The look is symbolic in the sense that it marks our implication as viewers in a network of looks constructed for us but not by us. By identifying with the look of a character we surrender our position of overviewing "everything" in the world of the film. However, the conventions of the Hollywood cinema always subordinate the look to the all-seeing point of view. We risk giving up our exalted visual position only because we know it will be restored to us. Like the infant who plays with a toy on a string by endlessly tossing it over the side of the crib and pulling it back in again, the pleasure of giving it up resides in our knowledge that we will get it back.

McCabe then analyzes *American Graffiti* in terms of the imaginary and the symbolic: point of view and the look. The glance of the girl in the "T-Bird" fragments our point of view in the film by introducing a look. In order for us and for the recipient of the look (Curt Henderson, the character played by Richard Dreyfuss) to be restored to the realm of the imaginary,

> ...we must find a father, someone who will figure as that moment of originating identity and power which will deny the possibility of the interplay of looks. It is this search that Curt Henderson undertakes. His progress from the school-teacher to the Pharaohs to Wolfman Jack is the search for a father who will confirm him in his identity and expunge the possibility of difference; who will reassert the point of view over the look.

As McCabe admits, this Lacanian interpretation of the psychological nature of cinematic vision might seem quite removed from any discussion of the social dimensions of film. At the end of his essay, however, he makes the case that the Hollywood film, by asserting an imaginary unity between viewer and film, removes the spectator from "the realm of contradiction." Here McCabe relates the Lacanian notion of the contradiction between the imaginary and the symbolic to the Marxist notion of ideology as a process of masking or displacing certain basic contradictions within capitalist culture. Just as the Hollywood film style smoothes over any potential disruptions to the power of our point of view, so certain social contradictions within Hollywood films are smoothed over. In the case of *American Graffiti*, the contradictions that are carefully removed from the spectator are those raised by the impact of the Vietnam War on American society. From our position in the post–Vietnam War age we look back on the America of *American Graffiti* as an era of innocence. The passing of innocence is not seen in the film as the imposition of external forces (the war) upon small-town life in the early 1960s, but rather a result of "growing up."

> Toad grows up and goes off to die at An Loc but this is simply part of a human cycle. The position of the viewer after the Vietnam War is simply held to be the same but different—the position of the imaginary. The Vietnam War is repressed and smoothed over.

The preceding discussion of Lacan and the applications of his theories to film study have done neither justice. It is impossible to outline here the many objections raised and qualifications made to this approach since 1976. The thrust of this line of research, however, is that films function to express in disguised form that which we cannot consciously articulate. Furthermore, the very act of viewing a film is emblematic of the more general way we negotiate the social world into which we are inserted in infancy. Freudian psychology is used to explain how aspects of our immediately lived experience are relegated to the unconscious and expressed partially and obliquely through language and art, while Marxism is invoked to explain the repression of social contradictions by the dominant ideology and their disguised and displaced expression.

Thus far theorists like Colin McCabe, Stephen Heath, Laura Mulvey, and others have concentrated on the relationship between psychoanalysis and the cinema in general, and much of this work has been—perhaps necessarily —ahistorical. It would be difficult to argue, for example, that the basic nature of human personality has changed in any significant way since the time of Freud. That this orientation might be changing is suggested by Stephen Heath in the concluding essay in his recent book, *Questions of Cinema*. Heath contends that the "major error" of psychoanalytic interpretations of the cinema has been its ahistorical nature. The degree to which psychoanalysis can be historicized and how this will be accomplished remain at this point to be seen.[25]

WHAT HAS BEEN SAID ABOUT THE MOVIES, BY WHOM AND FOR WHAT PURPOSE?

Jarvie's fourth sociological question about film has been altered and expanded to take into account the fact that movies have not just been evaluated by critics and reviewers but have been the subject of a much wider range of discourse as well. In the 1920s, for example, Hollywood was the third most important source of news in the United States (behind New York and Washington). Over 100 novels have been written about the movie colony, from *Merton of the Movies* to *The Last Tycoon*. The American film industry has been the subject of a number of Congressional investigations. Films from the *Birth of a Nation* to *Deep Throat* have engendered intense controversy, and prompted public demonstrations, riots, sermons, and editorials. For the historian, understanding the social discourse about film at a given time helps to establish the context in which films were produced and consumed. Not to be excluded as social discourse is the study of film in universities and high schools, a subject touched upon in Chapter 2.

A few studies have dealt with aspects of the history of social discourse on the cinema in America. Robert Davis's *Response to Innovation* examines the public response to the advent of the movies, radio and television in the United States. Jonas Spatz's *Hollywood in Fiction: Some Versions of the American Myth* is a history of the Hollywood novel. Larry Ceplair and Steven Englund's *The Inquisition in Hollywood* presents a fascinating account of the attack on Hollywood in the late 1940s and early 1950s by those who considered the movie colony infiltrated by communists.[26]

WHAT HAS BEEN THE RELATIONSHIP BETWEEN THE CINEMA AS A SOCIAL INSTITUTION AND OTHER SOCIAL INSTITUTIONS?

A fifth question needs to be added to Jarvie's list to take into account the fact that at any given time the cinema participates in a complex network of relationships with other social institutions. At a number of points in the history of the

American cinema, the most important of these relationships has been that between the cinema and various levels of government. During World War I, for example, the movie industry worked hand-in-hand with President Wilson's propaganda agency, the Committee on Public Information (CPI). Not only did Hollywood studios abide by guidelines of acceptable film content issued by the CPI, they voluntarily turned over foreign distribution of many of their films to this agency for the duration of America's involvement in the war.[27] As has been mentioned, the "Red Scare" of the Cold War period prompted investigations of Hollywood by the FBI, Congress, and other governmental agencies. Screenwriters, producers, directors, and actors were called to Washington to testify before the House Un-American Activities Committee as to their political affiliations and those of their colleagues. The Hollywood studios cooperated by "blacklisting" those who refused to testify and others who were merely suspected of leftist sympathies.

Part of the history of the cinema's institutional relationships would have to include the legal status of the movies. In 1915 the Supreme Court ruled unanimously that the movies were "not to be regarded, nor intended to be regarded as part of the press of the country or as organs of public opinion."[28] This decision effectively removed First Amendment protection from the movies and forced filmmakers to operate for decades under the fear of national censorship and the actuality of state and local censorship.

Nongovernmental social institutions, particularly religious and civic organizations, have tried to influence the production and exhibition of films. In *Slow Fade to Black*, Thomas Cripps details the continuing efforts of the NAACP to persuade Hollywood to change its portrayal of blacks and open up the studios to more employment opportunities for blacks.[29]

While this chapter has treated social film history as a number of separate questions that a film historian might ask, these questions are not really autonomous, but are interrelated. It is at the social level that the systemic nature of the cinema stands out most clearly. Film content does not appear by magic, but as a result of the film production process; audiences do not make choices among films at random, but on the expectation of being pleased or edified in certain ways; producers do not make films at random, but on the basis of audience feedback.

As was pointed out at the beginning of this chapter, films have long fascinated historians, sociologists, and others as a source of insight into aspects of society otherwise hidden from view. It should now be clear, however, that the relationship between the films of a given era and the "society" within which they were produced and consumed is both complex and uncertain. Once the historian attempts to put into practice the long-held notion that films are somehow privileged social documents, he or she discovers just how problematic such a seemingly commonsensical assertion really is. To ask What does this film or group of films reveal about society? is also to ask, among other things, Who saw these films? How are films read? What is the relationship between the movie audience and "society" in general? How do people decide to see one film and not another? And even, Is society a thing about which we can talk in any useful historical terms at all? The promise held by *From Caligari to Hitler* is no less tantalizing after nearly forty years, but the fundamental questions it raises have by no means been neatly answered.

CASE STUDY: THE ROLE OF THE STAR IN FILM HISTORY

If social film history has not produced a simple, universally recognized formula for extracting the social meaning from films, it has engaged in the less ambitious but more achievable task of identifying, describing, and understanding some of the social dimensions of film history. It is one of these dimensions, stardom, that will be discussed in the case study for this chapter. Using an approach adapted from that of Richard Dyer in his book *Stars*,[30] this case study asks, How have movie stars been social phenomena? and How can any particular star be studied historically?

What Is a Star?

Since the early 1910s, the movie star has been one of the defining characteristics of the American cinema. Stars have also been and continue to be prominent features of other national cinemas as well—from Berlin to Bombay. In the early 1920s it is quite probable that Mary Pickford and Douglas Fairbanks were the most famous living people in the world. For well over a half a century, the smallest details of the off-screen lives of stars have been broadcast (both literally and figuratively) to millions.

The term "star," now applied to rock stars, athletes, and soap opera actors, has been so overused as to become almost meaningless. Viewed in terms of film history, however, we can define the constituent elements of stardom more precisely. At its most basic, the concept of stardom would seem to involve a duality between actor and character. To audiences of *Casablanca*, Humphrey Bogart *is* the character Rick, but he is also the actor Humphrey Bogart *playing* the character of Rick. In *Les Stars*, sociologist Edgar Morin defines a star as the combination of screen role and actor, of filmic persona and off-screen personality. "Once the film is over, the actor becomes an actor again, the character remains a character, but from their union is born a composite creature who participates in both, envelops them both: the star."[31] In this sense, stars are, to use the terminology of Chapter 4, actors "with biographies." In some cases (Jayne Mansfield or Brigette Bardot, for example) their "biographies" almost completely overshadow their "works." Essential to the concept of stardom, says Morin, is that the stars' private lives must be public.

It is also clear that the public does not "know" a star's off-screen personality directly, but only certain representations of that star mediated through a variety of sources: the films themselves and their attendant publicity materials, gossip columns, interviews, newspaper articles, and so on. What the public knows, in short, is not the star as a person, but rather the star as an image. To Dyer, a star is a "structured polysemy": "the finite multiplicity of meanings and affects they [stars] embody and the attempt so to structure them so that some meanings and affects are foregrounded and others masked or displaced."[32]

Stars, then, are complex images containing multiple meanings. Their polysemic (literally: many-meaning) nature enables different people to see different things in the image of a particular star. However, the star image is not a random jumble of representations and qualities open to any interpretation. It is a *structured* polysemy, the decoding of which is conditioned by the reinforcement of some aspects of the image and the suppression of others. Thus the social film historian derives the image of a star from the texts that collectively embody that image, not for the purpose of determining the "correct" meaning of that star, but rather to determine how the image has been structured, the range of possible meanings at any given time, and the changes that might have occurred to that image over time. This type of historical analysis leaves aside the important but more difficult question of how the various possible meanings of a star are used by various groups within society (how, for example, the meanings of Marilyn Monroe might have been different for men and women), but it does enable us to better understand what meanings were available *to be used* by individuals and groups within society at a point in history.

It is clear that stars form an aesthetic intertext that audiences use to derive meaning and pleasure from films, but we have not yet addressed the question of what makes stars *social phenomena* as well. Several writers on the subject have made the case that stars exist because they crystalize in their personae certain collective needs, dreams, fantasies, and obsessions. To Richard Griffith, for example, stars are "made" "in the depths of the collective unconscious." According to this view, studying the most popular stars of a particular era would reveal to us something of the inner workings of society—a desire for innocence in the 1910s as evidenced by the meteoric ascendancy of Mary Pickford, or, perhaps, repressed rebelliousness in the 1950s expressed by Marlon Brando. While startypes have changed over time, the assumption that this change is a direct result of changes in the "collective unconscious" is just that—an assumption. As an assumption it begs many of the same questions (because it makes the same basic claim) as *From Caligari to Hitler*; nor is the mechanism by which stars are empowered to express the inner workings of society any more clear.[33]

Dyer's analysis of stardom is basically Marxist. Hollywood films, he says, are produced within and convey the dominant ideology of Western society. Like any dominant ideology, that of Western society establishes itself not as *one* way of looking at the world acting in the interests of *one* class in society, but rather as *the* natural and consensual assumptions of the entire society. In order to maintain the status quo (its dominance), the dominant ideology must deny the validity or relevance of opposing ideologies and continually disguise or displace its own inevitable contradictions. These contradictions arise from the fact that the dominant ideology must always appear to be that which it never is: the one "correct" world view equally valid for all members of society.

The overall ideological function of the movie star is to help preserve the status quo and thereby the power of the dominant ideology. The star image represents to Dyer an attempt to manage, mask, or displace some of the contradictions inherent in the dominant ideology; it renders fundamental problems unproblematic, defuses possible threats to the dominant ideology, and makes social-class issues appear to be personal ones. Dyer recognizes that not all star images successfully reconcile their oppositions and that some stars' images can even be read as subversive (Mae West or James Dean, for example), but these, he says, are exceptional cases.

One does not have to share Dyer's Marxism to see his formulation of the star (as polysemic image structured around a set of contradictions) as a useful starting point for the historical analysis of stardom and individual star-images. Non-Marxist sociologist Francesco Alberoni views the notion of stardom as inherently anomolous and contradictory. Stars constitute a "powerless elite," in that their actual political or social power is almost nonexistent, but their "charisma" enables them to be the objects of tremendous public fascination. Furthermore, he says, stars are idolized but not resented. They enjoy wealth and prestige far beyond that of their fans, but because the social position of stardom is, theoretically at least, open to all, even stars' most outrageous extravagances do not provoke the antagonism of their fans.

Nearly every scholar who has investigated the phenomenon has commented on the set of paradoxes that lie at the basis of stardom. The star is powerless, yet powerful; different from "ordinary" people, yet at one time was "just like us." Stars make huge salaries, yet the work for which they are handsomely paid does not appear to be work on the screen. Talent would seem to be a requisite for stardom, yet there has been no absolute correlation between acting ability and stardom. The star's private life has little if anything to do with his or her "job" of acting in movies, yet a large portion of a star's image is constructed on the basis of "private" matters: romance, marriage, tastes in fashion, and home life.

These and other paradoxes or contradictions are by their very nature social. The individual star image—ostensibly a single member of society—provides a convenient focus for a set of issues that reverberate within the society as a whole: success, wealth, romance, "acceptable" social behavior, and consumption, among others. This is not to say that an individual star-image somehow reflects the hidden desires of an entire society, but as structured polysemies, stars do form a social as well as an aesthetic discourse. Within this social discourse of stardom, the historian can see certain social tensions or paradoxes or contradictions (depending on one's viewpoint) at work. Dyer sees the very concept of stardom as organized around the themes of success, consumption, and romance. These themes or social issues provide a consistent framework within which any given star-image is constructed. Obviously, each star-image structures these themes differently and might involve other themes as well—for example, in the case of Garbo, the desire of a "public" figure to have a private life; in the cases of Jane Fonda and Ronald Reagan, the overt political dimensions of stardom.

How does the film historian go about reconstituting the image of a particular star? According to Dyer, the star image is embodied in four categories of texts: (1) promotion, (2) publicity, (3) films, and (4) criticism and commentary. In examining the role each plays in establishing and maintaining the star persona, we will draw examples from the star-image of Joan Crawford, whose career spanned more than forty years (1926–1970) and eighty films. In the words of her filmographer, she was "a typically American film star."[33] Obviously, space does not allow a full consideration of the Crawford image (a fascinating task yet to be tackled), rather the references below are meant merely as illustrations of more general points.

Promotion

Dyer defines promotion as "texts which are produced as part of the deliberate creation/manufacture of a particular image or image context for a particular star." Promotional materials would include those designed to establish the general contours of the star persona (studio press releases, posed photographs arranged for and distributed by the studio, and public appearances), plus advertising matter accompanying particular films of that star (advertisements, lobby cards, posters, and trailers).

The enormous amount of control the Hollywood studios exercised over the creation of the star persona in the 1920s and 1930s was given legal sanction through the terms of the standard actor's contract. The actor's agreement to "act, pose, sing, speak or otherwise appear and perform solely and exclusively" for the contracting studio was only the beginning of the actor's commitment to the studio and the studio's power to fashion, change, and exploit his or her public image. The contract barred the actor from making any public or private appearance in any way connected with the movies, sound recording, or the theater, *and* from engaging in any other occupation without the written consent of the studio.

When sound was innovated in the late 1920s, contracts were amended to allow the studio to substitute the voice of another person for that of the actor under contract. The actor agreed not only to act in films over whose selection he or she had no control, but to promote these films through personal appearance tours arranged by the studio. The actor relinquished to the studio all control over the use of his or her name and physical likeness, which the studio could use in advertising, publicity (whether or not connected with the actor's films), or even to sell other products through advertising "tie-ins." Bette Davis described her legal battles against the studio contract system in the late 1930s as

> . . . a fight against slavery from the standpoint that, according to the standard motion picture contracts of the day, I could be forced to do anything the studio told me to do. They could even ask a contract player to appear in a burlesque house. The only recourse was to refuse, and then you were suspended without pay. These original documents were so one-sided in favor of the studio that . . . when under suspension from your contract, with no salary, you could not even work in a five-and-dime store. You could only starve, which of necessity often made you give in to the demands of the studio.[34]

Perhaps most indicative of the power of the studio to create a star-image out of the "raw material" provided by the actor is this paragraph from a typical studio contract of 1936.

> The Producer [studio] shall have the privilege at all times during the term of this contract, or any extensions thereof, to change the name of the Artist [actor] from time to time and at its discretion to such professional name or names as the Producer might think best, and should the Producer use a professional name for the Artist in connection with any pictures produced hereunder the Producer shall be entitled to at all times use such professional name or names, even after the expiration of this contract and after any and all extensions thereof, it being the intention of the parties hereto that any professional name used by the Artist during his term of employment hereunder shall be a property right belonging exclusively to the Producer and in which no one other than the Producer shall have any right, title or interest.[35]

When Joan Crawford arrived in Hollywood in January of 1925, her name was Lucille Le Sueur. It was as Lucille Le Sueur that she signed a contract with MGM for $75 per week (which obligated her to the studio for five years but obligated the studio to her for only six months at a time), and that she appeared in her first two films. When she was cast in her first major role opposite child-star Jackie Coogan, the MGM publicity department decided that her name did not "fit." At this early point in Le Sueur/Crawford's career it was unclear what her image would be, but fairly clear what it would *not* be. She would not be molded as the exotic foreign beauty—as was Greta Garbo, who also signed with MGM in 1925. Le Sueur's dancing ability, photographic image as the active "modern girl," and initial screen role as the poor but wholesome friend of Jackie Coogan lent themselves more to the creation of an "All-American" persona. "Lucille Le Sueur" was too foreign in its connotation, and the MGM publicity department feared fans would find it too difficult to spell and pronounce. However, rather than simply give her a more appropriate name and present it to the public as a *fait accompli*, MGM decided to allow the public to help "create" one of its stars by selecting Le Sueur's new name.

Through an article in *Movie Weekly*, MGM offered fans an opportunity to win $1000 by suggesting the best new name for Lucille Le Sueur. Even at this early stage in the creation of Crawford's persona there were the outlines of an image of which her name was to be a part. Readers of the *Movie Weekly* article were told that she "is an auburn-haired, blue-eyed beauty . . . of French and Irish descent. Second only to her career is her interest in athletics and she devotes much of her spare time to swimming and tennis." She had been selected by MGM executives from among hundreds of young women in New York as the one who best personified the "ideal young American girl of today." Le Sueur herself, the article said, was "thrilled" by the prospect of a new name and would "personally favor one which is easy to pronounce and spell and also easy to re-member." "Joan Crawford" was the name given to Lucille Le Sueur, despite the fact that she objected to it so much that she introduced herself for several years as "Jo-Ann" Crawford.[36]

Lucille Le Sueur before she became Joan Crawford (1925).
MGM offered fans the opportunity to win $1000 by
suggesting the best new name for this star.

The Museum of Modern Art/Film Stills Archive

Publicity

Dyer defines publicity as publicly disseminated material on stars that does not appear to be directly promotional. Publicity would include star interviews, stories about a star's private life and plans, and gossip column items. Obviously there is considerable leakage between the two categories. Articles about stars were frequently "planted" by studio publicity departments, and interviews were (and are) often arranged by the studio as a pretext for promoting the star's latest film. As Dyer points out, however, the importance of publicity in generating the star-image lies in its *appearance* of being uncontrolled by the studio and hence of being more authentic. Publicity, as Dyer uses the term, is material generated in the "news" coverage of the star as celebrity. Through publicity we like to think we are able to pierce through the facade constructed for the star by the studio and get at the inside and unauthorized details of the star's persona—hence the exposé quality of much star publicity.

Although a full examination of the publicity devoted to Crawford between her signing with MGM in 1925 and and her death in 1977 is well beyond the scope of this study, a look at the articles published on her in *Photoplay* during her tenure at MGM (1925–1943) helps to establish the framework, at least, within which the Crawford image was constructed.

Veteran Hollywood reporter and gossip columnist Louella Parsons is quoted as saying that Crawford "manufactured herself," that she "drew up a blueprint, decided what she wanted to look like and sound like, and then put that person into existence."[37] The manner in which Crawford received her name testifies to the fact that she was by no means solely responsible for the creation of her star persona. However, in the articles on and interviews with Crawford in *Photoplay* in the 1920s and 1930s it is clear that the idea of the "self-made star" becomes one of the structuring elements of the Crawford image.

It took several years for a distinctive Crawford image to emerge. Initially, her persona was fashioned in terms of the "flapper": the modern American young woman who was carefree, single, fun-loving, and, in terms of the 1920s at least, "liberated." Paramount's Clara Bow enjoyed considerable success playing flapper roles in several films of the mid-1920s, and Crawford was represented as a Clara Bow "type." A fan magazine described her in 1926 as

> ...the symbol of everything the younger generation is supposed to be. You look at her and automatically stock phrases come to mind: bobbed hair—rolled stocking —defiance—topless roadsters...."Hey-Hey"—jazz—short skirts—slang—little hats banged over one eye—high heels and all the rest.[38]

Crawford's image as the "Hey-Hey Girl" was solidified by frequent mention in gossip columns of her penchant for dancing and by her role as "Dangerous Diana," the quintessential flapper in *Our Dancing Daughters* (1928). The success of Crawford in that film lifted her out of the ranks of contract-players and established her as a potential star.

The year 1928 also marks the beginning of the process by which Crawford became an individuated star-image—a persona distinguishable from the "type" to which it might have once belonged. The more negative facets of Crawford's flapper image (harding-drinking, fun-loving, reckless, cynical) were quickly suppressed and a set of more positive qualities took their place. Crawford became an object lesson in perseverance and proof that strength of character could overcome all material obstacles. In the fall of 1928, *Photoplay* ran a three-part autobiography of Crawford, "The Story of a Dancing Girl," in which she describes a "childhood as cheerless as any depicted by Charles Dickens," degrading jobs as a chorus girl, navigating her way through "a cesspool of all licentiousness" on Broadway, and, finally, the screen test that resulted in her MGM contract and a chance for stardom. From all accounts it does appear that Crawford's early years were miserable. Her father left the family while she was but an infant. Her mother was forced to put Crawford to work in a boarding school at the age of ten, where she was overworked and mistreated.

The truth or falsity of the events related in these and subsequent accounts of Crawford's life is not at issue here. What is important in terms of the image of Joan Crawford is how the revelation of events of her life functioned to help structure her public persona. Positing Crawford's dogged determination and indomitable spirit as reasons for her rapid rise to stardom helped to offset the devil-may-care aspects of her persona, which her on- and off-screen escapades had foregrounded. The first installment of the *Photoplay* series was headlined, "Every ambitious girl who is struggling for success against odds should read this story of Joan Crawford's brave fight."[39]

This shift in Crawford's image in 1928 also prepared her public for the announcement of her engagement to Douglas Fairbanks, Jr.—an announcement made in the final installment of the *Photoplay* series. Fairbanks, son of the famous silent film star and stepson of Mary Pickford, belonged to the most socially prominent family in Hollywood and one of the most famous families in the world. Fairbanks and Pickford regularly entertained diplomats, royalty, and powerful industrialists. They were the very embodiment of propriety, rectitude, and status. As Crawford the "Hey-Hey Girl," whose highly publicized engagement to a Detroit meat-packing heir had been ended by the objections of his mother, and who had been named as correspondent in several divorces, she made an incongruous match for the urbane and well-connected Fairbanks. However, as Crawford the star, undeterred by a tragic past, her marriage to Fairbanks seemed a fitting reward for her struggles. Crawford (through her ghost writer, Ruth Biery) wrote in the concluding installment,

> I have said that I would never marry. . . . But then I had not met the man I wanted to marry. I made that statement in all honesty. But there is always one man who answers every need for a woman. I am going to marry Douglas Fairbanks, Jr. This is an announcement of our engagement.

The contradiction in Crawford's image between the values represented by the "Hey-Hey Girl" and those of the wife of Douglas Fairbanks, Jr., was addressed directly in a 1931 *Photoplay* article entitled "Why They Said Joan was 'High Hat,' " by Katherine Albert. Albert defends Crawford against charges that her success as an actor and her marriage to Fairbanks had made her an elitist snob. Crawford's flapper manifestation, says Albert, was merely indicative of the difficulty anyone would have in adjusting to life in Hollywood, especially someone whose recent past had been one of "keen misery." What Crawford needed at this time was someone who could see through her veneer of gaiety to "the deep, latent powers of the girl, the fine uncultivated brain she had."

This process of self-realization was begun by MGM producer Paul Bern, who taught her "the beauty of words on paper, the feeling for musical harmony, the appreciation of form and color upon canvas." The transformation begun under Bern's tutelage was now being completed by Fairbanks, she says, so that "today Joan Crawford is no more Lucille Le Sueur than Will Rogers is Mahatma Gandhi." In short, as Mrs. Douglas Fairbanks, Crawford is a new person who has "done everything to improve herself."[40]

Even as one contradiction is "resolved" by this article, however, another is exposed. Crawford's metamorphosis is seen as both the result of self-creation ("Joan has become a woman. . . . She has done everything to improve herself.") *and*, at the same time, as the product of the shaping influence of some other, significantly male person. The Pygmalion analogy is nearly explicit in the final line of the article: "Her loyalty to those who have stood by her and gloried for her in her blossoming is like some fine marble statue." This self-made/ "man"-made dichotomy is also present in the autobiographical essays and recurs throughout publicity on Crawford through the 1930s. Describing her decision to leave Kansas City for a stage career, Crawford speaks in the 1928 *Photoplay* series of having to leave behind her sweetheart, the only person to have faith in her dancing abilities:

> How often does ambition force a woman to face such a separation? Yet, if she subjugates her career for a man, she may spend the rest of her life wondering to what heights she might have climbed had she followed her inclinations. And if she goes, there comes a time when she wonders if, after all, home and innocence-of-the-world might not have meant a more pacific, happy existence.

The implication of the above—reinforced by Crawford's screen persona of the 1930s—is that a woman is doomed either way. Except, perhaps, in Hollywood. Publicity on Crawford's marriages (to Fairbanks in 1929, Franchot Tone in 1935, Phillip Terry in 1943, and Alfred Steele in 1955) emphasizes her domesticity (she waxes her own floors, makes some of her own clothes) and the role played by her current husband in expanding her horizons. In a 1936 *Photoplay* article Tone is given almost the identical role as that played by Fairbanks in Crawford's development. Crawford is quoted as saying, "He began showing me things in books and music that I'd never known were there. It was like a new world opening before me. . . . It was as if I'd been hungry all my life without-realizing it, and now I was being fed."[41] Articles on Crawford's married life mask the tensions between ambition and marriage (as seen by 1930s society) by suggesting that in Crawford's case the latter aids in the realization of the former.

Especially during the times in the 1930s when Crawford was not married (1933–1935 and 1938–1943) the self-made, independent woman side of her image reasserts itself in publicity on her. A 1935 *Photoplay* profile begins, "She had carved a monumental career out of nothing. She had satisfied a consuming inner demand to be somebody." It goes on to describe how her every spare minute is spent improving herself through dance lessons, experimental drama performances in her backyard theater, and operatic voice training. Interestingly, she is depicted here as Tone's mentor: "She even started [him] . . . singing, thereby uncovering a very impressive basso-profundo voice."[42]

By the mid-1930s, Crawford had become not only the self-made star, but the regenerating star. Each new marriage, phase of her career, and avocational interest was seen as evidence of Crawford's unique power to transform herself to meet whatever new set of demands presented itself. In the accounts of her self-renewals there is both an invocation and an erasure of her past. For example, in "Adela Rogers St. Johns Presents Joan Crawford Starring in 'The Dramatic Rise of a Self-Made Star,' " a three-part *Photoplay* series of 1937, St. Johns once again tells the story of Crawford's early tribulations, explaining Crawford's continuing success in terms of the "instincts" she developed as a child. Each "new" Crawford is but another facet of the ever-struggling Lucille Le Sueur:

> You're a great movie star, but you're a great person because you, alone and
> unaided, pulled yourself up by your bootstraps, you aspired to better things, you
> dreamed better dreams, and you made them come true. If you'd always been just
> what you are today, you couldn't possibly be so closely identified with us, with all
> that's American in us, with all that's human in us.

In a 1935 article, however, Crawford is described as "the girl without a past," in the sense that her longevity derives from her unique ability to escape from the past: "Every phase of Joan is a stranger to the last one."[43]

Films

As Dyer points out, the films of stars are frequently "star vehicles," in that the film has been fashioned to provide a character or genre associated with its star. Certainly in the 1930s, Hollywood studios attempted to "fit" a property to the image of their biggest stars. Warner Bros., for example, continually had difficulty finding the "right" films for Bette Davis, in part because she did not conform to any existing star-type.[44]

By the mid-1930s Joan Crawford had become identified with one cinematic genre, the woman's film, which drew from and reinforced her star-image. As

Jeanine Bassinger has defined it, the woman's film focuses on a contemporary woman as its central character. The plots of these films, staples of Hollywood production in the 1930s and 1940s, concerned

> . . . women who were struggling to get on their own two feet. Then when they got on them, they struggled to forge ahead and struggled some more to get on top. After they got on top, they struggled with themselves and their guilts. Finally, society overcame them. They went down struggling, found "true love," and prepared to resume life's struggle in a state that was acceptable to society.[45]

The woman's film was also designed to appeal to a female audience. Within the woman's film genre, the role played most often by Joan Crawford was the "independent" woman: the woman who through choice or circumstance was forced to survive in modern society on her own. Her social station varied from film to film. She was a prostitute in *Rain* (1932), a maid in *Sadie McKee* (1934), and a factory worker in *Possessed* (1931), but a wealthy socialite in *Letty Lynton* (1932), *No More Ladies* (1935), *I Live My Life* (1935), *Love on the Run* (1936), and *The Last of Mrs. Cheyney* (1937). The nature of her dilemma, however, did not change. Her problems were what were thought to be "women's problems" in the 1930s: finding the "right" man, being in love with the "wrong" man, raising children, and earning a living in a "man's world." Bassinger argues that the "message" of these films was that a woman who achieved economic or sexual power did so at the expense of her ability to have a meaningful relationship with a man. Thus in many of the woman's films what the heroine strives so hard to achieve is given up at the end of the film in favor of the "happy ending": a chance to be a traditional wife and mother. Audiences, Bassinger says, "felt reassured by the endings in which the woman they admired on screen told them that what they had was better than what they had just enjoyed watching." Crawford's own image provided a "happy ending" to her films even where their narratives did not, and the constant reiteration of Crawford's own early struggles in publicity about her no doubt made her screen roles all the more convincing. It is unnecessary (not to mention simplistic) to draw point-to-point correspondences between the woman's film heroines Crawford played and her off-screen persona; however, it is clear that both were structured around the same themes: the "choice" between career and romance, finding the "right" man, climbing the social ladder—in short, asking the question, How independent can a woman be and at what price?

Crawford's woman's film roles are related to her more general star-image iconographically as well as narratively. As Joanne Yeck has pointed out, visually the woman's film genre was singularly uninnovative, occupying a position near the most conservative pole of the classical Hollywood narrative style. The pace of the woman's film was slow, locales confined to interior spaces, and actions limited to dialogue.[46] The stylistic featurelessness of the woman's film functioned to focus attention on the star's face *and* costume. Kay Francis, the Warner Bros. woman's film star of the early 1930s, remarked of one of her vehicles, "If [it]...does better than my other films, it's because I parade thirty-six costumes instead of sixteen."[47] Similarly, by the mid-1930s, Crawford had become, in the vernacular of the industry, a "clothes-horse," and her wardrobe frequently drew more (and more positive) critical response than her acting. *Motion Picture Herald* wrote of *Letty Lynton* (1932), "The gowns which Miss Crawford wears will be the talk of your town for weeks after...." *Chained* (1934), in which Crawford appeared in a different dress and hairstyle in almost every scene, prompted the *New York Times* critic to remark, "Miss Crawford adds to the general attractiveness of...this offering by an unusually extensive wardrobe and a variety of changes in her coiffure."[48]

Crawford became associated with a single "look": heavily lined eyes, emphasized cheekbones, dramatically outlined and darkened lips, and, especially, the square-shouldered dresses and "masculine" tailored suits designed for her by MGM's top designer, Adrian. Crawford's costumes provided an appropriate visual correlative to the "independent woman" character she so frequently played. Visually, if not narratively, her heroines overwhelmed their male counterparts. Less remembered about Crawford's screen iconography is the fact that

"The Clothes Horse": Joan Crawford in the 1930s

The Museum of Modern Art/Film Stills Archive

her look "above the neck" changed enormously from film to film. She wore her hair in almost every conceivable style, length, and color. Her eyebrows went from narrow, plucked, and penciled in the early 1930s to full and heavily darkened in *Mildred Pierce* (1945). The platinum-blonde Crawford of *This Modern Age* (1931) looks no more than a distant relative of the Crawford in *The Bride Wore Red* (1937). Thus while Crawford's roles helped to anchor her "independent woman" image, the changes she was able to effect in her very appearance from film to film contributed to the notion of self-regeneration found in publicity representations of her in the 1930s. Crawford constantly seemed to be making herself over on-screen and off.

Criticism and Commentary

Dyer defines this category as appreciations or interpretations of the star's performances. Included would be reviews, books and articles on the star's films, obituaries, and media profiles of the star's work. Although reviewers and critics frequently work for the same media industries that promote and publicize stars, their role in the construction of the star-image is distinctive in that they appear to be speaking on behalf of the audience. Their voice is that of response to an image rather than, ostensibly at least, creation of it. For this reason, says Dyer, criticism helps to add complexity to the star-image and helps to account for changes in public reception of a star. Criticism can also act back upon both promotion and publicity. Favorable reviews might influence the selection of future star vehicles or co-stars. Critics might pick up on one aspect of a star's screen performance, which is then foregrounded in publicity materials.

Until the late 1940s, Joan Crawford's screen performances received much less critical attention than those of her contemporary stars. For the most part, the films she appeared in were not highly regarded by critics. As has been noted, the style of the woman's film was invisible, and films of that genre were seldom adapted from critically acclaimed novels or plays. The public appeal of Crawford's films was seen by critics to be based on her screen presence and wardrobe rather than on any extraordinary acting ability.

Ironically, the most important "review" Crawford received in the 1930s came not from a critic per se but rather from a poll of theater owners. In May of 1938 the trade paper *Hollywood Reporter* ran the results of a survey conducted of the membership of the Independent Theatre Owners Association. In it, she (along with Mae West, Greta Garbo, and Katharine Hepburn) was voted "box-office poison," meaning that her star status and correspondingly high salary were unjustified by ticket sales of her films. One of the top ten box-office attractions each year between 1933 and 1936, Crawford had declined in popularity by 1938. Critics complained that the films she was given by MGM were hackneyed and her roles stale—a view she privately shared. Crawford's biographer argues the MGM studio head Louis B. Mayer believed the public to be tired of the older stars on his roster (Crawford, Garbo, Norma Shearer) and wanted to replace them with fresh faces (Judy Garland, Lana Turner, Hedy Lamarr, and Greer Garson). The "box-office poison" designation gave him all the more reason to invest more in the company's younger stars and consign Crawford and other "declining" MGM luminaries to the oblivion of program pictures. Crawford asked to be released from her MGM contract in 1943 and signed with Warner Bros. For two years she did not appear on the screen, waiting for the appropriate vehicle to serve as her first non-MGM film.

The film she finally did agree to make in 1945 was *Mildred Pierce*, based on the 1941 James M. Cain novel. During her hiatus, Crawford had hired a new agent. Even before shooting on the film was finished, he planted the rumor among gossip columnists that Crawford's performance was such that she was sure to be nominated for an academy award. By the time *Mildred Pierce* was released in October 1945, Crawford was being prominently mentioned as an Oscar candidate, and, as Bob Thomas, Crawford's biographer, puts it, "reviewers joined the bandwagon" by lauding her performance.[49] In the spring of 1946, Crawford vindicated the self-appointed prophets of her success by winning the "Best Actress" award.

At issue here is not the merit of Crawford's acting or whether the Oscar was "deserved," but how both the charge that she was poison at the box office and the accolades given her performance in *Mildred Pierce* functioned in her overall star-image. At the time, the "poison" label seemed to many to signal the end of Crawford's career. In 1938 Crawford had been appearing in films for more than a decade, outlasting most of the stars whose careers had begun before the introduction of sound. Furthermore, at age thirty-two she was considerably older than the top female stars of the day (Shirley Temple, Sonja Henie, Alice Faye, and Myrna Loy), and the ingenue roles most female stars were expected to play became less plausible for Crawford with each passing year.

With the critical success of *Mildred Pierce*, however, the "poison" episode was integrated into the Crawford image as one more obstacle she had been able to overcome. Crawford had done it again, triumphed against all odds, renewed herself once again—this time Phoenix-like out of the ashes of her nearly extinguished career. Columnist Louella Parsons wrote in *Photoplay* that "the too-plump chorus girl, who had come here twenty years ago and who had known triumph and defeat in that time, had come back after two years of idleness to be crowned queen of them all!" Parsons could not help but remind readers that even in this moment of Crawford's greatest success she was undergoing yet another tragedy, her divorce from Phillip Terry.[50]

CONCLUSIONS

This case study has merely hinted at the complex polysemy that is the image of a star such as Joan Crawford. Stars do not reflect society in some magical but straightforward way; rather, they embody in their images certain paradoxes or contradictions inherent in the larger social formation. In the case of Crawford these contradictions involve notions of success and how it might be achieved, and expectations about women and their roles in society. Dyer's formulation of promotion, publicity, films, and commentary provide the film historian with a means of locating the star image, examining it in its complexity, and charting changes over time.

Recognition of the star as a "structured polysemy" also suggests something of the complexity of social film history in general. Of the four traditional categories of film historical research, social film history presents the greatest challenge. Since films were first publicly shown in the 1890s, the film viewing situation has represented the point of convergence for three distinct social processes: that which produced the film on the screen, that which brought the audience to the theater, and the process of social representation occurring on the screen within the filmic text. Hence, the seemingly straightforward questions posed at the beginning of this chapter (Who made the movies and why? and so forth) lead inevitably from this point of convergence in the movie theater outward to larger social processes and institutions.

By multiplying the social event enacted at every public film screening by the number of those screenings since 1896 and then by the number of persons participating in them over the past ninety years, we can begin to sense the dimensions of the social phenomenon film production and reception represent. To this must be added our encounters with "the movies" outside the theater: reportage, publicity, advertisements, and the promotion of stars, among other forms of discourse about the movies. The scope of social film history is not limited to these aspects, however, for we have yet to consider the social dynamics of the typical viewing situation in most countries of the world for most of the course of film history: an audience from one culture confronting a filmic text produced not within and for its own culture, but imported from abroad.

The enormous popularity of the movies throughout the world and their centrality as a form of entertainment and leisure activity in Western culture for nearly a century have long tempted film and cultural historians to construct grand explanations of our fascination with the movies and to regard films as coded messages from the cultural unconscious. However, the complexity of the social processes involved in film production and reception precludes easy generalizations. Nowhere is the "open system" quality of the film historian's object of study more apparent than in social film history.

NOTES

1. Walter Prichard Eaton, *American Magazine* (September 1909): 498, quoted in Robert E. Davis, *Response to Innovation: A Study of Popular Argument About New Mass Media* (New York: Arno Press, 1976), p. 15.

2. Hugo Munsterberg, *Good Housekeeping* (April 1910), quoted in Davis, *Response to Innovation*, p. 184; see also, Hugo Munsterberg, *Film: A Psychological Study* (New York: Dover, 1970), p. 94.

3. Ian Jarvie, *Movies and Society* (New York: Basic Books, 1970), p. 14.

4. Andrew Tudor, *Image and Influence* (New York: St. Martins, 1974), p. 43.

5. Robert Sklar, *Movie-Made America* (New York: Random House, 1976), p. vi; and Lewis Jacobs, *The Rise of the American Film* (New York: Teachers College Press, 1939).

6. Bosley Crowther, *The Hollywood Rajah* (New York: Holt, Rinehart and Winston, 1960); Charles Higham, *Warner Brothers* (New York: Charles Scribner's Sons, 1975); Bob Thomas, *King Cohn* (New York: Putnam, 1967); and Tino Balio, *United Artists* (Madison: University of Wisconsin Press, 1975).

7. Leo Rosten, *Hollywood: The Movie Colony, the Movie Makers* (New York: Harcourt, Brace, 1941); and Hortense Powdermaker, *Hollywood the Dream Factory* (Boston: Little, Brown, 1950).

8. Lillian Ross, *Picture* (New York: Rinehart, 1952); Donald Knox, *The Magic Factory: How MGM Made "An American in Paris"* (New York: Praeger, 1973); and Dore Schary, *Case Study of a Movie* (New York: Random House, 1950).

9. Tudor, *Image and Influence*, p. 78.

10. Herbert Blumler, "Collective Behavior," in *New Outline of the Principles of Sociology*, A. M. Lee, ed., quoted in Jarvie, *Movies and Society*, p. 89.

11. Molly Haskell, *From Reverence to Rape* (New York: Holt, Rinehart, Winston, 1974). See also, Marjorie Rosen, *Popcorn Venus* (New York: Coward, McCann, Geoghegan, 1973).

12. James P. Murray, *To Find an Image: Black Films from Uncle Tom to Super-Fly* (Indianapolis: Bobbs-Merrill, 1973). See also, Daniel Leab, *From Sambo to Superspade* (Boston: Houghton Mifflin, 1975); and Edward Mapp, *Blacks in American Films: Today and Yesterday* (Metuchen, N.J.: Scarecrow Press, 1971).

13. Thomas Cripps, *Slow Fade to Black* (New York: Oxford University Press, 1977).

14. Siegfried Kracauer, *From Caligari to Hitler* (Princeton, N.J.: Princeton University Press, 1947), p. v.

15. Kracauer outlines his method in the Introduction to *From Caligari to Hitler*, pp. 3–11.

16. Phil Slater, *Origins and Significance of the Frankfurt School: A Marxist Perspective* (London: Routledge, Kegan Paul, 1977), pp. 23–25. On the research program of the Frankfort School, see also, David Held, *Introduction to Critical Theory* (Berkeley: University of California Press, 1980).

17. Kracauer, *From Caligari to Hitler*, p. 272.

18. Andrew Bergman, *We're in the Money* (New York: New York University Press, 1970), pp. xi–xvii; and Paul Monaco, *Cinema and Society* (New York: Elsevier, 1976), pp. 1–16, 160.

19. David H. Fischer, *Historians' Fallacies* (New York: Harper and Row, 1974), p. 166.

20. William Aydelotte, "Quantification in History," *American Historical Review* 71 (April 1966): 805, reprinted with other of Aydelotte's essays on history in *Quantification in History* (Reading, Mass.: Addison-Wesley, 1971).

21. Dorothy B. Jones, "The Quantitative Analysis of Motion Picture Content," *Public Opinion Quarterly* 16 (1942): 411–428. See also, Edgar Dale, *The Content of Motion Pictures* (New York: Macmillan, 1935). For a work that attempts to wed the

methods of quantitative analysis of manifest movie content to a psychological theory that might explain that content, see Martha Wolfenstein and Nathan Leites, *Movies: a Psychological Study* (Glencoe, Ill.: The Free Press, 1950).

22. Wolfgang Iser, *The Act of Reading* (Baltimore: Johns Hopkins University Press, 1978), p. 61.

23. Anika Lemaire, *Lacan* (London: Routledge, Kegan Paul, 1977); and John P. Mueller and William J. Richardson, *Lacan and Language* (New York: International Universities Press, 1982), p. 6.

24. Colin McCabe, "Theory and Film: Principles of Realism and Pleasure," *Screen* 17 (Autumn 1976): 7–27.

25. Stephen Heath, *Questions of Cinema* (Bloomington: University of Indiana Press, 1981), p. 243.

26. Davis, *Response to Innovation*; Jonas Spatz, *Hollywood in Fiction: Some Versions of the American Myth* (Brussels: Mouton, 1969); and Larry Ceplair and Steven Englund, *The Inquisition in Hollywood* (New York: Anchor Press, 1980).

27. Hollywood's relationship with the CPI is discussed in a memoir written by its chairman, George Creel, *How We Advertised America* (New York: Harper and Row, 1920).

28. *Mutual Film Corporation v. Ohio.* Quoted in Richard Randall, *Censorship of the Movies* (Madison: University of Wisconsin Press, 1968), p. 19.

29. Cripps, *Slow Fade to Black*, pp. 360–388.

30. Richard Dyer, *Stars* (London: British Film Institute, 1979).

31. Edgar Morin, *Les Stars*, trans. Richard Howard (New York: Grove Press, 1960).

32. Dyer, *Stars*, p. 3.

33. Lawrence J. Quirk, *The Films of Joan Crawford* (New York: Citadel Press, 1974), p. 79.

34. Quoted in Whitney Stine, *Mother Goddam* (New York: Hawthorne Books, 1974), p. 79.

35. Contract between Warner Bros., Inc. and Olivia de Haviland, April 14, 1936, Warner Bros. Collection, University of Southern California. De Haviland managed to have this paragraph struck from her contract and thus preserved the right to keep her own name.

36. The *Movie Weekly* article is reproduced in Larry Carr, *Four Fabulous Faces* (New York: Penguin, 1978), pp. 224–225. See also, Bob Thomas, *Joan Crawford* (New York: Bantam Books, 1979), pp. 28–43.

37. Quoted in Carr, *Four Fabulous Faces*, p. 218.

38. Ibid., p. 232.

39. *Photoplay* (September 1928): 34. The other two installments appeared in the October (pp. 68–69, 114+) and November (pp. 42–43, 133) issues.

40. Katherine Albert, "Why They Said Joan Was 'High Hat,'" *Photoplay* (August 1931): 64–65, 112.

41. Ida Zeitlin, "Why Joan Crawford Remains Great," *Photoplay* (October 1936): 44–45, 96–97. See also, Dorothy Manners, "Second Marriage and Joan Crawford Tone," *Photoplay* (May 1936): 24–25, 122.

42. "The New Ambitions of Joan Crawford," *Photoplay* (February 1935): 76–77, 101. See also, "Fan Experiences with the Stars," *Photoplay* (December 1936): 16; and Frazier Hunt, "I Meet Miss Crawford," *Photoplay* (October 1934): 36–37, 114.

43. Adela Rogers St. Johns, "Adela Rogers St. Johns Presents Joan Crawford Starring in 'The Dramatic Rise of a Self-Made Star,' " *Photoplay* (October 1937): 26–27, 69–70; (November 1937): 64–65, 75–76; (December 1937); 70–71, 91. Dorothy Manners, "The Girl Without a Past," *Photoplay* (October 1935): 32–33, 56.

44. Joanne L. Yeck, "The Woman's Film at Warner Bros., 1935–1950," Ph.D. dissertation, University of Southern California, 1982, p. 48.

45. Jeanine Bassinger, "When Women Wept," *American Film* 2 (September 1977): 52–57.

46. Yeck, "The Woman's Film," p. 71.

47. Ibid., p. 47.

48. Quirk, *Films of Joan Crawford*, pp. 100, 113.

49. Thomas, *King Cohn*, pp. 135–138.

50. Louella Parsons, "You're Welcome, Joan," *Photoplay* (June 1946): 34–35, 128.

PART THREE

Doing Film
History

8

Writing
Film History

One of the premises of this book is that as a reader of film history, the more one understands about the process by which film history (and history in general) is researched and written, the more enjoyable one's study of the history of the cinema can become. There is no better way to assess the problems and opportunities presented by film historical research than to put oneself in the position of a writer of film history, to become (for however brief a time) a film historian. Obviously, some film historical tasks require access to rare films, business records, or production documentation. Such is *not* the case with local film history, however. Film historians in nearly any area can ask (and reasonably expect to answer): How did film function in a given community? Who owned the local movie house? What technology did it use? What films did it show? Were films ever censored?

In addition to making one a more discerning reader of film histories, conducting local film historical research has several other benefits. It is a large and hitherto virtually untapped source of original film historical investigation. Rather than merely sift through the interpretations of others, the local researcher has the opportunity to find and use a great variety of primary materials. Since so little has been done to document film-going at a local level, it is possible to make a contribution to the state of film historical knowledge. The accumulation of local histories should help reshape our thinking on vital questions of economic and social history. Also, as an important fringe benefit, local film histories not only yield information regarding the history of film, but can also lead to a more general understanding of a particular city or town: Where and how various groups of people lived, how and why cities developed as they did in the twentieth century, and what sorts of leisure and cultural activities were available to citizens at particular points in a city's history.

Of the four major avenues of film historical research—aesthetic, social, economic, and technological—at least three* can be pursued by the inexperienced researcher at the local level. For example:

How did movie exhibitors make money? Showing what films? At what prices? When? (*economic*)

What technology was used to show movies? How was technological change introduced into a community? What was the local response to technological change? (*technological*)

Where were movie theaters located in a community? Who went to the movies? How did patterns of movie going vary within a community and/or change over time? (*social*)

These might seem to be extremely elementary questions, but as most local researchers will quickly discover they have never been asked about a *particular locality*.

Three local film historical research projects comprise the rest of this chapter. They are presented not so much as paths to be followed, but as preliminary forays into the as yet virgin territory of local film history. They suggest a few of the research questions that might be posed, the sorts of local data available for use, and ways of interpreting these data.

PROJECT I
HISTORY OF TECHNOLOGICAL CHANGE:
THE TALKIES COME TO MILWAUKEE

Most historians of technological change in the cinema emphasize the origins of change. Less frequently asked is, How does the diffusion of technological change occur at the local level? Perhaps the most dramatic technological change in the history of American (and, for that matter, world) cinema was the advent of synchronous-sound films—the "talkies"—in the late 1920s. The impact of the coming of sound upon Hollywood film production has become the material of film historical legend: acting careers shattered and created "overnight," theater

---

*Aesthetic film history is omitted from this list not because it is irrelevant at the local level, but because generally it involves the use of data—prints of old films—that are much more difficult to locate. Also, while historically, movie-going in America admits of considerable variation between communities, the production of entertainment films in the United States since 1915, at least, has been a national rather than local phenomenon. The expense of producing films has for the most part precluded the making of local films for local audiences. It would be possible to study the production of newsreels on the local level as well as cine clubs and experimental films.

directors imported from New York by the train-car loads, studio fortunes made and lost. The analysis of the economics of Hollywood's conversion to sound in Chapter Five paints a more accurate picture than traditional accounts. Still to be asked is what happened to the "talkies" once they left Hollywood and entered local movie theaters across the country?

Many survey historians of the American cinema deal with this technological change at the local level in terms of a single event: the day (variously given as October 5, 6, and 24) when Al Jolson's voice burst forth from the movie screen at the Warner Theatre on Broadway in New York City in *The Jazz Singer*. The immediate success of this film on this day "marked the end of an era," says Arthur Knight in *The Liveliest Art*.[1] "The success of *The Jazz Singer*," says Gerald Mast, "ripped apart the film industry of 1927 with incredible speed."[2] This event has become so associated with the American audience's initial exposure to sound that the U.S. Postal Department issued a stamp commemorating its 50th anniversary in October 1977.

But what happened outside New York City—in, let us say, Milwaukee, Wisconsin? How and when did sound come to that midwestern city? For this project only one local data source will be used: the accounts of movie activities contained in a daily newspaper, *The Milwaukee Journal*. This self-imposed limit demonstrates how much a researcher can learn from even the most accessible materials. From this one source the historian can conclude that the coming of sound to Milwaukee was a more complex and gradual process than the "instant success" *The Jazz Singer* implies.

Sound came to Milwaukee not via *The Jazz Singer* nor in October 1927. Milwaukee audiences first heard voices emanating from the screen on September 3, 1927, when veteran Milwaukee showman L. K. Brin reopened the downtown Garden Theatre with a program of several short Vitaphone talking films and a feature film (*When A Man Loves*) with recorded musical track. In the first talking film presented that day, Motion Picture Producers and Distributors Association president Will Hays stood stiffly before the camera and congratulated Warner Bros., makers of the short films, and Western Electric, suppliers of the special equipment. The entertainment proper opened with popular vaudeville comics Van and Schenck in filmed versions of their best-known routines, followed by soprano Mary Lewis and tenor Giovanni Martinelli. The program concluded with the feature. Brin hoped the novelty of talking films would enable him to make a crack in the local exhibition monopoly held by the Saxe Bros. chain. Since the shorts took the place of the regular live stage show, and recordings provided accompaniment for the feature, Brin eliminated the need for a theater orchestra at, we can guess, a considerable savings.[3]

The *Journal's* unnamed reviewers praised the whole concept. They wrote the next day that the audience had cheered after Hays's first words and remained on the edge of their seats all night. The hit of the show was Martinelli, his recorded voice flowing crystal-clear across the house. "Milwaukee liked the Vitaphone," the *Journal's* reviewer concluded. "It would seem that the Vita-

phone is best in the particular medium of the dramatic song [Martinelli's aria]."
Brin's advertising stressed entertainment value to frugal Milwaukeeans: New
Yorkers paid $2.20 for the talkies, while the Garden charged only 50¢ for adults
and 25¢ for children.[4]

Throughout the fall of 1927 the Garden presented sound shorts and silent
feature films with a recorded musical accompaniment. The shorts provided
quite a draw. The most famous performers of the day appeared in them: Fred
Waring and his Pennsylvanians, George Jessel, Mischa Elman, John Charles
Thomas, Willie and Eugene Howard, and even Al Jolson. The Garden's advertisements proclaimed "Vitaphone is better than seeing the stars in person." It
certainly was cheaper—one-half of the price of admission to an evening show at
Milwaukee's Palace vaudeville theater.[5]

On December 31, 1927, Milwaukeeans finally were able to see *The Jazz
Singer*, nearly three months after its "historic" New York opening. Brin raised
prices to 50¢ for children and 75¢ for adults. Despite that fact and a typically fri-
gid Milwaukee January, *The Jazz Singer* made quite a hit: The Garden held it
over for an unprecedented four weeks. The *Journal's* legitimate theater critic,
Nancy Lee, praised the Vitaphone as a "wonder" of the screen. With it, she said,
great dramas could finally come forth from the motion picture screen.[6]

But then nothing! Could the Garden not get other Warners sound features,
and so reverted back to silent features and "Vitaphoned" vaudeville acts? If
there truly was a "revolution" in the coming of sound, Milwaukee was slow to
experience it. It wasn't until March 1928, a full five months after New York's
debut of *The Jazz Singer*, that Milwaukeeans saw *Solomon's Children*, "the first
all-synchronized two-reel feature." Later that month, the Garden added Movietone newsreels with sound. However, the first program of talking newsreels
shown at the Garden was hardly "news": It included speeches by Charles
Lindbergh and President Calvin Coolidge, recorded in June 1927.[7]

In late April *The Jazz Singer* returned to the Garden for two weeks. At the
end of that run (on May 6) Fox Theatres, owner of the biggest chain in the city,
announced an "all-sound film" policy at five of its larger (2000+ seats) neighborhood picture palaces. Fox would experiment with sound in these second-run
neighborhood houses and then, if it proved successful, go downtown. Work-
men labored from midnight to 9 A.M. for a full week to install the necessary
equipment, and on Sunday, May 13, 1928, sound came to the neighborhoods of
Milwaukee. For a Mother's Day special the Oriental, Garfield, Tower, Modjes-
ka and Uptown offered facsimiles of the Garden's more expensive downtown
shows: sound shorts with a silent (mechanical music accompaniment) film.
Milwaukee now had 6 of America's 300 theatres wired for sound.[8]

Total conversion to sound did not occur in Milwaukee until the fall of 1928,
a full year after the New York debut of *The Jazz Singer*. The Garden, with its
ties to Warner Bros., led the way. On July 20, 1928, it presented *Lights of New
York*, the first "all-talking" feature film, for a three-week engagement. In August the Garden became the first Milwaukee theater to switch completely to all-

sound movies.[9] In September the Fox chain, satisfied with the results of its sound policy in neighborhood theaters, converted its large downtown theaters to sound.

As one can see from this account, there is no "date" that signaled the coming of sound to Milwaukee. If we were forced to choose one, however, it would be September 22, 1928, not October 6, 1927. That date marks the adoption of an all-sound policy at Fox's Wisconsin theater, the largest in Milwaukee. If we were forced to choose *one* film to represent Milwaukee's acceptance of sound, it would be *The Singin' Fool*, Jolson's *second* film, and not his first (*The Jazz Singer*). *The Singin' Fool* played for an unprecedented six weeks at the Garden during the fall of 1928—L. K. Brin claiming that 400,000 citizens passed through the turnstiles during its engagement.

The fairly rapid conversion of the downtown theaters in the fall of 1928 and the success of "all-talking," "all-singing" features at these houses did not, however, mark the demise of the silent film in Milwaukee. Approximately 25 percent of Milwaukee's smaller neighborhood theaters continued showing silent films well into 1930.[10]

This brief exercise, based on information from but a single source, highlights the dynamics of technological change at the local level. It should also caution us against a sweeping generalization—however oft-repeated—concerning film exhibition. As we shall see again in another project, New York City is *not* the entire country. In Milwaukee, sound shorts seem to have fostered the changeover to sound. *The Jazz Singer* was popular, but most Milwaukeeans saw and heard vaudeville shorts months before they ever experienced feature-length sound films. If revolution means rapid, complete, and drastic change, then the term must be stretched considerably to apply to the coming of sound in Milwaukee. Over the course of a year one theater, then five more, introduced Milwaukee's moviegoers to sound movies. It took more than three years after Will Hays's voice was first heard in a Milwaukee theater for the conversion to sound to be completed.

PROJECT II
THE ECONOMICS OF LOCAL EXHIBITION: THEATER CHAINS

As with technological film history, most examinations of the American film industry have focused on Hollywood and the economics of film production. While much remains to be added to our understanding of the workings of the Hollywood studios, we know that the film industry in the United States has long been characterized by a high degree of economic concentration. That is, a few firms—by 1930 the five "major" studios and the three "minors"—controlled most of the market for commercial entertainment films. The power of this eight-member oligopoly originated in exhibition; in 1948 the Supreme Court found that it was through their control of large theaters in major cities that the studios maintained their monopoly power. Hollywood's control over exhibition was accomplished gradually between the 1910s and the 1930s. It was based largely on the purchase of local and regional chains or circuits of theaters. Ironically, then, Hollywood's steps toward vertical integration (control over production, distribution, and exhibition) were facilitated by local entrepreneurs' efforts in horizontal integration (the formation of individual theaters into chains). Despite the fact that circuit building was a phenomenon in most localities, we understand little about how theater chains developed and prospered.

Using publicly available documents (urban histories, government reports, trade papers, journal articles, and interviews), this local research project examined the rise of America's most powerful regional theater chain during the 1920s: Babalan and Katz (hereafter B&K) of Chicago.

From 1926 to 1946 Babalan and Katz completely controlled first-, second-, and third-run releases in Chicago, and established what became known as the "Chicago System of Film Release." Under this system B&K—with only one-fourth of the seats in Chicago—generated an average of 65 percent of that city's film rentals. Since during this period revenues from Chicago accounted for nearly 10 percent of the gross of any film, it is reasonable to assume that 3 to 5 percent of any film's revenue from the United States flowed through the accounts of Babalan and Katz. Moreover, B&K achieved its vast power in six short years, from 1919 to 1925. In 1919 B&K owned only six theaters, just one of which was considered first-run. Yet by the end of 1925 B&K possessed complete control of the Chicago market and merged with Famous-Players Lasky to form Publix Theatres.[11] How did B&K, in the space of six years, rise from one of many Chicago theater chains to become the area's dominant corporation?

The short answer to this question is that B&K innovated a strategy that generated immense revenues while keeping costs in line. Specifically, because in its early years the then tiny B&K could not get the most popular first-run films, it was forced to fashion an economic strategy that stressed *nonfilmic* features. There were five parts to this hugely successful growth plan.

First, B&K recognized important socioeconomic changes taking place in Chicago (and other American cities). The construction of mass transit in the late nineteenth and early twentieth centuries enabled members of the middle and upper-middle classes to flee to "street-car suburbs." Thus, B&K did not build its first large theater, the Central Park, downtown, but on Chicago's far west side (a crowded "suburban" neighborhood created by the expansion of Chicago's elevated train system in 1902). The prosperity of the Central Park prompted B&K to build its second theater, the Riviera (1918), in Uptown (a northside neighborhood). Controlling picture palaces that could draw from Chicago's north and west sides, B&K's management now moved into the southern suburbs and the central business district. B&K built its first downtown house, the Chicago Theatre, in the Loop. Once this matrix of four palaces was in operation, B&K could attract patrons from all parts of Chicago. Using the elevated or streetcar system, any potential customer could reach a B&K theater within thirty minutes. And, with the addition of more theaters, travel time was soon reduced to fifteen minutes. By 1925 B&K had monopolized exhibition revenues in Chicago, not by owning all of the theaters, but by controlling large picture palaces in the major outlying business centers and downtown.[12]

B&K began the "show" long before the scheduled entertainment program; the building itself functioned as a significant part of the "moviegoing" experience. From the outside, B&K theaters resembled baronial halls—palaces fit not so much for a seventeenth-century king as a twentieth-century business tycoon. Gigantic three-story electric signs identified the theater, flashed its attractions in several colors, and served as massive advertisements. Contrasting with the spectacular if somewhat gaudy electrical displays, the stolid facades and stained glass windows of B&K theaters aligned them with the most conservative and respectable of community institutions—churches and banks.

The exterior of Balaban & Katz's Central Park Theatre in Chicago. From the outside, B&K Theatres resembled spectacular baronial halls.

Theatre Historical Society

Inside, luxurious foyers accommodated a waiting crowd large enough to fill the theater. Chandeliers, paintings, and rich draperies decorated the anterooms where pianists entertained those waiting. No B&K ticket holder needed to stand outside in inclement weather. Numerous ushers serviced the patrons and an intricate network of passageways enabled thousands to enter and exit with relative comfort and speed. Nor did B&K ignore a theater's auxiliary services. Restrooms were spacious, clean, and decorated with paintings and sculpture. B&K even provided child care; at each theater a trained attendant and a nurse presided over a mini-kindergarten.[13]

The third part of B&K's formula made their theaters unique among public buildings in the 1920s: air conditioning. Cooling theaters in the summer had been a problem for decades; most theaters simply closed their doors between June and September. By 1911, however, thanks oddly enough to the need to refrigerate beef in Chicago's stockyards, engineers there had perfected the necessary technology to safely cool large spaces. In 1917 B&K's Central Park became

The interior of Balaban & Katz's Tivoli Theatre in Chicago. Amidst luxurious surroundings, B&K patrons enjoyed many auxiliary services along with the scheduled entertainment program.

Theatre Historical Society

the nation's first air-cooled movie house, and by 1925 motion picture trade papers frequently cited air conditioning as one reason for B&K's huge summertime grosses. Summer ads for B&K theaters featured the theater's name encased in icicles and helped to make summer box-office takes frequently higher than those in the winter months.[14]

The fourth aspect of B&K's strategy was personal service—and lots of it. Each theater employed more than 100 persons, a third of them ushers and doormen. B&K recruited college men for their usher corps, dressing them in red uniforms with white gloves and yellow epaulets. Ushers were expected to be models of politeness. Patrons were to be referred to as gentlemen, ladies, and children, and each request to a customer ended with "thank you." No matter how obliging the service or grateful the customers, ushers were never permitted to accept tips.[15]

Finally, the entertainment offered in a B&K theater consisted of much more than motion pictures. A large orchestra accompanied all films and the live stage shows that filled at least one-half of any show's allotted two hours. By attracting top-flight vaudeville acts to its theaters B&K was able to insure a constantly attractive entertainment package to its customers. Especially in B&K's early days, the drawing power of the stage show was used to offset the company's frequent inability to secure popular films from distributors. In time, B&K became more famous for its stage attractions, orchestras, and organists than for any of the movies it presented. The stage shows featured the best show business talent, elaborate costumes and sets, and intricate multicolored lighting effects. These live spectaculars were expensive to produce, but B&K kept the cost for each individual theater low by rotating shows and dividing expenses among its theaters.[16]

In November 1925 B&K merged with Famous Players (later Paramount), and Sam Katz moved his management team to New York to institute the Balaban and Katz system for the newly formed Paramount-Publix chain which rapidly became the country's dominant chain. In the case of Balaban and Katz, we find an example of one company in one city (neither New York nor Hollywood) significantly altering the history of the American film industry. Recognition of this fact was the ultimate result of asking a simple question about a local phenomenon: How did Balaban and Katz become the most powerful theater circuit in Chicago?

This attempt to present the B&K economic strategy as succinctly as possible has smoothed over the somewhat tortuous research route that was followed in the collection of data for this project. It began with various editions of Chicago city directories, which yielded the names and locations of the Balaban and Katz theaters. Because Chicago has been one of the most studied cities in the world, it was relatively easy to fill in the geographic and socioeconomic contexts of theater location. This led to the realization of the importance of location for any retail enterprise. Several books on movie palace design in the 1920s stressed the importance of B&K's resident theater architects, W. W. and George Rapp. A bit of digging in the Chicago Historical Society unearthed a manual prepared by B&K for its theater managers. Material in this manual prompted a trip to a university's engineering library to research the development of air conditioning for theaters. Providing additional bits of information on movie-going in Chicago and the operations of B&K were general and trade newspapers: the *Chicago Tribune, Variety, Motion Picture News,* and *Moving Picture World.* All are on microfilm. Interviews with former B&K executives provided information in clearing up questions print sources failed to address.

Balaban & Katz is a somewhat privileged example of local film economic history. It became the most important (though by no means the largest) regional chain of movie theaters and did so in a city with a strong sense of its own past and development. On the basis of other preliminary studies, however, it appears that local circuit building was a widespread phenomenon and began in some cities earlier than in Chicago. In short, there is a great deal of local economic history to be researched—all beginning with someone someplace asking "Who has owned movie theaters in my town?"

PROJECT III
LOCAL SOCIAL HISTORY: EARLY PATTERNS OF
MOVIE-GOING IN TWO CITIES

Since its American debut in vaudeville theaters in 1896, the cinema has been the locus for a social experience. Within two decades movie-going had become the primary form of entertainment for millions of Americans. Who constituted the movie-going public at various historical moments? Where were the movie theaters they attended? What were these theaters like? We know surprisingly little about the movie audience or movie-going as a social experience in national terms, except in the grossest demographic sense. At the local level we know even less.

This project in social film history asks two related questions: Who went to the movies, and where were theaters located? The period we have chosen is 1905 to 1915—the so-called nickelodeon era—and the cities are New York and Durham, North Carolina.

Despite a dearth of primary research on early exhibition, survey histories of the American cinema paint remarkably similar pictures of movie-going prior to 1915. Following their use in vaudeville theaters for nearly a decade, we are told, the movies became an autonomous entertainment form with the establishment of thousands of nickelodeon theaters which sprang up in the poorer sections of American cities beginning in 1905. Nickelodeons were little more than converted storefronts where, for five cents, one crowded into a small room fitted with a few hundred chairs and watched a brief program of short films projected onto a sheet. We can summarize the description of the nickelodeon era in most survey histories as follows:

1. The nickelodeon "boom" began around 1905 and lasted for a decade or until the advent of the picture palace around 1915.

2. Nickelodeons were located in working-class neighborhoods in major urban centers, and were frequented by poor people, especially newly arrived immigrants.

3. Since they appealed to the proletariat, the nickelodeon theaters were at best spartan, but were often dank, dingy converted stores, seating fewer than 300 persons.

Since the data that serve to back up these generalizations seem to come from New York City, it is best to begin a reconsideration of the nickelodeon phenomenon by closely examining the exhibition situation there between 1905 and 1915. The most basic questions are: Where were early movie theaters located in New York and who attended them? As with Chicago, city directories for New York list the names and addresses of all business establishments in the city—including (beginning roughly in 1906) movie theaters.[17] Using these reference tools for the years 1905 to 1910 and a contemporaneous street map, it is possible to locate nickelodeons, and changes in operation, year-by-year. Nickelodeons, it seems, were not evenly distributed throughout Manhattan, but were clustered in the Lower East Side, around Union Square (14th Street), along the Bowery, on the Upper East Side, and along 125th Street in Harlem. This pattern remained constant (as did the total number of nickelodeons: 150) from 1906 to 1912.

The next step is to translate these data into answers for the questions posed earlier. Nickelodeons, it seems, were not evenly distributed throughout Manhattan; some areas contained clusters of theaters, others not a one. There were a sizable number of nickelodeons (about 25 percent) where survey history accounts would predict: in the densely populated Jewish immigrant ghetto of the Lower East Side. However, groups of nickelodeons were found in traditional entertainment areas (the Bowery and Union Square), along retail shopping thoroughfares (especially on 125th Street in Harlem), and along public transportation routes (Second and Third Avenues). In terms of social class, more nickelodeons were located in or near middle-class neighborhoods than in the Lower East Side ghetto.

It is important to explain where nickelodeons were *not* located. It is surprising that only a handful were situated in the Italian enclave adjacent to the Lower East Side neighborhood. Both areas were populated by the city's poorest, most recent immigrants. Why the difference? The answer seems to lie in different patterns of immigration for the two groups.

The great migrations of Eastern European Jews to the United States around the turn of the century came about as whole families sought permanent escape from religious and political persecution. The corresponding Italian immigration movement was comprised largely of men between the ages of fourteen and forty-four (roughly 80 percent of the total) who came to the United States to earn money for themselves or their families back in Italy. Most telling is the repatriation rate—the extent to which immigrants returned to their country of origin. Between 1907 and 1911, 73 out of 100 Italians landing at Ellis Island eventually returned to Italy. Among Jews the repatriation rate was only 7 percent. It is plausible, therefore, that many of the Italian men living in the tenements of lower Manhattan were unlikely to spend part of their paltry earnings on something so frivolous as the movies. On the other hand, the family-oriented, American-minded Jewish community next door was a far more lucrative location for movie theaters.[18]

Business directories and urban demographic data can tell us some things about early film exhibition; other things, however, it cannot. How large were the nickelodeons? How elaborate were they? Were they designed only for the showing of movies? To answer these questions we must search for additional sources of information. Memoirs, contemporaneous newspaper articles, and motion picture trade papers provide descriptions of some movie theaters. Nickelodeons were not always the dark, smelly, sawdust-floored storefronts of traditional film-lore, but many were elaborately decorated theaters, complete with uniformed ushers, seating 1000, featuring a two-hour program of movies and vaudeville. These "small-time" vaudeville theaters, as they were called, sprang up in Manhattan as early as 1908 and mark a major qualitative shift in early film exhibition.[19]

Further documentation for the trend toward larger, more commodious theaters is available from, of all places, fire insurance maps. Fires threatened American cities then as now, making fire insurance for dwellings and business an important economic activity. Insurance companies needed information on the nature of the structure itself, the type of adjacent buildings, and its distance to water sources. To assist local insurance agents in arriving at a rate for a customer, the Sanborn Map Company prepared block-by-block maps for larger American cities. These maps, revised every ten years or so, indicated a structure's location, building material (stone, wood, or brick), size, peculiar structural features (skylights or theatrical stages, for example), and use (store, factory, dwelling). From such maps, it is apparent that most of the theaters in the Lower East Side were small storefront operations. Other theaters, however, in more affluent neighborhoods, were made of masonry, displayed elaborate facades, had large stages, dressing rooms, and flies, and accommodated 1000 or more patrons. Our picture of the "average" theater for the nickelodeon decade certainly seems to need revision.

In sum, for Manhattan Island, the three generalizations noted earlier must be revised:

1. Nickelodeons were not just located in working-class neighborhoods. They seemed to be clustered in middle-class sectors, as well as *certain* poor neighborhoods. Our example of "Little Italy" underscores this latter point most vividly. Proximity to existing retail operations, traditional entertainment districts, and public transportation seem to account for the location of many nickelodeons.

2. Nickelodeons were not all dingy storefronts. Many were quite attractive, often modeled on or part of a vaudeville operation.

3. By 1910 the storefront theaters were on their way out, to be replaced by larger and more commodious houses. The period between 1910 and 1915 is better characterized as the "rise of the picture palace."

While the findings of the Manhattan study seem to hold for other large American cities, to what extent can they account for patterns of movie-going in smaller towns? To the New Yorker in 1906, movies would have been commonplace for a decade as a vaudeville attraction, but what was the situation in towns where there was little or no theatrical tradition to precede the rise of the movies? How does the absence of large ethnic enclaves affect the location of movie theaters in more homogeneous communities? Obviously a single study cannot satisfactorily answer these questions. However, an examination of the nickelodeon period in one small southern city, Durham, North Carolina, shows both similarities and important differences in movie-going.

New York and Durham differ not only in size, but also in growth pattern, cultural history, geography, and racial makeup—factors that underlie differences in the two cities' initial experiences with the movies. In 1865 Durham was a settlement of fewer than 100 persons; by 1910 the population had exceeded 26,000. Two factors account for this remarkable growth: the expansion of the railroad service, and the growth of the tobacco industry. By the turn of the century Durham was one of the world's most important centers of cigarette production. Durham's citizens were nearly all native-born Americans; in 1910 only 258 Durham residents were immigrants. About 35 percent of the population in 1910 were black. A single six-block business and retail district along Main Street served the town. Most white working-class residents lived in outlying neighborhoods called mill villages—each serving a different mill or factory.[20]

The black community was concentrated southeast of downtown in a district called "Hayti." Blacks in Durham were more affluent than most of their southern counterparts. In other cities blacks were excluded from skilled and semi-skilled factory jobs, but rapid expansion of the textile and tobacco industries in Durham forced the white factory owners to "open up" these jobs to black workers. In 1904, the Durham Hosiery Mill became the first such mill in the country to employ an entirely black work force. By 1909 blacks owned land in Durham County assessed at more than $500,000. Black writer and activist W. E. B. Dubois remarked of Durham, "There is in this small city a group of five thousand or more colored people whose social and economic development is perhaps more striking than that of any similar group in the nation."[21]

Films came later to Durham than to New York. The first recorded showing in Durham came during the summer of 1903 at an amusement park. In 1902 Lakewood Park had been constructed by the local streetcar company at the terminus of one line. (Such a practice was common at this time for it encouraged ridership.) Screenings continued off and on at Lakewood Park throughout the decade, but only during the summer. Durham's first permanent movie house did not open until December 1907. The Electric Theatre commenced operations on Main Street at an admission price of 10¢ for adults and 5¢ for children. A year later the Edisonia and Dixie opened nearby. When the latter premiered, the Durham *Morning Herald* reported in a front-page story that there was a "tremendous rush" to enter this amusement marvel. The movies came late to Durham, but hit with an immediate impact.[22]

In New York and Chicago a great deal of early movie exhibition took place in vaudeville theaters. Movies became one of the eight vaudeville acts. However, Durham had no vaudeville house. In fact, the first permanent theater of any kind, the Durham Opera House, was not built until 1897. It offered plays by touring stock companies. A second theater, the Academy of Music, opened in 1904. It, like many counterparts in other small cities, presented a potpourri of entertainment—drama, vaudeville, minstrel shows, and musical concerts. The absence of regular vaudeville in Durham was caused as much by inconvenient rail connections as the town's small size at the turn of the century; to big-time vaudeville performers, who traveled exclusively by rail, Durham would have been an out-of-the-way stop.

Between 1908 and 1913 Durham was served by at least three and at various times four movie theaters (not including summer shows at the Lakewood). By 1909 all Durham's movie theaters had added vaudeville acts to their programs. As was the case in larger cities, the addition of vaudeville seems to have been a response to sharp competition among theaters. It was one way a theater manager could differentiate his or her house from the others in town.

Prior to 1913, all movie theaters in Durham (with the exception of the Lakewood) were located along a four-block stretch of Main Street in the heart of the city's business and retail district. Unlike Manhattan, where some theaters were situated in working-class residential neighborhoods, there were no movie houses in Durham's mill villages. One reason for the establishment of downtown theaters exclusively was certainly the heavy pedestrian traffic that passed along Main Street. Advertisements invited shoppers to pop into the movies for a bit of relaxation. Downtown was also the easiest place in the city to reach by public transportation—the north–south and east–west streetcar lines intersected at the center of town. The concentration of theaters downtown and their absence in the outlying working-class neighborhoods suggest that movie theater managers appealed to middle- and working-class patrons. This is also indicated by newspaper advertisements, which stressed cleanliness, the suitability of programs for women and children, and, on occasion, the literary or historical origins of particular films.[23]

In 1913 the first of several black-oriented theaters opened in the Hayti community. It should not be assumed that black theaters were established in Durham merely because enterprising entrepreneurs saw opportunities to go into the movie business or that the black citizens necessarily preferred neighborhood theaters to those downtown. Blacks were not allowed in most downtown theaters, and the few that admitted blacks forced them to sit apart from white patrons in the balcony. Forced segregation continued in many southern movie theaters well into the 1960s.

Tracing the history of black exhibition in Durham or any city is extremely difficult. Black theaters were listed in city directories, but, in Durham, at least, black theaters seldom advertised in the white-owned newspapers. Hence it is difficult to determine if black theaters differed in terms of environment or programming from the white movie houses. There were black newspapers from time to time in Durham, but copies of them could not be located. In many cases oral histories are the only recourse researchers have in attempting to document this important aspect of exhibition (and local cultural) history.

The early history of film exhibition in Durham evinces patterns different in several respects from those found in large cities.

1. Regular film exhibition came much later to Durham. Amusement parks and traveling showmen (rather than vaudeville) provided what movie-going opportunities there were prior to 1907.

2. The establishment of storefront theaters occurred at about the same time as in larger cities (c. 1907), but in Durham theaters were located exclusively in the downtown business district, not in working-class residential areas.

3. Theater location, programming, and advertising strategies suggest Durham theater managers sought from the beginning to attract middle-class patrons.

4. Admission to most movie theaters was denied or restricted to over one-third of Durham's population on the basis of race. Exhibition in the black community began as early as 1913.

Whether or not the "Durham pattern" holds for other small cities and towns necessarily awaits further research. However, both the New York and Durham projects reveal considerably more complexity and local variation in exhibition history than survey histories account for.

POSSIBLE RESOURCES FOR LOCAL HISTORY

This chapter concludes with a list of easily accessible data sources that have proved useful in conducting local film histories. It cannot be a complete catalog of materials, since the selection of pertinent data depends on the question posed and should be limited only by the resourcefulness of the historical investigator.

Directories

These reference volumes come in two types: city and business. City directories typically include several different listings: an alphabetical index of a city's residents or property holders, a street-by-street inventory of residences and businesses, and a generic listing of businesses. The business directory is more limited, usually containing only a generic and alphabetical list of commercial establishments. Both types of directories date back to the nineteenth century and were prepared annually. Municipal libraries and local historical societies are likely places to find them. Directories should provide the names and street addresses of movie theaters for a given year. Prior to 1910, movie houses might be listed under "amusements" or "theatres." These reference tools also include the names of the owners and managers of movie houses (and distributors and producers for some time periods). From the street-by-street lists of businesses one can easily establish the sorts of retail establishments near the theaters in question.

Fire Insurance Maps

These reference tools date to the 1880s for towns as small as 10,000 people. Usually a complete new edition appeared every ten years. Using these atlases (the Sanborn Company was the principal supplier), it is possible to determine the size, age, and architectural features of a given theater. They also serve to verify addresses and names found in less reliable directories. One warning: In between issues of the Sanborn atlases, the Sanborn Company sent to its subscribers paste-on decals with which to update their maps. A decal might mark the construction of a new building in 1912, but have been placed on a 1907 map. Often the decals did indicate a date, but if one encounters a map with decals, one cannot be sure these paste-ons represent the same year as that of the map itself. The Sanborn Company has published a list of the cities covered by its atlases and the dates of issue. Municipal libraries, university libraries, and state and local historical societies are the best places to look for fire insurance maps. (Some libraries have obtained permission to make microfilm copies of the Sanborn maps, but since the microfilm copies will not be in color, you will not be able to read certain color codes on the maps, building materials, for example.) Another place to check for fire insurance maps is the city hall of records, building departments, zoning commissions, or fire departments.

Local Histories

As one uses directories and fire insurance maps, it is important to become familiar with basic social-cultural-economic data from a community's past. Local histories can be valuable sources for this sort of contextual information, but beware. The quality of such writing (in books or from articles in local history journals) varies widely. They must be read skeptically. Far too often they are self-congratulatory, or written simply to please the local chamber of commerce. Frequently more useful are special studies on commerce, marketing, or architectural preservation commissioned by local governments or private agencies.

Here we find "snapshops" of housing patterns, population migrations, retail sales distribution, crime rates, and/or traffic problems. All can help to situate movie-going as a part of the larger fabric of the community.

Local Newspapers

Newspapers offer a veritable ocean of information. Before the Great Depression many communities had five or more daily newspapers. By 1915 most included extensive advertisements for local movie shows, and when a theater opened it often was front-page news. Advertisements typically contained the names of the films shown and any added attractions (for example, a stage show), times and cast of the show, the enterprise's owner, and even the type of clientele sought. Local municipal or university libraries usually hold complete runs of local papers on microfilm, but rarely are they indexed. (Some have very good indexes, the *New York Times* or the *Washington Star*, for example.) This lack forces the researcher to begin with city directories, fire insurance maps, and other sources to help spot a theater's opening day, thereby helping to date possible newspaper accounts. In addition, many U.S. municipal libraries maintain a clipping file. Try that first. *Newspapers on Microfilm* inventories all U.S. newspapers preserved on microfilm and gives their locations.

Motion Picture Trade Papers

Since 1907 the motion picture industry has supported specialized magazines and newspapers aimed at producers, distributors, and exhibitors. Basically there are five:

1. *Moving Picture World* (1907–1928)
2. *Variety* (1905–date)
3. *Motion Picture News* (1907–1930)
4. *Motion Picture Herald* (1915–1972) (In 1928 the *Herald* absorbed the *World* and in 1931 the *News*.)
5. *Boxoffice* (1932–date)

All contain, at one time or another, columns for the local exhibitor, usually divided by region, plus "tips" on the best way to run a theater. When a major theater opened, one or more of these trade papers would present an article. There are *no* indexes here, however, so be sure to have a very specific idea of what you are looking for before you plunge in. All, save *Boxoffice*, are on microfilm.

Public Records

One of the functions of local government is to regulate local commercial activities. New construction needs permits; regular inspections for fire hazards are required; taxes must be paid. Movie theaters are no exception. In some cities, theaters (including movie theaters) were licensed by the municipal government. The issuance and renewal of licenses would have been duly recorded as would the purchase or sale of the property. The great thing about city documents is that they are matters of public record and hence, in theory at least, available to anyone who wishes to examine them. The problems are (1) determining if the documents you wish to look at still exist, (2) finding where they are stored, and (3) persuading a city employee to assist you. Here there is an advantage in researching a smaller city—the city bureaucracy is apt to be smaller and less complex. Idiosyncrasies in municipal record-keeping are such that there is no one method of researching city records for what they might reveal about local exhibition—a lot of it you will have to discover for yourself. But here are a few pointers. The hall of records, city clerk's office, or register of deeds should have records of the sale of individual pieces of real estate. The city tax or revenue office should have property tax listings, how much was paid, and by whom. The city building department should have records of the issuance of building permits, and maybe blueprints. The mayor's office, city (or county) executive's office, and sometimes the local library hold copies of ordinances and codes. Check for special taxes or levies, licenses, fire regulations, and censorship boards.

Interviews

Armed with information from the preceding sources (and numerous unsolved questions), you are ready to approach former theater employees, city officials, and avid movie-goers—anyone who might remember first-hand experiences with earlier movie houses. Most are genuinely pleased to talk about their experiences. Again, a warning: Our memories constantly play tricks on us. We tend to remember what we like, and suppress much of the rest. So check and verify all you learn, however earnest and well-meaning the interviewee.

Photographs

Finally, do not overlook the value of even one photograph of the buildings, persons, or events you attempt to study. You can examine architectural styles, relative structural size, nearby buildings, and even those people standing in line. Again, try the local public library and historical society. Two other sources deserve special mention. First, in every community there exists at least one hobbyist interested in old movie palaces. Ask around. Usually he or she will be glad to talk and show off a unique picture collection. These enthusiasts have their own magazine, *Marquee*. Few libraries have a complete run so try writing the editor, Robert K. Headley, 6510 41st Avenue, Hyattsville, Maryland 20742. *Marquee* has a policy to consider any article on a theater in the United States.

NOTES

1. Arthur Knight, *The Liveliest Art* (New York: New American Library, 1979), p. 145.
2. Gerald Mast, *A Short History of the Movies*, 3rd edition (Indianapolis: Bobbs-Merrill, 1981), p. 185. See also, Charles Higham, *The Art of the American Film* (New York: Anchor Press, 1974), p. 86; and Lawrence Kardish, *Reel Plastic Magic* (Boston: Little, Brown, 1972), p. 103.
3. *Milwaukee Journal*, September 3, 1927, pp. 7, 11.
4. *Milwaukee Journal*, September 4, 1927, II, pp. 10-11.
5. *Milwaukee Journal*, September 22, 1927, p. 4; October 4, 1927, p. 26; and November 4, 1927, p. 9.
6. *Milwaukee Journal*, December 29, 1927, p. 10; January 13, 1928, III, p. 4; and January 22, 1928, III, p. 4.
7. *Milwaukee Journal*, February 5, 1928, VII, p. 7; March 1, 1928, II, p. 6; and March 22, 1928, II, p. 11.
8. *Milwaukee Journal*, April 26, 1928, III, p. 8; May 6, 1928, VII, pp. 5 and 9; and May 13, 1928, VI, p. 9.
9. *Milwaukee Journal*, May 18, 1928, II, p. 7; May 27, 1928, VI, p. 11; June 22, 1928, III, p. 7; July 20, 1928, II, p. 10; and August 14, 1928, II, p. 10.
10. *Milwaukee Journal*, September 21, 1928, III, p. 5; September 28, 1928, III, p. 7; October 12, 1928, III, p. 4; November 9, 1928, III, p. 5; December 12, 1928, III, p. 8; and April 3, 1930, III, p. 6.
11. Michael Conant, *Antitrust in the Motion Picture Industry* (Berkeley: University of California Press, 1960), pp. 155-161; and Martin Quigley, ed., *Motion Picture Almanac—1931* (New York: Quigley Publications, 1932), p. 300.
12. Homer Hoyt, *One Hundred Years of Land Values in Chicago* (Chicago: University of Chicago Press, 1933), pp. 225-263; Chicago Plan Commission, *Forty-Four Cities in the City of Chicago* (Chicago: Chicago Plan Commission, 1942), pp. 12-40; Chicago Historical Society, Arthur G. Levy Collection, "Largest Motion Picture Theatres in Chicago and Vicinity," July 12, 1935 (Mimeo), n.p.; and Chicago Recreation Commission, *The Chicago Recreation Survey*, Volume II (Chicago, 1938), pp. 1-37.
13. Barney Balaban and Sam Katz, *The Fundamental Principles of Balaban & Katz Theatre Management* (Chicago: Balaban & Katz, 1926), pp. 90-101; *Motion Picture News* (April 9, 1921): 2485-86; and George L. Rapp, "History of Cinema Theatre Architecture," in *Living Architecture*, ed. Arthur Woltersdorf (Chicago: A. Kroch Publisher, 1930), pp. 62-64.

14. Barney Balaban, "My Biggest Mistake," *Forbes* 50 (February 1, 1946): 12–16; "Air Conditioning in a Motion Picture House," *Ice and Refrigeration*, LXIX (November 1925): 251–252; and "Heating, Ventilating and Cooling Plant of the Tivoli Theatre," *Power Plant Engineering* 26 (March 1, 1922): 249–255.

15. David Wallerstein, interview held in Slinger, Wisconsin, August 28, 1977; Balaban and Katz, *Fundamental Principles*, pp. 14–73; and Arthur Mayer, *Merely Colossal* (New York: Simon & Schuster, 1953), pp. 71–103.

16. *Variety*, numerous dates 1922–1925, reviews of stage show performance column; and Ben M. Hall, *The Best Remaining Seats* (New York: Bramhall House, 1961), pp. 187–188.

17. Specifically, we used *Trow's Business Directory of Greater New York* as well as theatrical and motion picture trade journals from the period. To double check we compared the 1908 Trow's list with one prepared by Edision employee Joseph McCoy (Edison Archives, West Orange, New Jersey). The correlation is very high.

18. Thomas Kessner, *The Golden Door: Italian and Jewish Immigrant Mobility in New York City* (New York: Oxford University Press, 1977); and Grace Mayer, *Once Upon A City* (New York: Macmillan, 1958), p. 50.

19. *Variety* and *Moving Picture World*, various issues, 1908–1912.

20. Herbert Swan, *The Durham Plan* (Durham, N.C.: Durham City Planning Commission, 1925); and *Durham County Economic and Social: A Laboratory Study in the U.N.C. Department of Rural Economics and Sociology* (Durham: n.p., 1918), p. 20.

21. Hugh Penn Brinton, "The Negro in Durham: A Story of Adjustment to Town Life," Ph.D. dissertation, University of North Carolina, 1930, pp. vii–43.

22. *Durham Morning Herald*, December 13, 1907; December 1, 1908, p. 1; and December 12, 1980.

23. *Durham Morning Herald*, various issues 1908–1913.

9

Reintegrating
Film History

In Chapter 1 it was suggested that Realism might provide a philosophical approach to film history that would take into account its systemic nature. As a theory of science, Realism posits generative mechanisms as the objects of scientific study and regards reality as an open system. While Realism maintains that the generative mechanisms responsible for specific events have an existence independent of the mind of the scientist studying them, it also stresses the role of theory in providing testable models for explaining the operation of generative mechanisms and their interrelation. As was further pointed out in Chapter 1, Realism is only beginning to be applied to historical study, so that any application of Realism to film history is necessarily preliminary, tentative, and, perhaps, crude. However, Realism does provide a general perspective on history out of which more specific film historical methods might be constructed, and, by the principle of noncontradiction, tested.

At the core of a Realist approach to film history is the recognition that the cinema is a system, a complex phenomenon made up of many interactive elements. In historical terms, the concept of the cinema as a system means that the historian wishing to understand how the cinema has functioned as an art form, for example, must ultimately investigate the historical relationship between cinema as art and cinema as technology, economic institution, and cultural product. This is because the former (the historical development of cinema art) is explained to some degree in terms of the latter (the interaction among aesthetics, economics, technology, and culture). In Chapters 4 through 7 it might seem that this historical precept was violated by treating aesthetic, economic, technological, and social film history as separate branches of film history. These four categories of film history were maintained in those chapters for two reasons. First, much of American film history has been written in terms of this division. Also, different sorts of film historical questions *do* require different sorts of data and skills. A producer's correspondence file yields different historical evidence than the film that correspondence discusses. However, to foreground the aesthetic or technological history of the cinema is not at all to claim that the two have no relation to each other. In other words, focusing on one element of a system does not deny the existence or relevance of the other elements.

This chapter provides a case study that reasserts the fundamental systemic nature of cinema as a historical phenomenon. Viewing the history of cinema as the history of an open system has several historiographic consequences. "Explaining" a film historical event involves specifying the relationships among the various aspects of cinema (economic, aesthetic, technological, cultural) as well as the relationships between cinema and other systems (politics, the national economy, other media of mass communication, other art forms). Assigning "causes" within an open system becomes a challenging task for the film historian because relationships among elements in that system are mutually interactive, not simply linear. The lines of force or influence between film as business and film as cultural phenomenon, for example, go in both directions, not just from one to the other. Although the historian might wish it were not so, the network of relationships that make up the generative mechanisms of any historical event themselves change over time. The Realist historian is by no means absolved of the responsibility of assigning causes to historical phenomena. Without some notion of causality there would be no criterion for the selection and interpretation of data; each "fact" would be equally important. Rather, it means that complex phenomena usually are the result of complex causes. It is very infrequent in film history that phenomenon *B* can be said to be the direct and inevitable effect of cause *A*.

Realism as applied to film history can accommodate a number of more specific methods. Classical economic theory (of the sort appied to the study of technological change in Chapter 5) implicitly recognizes the systemic nature of the cinema. On the other hand, in *Pictures of Reality* Terry Lovell argues for a Marxist Realism. Thus what is suggested here by a Realist approach to film history is hardly revolutionary, nor are most of its basic assumptions new. It is merely a starting point for the historical study of film, a recognition of the network of relationships within which any film or film historical event is embedded. It is also a reminder to readers and writers of film history that the responsibility of the historian extends beyond giving a chronological catalog of "one damn thing after another." History is interpretation.

CASE STUDY: THE BEGINNINGS OF
AMERICAN CINEMA VERITÉ

In Chapter 1 a four-step historical method was extrapolated from the basic premises of Realism: (1) a redescription of the event to be explained so as to uncover the possible generative mechanisms responsible for it, (2) analysis of these mechanisms, (3) consideration of interrelationships among the generative mechanisms, and (4) assessment of the relative force of the mechanisms. This method will be applied here in an examination of the origins of a stylistic movement in American documentary filmmaking that came to be called direct cinema, or *cinema verité*. This style of cinema will be defined in more detail later, but basically cinema verité was and is an attempt to present uncontrolled events as faithfully as possible by using synchronous sound, no voice-over narration, and unmanipulative editing. In short, verité films aspire to give the audience the sense that "they are there" as the events in front of the camera unfold. The specific film historical event to be analyzed is the first use of this style in America: films made for television in the early 1960s by a production team headed by Robert Drew. In his book *Cinema Verité in America* Stephen Mamber notes that these films "demonstrated the possibilities in spontaneous, uncontrolled shooting and first came to grips with major aesthetic questions growing out of the commitment. In effect, Drew Associates defined American cinema verité, establishing so strong an approach that its influence continues to dominate."[1]

Redescribing Cinema Verité

Most scholars have seen documentary as a type of filmmaking that can be set against fiction films. Fiction films use actors and scripts, while documentaries attempt to show "what really happened." For example, to Richard Barsam the documentary filmmaker "presents actual physical reality in a form that strives to be faithful to actuality...[he or she] creatively records and interprets the world without substantially altering it." Bordwell and Thompson find it more useful to define documentary as the result of a filmmaker's decision to give up a certain measure of control over his or her material.[2]

We might think of all types of film production as involving three distinct "levels" of control. The first (in descending degree of control) would include control before, during, and after filming. Most Hollywood films would fall into this category. The filming of a particular scene is done on the basis of a preexistent script, often on a set built exclusively for that scene. During filming, the filmmaker determines where the camera and lights should be placed, where the actors should stand and move, and when the action will begin and end. Following the filming, the filmmaker shapes what has been shot through editing.

In some cases a filmmaker might choose to give up control over the planning of an event to occur in front of the camera (the profilmic event, as it is called), but to retain control over how that event is to be recorded and how the film of it is to be edited. We usually think of documentary films as belonging in this second level of control. We presume, in other words, that while the documentary filmmaker can decide where the camera should be placed relative to the action, which lens to use, and how the film should be edited, the profilmic event has been left uncontrolled.

There are instances, usually by necessity rather than choice, where the filmmaker has control over a film only after it has been shot. Such films, which rely on editing alone (the third level of control), are called compilation films. A filmmaker who wished to make a film on a particular battle of the Vietnam War (or any other historical event, for that matter) would have to use filmed material shot at that time, since shooting "new" footage would be impossible.

This definition of documentary as films of the second and third levels of control is not without problems. An interview, for example, is both controlled by the filmmaker in the sense that he or she asks the questions, and uncontrolled in that responses are not predetermined. Uncontrolled material—footage of a riot, let us say—might be used to illustrate a point made by the voice-over narrator of the film who is reading from a script. However, this definition does recognize documentary as a form of cinema in which the filmmaker has relinquished *some* measure of control over *some* aspects of the filmmaking process and by doing so implicitly claims *some* degree of "truthfulness" or "believability" for that film. Whether or not that film actually *deserves* to be called "true" or "accurate" is quite another matter, which we will leave to documentary theorists and critics.

Cinema verité is a style of documentary filmmaking that emerged in the early 1960s in the United States and Canada. Its basic goal is to capture an ongoing event as accurately as possible with a minimum of filmmaker interference or interpretation. Stephen Mamber summarizes the goals of cinema verité as follows:

> Cinema verité . . . is an attempt to strip away the accumulated conventions of traditional cinema in the hope of rediscovering a reality that eludes other forms of filmmaking and reporting. . . . The filmmaker attempts to eliminate as much as possible the barriers between subject and audience. . . . [It] is a practical working method based upon a faith in unmanipulated reality, a refusal to tamper with life as it presents itself.[3]

Among the specific filmmaking strategies used to implement these goals are:

1. Reliance on synchronous sound recording and avoiding the "interpretations" provided by voice-over commentary or music.

2. Minimal interference by the filmmaker in the profilmic event. The filmmaker in no way attempts to influence what subjects say or how they behave. The process of filmmaking is made to be as inconspicuous as possible.

3. Avoidance of "editorializing" in the editing process. That is, editing is not used to present the filmmaker's attitude toward the film's subject, but to represent as faithfully as possible what viewers would have seen and heard for themselves had they witnessed the events depicted in the film.

Some of the first films to exhibit this new style were those made by a team of filmmakers headed by Robert Drew. In the late 1950s Drew secured the support of Time, Inc. to produce documentary films for television that could serve as the cinematic counterparts of *Life's* pictorial style of journalism. Drew attracted to his team many of the filmmakers who were to become key figures in the cinema verité movement in America: Donn Pennebaker, Albert and David Maysles, Richard Leacock, James Lipscomb, and Hope Ryden.

The first of these films were shown as brief segments on network television shows ("The Ed Sullivan Show," "The Tonight Show"). Time-Life then ran a few of the Drew films on the local television stations it owned. In 1960 ABC Television contracted with Time-Life for the Drew production team to produce a series of documentaries for its "Close-Up" public affairs series. After four films, ABC established a policy of airing only those documentaries produced by its own news department, and since then cinema verité in America has been dependent on public television, occasional theatrical release, and distribution through nontheatrical channels for reaching an audience.

By examining the films themselves, critical discourse on them and on later cinema verité works, trade paper coverage of commercial broadcasting in the late 1950s and early 1960s, and the articulated positions of Drew and other cinema verité practitioners, it is possible to identify several generative mechanisms—aesthetic, economic, technological, and political—whose interaction was responsible for the origins of cinema verité in America.

Cinema Verité as Alternative Practice

Aesthetically, cinema verité represents an alternative cinema practice, much in the way that German films of the 1920s were marked by the deviations from standard Hollywood practice. Unlike the so-called "art" films of the German Golden Age, however, cinema verité emerged in the early 1960s as a full-fledged *avant-garde* aesthetic movement: not only a body of works with common stylistic characteristics, but also, as David Bordwell puts it, "polemics, theories, and activities which constitute both internally coherent positions and explicit challenges to already existing styles."[4]

The "position" of cinema verité filmmakers has already been sketched: the cinema should be used as a device for exploring social reality, recording ongoing events as accurately as possible without prejudgment or filmmaker interference, and edited in such a way that the meaning of the film emerges from its subject matter, not from the filmmaker's imposition of a theme on the material. Filmmakers and sympathetic critics articulated this position through interviews, speeches, and articles in the early 1960s. Richard Leacock, perhaps the most important filmmaker on the Drew team, told an interviewer in 1965:

> What is it we filmmakers are doing then? The closest I can come to an accurate definition is that the finished film. . . is an aspect of the filmmaker's perception of what happened. This is assuming that he does no directing. No interference. . . . Now, why are we filmmakers doing this? To me it's to find out some important aspect of our society by watching our society, by *watching how things really happen* as opposed to the social image that people hold about the way things are *supposed* to happen. (Italics in text)

Patricia Jaffe, an editor for some of the Drew verité films, wrote that same year:

> Direct cinema. . . is based on *recording life as it exists at a particular moment before the camera*. The role of the filmmaker in this instance is never to intrude by directing the action—never to alter the events taking place. . . . His job is simply to record what is there as he sees it.[5] (Italics in text)

The "existing styles" challenged by the practitioners of cinema verité were both the Hollywood cinema and the traditional documentary style. Cinema verité films were but one manifestation of a more general reaction against Hollywood fiction filmmaking that surfaced in the years immediately following World War II. In Italy so-called neo-realist directors (championed, we might note, by André Bazin) rejected the glossy Hollywood imitation films of the Fascist-controlled Italian cinema of the 1930s and early 1940s by "taking their cameras into the streets." In *Open City, Paisan, Bitter Rice, The Bicycle Thief,* and other neo-realist films, the studio was given up for shooting on location wherever possible, nonprofessional actors, improvised dialogue, and straightforward editing and camera work. The subject matter of neo-realism was not the love-life of the rich, as in so many Italian films of the previous era, but the contemporary social and economic problems of the post-war Italian working class: feeding one's family, economic oppression, interracial marriage. Cesare Zavattini's neo-realist manifesto, published in 1953 as the movement was waning, prefigured the concerns of Leacock and Jaffe a decade later.

> The term neo-realism. . . implies, too, elimination of technical professional apparatus, screenwriter included. Handbooks, formulas, grammars, have no more application. There will be more technical terms. Everybody has his personal shooting script. Neo-realism breaks all the rules, rejects all those canons which, in fact, only exist to codify limitations. Reality breaks all the rules, as can be discovered if you walk out with a camera to meet it.[6]

A few years later in England young filmmakers such as Tony Richardson, Karel Reisz, Jack Clayton, and Lindsay Anderson continued this trend of gritty, simply shot, socially oriented filmmaking in *Room at the Top, Saturday Night and Sunday Morning, Look Back in Anger,* and *A Taste of Honey.* Both neo-realism and the "Angry Young Man" cinema in England, as the latter came to be called, retained a fictional plot and other trappings of traditional commercial filmmaking, but in their subject matter, use of locations, stylistic simplicity, and resolute refusal to satisfy the audience with a happy ending, they represented a radical departure from the Hollywood-style film. Furthermore, both "alternative" styles were very well received by American critics and "art" cinema audiences in the 1940s and 1950s. Neo-realist films were in general more financially successful in the United States than in Italy. Even the Hollywood establishment recognized the merits of the "Angry Young Man" films by bestowing Academy Awards upon several of their stars.

Whether articulated by Italian, English, or American filmmakers, the postwar reaction against Hollywood-style films shared several basic tenets: (1) Hollywood films run counter to the "true nature" of the cinema in that they substitute a fictional illusion for reality. (2) The technical complexity of Hollywood filmmaking interposes an unnecessary barrier between filmmaker and subject and between subject and audience. (3) Hollywood films exist to make money for their producers, not to use the cinema for any higher purpose. (4) The social world of the Hollywood film is one of glamour, luxury, stars, and success. It ignores the "real" problems of society: poverty, injustice, political struggle, and racism. (5) Whenever Hollywood films *do* deal with social issues their artifice and conventions (the happy ending) render them merely one more "unreal" fiction.

Documentary filmmaking did not begin with cinema verité in the 1950s. Since the 1920s filmmakers like Robert Flaherty, Dziga Vertov, and John Grierson had used the documentary form to create an alternative to commercial narrative filmmaking. In fact, Leacock had worked with Flaherty on the making of one of his last films, *Louisiana Story,* in 1948. In several respects, however, cinema verité represented as much of a challenge to traditional documentary filmmaking as it did to the Hollywood cinema. The verité filmmakers believed that many documentarists of the past were not really interested in presenting unmanipulated reality but rather in manipulating that reality to make a polemical point through editing or narration. The images captured on film might be "uncontrolled" in the sense that the filmmaker did not attempt to influence the action in front of the camera, but the meaning of that image in the finished film was created primarily through its relationship to the scripted narration, musical score, and to other images edited together.

Through his connection with Flaherty, Leacock learned that the pioneer documentarist was not averse to "staging" a scene when he could not get what he wanted by uncontrolled means or to creating a scene through editing if necessary. The filmmaker's vision seemed more important than what he saw through the camera. Particularly annoying to verité filmmakers about traditional documentaries was the use of documentary images merely as illustrations of scripted narration. Again reality was not allowed to speak for itself, but only to speak as the filmmaker or, heavens forbid, the scriptwriter wanted it to speak. Given what verité fimmakers saw as the manipulative nature of most documentaries, it is not too surprising that Patricia Jaffe saw cinema verité as closer in spirit to the fictional works of neo-realism than the "nonfiction" of traditional documentary.[7]

The Technological Context of Cinema Verité

The style of traditional documentaries, particularly their use of sound, was to a large degree a matter of technological limitation rather than aesthetic choice. Recording synchronous sound outside of a movie studio was extremely difficult. Until the 1950s, movie sound was recorded on phonograph records (discs), or optically on film, using large, heavy, and relatively immobile equipment. The Hollywood industry, which sought rather than abjured control over the filmmaking process, had little reason to innovate sound equipment that could be used to record uncontrolled situations. Similarly, the 35mm cameras used in Hollywood production were designed to be mounted on stationary tripods. When movement was necessary, it was achieved by means of mechanized dollies or cranes. Smaller cameras did exist for newsreel work but they were not designed for shooting synchronous sound. Most newsreels were shot silent with narration and music added later in the studio.

The difficulties in shooting synchronous sound on location stand out clearly in both neo-realist and traditional documentary films. The images of the former might be recorded in a rice paddy or the slums of Rome, but the dialogue had to be "dubbed" by actors in a recording studio. For *Louisiana Story*, which dealt with the coexistence between an oil-drilling operation and a Cajun family in an idyllic Louisiana bayou, Flaherty shot most of the film silent, then imported a separate sound crew and equipment for the film's few synchronous sound sequences. Even this small use of location synchronous sound in a documentary film with a luxurious budget ($258,000) created nightmarish problems for editor Helen von Dongen. Flaherty's biographer Alexander Calder-Marshall describes the synchronous dialogue sequences as "blocks of concrete that had to be set in a structure as pliant as woven bamboo."[8]

With unwieldy 35mm cameras and sound recorders weighing 200 pounds, even the most innovative of documentary directors were extremely limited in the kind of "reality" they could represent on the screen. What were required were lightweight, mobile cameras and recorders that could be carried by one or two people and record sound and image in sync. One way to lighten the weight of camera equipment was to reduce the size of the film stock and thereby reduce the size of the camera and lenses needed to store and expose the film. Hollywood films were (and are) shot on 35mm film. A smaller gauge, 16mm, had existed since 1923, but only for amateur filmmaking. Hollywood had little reason to bring 16mm equipment up to professional standards. During World War II, however, both sides of the conflict soon recognized the need for lightweight, compact, durable cameras that could be carried by battlefield photographers, record equipment tests, and be mounted in the nose of bombers and fighter planes to verify target hits. These needs were met by 16mm equipment, which was quickly pressed into service. The formerly amateur gauge was "professionalized" during the war: The quality of the lenses improved and parts standardized and made interchangeable.[9]

Army technicians were not the only ones to view combat and test footage shot with 16mm cameras. Millions of soldiers were shown training films shot in 16mm and even more civilians back home viewed 16mm newsreel footage of the war. The widespread use of 16mm equipment under combat conditions had aesthetic consequences that extended well beyond the war itself. Noted Hollywood cinematographer James Wong Howe contended that the shaky, jerky, often blurred images that were a necessary result of hand-held combat motion photography became equated in the minds of the movie audience with realism. "The audience cannot help comparing them [newsreels from the front and Hollywood films] and can draw only one conclusion: that the Hollywood concept is artificial and therefore unbelievable."[10] The combat "style" of war-time cinematography might well have helped audiences to accept similar qualities of verité style twenty years later, as well as giving verité films an air of authenticity Hollywood films could not share. Developments in 16mm camera equipment continued after World War II primarily through its use in monitoring scientific tests (atomic bomb blasts and jet flights, in particular) and in television news reporting, which replaced the movie newsreel as America's primary source of "visual" news in the 1950s.

World War II also saw advances in sound recording. The first two magnetic tape recorders in America were captured from the Germans by General Patton's troops late in the war, following the Battle of the Bulge. Upon examination, the machines were found to be far superior in terms of reproduction quality than any sound recording process then in use in the United States. Magnetic sound recording not only proved to provide superior movie sound, it was also cheaper and less prone to mechanical problems than previous methods. Within a few years after its "discovery" by American sound technicians, tape recording became standard procedure in Hollywood. However, while tape recording gave better quality, until the mid-1950s it was of little more use to documentary filmmakers for synchronous recording than conventional methods. Heavy and energy-consuming vacuum tubes made magnetic recording little more suitable for location synchronous sound than disc or optical methods. Robert Drew recalls that the magnetic recorder available for synchronous sound in the mid-1950s required two men to carry it. "When you finally put it down," he recalled, "it became the center of the universe." The breakthrough in synchronous sound recording came around 1960 with the application of transistor technology to sound recording. By using transistors rather than vacuum tubes, the weight of the sound recorder could be reduced from several hundred pounds to only twenty.[11]

The technological context of documentary filmmaking in the late 1950s might be more easily understood if the state of technology then is compared with that a decade later, when the complete "rig" for shooting cinema verité was in common use. By the late 1960s the cinema verité documentarist was using a lightweight, shoulder-mounted 16mm camera (usually an Eclair or Arriflex), which allowed him or her reflex viewing and on which was mounted a zoom lens. The reflex (through-the-lens) viewing system enabled the filmmaker to observe action through the camera itself and to adjust exposure and focus while shooting. The zoom (variable focal length) lens made it possible to go from a long-shot to a close-up by simply turning a ring on the camera lens.

The sound recorder in use by the late 1960s was also compact and lightweight, recording high-quality sound on ¼-inch magnetic tape. The recorder

The technology of verité: Robert Drew carries a Nagra tape recorder and microphone. Frank Simon is shown with a shoulder-mounted camera.

Drew Associates

(the Swiss-made Nagra was the most popular brand) was powered by batteries and kept in sync with the camera by means of a tiny radio transmitter. Camera operators and sound recordists were by this time completely unencumbered by cables connecting camera to recorder and were free to move about independently of each other. In the late 1950s the technology that would make the verité rig of the late 1960s possible was still in the invention and innovation stages. Issues of the *SMPTE Journal* (Society of Motion Picture and Television Engineers) in the late 1950s and early 1960s were filled with new product announcements as a number of product manufacturers proposed ways of solving film production problems that had arisen from Hollywood studio filmmaking, scientific experimentation, and television news.

The Origins of the Drew Team

Robert Drew came to documentary filmmaking from journalism and photography, specifically from ten years as a *Life* magazine reporter and editor. In 1954, Drew took a leave of absence from *Life* to prepare a sample magazine-style documentary program for NBC. The idea was to bring to television the excitement and spontaneity of the still photo-essays that had made *Life* one of the most popular magazines ever published. However, spontaneity was not possible with the cumbersome equipment then available. "The only real surprises that took place in front of the camera," Drew recalled later, "were the shock of the clap sticks and outburst of the sound man shouting 'Cut!' " NBC was unable to sell the pilot Drew prepared, and he returned to *Life*. Shortly thereafter Drew took another leave to become a Neiman Fellow at Harvard for one year. This sabbatical gave Drew the opportunity to discuss television, drama, philosophy, politics, and film with the other journalists studying under Neiman Fellowships. The problem with the documentary in particular, Drew concluded, was that in traditional documentary films the logic and rhetorical power was carried by the narration rather than by the images themselves, reducing documentaries to little more than illustrated lectures.[12]

Following his return to *Life*, Drew spent several years producing a series of short films financed by the publishers of the magazine. Drew persuaded the company that early involvement in television programming was in keeping with Time-Life's pioneering journalistic tradition: *Time* had been the first weekly news magazine in the United States, and *Life* had set the pattern for modern photo-journalism. *Life* would put up the money for films, which could then be sold to network television. Revenues from television and the promotional value of the films, whose subjects would be tied to *Life* stories, would make Drew's efforts self-sustaining, if not profitable. A film on bullfighting in Spain, timed to coincide with a *Life* cover story, was shown on "The Tonight Show." "The Ed Sullivan Show" used a ten-minute film on NASA experiments on weightlessness, footage that was used the next day by CBS news.

Early in 1960 Drew was asked to move from *Life* to its parent company's television division; Time, Inc. owned television stations in Denver, Minneapolis, and Grand Rapids. In return for sharing his ideas on television documentary with the stations' staffs, Drew would be given money to make longer films and to develop the mobile, lightweight equipment his team was still lacking. Drew had already added to this "team" several filmmakers who would later become important cinema verité documentarists in their own right: Richard Leacock, Donn Pennebaker, and Albert and David Maysles, among them. Leacock and Pennebaker were put in charge of modifying equipment to fit the needs of "candid" filmmaking. A television news camera, the Auricon, was stripped of its excess weight and synced to a new Perfectone ¼-inch sound recorder, a precursor of the Nagra. Sync was maintained by a Bulova watch's tuning fork, mounted on the side of the Auricon. This patchwork rig would finally allow documentary filmmakers to "stop talking and let the action within the frame tell the story," Drew felt.[13]

The subject of the first film made with this new equipment was the 1960 Democratic presidential primary in Wisconsin between John F. Kennedy and Hubert Humphrey. The two were in a close race for the Democratic nomination, and Wisconsin was a crucial test for both candidates. Although *Primary* contained some voice-over narration and considerable nonsynchronous footage (the latter necessitated by equipment problems), it was a documentary unlike anything most Americans had ever seen on television or in movie theaters. Cameras and microphones followed the candidates as they spoke at rallies, handed out leaflets on street corners, dropped in at cafes, prepared for radio interview shows, stole naps in cars and hotel rooms, and watched the election returns on television. French documentary critic Louis Marcorelles, who saw Leacock as the primary creative force behind the film, described its aesthetic significance as follows:

> Leacock was not content to isolate a single detail arbitrarily and later select it for special treatment at the cutting stage, on the contrary, he caught, while it was happening, the small revealing point, the sentence or part of a sentence that might throw light on a situation or a character, the visual detail that cannot be treated separately from the sound that accompanies it. This technique had never been used so rigorously before and it forces us to look at the cinema in an entirely new way, to redefine it in the way that Leacock, at his best, conceived it.[14]

Cinema Verité and the Television Networks

While *Primary* was a landmark film in the aesthetic development of cinema verité, it was seen by relatively few Americans, compared with the viewing audience for the documentary vignettes Drew and company prepared for "Today," "The Tonight Show," and "The Ed Sullivan Show." *Primary* did not receive a network airing, and hence was seen by few people outside the viewing markets served by Time, Inc.'s television stations. Time, Inc. hoped Drew's films would eventually produce a profit for the company, and the only distribution channel in 1960 that could be used to achieve this goal was network commercial television. Certainly there was no place for the type of documentary Drew was producing in movie theaters. Except for newsreels, which were themselves moribund in 1960 because of television, Hollywood had never had much use for documentary films. To establish cinema verité documentaries as an innovative form of television programming, Time, Inc. needed access to prime-time network air time.

In moving from the occasional brief film novelty that could be accommodated on entertainment programming (Drew recalls that the weightlessness film followed a trained dog act on "The Ed Sullivan Show") to longer, self-contained works such as *Primary*, Time, Inc. encountered an institutional barrier. Television documentaries fell into the programming category of "public affairs," and

Primary was made with a modified Auricon camera synced to a Perfectone ¼-inch sound recorder. Shown here in 1960 is Hubert Humphrey, candidate for the Democratic presidential nomination; Robert Drew with microphone; and Albert Maysles with camera.

From the film *Primary*, produced by Robert Drew

hence in the domain of the network news departments. In 1960 all three networks had formal or informal policies against accepting public affairs programming not produced by their own news operations. Otherwise, they felt, the authenticity of the programming could not be assured. In late 1960, however, ABC rescinded this policy and contracted with Time, Inc. for the Drew team to produce four hour-long documentaries for its public affairs series, "Close-Up." This decision prompted the resignation of ABC's Vice President for News, John Daly.

Why was ABC willing to take this controversial step? To understand how cinema verité received its resultant exposure on network television we must examine the economics and politics of television at this time and, specifically, ABC's place within this context. Among the three commercial television networks, ABC was in the best position to innovate in the area of programming. Put another way, as a distant third in the ratings race, ABC had the most to gain and the least to lose by taking programming risks. In the fall of 1959, ABC was for the first time in a position to compete with NBC and CBS for the national television audience. ABC's programming philosophy, developed by president Oliver A. Treyz, was to "counter-program" against the offerings of the other two networks. Against CBS's situation comedies and variety shows, ABC scheduled westerns and action/adventure dramas ("Cheyenne," "77 Sunset Strip," "The Untouchables"). ABC's only chance to compete, Treyz felt, was to offer an alternative to whatever was running on NBC or CBS at any given time-slot. In economic terms Treyz attempted to differentiate his product as much as possible from that of the competition.[15] "The Untouchables" had shown that violence could be used to attract audiences. ABC even tried an animated cartoon series, "The Flintstones," as a viewing "alternative"; it worked.

ABC hardly anticipated "Close-Up" would generate the ratings of "The Untouchables" or "The Flintstones." Public affairs programming in the 1950s drew significantly fewer viewers than almost any other program genre, but by 1960 advertisers were showing increased interest in public affairs as advertising vehicles. In April of that year a panel of 282 advertising agency buyers surveyed by NBC expressed the belief that "broadcasters are neglecting their pocketbooks as well as their prestige by not putting more emphasis on public service programming." Nine out of ten polled thought advertising in public affairs programming a good way to build a company's public image, and two-thirds believed it effective in selling high-cost products. In addition, 73 percent felt public affairs programming attracted a new audience to television: the young, highly educated, upper-income person who rarely if ever watched entertainment programming. When asked which type of public affairs programming would have the greatest audience appeal, the panel named documentaries second only to hard news programs.[16]

ABC's decision to air the Drew documentaries also must be seen in light of the regulation of American commerical broadcasting by the Federal Communications Commission. Since the establishment of the Federal Radio Commission (later the FCC) in 1927, that agency had been charged with the responsibility of assuring that the holders of broadcasting licenses served "in the public interest, convenience, and necessity." Even before the advent of commercial electronic television in the late 1940s, this had been interpreted to mean that broadcasters had a responsibility to address issues of general public interest through informational or public affairs programming in addition to offering the far more lucrative entertainment fare.

In the late 1950s, commercial television was frequently criticized for providing extremely limited public affairs programming and for offering what little they produced in the so-called "cultural ghetto" time period of Sunday afternoons, when very few viewers watched television. Among these critics was FCC Chairman John C. Doerfer, who favored requiring broadcasters to run a set quantity of public affairs and "cultural" programming during prime time. Since the FCC itself was unsure of its legal ability to regulate television programming, Doerfer proposed instead that the three networks voluntarily agree to set aside one-half hour of prime-time programming each weekday for public affairs on a rotating basis (CBS would offer the programming one week, NBC the next, and so forth). "I would not hesitate to urge the Commission to require such programming if I were certain we had that power and could effectively set understanding and enforcement standards," he declared in January 1960. The networks, fearful of increased government regulation of television, responded by doubling the amount of prime-time public affairs programming for the 1960–1961 season over 1959–1960 levels. ABC's fall public affairs offerings, announced in the summer of 1960, included a documentary series based on Winston Churchill's memoirs and fifteen editions of "Close-Up."[17]

Also, broadcasters were eager to improve their status both with the viewing public and with the FCC in the wake of several recent public relations disasters. A top-rated television quiz show, "The $64,000 Question," was found to be "rigged;" contestants were advised of the answers to questions in advance. In radio, disc jockeys, broadcast executives, and recording companies had been charged in the "payola" scandals—the illicit proffering of money or gifts to radio personnel for the inclusion of a record company's song on its play-list. Both episodes had prompted Congressional investigations and hearings by the FCC on the extent of the FCC's regulatory powers.[18]

Of the three networks, ABC was in the worst position to respond to FCC and public pressure to increase its public affairs offerings. Both CBS and NBC had extensive news operations built upon radio news departments that had been in existence since the late 1920s. ABC had no such news tradition, being a latecomer to both radio (the company was founded in 1943 from the sale of one of NBC's two radio networks) and television. ABC's news director, John Daly, doubled as the host of the television quiz show, "What's My Line?" ABC, with only a skeleton news staff, could not increase its public affairs programming immediately without purchasing programming produced outside its own news department. As ABC's Vice President for Administration, Alfred Scheider, stated in December 1960, "It's ABC's policy to develop wherever it can toward a 'vigorous' public affairs department even if it means hiring outside producers."[19]

Given its dilemma, ABC was fortunate to find as the principal sponsor for the "Close-Up" series the Bell and Howell Company, a Chicago photographic equipment manufacturer. Company chief executive officer Charles Percy (later U.S. Senator Percy) explained Bell and Howell's underwriting of "Close-Up" as follows: "One task that American business can undertake is the support of all types of responsible media that inform and enlighten and help us as a people to take a more responsible position on the burning issues of the day." In fact, by 1960 Bell and Howell had put nearly all its advertising budget into the sponsorship of televised public affairs programming.[20]

Bell and Howell's advertising strategy was prompted, however, by more than just the public-spiritedness of its management—as that management was willing to point out to others in the media industry, at least. In fact, Charles Percy and Bell and Howell advertising director, Peter Peterson, credited ads on public affairs shows with the company's overtaking of former industry leader Kodak in movie camera sales in 1960—despite a national recession, Kodak's much larger advertising budget, and the fact that Bell and Howell's home movie equipment was priced higher than competing models. Percy explained, "We had to take risks. . . . We are a relatively small company with a modest advertising budget and cannot afford the successfully established television vehicles used by mammoth budget advertisers." In other words, like ABC, Bell and Howell had much more limited resources than its competitors, and thus had to gamble on innovations to remain competitive. Of the three networks, ABC's was the least expensive "rate-card": the schedule of charges for advertising time. With fewer affiliated local stations carrying its programming, ABC commanded a smaller share of the viewing audience than either of the other two networks, and therefore could not charge as much for advertising time. Of all ABC's prime-time programming, public affairs were the cheapest to sponsor, both because of the low anticipated ratings of the programs and because ABC was willing to absorb part of the production costs of public affairs as the price to be paid for fending off FCC intervention in programming.

Despite the relatively small ratings ("Close-Up" never pulled more than 20 percent of the households with television sets), Bell and Howell had found an advertising bargain. Beginning in 1957 and continuing through the early 1960s, Bell and Howell introduced a number of new products for the 8mm home movie enthusiast: the "electric eye" (automatic exposure) movie camera (1957), an 8mm camera with zoom lens (1960), self-threading 8mm projector (1960), electronic zoom camera (1961), and, in cooperation with Dupont, 8mm color film for home movies (1961). In relation to current prices for home movie equipment, these new cameras and projectors were expensive. Thus, Bell and Howell needed to reach not the entire television viewing audience, but only those who in demographic terms (income, education, age) constituted the bulk of the potential market for "top of the line" home movie equipment. Bell and Howell marketing surveys revealed that "a significant correlation exists between buyers of photo equipment and the audience composition attracted to public service programming."[21]

With the Drew films on what became "Bell and Howell's Close-Up," the company got not only a match between the audience for the shows and the demographic profile of the home movie buff, but also a much more effective vehicle for their advertising than it could have obtained via entertainment programming. Through its sponsorship of "Close-Up," Bell and Howell hoped to establish the association: "quality programming = quality company products." Like other sponsors of public affairs programs (Purex, Ralston-Purina, and Prudential Life Insurance), Bell and Howell found that type of programming produced strong identification in the viewer's mind between program and sponsor. Despite a tag at the end of each "Close-Up" edition announcing that Bell and Howell exercised no control over the show's content, between 30 and 50 percent of the viewer mail generated by each show was sent not to ABC, but to Bell and Howell.[22]

Marketing experts also discovered that viewers could recall more about informational programming content and advertising than entertainment programming content. Max Banzhaf, advertising director of the Armstrong Cork Company, another sponsor of public affairs programming, put it this way, "Westerns are a form of amusement and escape, and so are most other shows. When the viewer is in that frame of mind, the commercials go in one ear and out the other. With meaty shows that have impact, most of the program and the accompanying commercial stay with the audience." In other words, information programming required greater attention on the part of the viewer—attention that carried over from the programming content to the commercials. This was very important to Bell and Howell, which used advertising time in "Close-Up" to demonstrate new product lines. "For movie equipment," said a Bell and Howell executive, "television is the ideal medium."[23]

Relationships among Generative Mechanisms

The aesthetics of cinema verité—sync-sound location shooting of uncontrolled situations, minimal narration, the "objectivity" of the filmmaker in editing —admirably fit the requirements of ABC for public affairs programming and of Bell and Howell for an advertising vehicle. One of the hallmarks of verité is that the structure of the film, both in terms of the relationship between images within a shot and the relationship between shots, is determined by "what happens" in the event being filmed, rather than imposed upon the material by the filmmaker. This aesthetic characteristic of verité was important both to ABC and Bell and Howell. To the former it meant a reduced risk that a film would be used to "editorialize" on a given topic—since in verité the filmmaker gave up much of the aesthetic opportunity to insert his or her views on the subject matter being filmed. As Richard Leacock said in an interview in 1965, "When I become intrigued by theatre or by film or even by education, it is when I am not being *told* the answer I start to find out for myself. . . . The moment I sense that I'm being *told* the answer I start rejecting it."[24] (Italics in text) Thus ABC did not have to worry about defending a "stand" on a controversial issue presented over its network or representing the views of filmmakers who were not under the direct scrutiny or control of network management.

This objectivity was important for several reasons. By presenting controversial subjects—anti-Americanism in Latin America (*Yanki No!*) and racial integration (*The Children Are Watching*)—ABC was fulfilling its obligation to "provide a reasonable amount of time for the presentation over their facilities of programs devoted to the discussion and consideration of public issues." However, ABC also had the obligation to abide by what came to be known as the FCC's "Fairness Doctrine," by which broadcasters were admonished to

Controversy presented objectively: a scene from "The Children Are Watching," which examined school desegregation in Louisiana.

From the film *The Children Are Watching,* produced by Drew Associates; executive producer, Robert Drew.

"afford reasonable opportunity for the discussion of conflicting views on issues of public importance." Thus verité allowed ABC to have its cake and eat it too: Controversial issues were discussed, but no ostensible position taken on them could be determined from the films. The "objectivity" of verité also assured that a sponsor would not be called upon to identify itself willingly or unwillingly with a particular social or political position. As one advertising executive commented in 1960, "[Broadcasting] has a deep underlying fear that a potential advertiser might be driven away by something the station or network says."[25]

To Bell and Howell the "objectivity" of verité meant that it could be perceived as a public-spirited company concerned with the presentation of important national issues, but, more importantly, the *disinterested* sponsor of these programs. Although the presentation of *The Children Are Watching* did result in some negative reaction against Bell and Howell from viewers in Louisiana (where the film was shot), in general mail to Bell and Howell in reaction to "Close-Up" shows ran a favorable forty to one. In fact, controversial programming worked to Bell and Howell's advantage in that it "tend[ed] to stimulate greater sponsor identification than the run of the mill format of most entertainment programs." The association in the viewer's mind of Bell and Howell with "controversial programs that will arouse as well as inform the viewing public" was all the more important because in addition to being a producer of photographic equipment, Bell and Howell was also a major manufacturer of audiovisual equipment for school use. The "current events" orientation of the Drew films fit in well with the education market Bell and Howell served.[26]

The resolute insistence of verité to *show* the viewer a situation rather than *tell* him or her about it bothered some reviewers. In his historical survey of television documentary, William Bluem says of *The Children are Watching*:

> Leacock went to New Orleans seeking to witness the same ugly miscarriage of justice which all thinking men knew was occurring there. But, while others were trying to explain the meaning of these events in order to invoke the sobriety of reason, he was predisposed to show only hate and fear at its most tumultous level, leaving us no room, no avenue, for thoughtful action.

Following a screening of a later Leacock film on capital punishment, *The Chair*, Louis Marcorelles commented that he found the film "oddly ambiguous in the comment it makes."[27] While the lack of "sober reason" and the presence of "ambiguity" in terms of the perceived relation between filmmaker and subject might have annoyed some critics, the "objectivity" of verité from which these qualities stem made the Leacock films consonant with network policy and advertiser requirements.

The increased viewer attentiveness needed to watch an informational program (relative to entertainment programming) has been noted. It could further be argued that within informational programming cinema verité documentaries required the highest level of viewer involvement. Deprived of a narrator, the viewer must make the logical connections between shots and scenes. Verbal information is carried not by a carefully scripted narration recorded in a studio, but through sync-sound dialogue recorded "on the run." Viewers cannot sit back and wait to be told the significance of the scene they are watching; they must actively read the screen to figure out the significance of a shot or piece of dialogue. To Bell and Howell, for which "depth" of an advertising impression was all-important, cinema verité must have seemed the perfect program style.

We should not overlook the relationship between verité as the outgrowth of cinematic technological innovation and Bell and Howell's use of commercial time within "Close-Up" to demonstrate its own cinematic innovations. Without access to the specific commercials run during the four Leacock/Drew "Close-Up" films it is dangerous to press this relationship too far, but there are certainly similarities in both spirit and effect between the technology that formed the basis for verité and that being introduced by Bell and Howell for the 8mm home movie market. The contention is not that Bell and Howell used the verité films shown on "Close-Up" as a means of encouraging the development of an army of 8mm verité documentarists, but the verité style did provide a model for the amateur filmmaker quite different from that of the Hollywood cinema. The slick glossiness of the Hollywood film has always been a tantalizing but unattainable goal for the amateur filmmaker. The effects that look so "natural" in the run-of-the-mill Hollywood film turn out to be impossible to achieve in one's backyard. Verité, on the other hand, implicitly offered the stylistic message: "It's o.k. to have jerky camera movements; it doesn't matter if you have to adjust focus in the middle of a shot; you can walk around with the camera running." Bluem describes *The Children Are Watching* as follows:

> Leacock resolved to remain as unobtrusive as possible and record the story to the finish. His hand-held camera gave us a sequence of unsteady pictures, as the loose pan, the zoom in and out (and the momentary adjustment of focus), and every other kind of externally imposed movement was introduced.

In his review of *Yanki No!*, entitled, "Look, Ma, No Light Meters," UPI correspondent Fred Danzig complained about the fuzziness of some of the images and the chaotic quality of footage shot on the run. As Julia Lesage has pointed out, cinema verité has profoundly influenced contemporary feminist filmmaking precisely because its style was more "accessible" to the inexperienced filmmaker.[28]

The stylistic characteristics of cinema verité—its avoidance of music and voice-over narration, and adherence to recording uncontrolled phenomena as faithfully as possible—would seem to make any connection between verité and politics a tenuous one, indeed. However, every use of the cinema is political in the broadest sense of that term, and even "objective" verité is no exception. Furthermore, every stylistic movement in film history has arisen within a specific political and social context. In the specific films of the "Close-Up" series and in the philosophical underpinnings of cinema verité in general one can see ties to a political outlook that has been called "American liberalism."

The goal of cinema verité as an *avant-garde* movement is to render the cinema as transparent a medium as possible, to give a true picture of the world by severely restricting the possibilities for filmmaker manipulation. The verité documentarist is a neutral observer, not a polemicist. The aspirations of cinema verité are not value neutral, however. The implicit philosophical basis for verité is a version of empiricism. Verité presumes the empiricist notion that the "truth" of a given situation can be determined by the dispassionate observing and recording of it by an unbiased observer. As Leacock noted in 1964, "More and more as I made films of situations that were out of control, I found things that I thought extraordinarily interesting. Not because they were clever, or chic or anything, but because they were true. They presented you with data to try to figure out what the hell was really going on." Both the scientific (and historical) empiricism discussed in Chapter 1 and the empiricism implied by Leacock's remark stem from the belief that if observed closely enough, reality will reveal itself to us; that "truth" resides "out there" in the data collected by our senses.

Leacock was not unaware of the objection that can be raised to the claim of "objectivity" on the part of the filmmaker (just as objections were raised in Chapter 1 to the objectivity of the historian), but he did insist that the "subjectivity" introduced into the filmmaking situation by the very presence of the camera could be limited by using the proper techniques. Furthermore, Leacock believed that this minimal intrusion by the filmmaker did not substantially alter the basic "truth" of what he or she shot.[29] One of the central aesthetic problems (and, by extension, philosophical problems) of verité filmmakers from *Primary* onwards has been how to minimize intrusion by the camera and filmmaker in the profilmic event, how subjects can be encouraged to ignore or forget the fact of the camera's presence—in other words, how to allow the cinematically recorded facts to "speak for themselves." The empiricism of American cinema verité makes it quite different from its French variant (also, confusingly enough, called cinéma vérité) developed at the same time by filmmaker Jean Rouch and sociologist Edgar Morin. In *Chronicle of a Summer* and other films, Rouch and Morin used portable camera and recording equipment as tools of provocation and confrontation rather than dispassionate observation.

A Marxist historian would maintain that the empiricist orientation of American verité already gives it a political point of view, since empiricism assumes that "the way the world works" can be learned through simple observation. A Marxist view would assert that all such empiricist observation tells us is how the world is *made to appear to work* by ideology. However, one need not be a Marxist to see more specific political implications within the subjects and style of the early cinema verité films, implications one could call "liberal."

As a political doctrine, American liberalism has not been articulated with a great deal of precision, and what has been called "liberal" in one era might be called "radical" or even "socialist" in another. Most political scientists and historians would agree, however, that in the 1950s and 1960s liberalism had come to stand for the belief that, as Edward Shills puts it,

> ...A government which draws on the resources of scientific knowledge could improve its performance and thus make itself more useful in the promotion of the common welfare....[It] affirms the possibility of improving social institutions through rational action...[and of] the desirability of gradual and piecemeal improvement rather than in a total and drastic resolution of all problems.

Similarly Irving Howe sees liberalism as a reformist tendency in American twentieth-century politics, which has sought to improve the lot of the disadvantaged in modern society through government regulation and intervention, rather than through a radical restructuring of society or the economic system. The effectiveness of Roosevelt's war-time leadership and that of his successor Harry Truman had convinced liberals of the need for a strong and aggressive executive branch and also of the potential of a powerful and well-intentioned federal government to solve massive problems: end poverty and discrimination at home, improve social conditions abroad, and, literally, reach out to the stars. Central to modern American liberalism has been belief in an "enquiring and critical press." The press is viewed as a sort of social watchdog, calling to the attention of citizens and their government tears and holes in the social fabric that required mending.[30]

American liberalism reached its apex with the election of John F. Kennedy in 1960. After eight years of conservative Republician administration, the liberal wing of the Democrats now had an opportunity to implement its goals, to "get the country moving again," as Kennedy's campaign slogan put it. During the next eight years, the White House (first with Kennedy, 1960–1963; then Johnson, 1963–1968) inaugurated the space program, supported the desegregation of public schools, launched the "War on Poverty," formed the Peace Corps, and increased foreign aid.

The very style of cinema verité documentary made it the perfect form for an "enquiring and critical press." Its technology (mobile and versatile cameras and synchronous-sound recorders) not only enabled the filmmaker to capture on film social problems hidden from public view, but it also allowed the subjects of the films to speak for themselves. The refusal of the filmmaker to inject himself or herself into the subject matter of the film heightened the perceived truthfulness of the images captured on film. To Leacock the purpose of the cinema verité was to "find out some important aspect of our society by watching our society, by watching how things really happen as opposed to the social image that people hold about the way things are supposed to happen."[31] The implicit assumption here is that if right-thinking people become aware of the way things "really are," they will take steps to correct injustices and inequities. The advocacy of a specific program of change is not the filmmaker's task; it is enough to reveal the "truth" of a social situation to the viewer.

Robert Drew has called himself an "apolitical" person. However, after his initial disappointing experiments in documentary filmmaking for NBC in 1954, Drew looked to the works of a number of philosophers, social critics, and filmmakers for "clues" as to the role the documentarist might serve on television: Walter Lippman, William Allen White, John Grierson, Henry Adams, Robert Flaherty, George Bernard Shaw, and Josiah Royce.[32] Two of them, Royce and Lippman, have special relevance to the relationship between verité and liberalism. Josiah Royce, a Harvard colleague of William James, wrote one book of philosophy for the general reader, *The Philosophy of Loyalty*, published in 1908. This work had, as Drew put it, an "inflammatory impact" on him. *The Philosophy of Loyalty*, Royce's major statement on ethics, discusses the question, What values are most worth living one's life by? To Royce the moral value to be prized above all others is loyalty. Royce defined loyalty as willing devotion to and service of a social cause. "Only a cause, dignified by the social unity that it gives to many human lives, but rendered also vital for the loyal man by the personal affection which it awakens in his heart, only such a cause can unify his outer and inner world."[33]

Drew does not tell us what social cause Royce's work might have prompted him to embrace, but his reading of Walter Lippman during his Neiman year at Harvard suggests a strong possibility. Lippman, whom Robert Bartley has called "a pillar of the liberal establishment,"[34] published *Essays in the Public Philosophy*, one of his most popular and controversial books, in 1955. In it he argued that the rapid pace of technological change in the twentieth century and the resulting complexity of domestic and international political problems cast serious doubt on Western democracies' ability to cope with these problems. Many issues required quick responses, but responses based on detailed analysis of complex alternatives. Democracy, with its cumbersome and slow process of deliberation, persuasion, and majority rule, was ill-equipped to handle problems of the atomic age. Central to Lippman's analysis of "the alarming failure of the Western liberal democracies to cope with the realities of this century" was the failure of journalism to inform the populace about complex social issues in such a way that rational decisions could be made, and, once made, acted upon by a unified nation.[35] Lippman's pessimism was interpreted as an attack on liberalism by many, but others looked upon his dire warnings as a challenge to repair the holes Lippman pointed out in the liberal edifice.

Drew has said that he shared Lippman's belief that democracies faced a crisis in decision making and hence a crisis in journalism, but believed further that innovative uses of new technology might help to deal with some of the problems technological innovation had created. Television might be used "to give the millions the commonly shared experience necessary to the workings of their democracies." The primary vehicle for his "commonly shared experience" Drew saw as the prime-time documentary. "What it can add to the journalistic spectrum is something absolutely unique—strong experience of what it is like to be somewhere else, seeing for yourself into the dramatic developments in the lives of people caught up in stories of importance."[36]

This is not an attempt to establish what Drew "intended" to do in his films or to demonstrate that his aim was the furthering of a specific political position through film and television. Remember that Drew has said he was "apolitical." However, it does appear that liberalism formed part of the political context out of which cinema verité emerged in both a general and a particular sense. To recall the case study from Chapter 3, the liberal victory helped to set the terms of political and social discourse of the period. More specifically, both Drew and Leacock's philosophy of filmmaking can be seen to grow out of a liberal concern over the proper role of the press in democratic societies.

Further evidence of how liberalism provided an important context for the early Drew films comes from the subjects of the "Close-Up" films themselves. The first, *Yanki, No!*, dealt with anti-Americanism in Latin America, an issue that was to become a major foreign policy concern for the Kennedy administration. *X-Pilot*, the second "Close-Up" film to be shown, looked at jet test pilot Scott Crossfield. The test flights of the "X planes" laid important groundwork for the space program, a priority of the Kennedy administration. The third, *The Children Are Watching*, examined school desegregation in Louisiana. Of it Drew has said, "I thought when people saw how vicious and awful they were in front of their own children, they'd all be converted."[37] The final film to be shown in the "Close-Up" series, *Adventures on the New Frontier*, was a "day in the life" portrait of President Kennedy. In the words of its opening narration, the film took the audience on a "personal adventure with the President as he confronts the great problems of the U.S. and the world."

Certainly cinema verité has been used to treat subjects other than social problems and other "liberal" issues. After leaving Drew Associates, Donn Pennebaker turned his attention to verité treatments of music and the arts: *Don't Look Back* (1966), *Monterey Pop* (1968), *Original Cast Album: Company!* (1970), and *Keep on Rockin'* (1970). Albert and David Maysles, members for several years of the Drew "team," have produced a series of cinema verité character studies in *Showman* (1962), *Meet Marlon Brando* (1965), *Salesman* (1969), and *Gimme Shelter* (1970). However, a number of other documentarists have found in verité an appropriate medium for expressing what we might call their "social commitment"—a commitment grounded in most cases in American liberalism's tradition of a "politics of conscience." In this category can be placed such films as Leacock's *Chiefs* (1969) on the attitudes of American police chiefs; Frederick Wiseman's series of films on American social institutions: *Titicut Follies* (1967), *Law and Order* (1969), *High School* (1969), *Hospital* (1970), and *Basic Training* (1971); William Jersey's *A Time for Burning* (1965) on church integration: Peter Davis's Vietnam War documentary, *Hearts and Minds* (1973); and Barbara Kopple's film on a Kentucky coal miner's strike, *Harlan County, U.S.A.* 1977).

Once again, what ties them to a liberal notion of the role of the press is not only their choice of subject matter but also their style. In Leacock's words, verité films "watch our society." By exposing social problems without explicitly commenting on them, verité documentaries leave solutions to problems outside the film. The advocacy of a specific program of change is not the filmmaker's task; he or she merely reveals the "truth" of a social situation to the viewer in as unbiased a way as possible. The style of cinema verité accommodates a liberal philosophical view in that it assumes that whatever inequities are revealed through the cinematic observation of reality can be solved by adjustments in the social system. Racial prejudice or anti-Americanism is not "explained" by the films or used as an illustration of the failure of the social system as a whole; rather, they are presented as flaws in the system that can be corrected by the action of the government or concerned citizens. The verité filmmaker has no specific alternative programmatic to present. In fact, where filmmakers do wish to use the documentary form not only to present a social problem but also to advocate a political or social plan of action, they find cinema verité an extremely restrictive style in which to work. Some feminist and Third World filmmakers have had to depart from the "objectivity" of verité because that quality rendered it incompatible with the filmmaker's desire to express his or her commitment to a specific political or social position.[38]

The Fate of Cinema Verité

After the initial four-film contract, ABC discontinued its association with Time, Inc. in documentary filmmaking. Drew recalls that the two companies squabbled over ownership of a local television station. It is also probable that ABC looked upon its brief association with Time, Inc. and Drew as a stopgap measure that bought the network some relief from FCC pressure while giving it time to bolster its own news division. At the same time ABC dropped its association with Time, it announced a return to its previous policy of not accepting public affairs programming from outside its own news operation. Except for a few isolated instances, that policy remains in effect at all three commercial networks.

Public television has provided the only network outlet for cinema verité documentaries (or independently produced documentaries of any kind, for that matter). A few cinema verité films have received commercial theatrical distribution (*Harlan County, U.S.A., Gimme Shelter, Monterey Pop, Gray Gardens, Best Boy, Gates of Heaven*). Others have been distributed nontheatrically to film clubs, cinema societies, and college film courses. As has been noted, some politically committed filmmakers have felt the need to move beyond verité and develop a more polemical style of filmmaking. Much of the movement's *avant-garde* character has been diluted, as frequently happens to "alternative" stylistic movements, by the adoption of verité techniques in Hollywood filmmaking. Ever since Haskell Wexler's *Medium Cool* (1968) used some uncontrolled footage and a verité "style" (hand-held camera work, location shooting) to lend a documentary feel to a scripted, fictional film, it has all but become a cliche in Hollywood filmmaking that when a director wants to convey a sense of spontaneity and immediacy in a particular scene, he or she uses a hand-held, restless, "verité" style of shooting.

Even in television public affairs programming, where verité first reached a mass audience in the United States, verité has not flourished. For one reason, since the days of Edward R. Murrow in the 1950s, television documentaries have been structured around the reporter, with whose voice and face the audience is familiar: Edward R. Murrow, Roger Mudd, Mike Wallace, Dan Rather, Geraldo Rivera, Barbara Walters. The inevitable mediation between audience and subject that the reporter creates is anathema to verité. On the other hand, networks do not pay their star reporters six-figure salaries to be "invisible" in prime-time documentaries. Hence, the typical prime-time television documentary is structured not around the principles of verité, but rather around Mike Wallace's leaping from behind a one-way mirror, Geraldo Rivera's pursuing a reluctant interviewee through a parking lot, and Dan Rather's masquerading as an Afghan rebel.

Conclusions: The Relative Force of Generative Mechanisms in Cinema Verité

Why did cinema verité emerge when and where it did? As this brief look at its historical context shows, it would be difficult to say that any one person, institution, or event "caused" cinema verité to develop as a style of documentary filmmaking. Rather, its early history in the United States is a result of the interaction of several mechanisms. Although he played a central role in getting cinema verité documentaries television exposure, it would be simplistic to say that Robert Drew was "responsible" for the development of verité. Similarly, although Richard Leacock seems to have been a major creative force in the shaping of the first American cinema verité films and although he and Donn Pennebaker fashioned the first practical verité recording equipment, it would be equally simplistic to assert that verité came about "because" of their efforts alone. The technology Leacock and Pennebaker adapted already existed (albeit in its nascent form) or was in the process of being developed. However, its invention and innovation were in response to World War II military needs and those of the broadcasting industry and space program rather than the needs of documentary filmmaking. Furthermore, the desire for a "cinema of truth" in the late 1950s cannot be credited to any single individual. Drew and Leacock form part of a larger movement in European and American cinema toward a "realist" alternative to the classical Hollywood narrative cinema.

It is unlikely that cinema verité in America would have emerged as a distinctive style of cinema as early as it did had it not been for the persistence and managerial abilities of Robert Drew and the artistic commitment of Richard Leacock. As in most historical phenomena, individuals do make a difference, but that "difference" is but one factor of many. Drew's efforts might well have gone for nought had it not been for the need of ABC to increase its output of public affairs programming—a situation that led to Time, Inc.'s being able to break through the networks' across-the-boards prohibition against using outside material. Nor might ABC have been willing to gamble on a type of public affairs programming so clearly different from the run-of-the-mill television documentary had it not been for its poor position *vis a vis* the other networks and for Bell and Howell's need to risk its tiny advertising budget in an attempt to capture a particular audience segment. Neither Drew or Leacock conceived of the "objectivity" of verité as an accommodation to the institutional needs of ABC or Bell and Howell. However, had the Drew "Close-Up" films "taken sides" in the issues they presented or explicitly advocated a social or political policy, it is highly unlikely ABC would have allowed the airing of outside public affairs material or that Bell and Howell would have provided sponsorship.

The fate of the verité films after "Close-Up" illustrates the changes that can occur to a film historical phenomenon as its generative mechanisms are altered. Furthermore, it suggests the primacy of film's relationship with commercial television as a causal factor in the history of cinema verité. In this case, for whatever reason(s)—a rift between ABC and Time, Inc. brass and/or a reversion to its initial policy regarding public affairs material—ABC discontinued its connection with Time, Inc., thus depriving cinema verité of the opportunity for national, mass-audience exposure on television. As a stylistic movement, cinema verité did not disappear, but after 1961, verité filmmakers were forced to look to public television, movie theaters, and film societies for exhibition outlets. It is easy to play the "what if" game of history with the post-"Close-Up" course of cinema verité history. "What if" ABC had continued to allow outside public affairs material on its network? "What if" the network news "star system" had not developed? Perhaps unfortunately for the verité document artists and television audiences, asking these questions *is* just a game. What *did* happen was that, because of the policies of commercial television networks, verité was forced into the position of a marginal filmmaking practice, seldom gaining access to movie theaters and less often to commercial television, its superficial stylistic characteristics appropriated by the dominant Hollywood and commercial television practices.

NOTES

1. Stephen Mamber, *Cinema Verite in America* (Cambridge, Mass.: MIT Press, 1974), p. 23.
2. Richard M. Barsam, "Nonfiction Film: The Realist Impulse," in *Film Theory and Criticism*, 2nd ed., Gerald Mast and Marshal Cohen, eds. (New York: Oxford, 1979), pp. 582–583; and David Bordwell and Kristin Thompson, *Film Art: An Introduction* (Reading, Mass.: Addison-Wesley, 1979), pp. 96–97.

3. Mamber, *Cinema Verite in America*, p. 4.

4. David Bordwell, *French Impressionist Cinema: Film Culture, Film Theory, and Film Style* (New York: Arno, 1980), p. 1.

5. James Blue, "One Man's Truth—An Interview with Richard Leacock," *Film Comment* 3 (Spring 1965): 16–23; and Patricia Jaffe, "Editing Cinema Verite," *Film Comment* 3 (Summer 1965): 43–47.

6. Cesare Zavattini, "Some Ideas on the Cinema," *Sight and Sound* 23 (July–September 1953): 64–70; quoted in Mamber, *Cinema Verite in America*, p. 15.

7. Jaffe, "Editing Cinema Verite," p. 43.

8. Alexander Calder-Marshall, *The Innocent Eye: The Life of Robert Flaherty* (Baltimore: Penguin Books, 1963), pp. 221–222.

9. Patricia Zimmerman, "With Cameras and Guns: Amateurs, 16mm, Hollywood, and World War II," unpublished paper, University of Wisconsin, 1980. I wish to thank Prof. Zimmerman for sharing her research on this topic with me prior to its publication.

10. James Wong Howe, "The Documentary Technique and Hollywood," *American Cinematographer* (January 1944): 10; quoted in Zimmerman, "With Cameras and Guns," p. 2.

11. Interview with Robert Drew by Robert C. Allen, December 11, 1981; Edmund M. Digiulio, "Development in Motion Picture Camera Design and Technology—A Ten-Year Update," *SMPTE Journal* 85 (July 1976): 483–486; and Loren L. Ryder, "Magnetic Sound Recording in the Motion Picture and Television Industries," *SMPTE Journal* 85 (July 1976): 528–530.

12. Robert Drew, "An Independent Among the Networks," unpublished paper, 1981.

13. Information taken from Drew interview; Drew, "Independent Among the Networks"; and Mamber, *Cinema Verite in America*, pp. 30–40.

14. Louis Marcorelles, *The Living Cinema* (New York: Praeger, 1973), p. 50.

15. "ABC-TV Assault on the Summit," *Broadcasting* 56 (March 16, 1959): 199–200; "Are CBS-TV and NBC-TV Copycats?" *Broadcasting* 60 (April 17, 1961): 46; and "Strategy for a Program Battle," *Broadcasting* 57 (August 17, 1959): 27–34.

16. "There's Money in Public Service," *Broadcasting* 58 (April 18, 1960): 29–32.

17. "This Way to the Escape Hatch?" *Broadcasting* 58 (January 18, 1960): 46; and "Big Swing to Information Shows," *Broadcasting* 59 (December 19, 1960): 39–40.

18. *Broadcasting* 58 (February 1, 1960): 31–33.

19. "Endorsement for Public Affairs," *Broadcasting* 59 (December 19, 1960): 39–40.

20. Quoted in "Bell and Howell Sticks to *Close-Up*," *Broadcasting* 61 (September 18, 1961): 34.

21. *Wall Street Journal*, January 8, 1960, p. 26; January 13, p. 10; September 21, p. 7; May 4, 1961, p. 4; May 26, p. 30; and "Bell and Howell Thrives on Controversy," *Sponsor* 15 (June 5, 1961): 43–44.

22. Ibid., p. 44.

23. "T.V. Documentaries: Will They Sell?" *Printer's Ink* 15 (May 1, 1959): 40–44; and "Bell and Howell Thrives on Controversy," p. 44.

24. Leacock interview, p. 16.

25. 13 FCC 1249, 1949; Amendment to Section 315, Communications Act, 1959; and Paul Silver, quoted in "There's Money in Public Service," *Broadcasting* 58 (April 18, 1960): 29–32.

26. "Endorsement of Public Affairs," *Broadcasting* 59 (December 19, 1960): 39–40; and ABC memo, Bert Briller to William Muller, August 8, 1960, quoted in Zimmerman, "With Cameras and Guns."

27. William Bluem, *Documentary in American Television* (New York: Hastings House, 1965), p. 130; and Louis Marcorelles, "Nothing But the Truth," *Sight and Sound* 32 (Summer 1963): 114–117.

28. Bluem, *Documentary in American Television*, p. 129; Fred Danzig, "Look Ma, No Light Meters," UPI Wire Story, December 8, 1960, quoted in Zimmerman, "With Cameras and Guns"; and Julia Lesage, "Political Aesthetics of the Feminist Documentary Film," *Quarterly Review of Film Studies* 3 (Fall 1978): 507–523.

29. Quoted in Marcorelles, *Living Cinema*, pp. 47–58.

30. Edward Shills, "The Antimonies of Liberalism," pp. 135–200; Robert Bartley, "Liberalism in 1976," pp. 61–80; Irving Howe, "Socialism and Liberalism," pp. 33–59; all in *The Relevance of Liberalism*, Staff of the Research Institute on International Change, Columbia University (Boulder, Colo.: Westview Press, 1978).

31. Leacock interview, p. 18.

32. Drew interview; and Drew, "Independent Among the Networks," p. 4.

33. Josiah Royce, *The Philosophy of Loyalty*, from *The Basic Writings of Josiah Royce*, Vol. II (Chicago: University of Chicago Press, 1969), p. 877.

34. Bartley, "Liberalism in 1976," p. 63.

35. Walter Lippman, *Essays in the Public Philosophy* (Boston: Little, Brown, 1955); and Larry L. Adams, *Walter Lippman* (Boston: Twayne, 1977), pp. 155–193.

36. Drew, "Independent Among the Networks," pp. 8–9.

37. Drew interview.

38. Lesage, "Political Aesthetics," p. 522.

10

A Selective Guide
to Reading

The following guide, organized according to chapter topics, provides suggestions for further reading. Space allows for only representative selections from the rapidly growing literature of film history. Examples focus on the American cinema for the most part. Purposely excluded are the numerous pop biographies, fan studies, and material concerning contemporary (post–1960) cinema. All citations should be available in any university or large public library.

CHAPTER 1: FILM HISTORY AS HISTORY

Film historians are just beginning to examine the nature and function of film historical research. Edward Buscombe has contributed three important essays: "A New Approach to Film History," *1977 Film Studies Annual, Part II* (West Lafayette, Ind.: Purdue University, 1978), pp. 1–8, "Introduction: Metahistory of Films," *Film Reader* 4, pp. 11–15; and "Notes on Columbia Picture Corp., 1926–41," *Screen* 16 (Autumn 1975): 65–82. Equally valuable are Robert C. Allen, "Film History: The Narrow Discourse," *1977 Film Studies Annual* (West Lafayette, Ind.: Purdue University, 1978); Michael T. Isenberg, "Toward an Historical Methodology for Film Scholarship," *The Rocky Mountain Social Science Journal* 12, no. 1 (January 1975): 45–57; Vance Keply, "Griffith's *Broken Blossoms* and the Problem of Historical Specificity," *Quarterly Review of Film Studies* 3, no. 1 (Fall 1977): 37–48; and Gerald Mast, "Film History and

243

Film Histories," *Quarterly Review of Film Studies* 1, no. 3 (August 1976): 297–314.

For a typology of approaches to film history, see Charles F. Altman's "Toward a Historiography of American Film," *Cinema Journal* 16, no 1 (Spring 1977): 1–25. Altman's article is particularly valuable because it presents an extensive survey of the various schools of method used by film historians. For an alternative, see Geoffrey Nowell-Smith, "Facts About Films and Facts of Films," *Quarterly Review of Film Studies* 1, no. 3 (August 1976): 272–275.

The nature of historical inquiry, explanation, and knowledge has been the subject of thousands of articles, monographs, and books. It is best to begin with one of the primers written for students in traditional history programs. They discuss philosophies of history as well as the process of doing historical research and writing. Among the best are Paul K. Conkin and Roland N. Stromberg, *The Heritage and Challenge of History* (New York: Dodd, Mead, 1972); Donald V. Gawronski, *History: Meaning and Method*, 3rd ed. (Glenview, Ill.: Scott, Foresman, 1975); Louis Gottschalk, *Understanding History* (New York: Knopf, 1969); and R. J. Shafer, *A Guide to Historical Method* (Homewood, Ill.: Dorsey Press, 1969).

A more general philosophical discussion of historiographic issues, but written in a straight-forward style, can be found in E. H. Carr's *What Is History?* (New York: Vintage, 1961). This is a collection of lectures on the nature of history, first delivered at Oxford in the late 1950s. Carr succinctly and clearly argues the case against the "common sense" (or empiricist) view of history.

David Hackett Fischer's *Historian's Fallacies: Toward a Logic of Historical Thought* (New York: Harper & Row, 1970) offers a virtual encyclopedia of the problems practicing historians encounter in their work. Fischer informs by example; his book would have been even more useful had he added a set of precepts in the conclusion. Still, *Historian's Fallacies* remains a great place to initiate the study of historiography.

Two useful anthologies contain the thought of historians (and philosophers) about the nature of historical inquiry: Fritz Stern's *The Varieties of History* (New York: Meridian, 1956); and Patrick Gardiner's *Theories of History* (Glencoe, Ill.: The Free Press, 1961). The latter is aimed at the specialist, and includes a fine bibliography.

Also suggested are two books by practicing historians commenting on their field work at a more advanced level; both are well worth reading. The best is Jacques Barzun and Henry F. Graff's *The Modern Researcher*, 3rd ed. (New York: Harcourt Brace Jovanovich, 1977). Indeed this book is for anyone who seeks to do quality research and writing. On the other hand, for a succinct summary of various approaches to historical analysis, read H. P. R. Finberg (ed.), *Approaches to History* (Toronto: University of Toronto Press, 1962). This collection provides a fine introduction to the value of specific methodologies.

Finally, where do modern American historians think their field is headed? John Higham's *Writing American History: Essays in Modern Scholarship*

(Bloomington: Indiana University Press, 1970) lays out one answer. Higham is one of America's most respected intellectual historians. For a collection of other perspectives, see Charles F. Delzell (ed.), *The Future of History* (Nashville: Vanderbilt University Press, 1977). These eleven essays cover the range of historiographic approaches as well as a discussion of the relationship between history and the social sciences.

One specific group of social historians in France has been working out an influential alternative to approaches taken in the United States and Britain. Their work, developed around and through the *Annales*, aims for an interdisciplinary, complete reconstruction of the past (*histoire totale*). Through the use of quantification, demography, sociology, economics, anthropology, biology, linguistics, and psychology, the *Annales* school has sought to bring "ordinary" people and "everyday" problems to the forefront of historical research and writing. Carefully dip into Marc Ferro (ed.), *Social Historians in Contemporary France: Essays from Annales* (New York: Harper & Row, 1972); Traian Storanovich, *French Historical Method: The Annales Paradigm* (Ithaca, N.Y.: Cornell University Press, 1976); and Fernand Braudel, *The Mediterranean and the Mediterranean World in the Age of Philip II* (New York: Harper & Row, 1976).

Professional philosophers have also addressed questions of historiography in many complex and interesting ways. They write for the specialist. Among the more accessible are R. F. Atkinson, *Knowledge and Explanation in History: An Introduction to the Philosophy of History* (Ithaca, N.Y.: Cornell University Press, 1978); Arthur C. Danto, *Analytical Philosophy of History* (Cambridge: Cambridge University Press, 1968); William Dray (ed.), *Philosophical Analysis and History* (New York: Harper & Row, 1966); and W. H. Walsh, *Introduction to the Philosophy of History* (London: Hutchinson, 1951).

The work of art historians also can help us with many of the same issues. For a survey of conventional approaches, see W. Eugene Klienbauer, *Modern Perspectives in Western Art History* (New York: Holt, Rinehart and Winston, 1971). For a radical perspective, examine Arnold Hauser, *The Philosophy of Art History* (New York: Meridian, 1959).

There has not been a great deal written by philosophers of science about empiricism and conventionalism. Robert Allen's particular discussion relies on three works that deal with advanced issues in the field: Ted Benton's *Philosophical Foundations of the Three Sociologies* (London: Routledge and Kegan Paul, 1977); Roy Bhaskaer's *A Realist Theory of Science* (Atlantic Highlands, N.J.: Humanities Press, 1978); and Russell Keat and John Unrry's *Social Theory as Science* (London: Routledge and Kegan Paul, 1975). This work is so new that even its supporters agree it only provides a first step. The only discussion in which this theory has been applied to film is Terry Lovell's book: *Pictures of Reality: Aesthetics, Politics and Pleasure* (London: British Film Institute, 1980). For philosophers of science, the work of Thomas S. Kuhn is more widely known in the United States. His key work appeared as Thomas S. Kuhn, *The*

Structure of Scientific Revolutions (Chicago: University of Chicago Press, 1962). For an analysis of how Kuhn sees his role in theory building see his article, "The Relations Between History and the History of Science," in Felix Gilbert and Stephen R. Graubaird (eds.), *Historical Studies Today* (New York: W. W. Norton, 1972), pp. 159–192. Gene Wise has attempted to convert Kuhn's theory into historical practice in *American Historical Explanations: A Strategy for Grounded Inquiry*, 2nd ed. (Minneapolis: University of Minnesota Press, 1980).

CHAPTER 2: RESEARCHING FILM HISTORY

There exists precious little written about the history of film study in the United States. A concise survey, "Film Study and Its Evolution," can be found in Nancy Allen's *Film Study Collections: A Guide to Their Development and Use* (New York: Frederick Ungar, 1979), pp. 3–10. For an analysis of the rapid expansion of the field during the past two decades, see Ronald Gottesman's, "Film Culture: The State of the Art," *Quarterly Review of Film Studies* 2, no. 2 (May 1977): 212–226. Periodic essays in the *Quarterly Review of Film Studies* survey the state of the film historical literature. For an up-to-date survey of the academic study of film, see The American Film Institute's *Guide to College Courses in Film and Television* (Princeton, N.J.: Peterson's Guides). It contains descriptions of film curricula in U.S. colleges and universities. This valuable reference tool is updated periodically. The Canadian Film Institute, headquartered in Ottawa, Ontario, publishes *A Guide to Film and Television Courses in Canada*. For a British perspective, examine articles in *Screen Education*, published by the Society for Education in Film and Television. In 1982 *Screen Education* was merged with *Screen* to form a bi-monthly publication.

There also has been far too little written about problems of filmic evidence. Gary Carey in *Lost Films* (Greenwich: New York Graphic Society, 1970) discusses some of the thousands of films that are forever lost because of nitrate disintegration. Although not directly concerned with the problem of lost films, Kevin Brownlow, *The Parade's Gone By...* (New York: Ballantine, 1969) does tell of the author's difficult quests to recover silent films. It also provides a delightful, anecdotal introduction to the history of the American silent film. Film storage problems are discussed in W. H. Utterback, Jr. "An Opinion on the Nitrate Fire, Suitland, Maryland, 7 December 1978," *Journal of the University Film Association* 32, no 3 (Summer 1980): 3–16.

Swedish film archivist Gosta Werner examines the problem of attempting to "reconstruct" lost films using photographs, shot lists, and other materials in "A Method of Constructing Lost Films," *Cinema Journal* 14, no. 2 (Winter 1974–75): 11–15. For an application of these principles, see Herman G. Weinberg's *The Complete Wedding March* (Boston: Little Brown, 1974), and *The Complete Greed* (New York: E. P. Dutton, 1972). In these two books, Weinberg has attempted to locate the various versions of these two films, and then reconstruct them using stills and description.

For more information on the deterioration of color films, see "Colour Problem," *Sight & Sound* 30, no. 1 (Winter 1980–81): 12–13; Paul Spehr, "The Color Film Crisis," *American Film* 5, no. 2 (November 1979): 56–61; and Harlan Jacobson, "Old Pix Don't Die, They Fade Away," *Variety*, July 9, 1980, p. 1.

There are two useful books on how archivists deal with the problems of maintaining the films that remain: Eileen Bowser and John Kuiper (ed.), *A Handbook for Film Archives* (Brussels: Federation Internationale des Archives du Film, 1980); and Ralph N. Sargent (ed.), *Preserving the Moving Image* (Washington, D.C.: Corporation for Public Broadcasting, 1974). The Bowser and Kuiper collection is based on the experience of members of the International Federation of Film Archives (FIAF), and lists numerous FIAF specialized pamphlets on individual problems of film preservation.

There exist no survey works concerned with the problems of textual variation. Much of the work done so far has centered on films made prior to 1910. Presently that area of film history is undergoing significant reevaluation. So by examining that new literature one can get an idea of how scholars have dealt with the problem of textual variation in terms of larger historical issues. See Charles Musser, "The Early Cinema of Edwin Porter," *Cinema Journal* 19, no. 1 (Fall 1979): 1–35; Jon Gartenberg, "Camera Movement in Edison and Biograph Films, 1900–1906," *Cinema Journal* 19, no. 2 (Spring 1980): 1–16; and Noel Burch, "Porter or Ambivalence," *Screen* 19, no. 4 (Winter 1978–79): 91–105. All take different approaches toward understanding the form and function of early cinema necessitating the reconstruction of proper versions of early films.

More and more film archives are opening in all parts of the United States. For surveys of the major archives of collections, refer to the following: Nancy Allen, *Film Study Collections: A Guide to Their Development and Use* (New York: Ungar, 1979); Robert A. Armour, *Film: A Reference Guide* (Westport, Conn.: Greenwood Press, 1980): and Ronald Gottesman and Harry M. Geduld, *Guidebook to Film* (New York: Holt, Rinehart and Winston, 1972).

Two sources help keep up with recent additions, new collections, and the opening of new centers: *The American Film Institute Guide to College Courses in Film and Television* from Peterson's Guides of Princeton, New Jersey; and Peter Cowie's annual *International Film Guide* published by Tantivy Press of London, England.

Finally, there exist two specific area guides: Linda Harris Mehr (ed.), *Motion Pictures, Television and Radio: A Union Catalogue of Manuscript and Special Collections in the Western United States* (Boston: G. K. Hall, 1977); and Bonnie G. Rowan *Scholars' Guide to Washington, D.C.: Film and Video Collections* (Washington, D.C.: Smithsonian Institution Press, 1980).

Nonfilmic evidence comes in many forms. The researcher seeks information generated as close as possible to the events of interest—in terms of both time and space. The written sources often come in the form of trade papers sold to industry participants. Indeed, as soon as motion picture technology was used for commercial enterprise, specialized newspapers began to cover business activities. At first, coverage was restricted to the trade papers for circuses and vaudeville: the still published *Billboard*, and the New York *Dramatic Mirror* (1879–1922). In 1905 *Variety* opened for business to cover vaudeville. Soon movies took up much of its space. *Daily Variety* for West Coast readers began in 1933. In 1907 came *Moving Picture World* aimed at exhibitors. It merged with *Exhibitor's Herald* (1914–1929) in 1929, and then with *Motion Picture Herald* in 1930. *Motion Picture Herald* lasted until 1972.

There have been other tradepapers aimed at exhibitors: *Boxoffice* (1932–present); *Film Daily* (1915–1970), and *Motion Picture News* (1908–1930). (*Motion Picture News* also merged with *Motion Picture Herald* in 1930.) There were many regional tradepapers that went in and out of business as conditions permitted. All were absorbed by *Boxoffice* by 1970.

In 1918 the Wid's organization began *Wid's Daily*, which later became *Film Daily*. In 1918 Wid's issued a yearbook, collecting in one place rosters of stars, technicians, directors, producers, other creators, corporations, and other useful information, to be updated yearly. Renamed *Film Daily Yearbook*, it lasted until 1970.

In 1929 the Quigley organization, publishers of *Motion Picture Herald*, printed the first *Motion Picture Almanac* yearbook. Now titled the *International Motion Picture Almanac*, this remains a useful compendium of information about the U.S. (and foreign) film industries. In 1964 Peter Cowie began his *International Film Guide* series (London, Tantivy Press) for the critic/teacher/scholar, not the industry participant.

Most university and large public libraries have complete runs of *Variety*, *Film Daily Yearbook*, and *International Motion Picture Almanac* on microfilm. Reviews of motion pictures began in earnest about 1910. Two valuable collections can be found in the *New York Times Film Reviews, 1913–1970* (New York: Arno Press, 1969–1971), updated; and the recently issued collected reviews of *Variety* (New York: Variety, 1983–1985). For collections of other primary written material, see George C. Pratt's *Spellbound in Darkness* (Greenwich, Conn.: New York Graphic Society, 1973); and Gerald Mast's *The Movies in Our Midst: Documents in the Cultural History of Film in America* (Chicago: University of Chicago Press, 1982).

There is, of course, a great deal of published secondary material. For specific information, seek out the array of guides and encyclopediae. Encyclopediae provide an overview. Look to Roger Manwell, *The International Encyclopedia of Film* (New York: Crown, 1972); and Ephraim Katz, *The Film Encyclopedia* (New York: Lippincott & Crowell, 1979).

Reference guides, usually concentrating on stars and their careers, abound. Try Cobbett Steinberg, *Reel Facts: The Movie Book of Records* (New York: Vintage, 1978); Leslie Halliwell, *The Filmgoers Companion*, 6th ed. (New

York: Avon, 1978); Georges Sadoul, *Dictionary of Filmmakers* (Berkeley: University of California Press, 1972); Richard Roud, *Cinema: A Critical Dictionary* (New York: Viking, 1980); Mike Kaplan, *Variety: International Showbusiness Reference* (New York: Garland, 1981); and William T. Stewart, Arthur F. McClure, and Ken D. Jones, *International Film Necrology* (New York: Garland, 1980). The latter is a valuable guide to the obituaries of people who worked in Hollywood.

Moreover, data relating to questions of film history often reside in sources on U.S. history in general. For help in that area, see Frank Freidel (ed.), *Harvard Guide to American History*, rev. ed. (Cambridge, Mass.: Harvard University Press, 1977); and John R. M. Wilson, *Research Guide in History* (Morristown, N.J.: General Learning Press, 1974).

Not all written information about cinema's past has been published or issued in microform. Personal and business papers often rest in specialized archives. For lists of such archives and their holdings, see Nancy Allen, *Film Study Collections: A Guide to Their Development and Use* (New York: Ungar, 1979); Robert A. Armour, *Film: A Reference Guide* (Westport, Conn.: Greenwood Press, 1980); Ronald Gottesman and Harry M. Geduld, *Guidebook to Film* (New York: Holt, Rinehart and Winston, 1972); and the other sources noted above under the section concerned with film archives. In addition, another useful guide on unpublished papers can be found in Louis A. Rachow (ed.), *Theatre and Performing Arts Collections* (New York: The Haworth Press, 1981).

A great deal of unpublished material can also be found in court records and government documents. For information and help with the former, see Morris L. Cohen, *Legal Research in a Nutshell*, 3rd ed. (St. Paul, Minn.: West Publishing Co., 1978); and Harvey L. Zuckman and Martin J. Gaynes, *Mass Communication Law in a Nutshell* (St. Paul, Minn.: West Publishing Co., 1977). For help with the latter, see Helen J. Poulton, *The Historian's Handbook: A Descriptive Guide to Reference Works* (Norman: University of Oklahoma Press, 1972).

As opposed to the written sources noted above, oral sources are much more difficult to investigate. Indeed, with the development of Hollywood, interviews with stars have been a cornerstone of the film industry's publicity mill. In recent years with the rise of the auteur theory, this impetus has extended to directors, producers, and others. Printed interviews have often been collected into anthologies. The classic for a director is François Truffaut's *Hitchcock* (New York: Simon and Schuster, 1966). With use of more than 500 questions, and nearly the same number of stills, noted director Truffaut paid homage to his favorite director.

Other collections for directors include Eric Sherman and Martin Rubin, *The Director's Event* (New York: Atheneum, 1969); Andrew Sarris (ed.), *Interviews with Film Directors* (Indianapolis: Bobbs-Merrill, 1967); Charles Thomas

Samuels, *Encountering Directors* (New York: Capricorn, 1972); and Charles Higham and Joel Greenberg, *The Celluloid Muse* (Chicago: Henry Regnery, 1969).

More and more nonstar types are being interviewed. For example, see Leonard Maltin's *Behind the Camera: The Cinematographer's Art* (New York: New American Library, 1971); Walter Wagner's *You Must Remember This* (New York: G. P. Putnam's Sons, 1975); and Bernard Rosenberg and Harry Silverstein's *The Real Tinsel* (New York: The Macmillan Company, 1970). The latter includes interviews with producers and corporate executives.

Unpublished interviews can be found in nearly all major archives. They have not been catalogued. One large collection is located in the Louis B. Mayer Oral History Collection at the American Film Institute Library in Beverly Hills, California, and is now available on microfilm through the Microfilming Corporation of America. The availability of other collections should be verified by contacting the specific archive. Since many figures in film history are still alive, the researcher can conduct his or her own interviews. For suggestions on the best procedures, see citations listed in Chapter 8.

CHAPTER 3: READING FILM HISTORY

The best place to begin reading history of American cinema is with the survey histories. Chapter 3 analyzes the first such works: Robert Grau, *Theatre of Science* (New York: Broadway Publishing, 1914); and Terry Ramsaye, *A Million and One Nights* (New York: Simon and Schuster, 1926). The work of Benjamin Hampton and Lewis Jacobs constitute the other major contributions in the first epoch of film historical writing in the United States. Hampton, a corporate insider, authored the first business history: *History of the American Film Industry* (New York: Covici, Friede, 1931). Jacobs, an active filmmaker writing during the Great Depression, produced a social history, *The Rise of the American Film* (New York: Teachers College Press, 1939).

Europeans also began to write histories with a great deal of their attention directed toward Hollywood. Filmmaker Paul Rotha produced *The Film Till Now* (London: Spring, 1930). This and Maurice Bardeche and Robert Brasillach's *A History of Motion Pictures* (New York: Norton, 1938) constitute part of an early appreciation of motion pictures by Europeans.

The transition to the current group of survey textbooks was fostered by five historians: Arthur Knight, Richard Griffith, Arthur Mayer, A. R. Fulton, and Kenneth MacGowan. Knight's *The Liveliest Art* (New York: New American Library, 1979—originally published in 1957) came first. This book, and Richard Griffith and Arthur Mayer's *The Movies* (New York: Bonanza, 1957), laid out what most people have come to think of as American film history. Both books emphasized the split between the great filmmakers of Europe, and the economic influence and power of Hollywood. A. R. Fulton, *Motion Pictures: The Devel-*

opment of an Art (Norman: University of Oklahoma Press, 1960); and Kenneth MacGowan, *Behind the Screen* (New York: Delta, 1965) were authored by academics, thus providing the first film history books for college and university film courses.

When the post-World War II baby boom generation began to matriculate to U.S. colleges and universities during the 1960s, sales of Knight's book began to soar. Soon the new teachers of film courses sought to write alternative survey texts. The first, Gerald Mast's *A Short History of the Movies* (Indianapolis: Bobbs-Merrill, 1971), became a best seller. After that came one new survey history per year: Lawrence Kardish, *Reel Plastic Magic* (Boston: Little Brown, 1972); Peter Cowie, *A Concise History of the Cinema*, 2 volumes (London: A. Zwemmer, 1971); Charles Higham, *The Art of the American Film* (Garden City, N.Y.: Anchor Books, 1973); Alan Casty, *Development of the Film: An Interpretative History* (New York: Harcourt Brace Jovanovich, 1973); David Robinson, *The History of World Cinema* (New York: Stein & Day, 1973); Basil Wright, *The Long View* (New York: Knopf, 1974); Eric Rhode, *A History of the Cinema* (New York: Hill and Wang, 1976); Thomas W. Bohn and Richard L. Strongren, *Light and Shadows* (Port Washington, N.Y.: Alfred, 1976); S. C. Earley, *An Introduction to American Movies* (New York: New American Library, 1978); Jack C. Ellis, *A History of Film* (Englewood Cliffs, N.J.: Prentice-Hall, 1979); Keath Reader, *The Cinema* (New York: David McKay, 1979); John L. Fell, *A History of Films* (New York: Holt, Rinehart & Winston, 1979); and David Cook, *A History of Narrative Film* (New York: W. W. Norton, 1981). There surely will be more. Cook, for the moment, is most valuable because of its complete bibliography. At the same time came the expected anthologies of articles on film history. See, for example, Lewis Jacobs (ed.), *The Emergence of Film Art*, 2nd ed. (New York: Norton, 1979); and Arthur McClure (ed.), *The Movies: An American Idiom* (Rutherford, N.J.: Fairleigh Dickenson University Press, 1971).

There are many survey histories of world cinema by European authors. The "deans" of film historical writing in France, Jean Mitry and Georges Sadoul, dominate. Both have authored multi-volumed works. Indeed, Mitry's critical history of world cinema has only reached the 1920s. See Jean Mitry, *Histoire du Cinema*, 3 volumes (Paris: Editions Universitaires, 1967–73). Georges Sadoul's *Histoire Generale du Cinema*, 6 volumes (Paris: Denoel, 1973–77) is more comprehensive. Neither has been translated. So far we have no multivolume histories in English.

Traditional historians have also begun to write about film. They are primarily interested in using film as a document, but often consider issues of film history. See, for example, John O'Connor and Martin Jackson (eds.), *American History/American Film* (New York: Ungar, 1979); Pierre Sorlin, *The Film in History: Restaging the Past* (New York: Barnes & Noble, 1980); Michael Clark (ed.), *Politics and Media: Film and Television for the Political Scientist and Historian* (Fairview Park, N.Y.: Pergamon Press, 1979); and Anthony Aldgate,

Cinema and History: British Newsreels and the Spanish Civil War (London: Scholar Press, 1979).

Fortunately there now exists a growing body of sources one can turn to learn of other writings in film history. Consider this list of bibliographic sources of books and monographs: Robert A. Armour, *Film: A Reference Guide* (Westport, Conn: Greenwood Press, 1980); Peter J. Bukalski, *Film Research: A Critical Bibliography* (Boston: G. K. Hall, 1972); Alan R. Dyment, *The Literature of the Film: A Bibliographic Guide to Film as Art and Entertainment* (New York: White Lion, 1976); Jack C. Ellis, Charles Derry, and Sharon Kern, *The Film Book Bibliography, 1940–1975* (Metuchen, N.J.: The Scarecrow Press, 1979); Ronald Gottesman and Harry M. Geduld, *Guidebook to Film* (New York: Holt, Rinehart & Winston, 1972); and Frank Manchell, *Film Study: A Resource Guide* (Rutherford, N.J.: Fairleigh Dickenson University Press, 1973).

The most comprehensive work on the bibliography of books on film in English has been done by George Rehrauer. He issued three volumes in his *Cinema Booklist* series during the 1970s, all from Scarecrow Press. In 1982 he combined and updated his work into *The Macmillan Film Bibliography* (New York: Macmillan Publishing, 1982). Volume I lists, with annotations, 6762 books; Volume II provides a subject and author index.

The United States Works Progress Administration underwrote the first guide to articles about film. See Harold Leonard, *The Film Index: A Bibliography* (New York: Museum of Modern Art, 1941, reprinted by Arno Press in 1970). Richard Dyer MacCann and Edward S. Perry edited a volume that updated the WPA's work: *The New Film Index: A Bibiography of Magazine Articles in English, 1930–1970* (New York: E. P. Dutton, 1975). Extending this coverage somewhat is John C. and Lana Gerlach's *The Critical Index: A Bibliography of Articles in English, 1946–1973* (New York: Teachers College Press, 1974). Linda Batty also has written a guide to articles from the same period: *Retrospective Index to Film Periodicals, 1930–1971* (New York: R. R. Bowker, 1971).

There are two major annual indexes to periodical articles. Vincent Aceto, Jane Graves, and Fred Silva began their service in 1973. Their *Film Literature Index* is published annually from Albany, New York. The other, *International Index to Film Periodicals* started in 1974, also comes out annually, and has had several editors.

In recent years a whole host of specialized bibliographies have appeared. The Scarecrow Press of Metuchen, New Jersey, seems to dominate in this area. Here are five examples: Thomas W. Hoffer, *Animation: A Reference Guide* (Westport, Conn.: Greenwood Press, 1981); Richard Stoddard, *Theatre and Cinema Architecture: A Guide to Information Sources* (Detroit: Gale Research, 1978); John G. Nachbar, *Western Films: An Annotated Critical Bibliography* (New York: Garland Publishing, 1975); Anne Powers, *Blacks in American Movies: A Selected Bibliography* (Metuchen, N.J.: Scarecrow Press, 1974); and Rosemary Ribich Kowalski, *Women and Film: A Bibliography* (Metuchen, N.J.: Scarecrow Press, 1976).

Finally, there exist several out-of-the-way sources any students of film history ought not overlook. Ian Jarvie's *Movies and Society* (New York: Basic Books, 1970) contains the best bibliography on that subject. For alternative views on film and society, see a series of three bibliographies published by International General of New York under the title of *Marxism and the Mass Media.* Further updates are promised. The catalogs of the two leading specialized cinema bookstores in the United States often reveal that difficult-to-find work on film history. Many libraries carry them: Cinemabilia of 10 West 13th Street, New York 10011; and Larry Edmunds Bookstore of 6658 Hollywood Boulevard, Hollywood, California 90028.

Current writing about film history appears in many different journals. The following list includes the more important film history-related journals:

American Film—Published by the American Film Institute. General reader.

American Quarterly—Published by the American Studies Association. Scholarly, with occasional articles on film history.

Cineaste—Independently published, Marxist orientation.

Cinema Journal—Published by the Society for Cinema Studies. Scholarly.

Film Comment—Published by the Film Society of Lincoln Center in New York. General reader.

Film and History—Published by the Historian's Film Committee. Scholarly. Treatments of both film historical issues and the use of film as evidence by traditional historians.

Film Quarterly—Published by the University of California Press. General reader.

Film Reader—Published by the Film Division, School of Speech, Northwestern University. Scholarly.

Film in Review—Published by the National Board of Review. For the film fan.

Historical Journal of Film Radio and Television—Published by International Association for Audio-Visual Media in Historical Research and Education. Scholarly.

Image—Published by the International Museum of Photography at the George Eastman House in Rochester, New York. Scholarly.

Journal of American History—Published by the Organization of American Historians. Scholarly.

Journal of Popular Film and Television—Published by the Popular Culture Center at Bowling Green University. Scholarly.

Journal of the University Film and Video Association—Published by the University Film and Video Association. Scholarly.

Jump Cut—Published independently, Marxist oriented.

Marquee—Published by the Theatre Historical Society. General reader.

Quarterly Review of Film Studies—Published by Redgrave Press through the Humanities Center at the University of Southern California. Scholarly.

Screen—Published by the Society for Education in Film and Television in the United Kingdom. Scholarly.

Sight and Sound—Published by the British Film Institute. General reader.

SMPTE Journal—Published by the Society of Motion Picture and Television Engineers. Technical.

The Velvet Light Trap—Independently published. Scholarly.

Wide Angle—Published by the Ohio University Press. Scholarly.

CHAPTER 4: AESTHETIC FILM HISTORY

For a first-rate survey of theoretical approaches to the cinema, see J. Dudley Andrew, *The Major Film Theories* (New York: Oxford University Press, 1976). Less helpful is Andrew Tutor's *Theories of Film* (London: Secker and Warburg, 1974). The formative position is best laid out in the work of Rudolph Arnheim and Sergei Eisenstein. See Arnheim's *Film as Art* (Berkeley: University of California Press, 1956). Translations of Eisenstein's writings now include *Film Form* (New York: Harcourt, Brace & World, 1949); *Film Sense* (New York: Harcourt, Brace & World, 1942); *Notes of a Film Director* (New York: Dover, 1970); and *Film Essays and a Lecture* (New York: Praeger, 1970).

Andre Bazin's realism informs the essays in the two volumes of the English translation of his many film reviews and articles, *What is Cinema?*, Volume I & II (Berkeley: University of California Press, 1968 and 1971). See also Bazin's *French Cinema of the Occupation and Resistance: The Birth of a Critical Esthetic* (New York: Ungar, 1981); and *Jean Renoir* (New York: Simon and Schuster, 1973). Siegfried Kracauer's brand of realism is rigorously set forth in his *Theory of Film* (New York: Oxford University Press, 1960). To learn of other positions on realism in the cinema see Christopher Williams, *Realism and the Cinema: A Reader* (London: Routledge & Kegan Paul, 1980).

There are two other fine collections of theoretical writings about cinema: Gerald Mast and Marshall Cohen (eds.), *Film Theory and Criticism*, 2nd ed. (New York: Oxford University Press, 1979); and Bill Nichols (ed.), *Movies and Methods* (Berkeley: University of California Press, 1976). David Bordwell and Kristin Thompson in *Film Art: An Introduction* (Reading, Mass.: Addison-Wesley, 1979) include a well-written analysis of the realist/formalist split as well as an excellent chapter on the aesthetic history of the cinema.

For examples of the masterpieces approach, take a look at any of the textbooks cited under Chapter 3, particularly Gerald Mast's *A Short History of the Movies*. Individual case studies can be found in Louis Giannetti, *Masters of the American Cinema* (Englewood Cliffs, N.J.: Prentice-Hall, 1981); William K. Everson, *American Silent Film* (New York: Oxford University Press, 1978); P. Adams Sitney, *Visionary Film: The American Avant-Garde, 1943–1978* (New York: Oxford University Press, 1979); and Richard Koszarski, *The Rivals of D. W. Griffith* (New York: New York Zoetrope, 1980).

The American version of auteurism was initially laid out in Andrew Sarris' *The American Cinema* (New York: Dutton, 1968). John Caughie (ed.), *Theories of Authorship* (Boston: Routledge & Kegan Paul, 1981) provides a collection of the basic writings about this particular approach. The seminal statement of the auteur approach is François Truffaut's "Un Certaine Tendence du Cinema Français," *Cahiers du Cinema* 31 (January 1954): 15–29, critiqued by John Hess in "La Politique des Auteurs: World View as Aesthetic," *Jump Cut* 1 (May–June 1974): 19–21.

The literature on semiotics and film makes for difficult reading. A good introduction can be found in Bill Nichols' *Ideology and the Image* (Bloomington: University of Indiana Press, 1981). The British journal *Screen* has been the center of the discussion of these issues for the past decade. Two recent anthologies now house much of the important work of this journal. See *Screen Reader 1: Cinema/Ideology/Politics* and *Screen Reader 2: Cinema and Semiotics* (both London: The Society for the Education in Film and Television, 1977 and 1981 respectively).

To place the work of *Screen* in some historical and philosophical perspective, read Phillip Rosen's article, "*Screen* and the Marxist Project in Film Criticism," *Quarterly Review of Film Studies* 2, no. 3 (August 1977): 273–287. *Screen's* dominant figure has been Stephen Heath. Heath's work is now collected in *Questions of Cinema* (Bloomington: Indiana University Press, 1981).

The work of Christian Metz, Roland Barthes, and Claude Levi-Strauss informs *Screen's* debate in general, and Heath's work in particular. Metz's work is available in translation in three volumes: *Film Language: A Semiotics of the Cinema* (New York: Oxford University Press, 1974); *Language and Cinema* (The Hague: Mouton, 1974); and *The Imaginary Signifier: Psychoanalysis and the Cinema* (Bloomington: Indiana University Press, 1982). Barthes' major texts are his *Writing Degree Zero* and *Elements of Semiology* (Boston: Beacon Press, 1968); *Mythologies* (New York: Hill and Wang, 1972); and *S/Z: An Essay* (New York: Hill and Wang, 1974). Levi-Strauss requires some preparation. For background, read Terence Hawkes, *Structuralism and Semiotics* (Berkeley: University of California Press, 1977); and Edmund Leach, *Culture and Communication: The Logic By Which Symbols Are Connected* (Cambridge University Press, 1976). For Levi-Strauss himself, try *Structural Anthropology* (New York: Penguin Books, 1972).

Two other works try to connect semiotics, film studies, and issues of technological change. They are Theresa Hak Hyung Cha (ed.), *Apparatus: Cinematographic Apparatus: Selected Writings* (New York: Tanam Press, 1980); and Terese de Lauretis and Stephen Heath (eds.), *The Cinematic Apparatus* (New York: St. Martins Press, 1980).

Other scholars have tried to reformulate and rework the basic issues of film studies, including film history. Jerry L. Salvaggio has labeled one new school, neo-formalism; see his "The Emergence of a New School of Criticism: Neo-Formalism," *Journal of the University Film Association* 33, no. 4

(Fall 1981): 45–52. Central to this approach is the work of David Bordwell and Kristin Thompson. Both have produced an incredible amount of important scholarly work. Most accessible in book form are Bordwell's *French Impressionism: Film Culture, Film Theory and Film Style* (New York: Arno Press, 1980); and *The Films of Carl-Theodor Dreyer* (Berkeley: University of California Press, 1981), Thompson's *Eisenstein's Ivan the Terrible: A Neoformalist Analysis* (Princeton, N.J.: Princeton University Press, 1981); and a jointly authored work, *Film Art: An Introduction* (Reading, Mass.: Addison-Wesley, 1979).

Linked to this methodology are the explicitly historical essays of Janet Staiger. She seeks to analyze the production setting of filmmaking. See Staiger's "Dividing Labor for Production Control: Thomas Ince and the Rise of the Studio System," *Cinema Journal* 28, no. 2 (Spring 1979): 16–25; and "Mass-Produced Photoplays: Economic and Signifying Practices in the First Years of Hollywood," *Wide Angle* 4, no. 3 (1980): 12–27.

Noel Burch also seeks a form of neo-formalist analysis. See his *Theory of Film Practice* (New York: Praeger, 1972); and *To the Distant Observer: Form and Meaning in the Japanese Cinema* (Berkeley: University of California Press, 1979). The subtle and important differences between Burch's and Thompson and Bordwell's methods can be seen by contrasting *To the Distant Observer* with Bordwell's essay, "Our Dream-Cinema: Western Historiography and the Japanese Film," *Film Reader* 4 (1979): 45–62.

Others have tried a more sociological alternative to the masterpieces approach. Begin with Siegfried Kracauer's *From Caligari to Hitler* (Princeton, N. J.: Princeton University Press, 1948); and George Huaco's *The Sociology of Film Art* (New York: Basic Books, 1965). More on the sociological perspective can be found under the listing of Chapter 7.

The final alternative presently in circulation utilizes statistical techniques. Barry Salt is the main exponent of this approach. See his "Film Form, 1900–1906," *Sight and Sound* 47, no. 3 (Summer 1978): 148–153; and a series of articles in *Film Quarterly*: "Film Style and Technology in the Forties," *Film Quarterly* 31, no. 1 (Fall 1977): 46–57; and "Film Style and Technology in the Thirties," *Film Quarterly* 30, no. 1 (Fall 1976): 19–32.

Finally, Nick Browne has attempted to reformulate a more global perspective. See his "The Politics of Narration: *Capra's Mr. Smith Goes to Washington*," *Wide Angle* 3, no. 3 (1979): 4–11; "The Spectator of American Symbolic Forms: Re-Reading John Ford's *Young Mr. Lincoln*," *Film Reader* 5 (1979): 180–188; and "Cahiers du Cinema's Rereading of Hollywood Cinema: An Analysis of Method," *Quarterly Review of Film Studies* 3, no. 3 (Summer 1978): 405–416.

Another widely used methodology for film historical analysis is genre history. Films are placed in appropriate categories, and then analyzed historically. Some categories are quite broad. These usually are labelled modes. Examples of studies of this form include studies of compilation films: Jay Leyda's *Films Beget Films* (New York: Hill and Wang, 1964); newsreels: Raymond Fielding's *The American Newsreel 1911–1967* (Norman: University of Oklahoma Press, 1972); comedy: Stanley Cavell's *In Pursuit of Happiness: The Hollywood Comedy of Remarriage* (Cambridge, Mass: Harvard University Press, 1981) and Gerald Mast's *The Comic Mind*, 2nd ed. (Chicago: University of Chicago Press, 1979); and animation: Leonard Maltin's *Of Mice and Magic* (New York: New American Library, 1980).

Genres familiar to all film-goers (the western, the gangster film, the detective film, the musical, and the melodrama) have been the subject of numerous books and articles. The best surveys are John G. Cawelti, *Adventure, Mystery, and Romance: Formula Stories as Art and Popular Culture* (Chicago: University of Chicago Press, 1976); Stuart M. Kaminsky, *American Film Genres: Approaches to a Critical Theory of Popular Film* (Dayton, Ohio: Pflaum, 1974); Stephen Neale, *Genre* (London: British Film Institute, 1980); Thomas Schatz, *Hollywood Genres: Formulas, Filmmaking, and the Studio System* (Philadelphia: Temple University Press, 1981), and Stanley J. Soloman, *Beyond Formula: American Film Genres* (New York: Harcourt Brace, 1976). Each has an extensive bibliography.

A collection of recent work on genre theory can be found in *Film Reader* 3 (1978). Individual studies of specific genres by and large repeat a masterpieces approach. Exceptions can be found in Rick Altman's *Genre: The Musical* (London: Routledge & Kegan Paul, 1981); John G. Cawelti's, *The Six-Gun Mystique* (Bowling Green, Ohio: Bowling Green University Popular Press, 1971); and Will Wright's *Six Guns and Society: A Structural Study of the Western* (Berkeley: University of California Press, 1975). Jane Feuer's use of intertexuality is examined in her article "The Self-Reflective Musical and the Myth of Entertainment," *Quarterly Review of Film Studies* 2, no. 3 (August 1977): 313–326, and her book *The Hollywood Musical* (Bloomington: Indiana University, 1982).

Little has been written about the creation of meaning through nonfilmic events (advertising, posters, and the like). A promising beginning can be found in Mary Beth Harolovich's article, "Advertising Heterosexuality," *Screen* 23, no. 2 (July–August 1982): 50–60. This is an area in which much research remains to be done.

Sunrise was the subject of a seminar project at the University of Iowa in 1976. Four papers were published from that group project. The professor, J. Dudley Andrew, authored a critical study, "The Gravity of Sunrise," and Robert C. Allen and Steven Lipkin wrote economic and social studies, "William Fox Presents *Sunrise*," and "*Sunrise*: A Film Meets Its Public." All three can be found in the *Quarterly Review of Film Studies* 2, no. 3 (August 1977): 327–387. Yet another was published as Mary Ann Doane, "Desire in *Sunrise*," *Film Reader* 2 (1978): 71–77.

CHAPTER 5: TECHNOLOGICAL FILM HISTORY

The best introduction to the writing on technological film history is Edward Branigan, "Color and Cinema: Problems in the Writing of History," *Film Reader* 4 (1979): 16–33. Branigan systematically compares four approaches. They are identified with the writings of Terry Ramsaye (see Chapter 3), Douglas Gomery, Patrick Ogle, and Jean-Louis Comolli.

For more on Ogle's method, see his "Technological and Aesthetic Influences Upon the Development of Deep Focus Cinematography in the United States," *Screen* 13, no. 1 (Spring 1972): 45–72. Gomery's approach is the one outlined in Chapter 5 in this book. For more detail, see his "Economic Struggle and Hollywood Imperialism: Europe Converts to Sound," *Yale French Studies* 60 (1980): 80–93; "Tri-Ergon, Tobis Klangfilm, and the Coming of Sound," *Cinema Journal* 16, no. 1 (Fall 1976): 51–61; and "Problems in Film History: How Fox Innovated Sound," *Quarterly Review of Film Studies* 1, no. 3 (August 1976): 315–330. Edward Buscombe has also analyzed Gomery's approach in "Sound and Color," *Jump Cut* 17 (April 1978): 48–52. Jean-Louis Comolli wrote a series of articles on the ideology of cinema technology for *Cahiers du Cinema*: "Technique et Ideologie," in no. 229 (May–June 1971): 4–21; no. 230 (July 1971): 51–57; no. 231 (August–September 1971): 42–49; no. 233 (November 1971): 29–45; nos. 234/35 (December 1971–January 1972): 94–100; and no. 241 (September–October 1972): 20–24. The first part has been translated by Diana Matios as "Technique and Ideology: Camera, Perspective, Depth of Field," *Film Reader* 2 (1977): 128–140. For an analysis of Comolli's method, see James Spellerberg, "Technology and Ideology in the Cinema," *Quarterly Review of Film Studies* 2, no. 3 (August 1979): 288–301.

Raymond Fielding in *A Technological History of Motion Pictures and Television* (Berkeley: University of California Press, 1967) has collected informative historical articles on all phases of film technology from the journals of the Society of Motion Picture and Television Engineers. James Limbacher's *Four Aspects of Film* (New York: Brussel & Brussel, 1968) is the only other book that could be considered a technological history of cinema; however, it is anecdotal and somewhat disorganized.

On particular technologies the study of color has attracted the most scholarly attention in recent years, including two books: R. T. Ryan, *A History of Motion Picture Color Technology* (New York: Focal Press, 1978); and Fred E. Basten, *Glorious Technicolor* (San Diego: A. S. Barnes, 1980). There are also two important articles: Gorham A. Kindem, "Hollywood's Conversion to Color: The Technological, Economic, and Aesthetic Factors," *Journal of the University Film Association* 31, no. 2 (Spring 1979): 29–36; and Dudley Andrew, "The Postwar Struggle for Color," *Cinema Journal* 18, no. 2 (Spring 1979): 41–52. There are several good sources of information on the history of sound in the cinema: Evan William Cameron's anthology, *Sound and the Cinema* (Pleasantville, N.Y.: Redgrave, 1980); Harry M. Geduld's *The Birth of the Talkies: From Edison to Jolson* (Bloomington: Indiana University Press, 1975); Alexander Walker's *The Shattered Silents* (New York: William Morrow, 1979); and a special issue of the *Yale French Studies*, No. 60, "Cinema/Sound," edited by Rick Altman. The latter source contains an extensive bibliography. Other aspects of the technological history of the cinema have so far been ignored.

On cinematography, there is Brian Coe's, *The History of Movie Photography* (New York: New York Zoetrope, 1982). On wide-screen processes, see Martin Quigley, *New Screen Techniques* (New York: Quigley, 1953); Charles Barr, "Cinemascope: Before and After," first printed in *Film Quarterly* 16, no. 4 (1963), but easily found in anthologies such as Gerald Mast and Marshall Cohen (eds.), *Film Theory and Criticism*, 2nd ed. (New York: Oxford University Press, 1979), pp. 140–168; and Derek J. Southall, "Twentieth Century-Fox Presents a Cinemascope Picture," *Focus on Film* 31 (1978): 8–26, 47. See also Kemp Niver's "Motion-Picture Film Widths," *Journal of the Society of Motion Picture and Television Engineers*, 77, no. 8 (August 1968): 814–818.

Finally, because of his substantial involvement in the early development of cinema technology and modern technology in general, Thomas Edison continues to attract scholarly attention. Wyn Wackhorst *Thomas Alva Edison: An American Myth* (Cambridge, Mass.: MIT Press, 1981) analyzes the public myths that have built around Edison in the 100 years since his birth. A good, general biography is Robert Conot, *A Streak of Luck* (New York: Seaview Books, 1979). Gordon Hendricks has contributed the most in the debate over the appropriateness of Edison's credit for the invention of the motion picture camera and projector: *The Edison Motion Picture Myth* (Berkeley: University of California Press, 1961); *Beginnings of the Biograph* (New York: Beginnings of the American Film, 1964); *The Kinetoscope* (New York: The Beginnings of the American Film, 1966); and *Eadweard Maybridge* (New York: Viking, 1975).

Two works on the technological history of related media are of interest to film historians. Raymond Williams takes a Marxist approach in *Television: Technology and Cultural Form* (New York: Schocken, 1974). Reese Jenkins takes an industrial analysis approach in his book on Eastman Kodak, *Images and Enterprise* (Baltimore: The Johns Hopkins University Press, 1975). His book includes one chapter on Kodak's relationship to the film industry.

CHAPTER 6: ECONOMIC FILM HISTORY

The best introduction in this area is an anthology of articles: Tino Balio (ed.), *The American Film Industry* (Madison: University of Wisconsin Press, 1976). It also contains an extensive bibliography. Gorham Kindem has collected a different set of articles—but from a similar perspective—in his *The American Movie Industry: The Business of Motion Pictures* (Carbondale: Southern Illinois University Press, 1982). The only other survey is an anecdotal narrative history: Robert Stanley's *The Celluloid Empire* (New York: Hastings House, 1978).

Three older studies, aside from Hamption's volume mentioned in the listing of Chapter 3, continue to hold our interest. Michael Conant, *Antitrust in the Motion Picture Industry* (Berkeley: University of California Press, 1960) remains a model for industrial analysis. Gertrude Jobs' *Motion Picture Empire* (Hamden, Conn.: Archon Books, 1966) is anecdotal, but does contain a great deal of interesting information. Howard T. Lewis' *The Motion Picture Industry* (New York: D. Van Nostrand, 1933) was the product of team research at the Harvard Business School. It provides a vivid "snapshot" of what the U.S. film industry was like in 1933.

For a Marxist perspective, see F. D. Klingender and Stuart Legg's *Money Behind the Screen* (London: Lawrence & Wishart, 1937). This analysis has been adopted by most film historians, Marxist or not. Janet Wasco has extended Klingender and Legg's work in her *Movies and Money: Financing the American Film Industry* (Norwood, N.J.: Ablex Publishing, 1982). Douglas Gomery has tried to reformulate the model all these authors utilized, finance capitalism, and apply an alternative framework: monopoly capitalism. See "Hollywood, the National Recovery Administration, and the Question of Monopoly Power," *Journal of the University Film Association* 31, no. 2 (Spring 1979): 47–52; and "Re-thinking U.S. Film History: The Depression Decade and Monopoly Control," *Film and History* 10, no. 2 (May 1980): 32–38.

For analysis of international economics of film, we only have Thomas Guback's *The International Film Industry: Western Europe and America Since 1945* (Bloomington: Indiana University Press, 1969). Janet Staiger and Douglas Gomery in "The History of World Cinema: Models for Economic Analysis," *Film Reader* 4 (1979): 35–44, tried to generalize to the level of method concerning international issues, but the article mainly serves to point out how difficult this area is to research.

There are numerous books that have been written about the Hollywood studios. However, only two are extensively based on primary documentation: Tino Balio's *United Artists: The Company Built by the Stars* (Madison: The University of Wisconsin Press, 1976); and Richard B. Jewell's *The RKO Story* (New York: Arlington House, 1982). Anthony Slide in *The Kindergarten of the Movies: A History of the Fine Arts Company* (Metuchen, N.J.: Scarecrow Press, 1980); and Richard M. Hurst in *Republic Studios: Between Poverty Row and the Majors* (Metuchen, N.J.: Scarecrow Press, 1979) do first-rate jobs from trade paper sources.

For the standard "great man" accounts, you might dip into Bosley Crowther's *The Lion's Roar* (New York: Dutton, 1957) on M-G-M, or Charles Higham's *Warner Brothers* (New York: Charles Scribner's Sons, 1975). A picture book series chronicles three studios: John Douglas Eames, *The MGM Story* (New York: Crown, 1975); Clive Hirschhorn, *The Warner Brothers Story* (New York: Crown, 1979); and Tony Thomas and Aubrey Solomon, *The Films of*

Twentieth Century-Fox (Secaucus, N.J.: Citadel, 1979). Each is valuable as a reference tool because of its extensive, annotated list of feature films produced and distributed through that studio.

Unions have long played an important role in Hollywood. Unfortunately, all surveys of unionization are out-of-date. Still, Murray Ross' *Stars and Strikes* (New York: Columbia University Press, 1941), and Hugh G. Lovell and Tasile Carter's *Collective Bargaining in the Motion Picture Industry* (Berkeley: Institute of Industrial Relations, University of California, 1953) prove useful guides. Louis B. Perry and Richard S. Perry's *A History of the Los Angeles Labor Movement, 1911-41* (Berkeley: University of California Press, 1963) does contain a valuable chapter on labor relations in Hollywood. Furthermore, it situates the Hollywood case in the world of southern California labor struggles. Recent work on Hollywood and labor has been more specialized. See Nancy Lynn Schwartz, *The Hollywood Writer's Wars* (New York: Alfred A. Knopf, 1982); and Ida Jeter, "The Collapse of the Federated Motion Picture Crafts: A Case of Class Collaboration," *The Journal of the University Film Association* 31, No. 2 (Spring 1979): 37-46.

CHAPTER 7: SOCIAL FILM HISTORY

The sociology of film is forcefully covered in Ian Jarvie's two books: *Sociology of the Movies* (New York: Basic Books, 1970); and *Movies as Social Criticism* (Metuchen, N.J.: Scarecrow Press, 1978). Andrew Tudor, *Image and Influence* (New York: St. Martins, 1974), also the work of a sociologist, is a survey of a variety of different sociological analyses of the movies. Garth Jowett's *Film: The Democratic Art* (Boston: Little Brown, 1976), and Robert Sklar's *Movie-Made America* (New York: Random House, 1975) are social histories of the American film and both contain extensive bibliographies. Jowett's approach is an application of Jarvie's methodology; Sklar comes out of the tradition of American Studies, closer in spirit to the work of Kracauer.

There are several useful case studies on Hollywood film production. See Donald Knox, *The Magic Factory: How MGM Made An American in Paris* (New York: Random House, 1956); and Lillian Ross, *Picture* (New York: Rinehart, 1952). In Leo Rosten's *Hollywood the Movie Colony* (New York: Harcourt, Brace, 1939) a sociologist examined a pre-World War II Hollywood. Hortense Powdermaker's *Hollywood: The Dream Factory* (Boston: Little Brown, 1950) offers an examination of the same Hollywood from the point-of-view of an anthropologist.

The movie mogul continues to hold the fascination of many interested in Hollywood's past. There are two surveys: Philip French's *The Movie Moguls: An Informal History of the Hollywood Tycoons* (Chicago: Henry Regnery, 1969); and Norman Zierold's *The Moguls* (New York: Avon, 1969).

Each major studio is associated with at least one mogul. For Paramount, it is Adolf Zukor. See Will Irwin's *The House That Shadows Built* (New York: Doubleday, Doran, 1928); and Zukor's own *The Public Is Never Wrong* (New York: G. P. Putnam's Sons, 1953).

For Twentieth Century Fox, there is founder William Fox: Upton Sinclair, *Upton Sinclair Presents William Fox* (Los Angeles: Privately Printed, 1933); and Glendon Allvine, *The Greatest Fox of Them All* (New York: Lyle Stuart, 1969). Succeeding Fox was mogul Darryl F. Zanuck: Leo Guild, *Zanuck: Hollywood's Last Tycoon* (Los Angeles: Holloway House, 1970); and Mel Gussow, *Don't Say Yes Until I Finish Talking* (New York: Doubleday, 1971).

Only Jack of the four Warner brothers emerged as a public figure. See his *My First Hundred Years in Hollywood* (New York: Random House, 1965).

MGM seems to have generated the most famous mogul archetypes, Louis B. Mayer, and Irving Thalberg. See Bosley Crowther, *Hollywood Rajah: The Life and Times of Louis B. Mayer* (New York: Henry Holt, 1960); Gary Carey's *All the Stars in Heaven: Louis B. Mayer's MGM* (New York: E. P. Dutton, 1981); Bob Thomas, *Thalberg's Life and Legend* (Garden City, N.Y.: Doubleday & Co., 1969); and Samuel Marx, *Mayer and Thalberg: The Make-Believe Saints* (New York: Random House, 1975).

The material on Walt Disney is voluminous. Elizabeth Leebron and Lynn Gartley located more than 600 bibliographic items written before 1977. See their *Walt Disney: A Guide to References and Resources* (Boston: G. K. Hall, 1979). The most accessible accounts of Disney's life are Richard Schickel's *The Disney Version* (New York: Simon & Schuster, 1968); and Bob Thomas' *Walt Disney* (New York: Simon & Schuster, 1976).

For Columbia, there is Bob Thomas' *King Cohn* (New York: G. P. Putnam's Sons, 1967).

For Universal, there is John Drinkwater's *The Life and Adventures of Carl Laemmle* (New York: G. P. Putnam's Sons, 1931).

Finally, Sam Goldwyn, never a studio boss, has generated much interest as the strong-willed, creative producer. See Carol Easton, *The Search for Sam Goldwyn: A Biography* (New York: William Morrow, 1976); Lawrence J. Epstein, *Samuel Goldwyn* (Boston: Twayne, 1981); and Arthur Marx, *Goldwyn: A Biography of the Man Behind the Myth* (New York: W. W. Norton, 1976).

The material on the history of American movie-going is sparse. From an empirical point of view, Leo A. Handel's *Hollywood Looks at Its Audience* (Urbana: University of Illinois Press, 1950) nicely sums up the statistical evidence on American audiences before 1950. There is no single book covering the three decades since then, but for a nearly comprehensive listing of monographs and articles, see Bruce A. Austin's "Film Audience Research, 1960–1980: An Annotated Bibliography," *Journal of Popular Film and Television* 8, no. 2 (Spring 1980): 53–80; and "Film Audience Research, 1960–1980: An Update," *Journal of Popular Film and Television* 8, no. 4 (Winter 1980–81): 57–59. A unique look at movie audience attitudes is available on microfilm from Scholarly Resources of Wilmington, Delaware in the form of its compilation of Gallup Poll surveys of audience preferences during the 1940s.

A second method for audience study looks at the cultural appeals of exhibition; the historian then "works backward" to figure audience composition. Lary May lays out such an approach in his *Screening Out the Past: The Birth of Mass Culture and the Motion Picture Industry* (New York: Oxford University Press, 1980). For more on exhibition practices, see the listing under Chapter 8; Ben M. Hall's *The Best Remaining Seats* (New York: Bramhall House, 1961); and David Naylor's *American Picture Palaces: The Architecture of Fantasy* (New York: Van Nostrand Reinhold, 1981).

A third approach to audience analysis, based on urban history and urban geography, is outlined in Douglas Gomery, "Movie Audiences, Urban Geography, and the History of the American Film," *The Velvet Light Trap*, No. 19 (1982): 23–29.

There is extensive literature on the image of minority groups, and social problems as depicted in feature films. Thomas Cripps has done the most work on the image of the black American in the Hollywood film. See his *Slow Fade to Black: The Negro in American Film, 1900–1942* (New York: Oxford University Press, 1977); and *Black Film as Genre* (Bloomington: Indiana University Press, 1979). Both contain extensive bibliographies.

Interested readers also should seek out Donald Bogle's *Toms, Coons, Mulattoes, Mammies and Bucks: An Interpretative History of Blacks in American Films* (New York: Viking, 1973); Daniel J. Leab's *From Sambo to Superspade: The Black Experience in Motion Pictures* (Boston: Houghton Mifflin, 1976); and Edward Mapp's *Blacks in American Films: Today and Yesterday* (Metuchen, N.J.: Scarecrow Press, 1972). In conjunction with the black in film, the reader might want to consult Edward D. C. Campbell, Jr., *The Celluloid South: Hollywood and the Southern Myth* (Knoxville: The University of Tennessee Press, 1981); and Warren French (ed.), *The South and Film* (Jackson: The University Press of Mississippi, 1981).

Native Americans have not been the subject of as much analysis. Helpful are Gretchen M. Bataille and Charles L. P. Silet, *The Pretend Indians: Images of Native Americans in the Movies* (Ames: The Iowa State University Press, 1980); Ralph Frair and Natasha Frair, *The Only Good Indian* (New York: Drama Book Specialists, 1972); and John O'Connor, *The Hollywood Indian: Stereotypes of Native Americans in Film* (Trenton: New Jersey State Museum, 1981).

Women in film has become the focus of a number of important studies during the 1970s. Three surveys of this material are Molly Haskell's *From Reverence to Rape: The Treatment of Women in the Movies* (New York: Holt, Rinehart and Winston, 1974); Joan Mellen, *Women and Their Sexuality in the New Film* (New York: Horizon Press, 1973); and Marjorie Rosen's *Popcorn Venus* (New York: Coward, McCann and Geoghegan, 1973). Much of the best work on women and film has been collected in two anthologies: Patricia Erens (ed.), *Sexual Strategems: The World of Women in Film* (New York: Horizon, 1979); and Karyn Kay and Gerald Peary (eds.), *Women and the Cinema* (New York: E. P. Dutton, 1977). Three helpful specialized works include Brandon French's, *On the Verge of Revolt* (New York: Ungar, 1974) on the 1950s; E. Ann Kaplan (ed.), *Women in Film Noir* (London: British Film Institute, 1980), and *Film Reader 5* on feminist film criticism, theory and history.

The portrait of homosexuals in film has inspired three books: Richard Dyer (ed.), *Gays and Film* (London: British Film Institute, 1980), Vito Russo, *The Celluloid Closet: Homosexuality in the Movies* (New York: Harper & Row, 1981); and Parker Tyler, *Screening the Sexes: Homosexuality in the Movies* (New York: Holt, Rinehart and Winston, 1973).

To mention all other "image" studies is impossible, but there also exist works on such topics as (1) images of war in film: Colin Shinder, *Hollywood Goes to War* (London: Routledge & Kegan Paul); and Lawrence H. Suid, *Guts and Glory* (Reading, Mass.: Addison-Wesley, 1978); (2) social problems: Peter Roffman and Jim Purdy, *The Hollywood Social Problem Film* (Bloomington: Indiana University Press, 1981); (3) imperialism: Jeffrey Richards, *Visions of Yesterday* (London: Routledge & Kegan Paul, 1973); and (4) alcoholism: Jim Cook and Mike Lewington, *Images of Alcoholism* (London: British Film Institute, 1979), to name but four more categories. The bibliographies in Jarvie, Jowett, and Sklar (cited in first paragraph of Chapter 7's listing) list the bulk of this form of analysis prior to 1976. Related literature on the history of film as a cultural document is as extensive, and also well covered in Jarvie, Jowett and Sklar.

The seminal work is undoubtedly Siegfried Kracauer's *From Caligari to Hitler* (Princeton, N.J.: Princeton University Press, 1947). Two works help place Kracauer's arguments in perspective: Paul Monaco, *Cinema and Society* (New York: Elsevier, 1976); and M. S. Phillips, "The Nazi Control of the German Film Industry," *Journal of European Studies* 1, no. 1 (1971): 37–68. American Studies follows in the film-as-cultural document approach. Sklar's aforementioned *Movie-Mode America* (New York: Random House, 1975) remains the central work. See also, Russell Merritt's "Dixon, Griffith, and the Southern Legend," *Cinema Journal* 12, no. 1 (Fall 1972): 26–45; and Lary May's *Screening Out the Past* (New York: Oxford University Press, 1980).

Classic studies of the psychology of film viewing include Martha Wolfstein and Nathan Leites' *Movies: A Psychological Study* (Glencoe, Ill.: The Free Press, 1950); and Harvey R. Greenberg, *The Movies on Your Mind* (New York: E. P. Dutton, 1975). Translations of Lacan's writings make for difficult reading. Try *Écrits: A Selection* (New York: W. W. Norton, 1977); *The Four Fundamental Concepts of Psycho-Analysis* (New York: W. W. Norton, 1978); and *The Language of the Self: The Function of Language in Psychoanalysis* (New York: The Johns Hopkins Press, 1968). A guide to the place of Lacan's work in new approaches to the cinema can be found in Rosalind Coward and John Ellis,

Language and Materialism: Developments in Semiology and the Theory of the Subject (London: Routledge & Kegan Paul, 1977). Much has been written on Lacan and his influence. Consult Anika Lemaire, *Lacan* (London: Routledge, Kegan Paul, 1977); and John P. Mueller and William J. Richardson, *Lacan and Language* (New York: International Press, 1982).

Screen took up questions of psychology and film in the mid-1970s. Representative work includes Colin McCabe's "Theory and Film: Principles of Realism and Pleasure," *Screen* 17, no. 3 (Autumn 1976): 7–27; Stephen Heath's, "On Suture" reprinted in *Questions of Cinema*, and "Difference," *Screen* 19, no. 3 (Autumn 1978): 51–112; and Claire Johnston's "The Subject of Feminist Film Theory/Practice," *Screen* 21, no. 2 (Summer 1980): 27–34. Christian Metz's *The Imaginary Signifier* (Bloomington: Indiana University Press, 1982) also relies heavily on Lacanian theory.

The history of discourse on the cinema is limited. Jonas Spatz, *Hollywood in Fiction: Some Versions of the American Myth* (Brussels: Mouton, 1969), and Walter Wells, *Tycoons and Locusts: A Regional Look at Hollywood Fiction of the Thirties* (Carbondale: Southern Illinois University Press, 1973) look at how novelists have treated Hollywood. One way to better understand the place of Hollywood in American society is to examine the debate about the place and influence of the Communist movement in the movies, a public issue in the late 1940s and early 1950s. There is a growing literature in this area. See, for example, John Cogley, *Report on Blacklisting, Volume I (The Movies)* (New York: Fund for the Republic, 1956); Larry Ceplair and Steven Englund, *The Inquisition in Hollywood* (New York: Anchor, 1980); and Victor S. Navasky, *Naming Names* (New York: Viking, 1980).

Studies of the relationship between film as a social institution and other social institutions is scattered in many areas of film studies as well as other disciplines. Students of film have long been fascinated by the relation of film and government. Early on, scholars realized film was effectively being used as propaganda. For studies on this question, see David M. White and Richard Averson, *The Celluloid Weapon* (Boston: Beacon Press, 1972); Richard Taylor, *Film Propaganda* (New York: Barnes and Noble, 1979); Anthony Rhodes, *Propaganda* (New York: Chelsea House, 1976); Richard A. Maynard, *Propaganda on Film: A Nation at War* (Rochelle Park, N.J.: Hayden, 1975); and Nicholas Pronay and D. W. Spring (eds.), *Propaganda, Politics, and Film, 1918–45* (Atlantic Highlands, N.J.: Humanities Press, 1982). These five studies cover American and European contexts.

The U.S. government has long produced documentary films for many purposes. This relationship is surveyed in Richard Meran Barsam's *Nonfiction Film: A Critical History* (New York: E. P. Dutton, 1973); and Erik Barnouw's *Documentary: A History of Non-Fiction Film* (New York: Oxford University Press, 1974). For specific data on the government's involvement, see Richard Dyer MacCann's *The People's Films: A Political History of U.S. Government Motion Pictures* (New York: Hastings House, 1973).

Many social thinkers have taken an interest in the American film industry because of its purported effects on social, moral, and religious values. Threats of and instances of actual censorship have been commonplace for more than seventy-five years. There are several good surveys of censorship and the movies: Ira H. Carmen's *Movies, Censorship and the Law* (Ann Arbor: The University of Michigan Press, 1966); Edward de Grazia and Roger K. Newman's Banned Films: *Movies, Censors, and the First Amendment* (New York: R. R. Bowker, 1982); and Richard S. Randall, *Censorship of the Movies: The Social and Political Control of a Mass Medium* (Madison: The University of Wisconsin Press, 1968). Older but still useful are Morris L. Ernst and Pare Lorentz, *Censored: The Private Life of a Movie* (New York: Jonathan Cape and Harrison Smith, 1930); and Ruth A. Inglis, *Freedom of the Movies* (Chicago: University of Chicago Press, 1947).

The practice of self-regulation has been a part of the Hollywood scene for half a century. For insight into how well that process has worked, see Stephen Farber, *The Movie Rating Game* (Washington, D.C.: Public Affairs Press, 1972); and Jack Vizzard, *See No Evil: Life Inside a Hollywod Censor* (New York: Simon and Schuster, 1970).

Little has been written about the effect of religious organizations in the censorship debate. A beginning can be found in Paul W. Facey's *The Legion of Decency* (New York: Arno, 1974). A perspective on foreign censorship efforts can be found in Neville March Hunnings' encyclopedic *Film Censors and the Law* (London: George Allen & Unwin, 1967).

The movie star may be the most written of and least understood phenomenon in film history. It would be impossible to list all the biographies and autobiographies of Hollywood stars. The bibliographies noted above provide a fair and accurate list. However, the star system itself has produced a surprisingly limited shelf of serious literature. Richard Dyer's *Stars* (London: The British Film Institute, 1978), and Edgar Morin's *The Stars* (New York: Grove Press, 1961) stand as the best surveys. Dyer's volume contains an extensive bibliography. For other treatments, see Alexander Walker's *Stardom: The Hollywood Phenomenon* (New York: Stein & Day, 1970); and Elisabeth Weis (ed.), *The Movie Star* (New York: The Viking Press, 1981). Charles Affron has provided useful insights into the star system in his *Star Acting* (New York: E. P. Dutton, 1977); and *Cinema and Sentiment* (Chicago: University of Chicago Press, 1982). An interesting study of female stars can be found in Janice Welch's reprinted Ph.D. dissertation, *Film Archtypes: Sisters, Mistresses, Mothers, Daughters* (New York: Arno Press, 1978).

CHAPTER 8: WRITING FILM HISTORY

Little has been written about how to research and write local film history. See Douglas Gomery, "Doing Film History: A Modest Proposal," *American Film Institute Newsletter* 5, no. 2 (October–November 1981): 1–2. However, there does seem to be a growing interest in this area by many scholars. See, for example, Robert C. Allen, "Motion Picture Exhibition in Manhattan: Beyond the Nickelodeon," *Cinema Journal* 18, no. 2 (Spring 1979): 2–15 (about New York City); Douglas Gomery, "The Growth of Movie Monopolies: The Case of Balaban & Katz," *Wide Angle* 3, no. 1 (1979): 54–63 (about Chicago); David O. Thomas, "From Page to Screen in Smalltown America: Early Motion Pictures in Winona, Minnesota," *Journal of the University Film Association* 33, no. 3 (Summer 1981): 3–14; Douglas Gomery, "Saxe Amusement Enterprises: The Movies Come to Milwaukee," *Milwaukee History* 2, no. 2 (Spring 1979): 18–28, Robert Headley, *Exit* (Washington: Privately Printed, 1973) (about Baltimore); Burnes St. Patrick Hollyman, "The First Picture Shows: Austin, Texas, 1894–1913," *Journal of the University Film Association* 29, no. 3 (Summer 1977): 3–8; and Richard Alan Nelson, "Florida: The Forgotten Film Capital," *Journal of the University Film Association* 29, no. 3 (Summer 1977): 9–21.

The standard guides to more information of all sorts for the local historian are Frank Freidel's *Harvard Guide to American History*, rev. ed. (Cambridge, Mass.: Harvard University Press, 1977); and David E. Kyvig and Myron A. Martz, *Nearby History: Exploring the Past Around You* (Nashville: The American Association for State and Local History, 1982).

Index